SPECIAL PUBLICATIONS

OF THE

NEW YORK ACADEMY OF SCIENCES

VOLUME II

NEW YORK
PUBLISHED BY THE ACADEMY
1942

Special Publications of the New York Academy of Sciences
Volume II
Wilbur G. Valentine, Editor

BALINESE CHARACTER
A PHOTOGRAPHIC ANALYSIS

By
GREGORY BATESON
AND
MARGARET MEAD

December 7, 1942

Copyright, 1942, by
The New York Academy of Sciences

Second Printing, 1962

PRINTED IN UNITED STATES OF AMERICA

1817–1942

THIS VOLUME IS ISSUED
IN COMMEMORATION OF

THE ONE HUNDRED AND TWENTY-FIFTH ANNIVERSARY

OF THE FOUNDING OF

THE NEW YORK ACADEMY OF SCIENCES

AND IS DEDICATED
TO THE GREAT ARMY OF EMINENT SCIENTISTS
WHO, BY THEIR ACHIEVEMENTS, DURING THAT
PERIOD HAVE GREATLY TRANSFORMED THE EN-
VIRONMENT AND INFINITELY EXPANDED THE PO-
TENTIALITIES OF MANKIND.

ACKNOWLEDGMENTS

This monograph is the first extensive publication based upon our combined researches in Bali where we worked from March 1936 to March 1938 and for a six-week period in February and March 1939. It represents one cross section of all the material collected, and so our acknowledgments are due to all the persons and organizations who have contributed to any part of the expedition or the subsequent organization of materials, to all of our collaborators in Bali and in New York upon whose concrete data or theoretical insights we have drawn, and to our research assistants whose patience and clarity have greatly facilitated our labors.

For general field funds and maintenance in the field we are indebted to: the Department of Anthropology of the American Museum of Natural History (and in particular to the Voss Fund and the South Seas Exploration Fund); to St. John's College and to the William Wyse Foundation of Trinity College, Cambridge, England. For special field funds and for funds directly devoted to the preparation of this monograph, we are indebted to the Social Science Research Council and the Committee for Research in Dementia Praecox supported by the Thirty-Third Degree Scottish Rite, Northern Masonic Jurisdiction. For the final publication of these materials we have to thank the New York Academy of Sciences and the Quain Research Fund. To the Government of the Netherlands East Indies we owe our thanks for many courtesies and substantial assistance.

For collaboration in the field, we have to thank Jane Belo, Katharane Mershon, and Colin McPhee, and also Walter Spies, C. J. Grader, R. Goris, and our invaluable Balinese assistant, I Made Kaler. For theoretical insights given us in the United States we have to thank Theodora Abel, Gordon Allport, Erik Erikson, Milton Erickson, Geoffrey Gorer, Harold Lasswell, Kurt Lewin, William Steig, and Marian Stranahan. Acknowledgment is due also to Claudia and Philomena Guillebaud and Audrey Burrows, whose unflagging interest accompanied the review of the diapositive collection, and to Karsten Stapelfeldt for his skillful retouching of the plates. Finally to our research assistants, Claire Holt who has done the analytical work on our collection of carvings and who assisted in the lay-out of the plates, and to Dorothy Minton who has systematized our records of child behavior, we make grateful acknowledgment.

GREGORY BATESON
MARGARET MEAD

New York, July 10, 1942

CONTENTS

	PAGE
INTRODUCTION	xi
BALINESE CHARACTER BY MARGARET MEAD	1
NOTES ON THE PHOTOGRAPHS AND CAPTIONS BY GREGORY BATESON	49
PLATES AND CAPTIONS BY GREGORY BATESON	56
ETHNOGRAPHIC NOTE ON BALI	256
BIBLIOGRAPHIC NOTE	264
GLOSSARY AND INDEX OF NATIVE WORDS AND PERSONAL NAMES	267

LIST OF PLATES

INTRODUCTORY

PLATES	FACING PAGE
1. Bajoeng Gede: Village and Temples	56
2. Bajoeng Gede: Agriculture	59
3. Communities with Irrigation	60
4. Anthropomorphic Offerings	63
5. Crowds (*Rame*)	64
6. Industrialization	67
7. Awayness	68
8. Official Trance	71

SPATIAL ORIENTATION AND LEVELS

9. Sharing and Social Organization	72
10. Elevation and Respect I	75
11. Elevation and Respect II	76
12. Elevation and Respect III	79
13. Elevation and Respect IV	80
14. Elevation and Respect V	83

LEARNING

15. Visual and Kinaesthetic Learning I	84
16. Visual and Kinaesthetic Learning II	87
17. Balance	88

INTEGRATION AND DISINTEGRATION OF THE BODY

18. Trance and *Beroek* I	91
19. Trance and *Beroek* II	92
20. Trance and *Beroek* III	95
21. Hand Postures in Daily Life	96
22. Hand Postures in Dance	99

PLATES	FACING PAGE
23. Hand Postures in Arts and Trance	100
24. The Surface of the Body	103
25. Hands, Skin, and Mouth	104

ORIFICES OF THE BODY

26. Attack on the Mouth	107
27. Defense of the Mouth	108
28. Fingers in Mouth	111
29. Eating Meals	112
30. Pre-chopped Food	115
31. The Body as a Tube	116
32. Body Products	119
33. Scavengers, Food, and Feces	120
34. Elimination by Scrambling	123
35. Suckling	124
36. Eating Snacks	127
37. Water and Drinking	128

AUTOCOSMIC PLAY

38. Autocosmic Symbols: The Baby	131
39. Genital Manipulation	132
40. Autocosmic Toys	135
41. Autocosmic Symbols on Strings	136
42. A Bird on a String	139
43. Cockfighting	140
44. Audiences and Autocosmic Symbols	143

PARENTS AND CHILDREN

45. The Child as a God	144
46. The Mother: Fear	147
47. Stimulation and Frustration	148
48. The Mother: Narcissism	151
49. Borrowed Babies	152
50. Sulks	155
51. Boys' Tantrums	156
52. Men Singin and Her Son I	159
53. Men Singin and Her Son II	160
54. Girls' Tantrums	163
55. Trance: The Setting	164
56. Trance: Attack on the Witch	167
57. Trance: Attack on the Self	168
58. Trance: Ecstasy and Recovery	171
59. Courtship Dancers	172
60. Courtship and the Witch's Cloth	175
61. Little Witches	176

BALINESE CHARACTER

PLATES FACING PAGE

62. Parents: Witch and Dragon 179
63. The Father-Child Relationship 180
64. A Father and His Daughter 183
65. The Father: Friendly Roughness 184
66. The Dragon (*Barong*) 187
67. The Dragon and Fear of Space 188
68. Fear and Sleep 191

SIBLINGS

69. Sibling Rivalry   I 192
70. Sibling Rivalry   II 195
71. Sibling Rivalry III 196
72. Sibling Rivalry IV 199
73. Each Parent with Three Children 200
74. Roles of Siblings 203

STAGES OF CHILD DEVELOPMENT

75. Infancy and Unresponsiveness 204
76. Small Girls' Play   I 207
77. Small Girls' Play   II 208
78. Small Girls' Play III 211
79. Child Nurse 212
80. Female Childhood 215
81. Female Adolescence   I 216
82. Female Adolescence   II 219
83. Male Childhood 220

RITES DE PASSAGE

84. 210-Day Birthday   I 223
85. 210-Day Birthday   II 224
86. Tooth-filing 227
87. Marriage 228
88. Death on the Stage 231
89. Funerals 232
90. Exhumation   I 235
91. Exhumation   II 236
92. The Lay-Out of the Body 239
93. The House and the Corpse 240
94. Carrying the Corpse   I 243
95. Carrying the Corpse   II 244
96. Burning the Corpse 247
97. Representations of the Body 248
98. Representations of the Soul 251
99. Farewell to the Dead 252
100. The Continuity of Life 255

INTRODUCTION

The form of presentation used in this monograph is an experimental innovation. During the period from 1928 to 1936 we were separately engaged in efforts to translate aspects of culture never successfully recorded by the scientist, although often caught by the artist, into some form of communication sufficiently clear and sufficiently unequivocal to satisfy the requirements of scientific enquiry. "Coming of Age in Samoa," "Growing up in New Guinea," and "Sex and Temperament"[*] all attempted to communicate those intangible aspects of culture which had been vaguely referred to as its *ethos*. As no precise scientific vocabulary was available, the ordinary English words were used, with all their weight of culturally limited connotations, in an attempt to describe the way in which the emotional life of these various South Sea peoples was organized in culturally standardized forms. This method had many serious limitations: it transgressed the canons of precise and operational scientific exposition proper to science; it was far too dependent upon idiosyncratic factors of style and literary skill; it was difficult to duplicate; and it was difficult to evaluate.

Most serious of all, we know this about the relationship between culture and verbal concepts — that the words which one culture has invested with meaning are by the very accuracy of their cultural fit, singularly inappropriate as vehicles for precise comment upon another culture. Many anthropologists have been so impressed with this verbal inadequacy that they have attempted to sharpen their comment upon other cultures by very extensive borrowing from the native language. This procedure, however, in addition to being clumsy and forbidding, does not solve the problem, because the only method of translation available to make the native terms finally intelligible is still the use of our own culturally limited language. Attempts to substitute terms of cross-cultural validity, while they have been reasonably successful in the field of social organization, have proved exceedingly unsatisfactory when finer shades of cultural meaning were attempted.

Parallel with these attempts to rely upon ordinary English as a vehicle, the approach discussed in "Naven"[†] was being developed — an approach which sought to take the problem one step further by demonstrating how such categories as ethos, there defined as "a culturally standardized system of organization of the instincts and emotions of individuals," were not classifications of items of behavior but were abstractions which could be applied systematically to all items of behavior.

[*] Mead, Margaret. William Morrow, 1928, William Morrow, 1930, William Morrow, 1935, respectively.
[†] Bateson, Gregory. Cambridge, England, Cambridge University Press, 1936.

The first method has been criticized as journalistic — as an arbitrary selection of highly colored cases to illustrate types of behavior so alien to the reader that he continues to regard them as incredible. The second method was branded as too analytical — as neglecting the phenomena of a culture in order to intellectualize and schematize it. The first method was accused of being so synthetic that it became fiction, the second of being so analytic that it became disembodied methodological discussion.

In this monograph we are attempting a new method of stating the intangible relationships among different types of culturally standardized behavior by placing side by side mutually relevant photographs. Pieces of behavior, spatially and contextually separated — a trance dancer being carried in procession, a man looking up at an aeroplane, a servant greeting his master in a play, the painting of a dream — may all be relevant to a single discussion; the same emotional thread may run through them. To present them together in words, it is necessary either to resort to devices which are inevitably literary, or to dissect the living scenes so that only desiccated items remain.

By the use of photographs, the wholeness of each piece of behavior can be preserved, while the special cross-referencing desired can be obtained by placing the series of photographs on the same page. It is possible to avoid the artificial construction of a scene at which a man, watching a dance, also looks up at an aeroplane and has a dream; it is also possible to avoid diagramming the single element in these scenes which we wish to stress — the importance of levels in Balinese inter-personal relationships — in such a way that the reality of the scenes themselves is destroyed.

This is not a book about Balinese custom, but about the Balinese — about the way in which they, as living persons, moving, standing, eating, sleeping, dancing, and going into trance, embody that abstraction which (after we have abstracted it) we technically call culture.

We are interested in the steps by which workers in a new science solve piecemeal their problems of description and analysis, and in the relationship between what we now say about Balinese culture, with these new techniques, and what we have said with more imperfect means of communication about other cultures. A particular method of presentation has therefore been agreed upon. Margaret Mead has written the introductory description of Balinese character, which is needed to orient the reader so that the plates may be meaningful. She has used here the same order of vocabulary and the same verbal devices which have been made to do service in earlier descriptions of other cultures. Gregory Bateson will apply to the behavior depicted in the photographs the same sort of verbal analysis which he applied to his records of Iatmul transvestitism in "Naven," and the reader will have the photographic presentation itself to unite and carry further these two partial methods of describing the ethos of the Balinese.

Former students of Bali have approached Balinese culture as peripheral to and derivative from the higher cultures of India, China, and Java, carefully identifying in Bali the reduced and residual forms of the heroes of the Ramajana or of the Hindoo pantheon, or of the characters of the Chinese theater. All those items of Balinese culture which could not be assimilated to this picture of Asiatic diffusion have been variously classified as "Polynesian," "Indonesian," "animistic," or *"Bali aga"* (a term which some Balinese have learned to use in contradistinction to *"Bali Hindoe"*). We, however, always approached the material from the opposite point of view; we assumed that Bali had a cultural base upon which various intrusive elements had been progressively grafted over the centuries, and that the more rewarding approach would be to study this base first. We accordingly selected for our primary study a mountain village, Bajoeng Gede, near Kintamani in the District of Bangli, where most of the conspicuous elements of the later, intrusive culture were lacking. In Bajoeng Gede one does not find use of Hindoo names for the Gods, the importance of color in relation to direction in offerings, cremation, caste, the taboo upon eating beef, or any relationship to a Brahman priestly household. Writing there was, but only a half-dozen semi-literate individuals who were barely able to keep records of attendance, fines, etc. The village boasted one calendrical expert who was skilled enough to advise the village officials on the intricacies of the calendar of multiple interlocking weeks and "months." Furthermore, Bajoeng Gede was ceremonially bare, even compared with other Balinese mountain villages. There was a minimum of that reduplication and over-elaboration of art and ceremonialism which is such a marked characteristic of Balinese culture. Reliance on the calendar and complication of offerings and *rites de passage* were all reduced to a meager and skeletal minimum — a minimum which would nevertheless seem highly complex in comparison with most of the known cultures of the world. In this locality, it was possible in the course of a year to get a systematic understanding of the ground plan of the culture.

This undertaking was facilitated by two circumstances: the population of Bajoeng Gede suffered from a pronounced thyroid condition, with about 15 per cent of the population showing various degrees of simple goiter; and the whole population was markedly slow both in intellectual response and in speed of bodily movement. These circumstances, which are no doubt interrelated, provided us with a community in which the cultural emphases were schematically simplified, and upon our understanding of this base it was possible to graft — as the Balinese had before us — an understanding of the more complex versions of the same essential forms which we encountered on the plains. (It is important to remember that Hindoo culture came by way of Java, where the culture was related to that of Bali, and that most of the elements probably reached Bali in a partially assimilated form, already somewhat adapted to Balinese emphases and social structures.)

After an initial two months of exploration and work on the language in Oeboed (district of Gianjar), we selected Bajoeng Gede, and we worked there with only a few short absences from June 1936 to June 1937 and intermittently till February 1938. In November 1936, we established a second camp in Bangli in a palace built by a former Rajah, from which we were able during various short stays to participate in the family ceremonies of the ruling caste of Bangli. Finally in 1937, we built a pavilion in the courtyard of a Buddhistic Brahman family in the village of Batoean, from which position we participated in and studied Brahman family life, simultaneously collecting the work and studying the personality of the large group of Brahman and casteless painters in the school of art which had sprung up in Batoean during the last ten years.

Through Miss Belo's work in Sajan, a peasant plains village dominated by feudal Kesatrya nobles; Mrs. Mershon's work in Sanoer, a coastal fishing village consisting mainly of Sivaistic Brahmans and casteless people; and from material provided by our Balinese secretary who came from a rising casteless family in Singaradja, the Dutch capital in North Bali, we were able to gather various sorts of comparative materials to round out the picture of Balinese culture which we had developed on the basis of observations in Bajoeng Gede. The discussions of Balinese culture in this book are based on these experiences, and on short excursions by ourselves and our collaborators to other villages and cities in Bali.

It is true that every village in Bali differs from every other in many conspicuous respects, and that there are even more striking differences between districts, so that no single concrete statement about Bali is true of all of Bali, and any negative statement about Bali must be made with the greatest caution. But through this diversity there runs a common ethos, whether one is observing the home of the highest caste, the Brahman, or of the simplest mountain peasant. The Brahman's greater ease, due to the fact that there are fewer of those who know much more than he, is but another version of the peasant's unwillingness to commit himself, of his "lest I err, being an illiterate man." The most conspicuous exceptions to this common ethos are the culture of the ruling caste, the Kesatryas, and the culture of North Bali which has been exposed to strong foreign influences during the last sixty years. In both of these groups may be found an emphasis upon the individual rather than upon his status, an ele-

BALINESE CHARACTER

ment of social climbing and an uneasiness of tenure which contrast strongly with the rest of Bali. For this reason, reference to these two groups, except for occasional bits of ceremonial which they hold in common with the rest of Bali, has been excluded from this discussion.

In the Plates, each single illustration is dated and placed, and it is not safe to generalize from its detailed content for other parts of Bali. The form, however, the ethological emphasis which is implicit, may be taken to apply to all those parts of Bali of which we have any knowledge, except for North Bali, the Kesatryas, and the Vesias, a lower caste which mimics the Kesatryas and upon which we did very little work. These groups we explicitly exclude and we avoid all detailed negative statements as such statements are virtually impossible to make about a culture which has found it possible to combine such extraordinarily divergent content with such a consistent ethological emphasis. There is no apparent difference in the character structure of the people in villages where trance is shared by all and those in villages where no one ever goes into trance; people in villages where every other woman is believed to be a witch and those in villages where no one is believed to be a witch. In most of the cultures of which we have systematic knowledge, such matters are intricately and inextricably part of the personality of every participant member of the culture, but in Bali the same attitude of mind, the same system of posture and gesture, seems able to operate with these great contrasts in content with virtually no alteration in form. So also for climatic contrasts, and contrasts in wealth and poverty: the mountain people are dirtier, slower, and more suspicious than the plains people; the poor are more frightened than the rich, but the differences are in degree only; the same types of dirtiness, of suspicion, and anxiety are common at all levels.

This volume is in no sense a complete account of Balinese culture, even in its most general outlines. It is an attempt to present, at this time when scientific presentations are likely to be widely spaced, those aspects of our results and those methods of research which we have judged most likely to be of immediate use to other students. A less pregnant period of history might have dictated another choice of subject matter for our first presentation. Balinese culture, even that of Bajoeng Gede, is very rich and complex, and our two years' work, with two American collaborators and three Balinese secretaries, can only claim to be a "sampling" of the Balinese scene. We attempted to make systematic samples of village organization, calendrical ceremonial and *rites de passage,* trance, painting, carving, the shadow-play puppets, death rituals, and child behavior, so as to provide a series of crosscutting pictures of the culture which could be fitted together and cross checked against each other. The discussion which follows is a synthetic statement based upon these various samples; the photographs are a carefully selected series, analyzed on the basis of the same sampling.

Finally a word about the relevance of such researches to the period of history in which we find ourselves. Balinese culture is in many ways less like our own than any other which has yet been recorded. It is also a culture in which the ordinary adjustment of the individual approximates in form the sort of maladjustment which, in our own cultural setting, we call schizoid. As the toll of dementia praecox among our own population continues to rise, it becomes increasingly important for us to know the bases in childhood experience which predispose to this condition, and we need to know how such predisposition can be culturally handled, so that it does not become maladjustment.

Meanwhile, we are faced with the problem of building a new world; we have to reorient the old values of many contrasting and contradictory cultural systems into a new form which will use but transcend them all, draw on their respective strengths and allow for their respective weaknesses. We have to build a culture richer and more rewarding than any that the world has ever seen. This can only be done through a disciplined science of human relations and such a science is built by drawing out from very detailed, concrete materials, such as these, the relevant abstractions — the vocabulary which will help us to plan an integrated world.

BALINESE CHARACTER

By Margaret Mead

Introductory (Plates 1 to 8)

Once every 400 days, Bali is quiet and empty. The whole thickly populated section of the little island lies silent for the New Year, which is spoken of as the "silence." One can traverse the length of Bali, along the excellent roads which the Dutch have built, through village after village, between the long mud walls punctuated every few feet by the high narrow gates built in the distinctive style of that particular village, and see no women squatting before their own or someone else's doorway in front of an ankle-high table covered with soft drinks and tidbits, no group of boys gambling for pennies, no cages of fighting cocks set out in the sun. The roads, at other times, are crowded with people coming and going from the markets, which are held every three days in the larger towns; crowded with people carrying rice, pulling carts loaded high with baskets or mats or pots being brought from a distance for sale; crowded with small boys driving oxen or water buffalo. On feast days, the roads are crowded with processions of people in silks and brocades, walking in easily broken lines behind their orchestras and their gods; gods represented by temporary minute images seated in small sedan chairs; gods represented by images made of leaves and flowers; gods which are masks or bits of old relics. With the processions mingle groups of people grimed from work, hurrying lightly beneath heavy loads; and theatrical troupes, their paint and fine costumes tucked away in little bundles, trudge wearily behind the two-man mask, the patron Dragon (*Barong*) who walks quietly with covered face.

But at the New Year, these same roads are empty, stretching up and down the frequent hills, between terraced fields holding green rice, to another district where the rice is golden, on to a third where the rice is so young that the flooded beds seem filled mostly with reflections from the sky. The air on every other day of the year is filled with sound, high staccato voices shouting the clipped ambiguous words of familiar speech or artificially prolonging the syllables of polite address, quips of passers-by to the vendor girls who make a professional art of repartee, babies squalling on the hips of their child nurses; and over and above and behind all these human sounds, the air on other days carries music from practicing orchestras, from an individual idly tapping a single metallophone, from children with jew's-harps, and from whirring musical windmills set on narrow standards high against the sky.

But at the New Year every sound is silenced. Even the dogs, which on every other day keep up a sharp, impersonal yapping at every passer-by, sense the need for silence and skulk away into the courtyards where each family, with fires out and offerings set out in the house temple, stays quietly by itself. In many villages a screen set squarely across the gate, a few inches inside it, not only misleads mischievous demons who are unable to negotiate such sharp turns, but also protects the family life from watchful eyes. Inside, there are doors to close between neighboring houseyards, if it happens that close relatives live side by side (and if relatives are to live near each other at all, it had best be side by side or else the unfortunate one who dwells between them will be "pinched" by the outraged ancestral gods). Between the courtyards of non-relatives there are high walls. Each household is a complete unit; in one corner is the house temple, planted with flowers for use in offerings, and set with small shrines where the ancestors and sometimes other special gods are honored.

No one enters lightly the house of another; only beggars whose low estate may be that of the houseowner in another incarnation, peddlers, relatives, and those who have some special errand, enter another's house in the course of everyday affairs. Only if the houseowner gives a shadow-play or a light opera to celebrate the birthday of a child, the validation of a new house temple, or some piece of good fortune, do all who live in the same village, and even those who are merely passing through, or working as the lowest of casual laborers, feel free to enter, to sit down, and enjoy the play until it is over. With this exception the houseyard is closed and for the individual member who wishes to exchange light stylized puns, or easy caricature, or merely stand and chew betel with others — the street lures him out. In the street, people meet and eat casually around the vendors' stalls, two-year-olds come with their pennies — worth a fourteenth of an American cent — and there is gay impersonal interchange, with little enough meat or matter in it.

The roads lead through small villages and large, cities in which the great courts of the ruling caste are conspicuous with their gilded and highly carved gates and their occasional many-tiered pagodas, and where innumerable temples are equally conspicuous. A few roads lead up into the mountain districts, where the terraced rice fields are replaced by fields of dry rice in a landscape that is more like Europe than the tropics. Here oxen replace water buffaloes, bamboo tiles replace the thick plump thatch which roofs the lowland houses. The temples become simpler and simpler, until a structure of only four posts furnished with a shelf and a roof thatched with black sugar-palm fiber is found instead of the elaborate overcarved rococo structures of the plains. In these mountain villages there are greater differences between one community and the next, but all contain fewer elements of the Hindooism which for centuries has seeped into Bali, carried by word of mouth, by priests, by the palm-leaf books, by pictures on cloth, by carvings. There are few people who have caste in the mountains — for in Bali only a small percentage of the people are spoken of as having caste, the others, "outsiders," simply lack this special hereditary ingredient of personality. But in the lowland villages and in the mountains alike one sees straight streets, walled courtyards, and gates through which, on every day except the New Year, children trickle in and out, and dogs bark at everyone who passes, not sparing the nearest neighbor their comment on his essential strangeness.

The significance of *Njepi*, the Silence, can only be realized against the Balinese preference for anything which is *"rame,"* a word which may be translated as "noisily, crowdedly festive." Roads packed with people all going in different directions; temple courts overcrowded with offerings and where three orchestras are playing different pieces within easy earshot of each other and two dramatic performances are going on a few feet apart; market places where gay shoppers can hardly thread their way among the endless trays of carefully sorted and arrayed fruits and foods, and the fresh flowers upon which strong manufactured scent has been put, and the little stands where ready-made offerings to the market gods are sold; a theatrical performance about which the audience packs so tightly that the smallest child cannot worm its way from the front row (where the smaller children sit by well accepted custom) to the outer edge where people break away and wander among the peanut vendors — that is *rame*. No matter if one knows no one in the whole crowd. Pressed tightly against the steaming bodies of strangers, the air heavy with scent and garlic and spices, and many rare forms of dirt, sharing no single emotion with those so close to him, the Balinese watches the play and revels in the occasion, when he can stand completely remote in spirit, yet so close in body to a crowd. Women are believed to love crowds more than men and to be less able to stand the silence of empty fields, while occasionally an overwrought man develops a hatred for crowds and becomes a solitary.

This crowd preference is seen everywhere in Balinese life — in the tendency to crowd too many offerings on an altar shelf, to pack too many flowers in a young girl's hair, or to carve too many scrolls and flowers on a stone gate. Single offerings or designs, lovely in themselves when taken out of context, occur in real life in a scrambled confusion of too many colors, too many intricate, unrelated patterns. But the Balinese, who enjoys the crowd without sharing in it, is not confused by such arrays, nor is he confused by interruptions in his elaborate patterns. When a motor car or a peddler thrusts into a long and stately procession, the European is shocked but the Balinese does not notice the intrusion. Never attending to the whole, which he wants nevertheless as packed and as rich as possible, the Balinese does not notice when that whole is broken, when the dancer pauses while someone from the crowd pins her sash back on, or when the priest pauses in the middle of a complex stylized gesture of prayer to slap an overeager dog.

All ceremonial work, work for the gods, and work for the village — the preparation of offerings or feast foods, or the roofing of a house — is done in groups in Bali. And there are two principles which run through all organized work; first, that there should be more than enough people for any task, and second, that the task should be simplified and broken down into small units, almost as the construction of a motor car is broken down for a modern assembly line. The club (*sekaa*) is the model for the working group, although the members of a village or the kin of a given household may also form such groups. The club, which may be to plant or harvest or thresh rice, to lay bricks, dance a ballet, or practice as an orchestra, is a formal organization with a recording secretary, no formal leader, and far too many members for any given task. There is no requirement which demands that the man who joins a dance club should be able to dance, or that the girl who becomes the member of a harvesting club should be deft and quick at cutting rice. Those who cannot dance can do other things — roll up the mats, carry the costumes, or help in pinning up the dancers' costumes. Those who cannot cut the rice quickly can be set to counting the bound sheaves. If tasks are broken down into enough simple units, then the smallest and the least skilled can take some part. Only the wise woman who knows a great deal about offerings can tell how many of each kind of colored and specially shaped cakes should be included in a given offering container. But if the containers are laid out — 300 of them — on stands, and each small girl is given a tray with hundreds of one of the proper kinds of cake and bidden to put a certain number in each of the 300 trays, the complex results can be obtained, while each relatively ignorant and completely relaxed participant strolls, dreaming, through the repetitious undemanding task.

Only when genuine skill is required, as when the carver is attending to his chisel or the painter to his brush, or the mother is intent for a fleeting moment on teasing her child, does the Balinese display genuine concentration, and even this can be followed with startling suddenness by a state of complete awayness, in which he stares off into space, vacant faced and bare of all feeling. In the most rapt crowds, when the clowns are performing some fascinating new version of an absolutely reliable joke, one can still see face after face which contains no response to the outside world.

Trance is such an experience, an interval of extremely narrow concentration, and this is especially true of the trances of those practiced seers whose task it is to let the gods or the ancestors speak through them, giving small, deft turns to the course of events by suggestions spoken when in a state of trance. Such a seer or priestess epitomizes during the trance period all the busy activity which characterizes Balinese ceremonial; and in the trance state exhibits emotions never otherwise appropriate except on the stage — tears and intense expressions of grief and striving. All these are lived through, until again vacancy and awayness supersede.

These trance states are an essential part of Balinese social organization, for without them life would go on forever in a fixed and rigid form, foreordained but unguessed in advance. In reply to questions about future events, e.g., whether a given ceremony will be performed, or who will dance as princess in a given theatrical performance, the Balinese will reply *"doëroeng terang"* — "it is not yet clear" — a phrase which implies that the future is fixed, but that, like the latent image on an exposed photographic plate, it has not yet developed.

This way of thinking is not in any sense a lack of orientation, but is rather an expression of very rigid orientation in time and space based on the articulate recognition of large numbers of permutations and combinations of contingent circumstances. They do not say that "other things being equal" or *"Deo volente,"* such and such will occur, but feel a need to specify the necessary circumstances. They will not answer a hypothetical question which envisages contingent circumstances known to be impossible. If, for example, we asked, "If Djero Baoe Tekek were the senior citizen of the village, would he retain the duties of calendrical expert?" the reply would always be, "But the Djero Baoe has ceased to be a citizen" (because his youngest child has married), and from this position the informant cannot be shifted by any amount of urging or inquiry as to what *would* have happened if the youngest child had not married. The contingent circumstance is past and clear, and the events could not have taken any other form.

This orientation among contingent circumstances is most clearly illustrated by the calendar. This is a complex cyclical system of days, grouped into concurrent weeks. If today is the 3rd day of the five-day week and the 4th day of the seven-day week, then tomorrow will be the 4th day of the five-day week and the 5th day of the seven-day week. And of these weeks they have a complete series from a two-day week to a ten-day week, of which the three-, five-, six-, and seven-day weeks are the most important.

Identical combinations of days in the five- and seven-day weeks recur every 35 days, the Balinese "month"; identical combinations for the three-, five-, and seven-day weeks recur every 105 days (the occasion for the celebration of a baby's "three-month" birthday); and combinations involving all four of the important weeks recur every 210 days. This 210-day period, the *oton*, defines the recurrence of a very large number of ceremonials, birthdays, temple feasts, the feast of *Galoengan*, etc.*

This calendric system is truly circular in the sense that the Balinese themselves pay almost no attention to the beginnings and ends of the constituent periods. They do not know how many *oton*s old a child is, but they do know on what combination of days it was born. The whole emphasis is upon the recombinations of contingent circumstances — a sort of emphasis which only crops up in our own culture when we attend to such matters as "Friday, the thirteenth of March."

Spatial Orientation and Levels (Plates 9 to 14)

Orientation in space, like that in time, is rigid and precise, and the same interest in overlapping contingencies is recognizable. There are two pairs of primary directions, east and west (determined by the rising and setting of the sun) and inland and coastward (determined by reference to the principal mountain on the island, the Goenoeng Agoeng, which is the home of the gods). *Kadja*, the inland direction, is, however, conventionally at right angles to the east-west line, so that in most of North Bali the "inland" direction is due south, and in most of South Bali it is due north. These four cardinal points have their ceremonial characteristics; inland and east are in some sense superior to coastward and west, and the combination inland-east (*kadja-kangin*) is the most sacred direction. The village temple is set in the inland-east quadrant of the village crossroads; while the cemetery is down toward the coastward-west. In every houseyard, the family shrines are on the inland or eastern side, while the kitchen and latrine are toward the coast or the west. And inside the house, the superior person should sleep to the east or inland of the inferior, and his head should be inland or east of his feet; for this system of orientation is a part of the code of respect as well as a frame of impersonal reference. The words for the cardinal points are among the first that a child learns and are used even for the geography of the body. A Balinese will tell you that there is a fly on the "west" side of your face.

Among persons, as with time and space, there is a fixed hierarchical plan by which the three castes, Brahmans, Kesatryas, and Vesias stand in order at the top, with the outsiders, the casteless people, below them. A Brahman high priest (*pedanda*) must

* This account of the calendar is necessarily very much simplified and omits, for example, all the complications involved in fitting the *oton* system to the astronomical system of twelve named months of various lengths which define the recurrence of the ceremonies for new and full moon and the ceremonies connected with the agricultural year.

always sit higher than anyone else present and he will, even in a European house, cast his eye about with practiced calculation to select the one chair that has a quarter-inch thicker cushion than any of the others. In the simple mountain village of Bajoeng Gede the hierarchy depends upon order of entry into full citizenship (which usually occurs after marriage). The order can never be altered by promotion of one man over another and the man who happens to stay in until all above him have died or retired becomes the chief priest and ceremonial head of the community. He and the seven who stand below him, and their eight wives, are called the *"doeloe"* or "heads" of the village.

When a man speaks to another whose caste is higher than his, he must use the "polished" language, stretching out and embellishing his sentences and using quite different words, even to the prepositions and adverbs, from those of "rough" speech. Only in talking to intimates or to those of lower caste or status can a man use this "rough" speech, clipping his words and coming straight to the point. Similarly in the mountains a simplified form of the "polished" language must be used in addressing the "heads."

Each man's place in the social scheme of his village is known; the contribution which he must make to the work and ceremonial of the village and the share of the whole which he will receive back again are likewise defined. For failure to receive what is due him, he is fined even more heavily than for failure to give that which is due from him. Just as a man must accept his privileges as well as discharge his duties, so is he also the guardian of his own status and if, as may happen to a high caste, that status is affronted, he himself must perform a ceremony to restore it. Similarly the elder of a village who may not come in contact with birth or death, must himself perform a costly ceremony, if someone enters his house fresh from contact with birth or death. And as order and status are maintained among men, so also, within the man, the head is the highest part of the body and not only must it be placed toward the gods, but a flower which has fallen to the ground may not be picked up and placed in the hair again. Younger brothers may not touch the head of an older brother, and nothing may be taken from above the head of one of higher status without much preliminary apology.

So also the cycle of life is scaled in degrees of sacredness and profanity. The newborn baby is too close to the other world to be quite fit company for men; it is addressed in polished language; and not until its 105th day may its feet touch the ground. On this day a name is given and the child is henceforth permitted to enter a temple. The body of a child who has his milk teeth must be buried in a separate cemetery. Between the cutting of the adult teeth and marriage, young men are spoken of as "flower youths" as long as they are not publicly known to have had sex experience, and they are especially fitted to serve the gods. With marriage they take a sudden plunge into the profane, from which they gradually recover after years of progressive ceremonial, until with the marriage of their children they begin a slower, but sure descent into social death. The birth of a great-grandchild or the marriage of one's youngest child terminates citizenship.

The strict and formal interrelationships between persons are expressed in the recurrent village ceremonials to which each member of the community contributes and from which each receives back a share. In the mountain villages these procedures constitute a large part of village life, but in the plains they may occur only once every 210 days, and sometimes each alternate occasion is dismissed with a small feast, and only after 420 days is there a big ceremony, in which the sharing of food among the villagers is only a minor part of the entertainment given to the gods. But in the village of Bajoeng Gede the sharing is very important. At the new moon and at the full, every 35 days in each temple and at a series of feasts connected with the agricultural year, the town criers, serving monthly on a rotating system, went through the village announcing: "Every household! Every household! Tomorrow citizens come to chop; the women to sweep; the young girls to lay out offerings; every household one coconut, a measure of rice, etc.," giving a list of the contributions required of every household. Certain households, in turn, would have to provide more substantial items — a pig or a fowl or a duck. In the temple kitchens, for large ceremonies (or in the home of the men whose turn it was, for small ceremonies) the food would be cooked, offerings would be made for the gods, and later, at the ceremony, the food would be spread out in formal order — the banana-leaf plates for the "heads" laid along the inland-east and those for the members of the temple club or of the village laid out in two lines running downward and west from there. These shares, called *kawes,* are symbols of participation so important that a man can be fined more heavily for refusing his share than for failing to contribute his share to any ceremony. The fines are small (unless payment is delayed and then they rise steeply) but the matter is never a light one, and from the early deliberations of the responsible heads, through the preparation and offering of the food, down to the final distribution when his exact share of the chicken is given to each according to his status, a mild threat of fussy, group pedantry runs through the proceedings. Even the simplest arrangement of offerings or distribution of food is so complicated that numerous small errors are almost inevitable. These small errors — when the neck of the chicken is not given to the special official entitled to it

— are matters of embarrassment, and stimulate a sort of garrulous scuttling of too many people trying to correct them. Failure in the proper arrangements for a feast, where the offerings are concerned, may bring misfortune, supernaturally sent. Yet so slight is the expectation that there will not be errors, that the folk belief grows that the flowers on the headdress of the great serpent, on which a priest rides for special large cremation ceremonies, would stay unwithered if the ceremony had been perfect.

Among the casteless people of the mountains, the preservation of status among those who by birth are equal, is a solemn and humorless business, conducted with a maximum dependence upon such external forms as details of food distribution and small permissions and prohibitions. Every individual must bear in mind a large number of these injunctions, which determine details of his costume and what temples he may enter, what houses he must avoid because they have not been purified since the last death or birth, etc. It cannot be said that any status is more "free" than any other — only that the list of permissions and prohibitions differs as between one status and another.

As in the plains, so also in the mountains, the niceties of language are invoked in the expression of status, with the only difference that the mountain system is simpler than that of the plains. The mountain people have the essential differentiation between the clipped speech addressed to intimates and the long-winded periphrases addressed to superiors; and this long-winded locution they use for all formal occasions, citizens' meetings, marriage negotiations, etc. This polite speech of the mountains is built up of everyday words and has not the complete and separate vocabulary of that used in the plains. But the pronouns are differentiated according to relative status.

Posture and gesture are also used to express status but very much less than in the plains, and expressions of respect lack the exaggeration characteristic of the plains. The gestures of obeisance, the clasped hands, the politely downward-pointing right thumb, all these are absent in the mountains, even when the gods are addressed. The mountain people experience these postures only in the theatricals which traveling companies of plainsmen bring to their villages, but here they learn enough of the overdone gestures of obsequiousness to be able to imitate them, at least for the next few months, when high persons enter their village. "But," say the people of Bajoeng, "high-caste people could never live long in the village of Bajoeng Gede, for the Bajoeng people would not be able to keep on being polite." And those of high caste who are treated without proper respect themselves suffer. Only in occasional instances are they strong enough to make others suffer.

In the mountains there is less use of levels to discriminate between man and man, but when we look at the relations between men and gods we find the same insistence upon the stratification of vertical space as in the plains. The higher an offering, the more the gods are honored. Shrines tower upward; the little sedan chairs of the gods are carried on the shoulders; little girls in trance are carried on the shoulders; and food may not be placed upon the ground but must be laid at least upon a mat (in the plains it would be stood upon a pedestal), thus raising it above the level where the eaters are seated — for food also is a god.

In the mountain village, space and time and social status form an orderly whole, with little stress or strain, and without a need to skit or overstate the points of difference. People dress in their best and wash their hair for ceremonies; they speak with respect when they meet the village heads on the street or approach them to ask to be excused from some village obligation. True, in Bajoeng, the exclusive distinction between those born in the village and those who have entered later is never forgotten, for a different first person pronoun is used by the birthright Bajoeng people, but here also there is so little strain that the people make no play with the idea themselves, and only laughed merrily when I would use it: *"Njonjah demen me-oke"* — "The *Njonjah** enjoys using *oke*," they would giggle. Similarly if a baby would pull at my hair, the mother would quickly remove him and apologize, but if I made a point of letting him play on, the people would relax and laugh. A flower that falls to the ground cannot be replaced in the hair, but everyone knows that — it is no great strain to remember. Children have to be watched until they learn the rules, and foreigners admonished lest they break the local regulations, like the vendor woman who became ill because she raised her umbrella too high in front of the village temple, and so was punished by the gods.

But within the village, within the fixed and complicated sets of regulations, obligations, and privileges, the people are relaxed and dreamy. Only occasionally, as when offerings have to be checked, fines counted, or food distributed, do they pay attention for a moment. And when the whole village travels as a unit to take their contributions to a ceremony held by the Rajah, they seem able to take this sense of complete orientation with them, and the simplest peasant sits quiet and relaxed, in a group, in the presence of his prince.

The minute, however, that caste enters the picture in the form of inter-personal relations, we find a different situation. The casteless Balinese man who, at home in his village, made only the necessary obeisances, becomes extravagantly overpolite in greet-

* Third person singular term of respect for a non-Balinese woman.

ing a high caste. Those who actually become servants in the palaces skit their position still further, going about with their clothes at fantastic and grotesque angles, clowning their subordinate role. It is significant that this clowning is always done from below. The superior person, whether a high caste in real life or a prince on the stage, remains aloof and self-contained, giving no sign that the clowning of his subordinate is a continuous warning to him not to diverge too far from his aloof role into assertiveness.

Between those whose status is not known to each other, there is a great chilly distance, the most formal of discourse, and an unsmiling countenance. Each takes the earliest opportunity to ask the questions necessary to place the other. In a strange village, where he does not know the cardinal points or the local customs, and if he does not know what day it is in at least three of the intercogging weeks, nor the caste and order of birth term* for the person with whom he is trying to converse, the Balinese is completely disoriented. To this state they apply the term *"paling"* which is used also for those who are drunk, delirious, or in trance. Orientation in time, space, and status are the essentials of social existence, and the Balinese, although they make very strong spirits for ceremonial occasions, with a few startling exceptions resist alcohol, because if one drinks one loses one's orientation. Orientation is felt as a protection rather than as a strait jacket and its loss provokes extreme anxiety. If one takes a Balinese quickly, in a motor car, away from his native village so that he loses his bearings, the result may be several hours of illness and a tendency to deep sleep.

Virtually the only context in which levels are skitted in Bajoeng Gede is in the relationship between elder and younger brother, when the mother borrows a baby to place on the head of her child, or deliberately places a younger sibling over her older child's head. The hierarchical position of brothers, in which the younger is supposed to use self-deprecating pronouns in addressing the elder, is one of the least stable and most uncomfortable points in Balinese inter-personal relations; and in the effort to adjust it Europeanized Balinese even mix Dutch pronouns in their native speech. Between castes, if the high caste wishes to be modern and to treat the casteless man politely, the courtesy language can be assumed, as between strangers. Between brothers, however, two systems cross: that which assumes that the "rough" language is the language of intimacy, and that which declares the younger brother must honor the elder and should use pronouns of polished subordination. The sibling relationship is also characterized by another anomaly; there is a certain insistence upon cherishing, upon

* The Balinese of the plains use four common terms of address (*Wajan, Made, Njoman, Ketoet*) to define order of birth. A fifth child usually starts a new "set" and is addressed as "*Wajan.*"

thoughtfulness from the elder to the younger. Now thoughtfulness, implying as it does identification with the other, is extraordinarily out of key with Balinese character. Placating another, teasing another, flirting with another, fending off the approach from another — these are all habitual enough. But cherishing and thoughtfulness are absent even from the mother-child relationship to an astonishing degree, being replaced by titillation and emotional exploitation. Yet, in the comment of parent to elder child, there recurs a sententious, out-of-key admonition — "Take care of your younger sibling," "Give that to your younger sibling," usually shortened to a sharp *"Adinne"* — "the younger sibling," whenever the older child shows signs of aggression or greed.

These various anomalies and points of contradiction in the use of fixed levels, between high-caste and servant, and between brothers, are all skitted in every theatrical performance. The stock theatrical servants are an elder brother, elegant, pompous, and dull, and a younger brother, gauche, mischievous, and hyperactive. The pair of them, after thoroughly confusing their relationship to each other, proceed to overdo and caricature their relationship to their prince, who remains charming and aloof and continues to sing unintelligible archaic words while the two brothers posture around him.

This freedom of theatrical caricature, from which neither the possessed seer nor the Brahman high priest escapes, though running the whole gamut of Balinese life, concentrates on the points of strain in the system, and so provides continual release in laughter for an audience which has learned to count upon the recurrence of just these themes. The very tone of the laughter is a further index of what the caricature does, for it has the unmistakable character of laughter at a pornographic joke. In every other culture in which I have worked, it has been possible to distinguish the sudden roar of pornographic laughter from laughter at themes other than sex. In Bali this cannot be done, the restrictions surrounding personal relationships in terms of seniority, caste, and directions and levels, seem to have the same quality as the restrictions which, in many cultures, surround sex; and the skits upon status, although rooted in inter-personal relationships, have some of their most satisfying expressions in inversions of the human body — dances in which people stand on their heads with feet doing duty as hands and with masks set on their pubes; carvings in which the head is set on a neck so elongated that it can be twisted around to fit between the legs. Probably the tie-up between the position of the head and the position of the older brother and the person of rank, impressed as it is upon the infant so that a child of eighteen months will shriek with rage if another child is held over his head, is responsible for the bodily ribaldry with which the Balinese can laugh at a joke involving a reversal of pronouns.*

Learning (Plates 15 to 17)

When the Balinese baby is born, the midwife, even at the moment of lifting him in her arms, will put words in his mouth, commenting, "I am just a poor little newborn baby, and I don't know how to talk properly, but I am very grateful to you, honorable people, who have entered this pig sty of a house to see me born." And from that moment, all through babyhood, the child is fitted into a frame of behavior, of imputed speech and imputed thought and complex gesture, far beyond his skill and maturity. The first time that he answers *"Tiang,"* the self-subordinating ego pronoun, to a stranger, he will be echoing a word that has already been said, on his behalf and in his hearing, hundreds of times. Where the American mother attempts to get the child to parrot simple courtesy phrases, the Balinese mother simply recites them, glibly, in the first person, and the child finally slips into speech, as into an old garment, worn before, but fitted on by another hand.

As with speech, so with posture and gesture. The right hand must be distinguished from the left; the right hand touches food, and the right thumb may be used in pointing; the left hand is the hand with which one cleanses oneself, or protects one's genitals in bathing, and must never be used to touch food, to point, or to receive a gift. But the Balinese mother or nurse carries a child, either in or out of a sling, on her left hip, thus leaving her own right hand free. In this position, the baby's *left* arm is free, while the right is frequently pinioned in against the breast, or at best extended behind the mother's back. Naturally, when a baby is offered a flower or a bit of cake, it reaches for it with the free left hand, and the mother or the child nurse invariably pulls the left hand back, extricates the baby's right hand — usually limp and motiveless under this interference with the free gesture — and extends the right hand to receive the gift. This training is begun long before the child is able to learn the distinction, begun in fact as soon as the child is able to grasp at a proffered object, and discontinued usually when the child is off the hip. A three-year-old may often err and

---

* This final paragraph summing up the themes of status joking involves three sets of psychological generalizations which are separately handled in the analytical captions.

1. Generalizations involving the psychological equivalence, for the Balinese, of sex and aggression. These appear in the captions in the form of statements about Balinese climax. It is stated, for example, that the Balinese child is frustrated whenever it tries to achieve *crescendo* and climax in inter-personal relations with the mother, and that this frustration occurs whether it be a *crescendo* of love or of anger.

2. Generalizations about the psychological role which birds on strings and actors on the stage play, for the Balinese, as autocosmic genital symbols.

3. Generalizations about the Balinese fantasies of bodily integration and disintegration.

G. B.

receive a casual present in his left hand, with no more punishment than to have some older child or nearby adult shout *"Noenas!"* ("Ask!") which means "Cup the right hand in the left," but the baby of four months is permitted no such leeway. Over and over again, the first spontaneous gesture is clipped off, and a passive, plastic gesture is substituted.

Meanwhile, the child in the sling, or supported lightly on the carrier's hip, has learned to accommodate itself passively to the carrier's movements; to sleep, with head swaying groggily from side to side, as the carrier pounds rice; or to hang limp on the hip of a small girl who is playing "crack-the-whip." Surrendering all autonomy, and passively following the words spoken in its name or the rhythm of the person who carries it or the hand which snatches its hand back from a spontaneous gesture, the child's body becomes more waxy flexible as it grows older; and gestures which are all echoes of an experienced pattern replace such spontaneous gestures of infancy as the pounding of the child's silver bracelets on any convenient board. This accommodation to the movements of others, to cues that come from a pattern rather than from a desire, is facilitated by the extent to which a Balinese child is carried. There is a strong objection to letting a child be seen crawling — an animal activity — by any but the family intimates; and babies, even after they are able to crawl and toddle, are still carried most of the time. The position on the hip limits spontaneity to the arms and the carrier's repetitive interference with hand gestures reduces it there.

Even at its 105-day birthday, the infant is dressed in full adult costume. The infant boy is seated in a parent's arms, and a headcloth ten times too large for him is arranged at least for a moment on his head. The infant's hands are put through the gestures of prayer, of receiving holy water, and of wafting the essence of the holy offering toward himself. By the 210-day birthday, the child will repeat these gestures himself, sitting dreamily, after the ceremony, clasping and unclasping his tiny hands, and then speculatively examining them, finger by finger. At this age also, before he can walk, he will be taught simple hand dance gestures, first by manual manipulation, and later he will learn to follow visual cues, as the parent hums the familiar music and gestures before the baby's eyes with his own hand. This situation, the child dancing in the sustaining arm of the parent and that arm vibrating rhythmically to the music, becomes the prototype of Balinese learning in which as he grows older he will learn with his eyes and with his muscles. But the learning with the eyes is never separated from a sort of physical identification with the model. The baby girl climbs down off her mother's hip to lift a bit of an offering to her head, when her mother or elder sister does the same.

BALINESE CHARACTER

Learning to walk, learning the first appropriate gestures of playing musical instruments, learning to eat, and to dance are all accomplished with the teacher behind the pupil, conveying directly by pressure, and almost always with a minimum of words, the gesture to be performed. Under such a system of learning, one can only learn if one is completely relaxed and if will and consciousness as we understand those terms are almost in abeyance. The flexible body of the dancing pupil is twisted and turned in the teacher's hands; teacher and pupil go through the proper gesture, then suddenly the teacher springs aside, leaving the pupil to continue the pattern to which he has surrendered himself, sometimes with the teacher continuing it so that the pupil can watch him as he dances. Learning with the eyes flows directly from learning passively while one's own body is being manipulated by another.

The Balinese learn virtually nothing from verbal instruction and most Balinese adults are incapable of following out the three consecutive orders which we regard as the sign of a normal three-year-old intelligence. The only way in which it is possible to give complex verbal instructions is to pause after each detail and let the listener repeat the detail, feeling his way into the instruction. Thus all orders tend to have a pattern like this. "You know the box?" "What box?" "The black one." "What black one?" "The black one in the east corner of the kitchen." "In the east corner?" "Yes, the black one. Go and get it." "I should go and get the black box in the east corner of the kitchen?" "Yes." Only by such laborious assimilation of words into word gestures made by oneself, do words come to have any meaning for action.

This same peculiarity is found in the pattern of story telling. The Balinese story teller does not continue gaily along through a long tale, as the story tellers of most cultures do, but he makes a simple statement, "There was once a princess," to which his auditors answer, "Where did she live?" or "What was her name?" and so on, until the narrative has been communicated in dialogue. A thread, even a simple verbal thread, in which one's body plays no role, has no continuous meaning.

There is rarely any discernible relationship between the conversation of a group of Balinese and the activity which they are performing. Words must be captured and repeated to have meaning for action, but there is no need at all to translate action into words. One might listen at a spy hole for an hour to a busy group, hearing every word spoken, and be no wiser in the end as to whether they were making offerings, or painting pictures, or cooking a meal. The occasional "Give me that!" is interspersed with bits of comic opera, skits and caricatures, songs and punning and repartee. As Americans doodle on a piece of paper while attending to the words of a lecture, so the Balinese doodles in words, while his body flawlessly and quickly attends to the job in hand.

All learning in Bali depends upon some measure of identification, and we may consider as prototype of such learning, the child's continuous adaptation to movements into which it is guided by the parent who holds it. Lacking such identification, no learning will occur, and this becomes specially conspicuous when one attempts to teach a Balinese some new foreign technique. Most Balinese will balk and make no attempt to copy a European, or to perform any act, no matter how simple, which only a European has been seen to perform. But if once one can persuade one Balinese to master a European skill, then other Balinese of the same or superior caste position will learn it very quickly. So in training our Balinese secretaries, we had no difficulty because I Made Kaler, our secretary, educated in Java, believed that he could do what Europeans did, just as he could speak their language, sit on their chairs and handle their tools. Other Balinese boys, seeing Made Kaler use a typewriter, learned to type accurately and well in a few days.

This particularistic identification with the movement and skill of other bodies, socially comparable to one's own, has undoubtedly served as a conservative element in Bali, maintaining the division of labor between the sexes, and partially limiting certain skills, like writing, to the high castes. Only by invoking some such explanation can we understand the division of labor in Bali. The system works smoothly and accurately but with a total absence of sanctions. In the few cases of women who become scholars or musicians, or men who become skilled in weaving, no one even bothers to comment on the odd circumstance. And those who cross the sex division of labor are not penalized; they are not regarded as more or less masculine or feminine nor confused with the occasional transvestite, although the latter includes the occupations of the opposite sex in his transvesticism. But without sanctions, with freedom to embrace any occupation, ninety-nine out of a hundred Balinese adhere simply to the conventions that spinning, weaving, making most offerings, etc., are women's work, whereas carving, painting, music, making certain other offerings, etc., are men's work.

Combined with this kinaesthetic type of learning and with the continuous insistence upon levels and directions, there is a preoccupation with balance, which expresses itself in various ways. When the young male child is still learning to walk, loss of balance or any other failure evokes a regular response: he immediately clutches at his penis, and often, to be sure of balance, walks holding on to it. Little girls clasp their arms in front of them, and sometimes hold on to their heads. As they grow older, an increased sense of balance makes it possible to stand motionless for quite a long time on one foot; but dancing on one foot, playing too freely with a preciously achieved and highly developed balance is associated with witches and demons. Just as in witchcraft, right and left are reversed, so also in witchcraft, the decent boundaries of body posture are trespassed upon.

Balinese children, especially little Balinese girls, spend a great deal of time playing with the joints of their fingers, experimenting with bending them back until the finger lies almost parallel with the back of the hand. The more coordinated and disciplined the motion of the body becomes, the smaller the muscle groups with which a Balinese operates. Where an American or a New Guinea native will involve almost every muscle in his body to pick up a pin, the Balinese merely uses the muscles immediately relevant to the act, leaving the rest of the body undisturbed. Total involvement in any activity occurs in trance and in children's tantrums, but for the rest, an act is *not* performed by the whole body. The involved muscle does not draw all the others into a unified act, but smoothly and simply, a few small units are moved — the fingers alone, the hand and forearm alone, or the eyes alone, as in the characteristic Balinese habit of slewing the eyes to one side without turning the head.

Integration and Disintegration of the Body (Plates 18 to 25)

These two habits, that of going waxy limp in the hands of a teacher and permitting the body to be manipulated from without, and that of moving only the minimum of muscles necessary to any act, find expression in the whole puppet complex* on the one hand, and in the fear of decomposition on the other. The animated puppet, the doll which dances on a string, the leather puppets manipulated by the puppeteer, and finally the little girl trance dancers who themselves become exaggeratedly limp and soft as they dance to the commands of the audience, all dramatize this whole picture of involuntary learning, in which it is not the will of the learner, but the pattern of the situation and the manipulation of the teacher which prevail. In the shadow-play, the puppet is set against the screen, and while he stands immobile, the flickering and swinging of the lamp give him a fiction of movement and the puppeteer recites a long speech, imputing it to the puppet. In the *sangiang deling* performance, little puppets with loaded feet are suspended from a slender string supported by sticks held in the hands of two performers. The hands of the performers tremble, set up a harmonic action in the string, and the puppets are said to "be in trance, and to dance uncontrollably," thus dramatizing the confusion which is involved in all Balinese activity — the blending of the teacher and the taught, the model and the copyist.

The fear of disintegration, epitomized in the shuddering horror at the rotting of

* Originally described by Jane Belo (MS on "Trance in Bali," to be published shortly by Columbia University Press).

the body after death, is equally understandable. This body, which moves only in parts and without volition, hardly seems like a unit at all, and may well be composed of a series of separate units, each with a life of its own. Such are the ideas of black magic, and of protection against black magic. Folk beliefs are filled with personified limbs, legs and arms, and heads, each animated by a mischievous will of its own, frequenting the cemetery and existing merely to torment man. And in a special set of *sangiang* performances in the District of Karangasem, there are trances in which only the hand of the performer is put in trance; it trembles independently, while he himself and the rest of his body remain uninvolved.

In the hands, more intensely than in any other part of the body, this disassociation, this independence of each small unit is seen. Balinese hands at rest rarely lie with the fingers in seriated regular flexion as our hands do, but one finger stays at one angle and another at another in a way which would prove infinitely tiring to us. As a Balinese sits watching two children play, or two cocks fighting, it is sometimes possible to see how the two hands become separate symbols of the two who are being watched, the hands twitching slightly as the scene shifts. Even when one of the fighting cocks belongs to the spectator and the other to his rival, still the two hands play out their dramatic counterpoint, and from watching them one can follow the action but not guess the winner. So when a painter was working with one hand, and the other lay on the table unused, it was sometimes found that that second hand provided the more interesting series of postures, as if the neglected hand were playing out a little counterpoint of its own.

Watching a Balinese crowd around a vendor's stall, an audience at play, a group sitting by the roadside, or a religious congregation, one is struck by the continuous fussing with the surface of the skin, the roving of the sensitive fingers, alert and searching over the skin, looking for something, some roughness or imperfection on which to pause. At first this appears to be mere fidgeting, but actually the people are unduly sensitive to skin imperfections. Every break in the surface of the body is a disaster; people with open sores cannot enter the temple and cannot prepare offerings for the gods, nor, if the sore is too bad, can they be buried in the proper cemetery. Imperfections in the skin are associated with loss of a body part, so no one who has lost a fingernail, or has broken an ear lobe, or has lost a finger joint is eligible to full temple membership in Bajoeng Gede. Skin lesions are ceremonially classed with pregnancy in Bajoeng — temporary distortions rendering one unfit for ceremonially pure occasions. And the Balinese skin heals too fast. The whole problem of treating a wound is how to keep the wound open against too quick healing followed by infection which develops beneath the light scar.

But as one watches these crowds with their fingers playing exploringly over the surface of the face, it becomes apparent also that wherever a rough spot is found, some abrasion sufficient to arrest that straying finger, a sort of closed circuit is set up — finger and point of body surface against which the finger presses, both entering consciousness. This circuit from own hand to own body can be diverted to inter-personal uses, e.g., in lousing, one of the few inter-personal contacts which may unite a whole group of girls and women during some long pause in a ceremony.

Orifices of the Body (Plates 26 to 37)

The Balinese have their fantasies of bodily disintegration, but as one watches an adult Balinese, one is impressed with a sense of the whole body, with the way in which the tip of the finger is an integrated part of the whole. Watching a member of our own culture, one receives quite a different impression; the body appears as a trunk and the arms and legs as appendages which are never quite in unison with it. Peoples differ strikingly in the emphases implicit in their handling of the body; some think of the human body as a trunk, with orifices at both ends, while others think of the trunk as merely a central element in a unified body. But the human infant at birth brings to his cultural experience an almost uncoordinated body and a series of orifices by which he initially meets and interprets the world. What his primary interpretation will be and whether this interpretation will persist, must depend largely upon the way in which those about him handle him.

In Bali, the infant is both suckled and fed from birth on, so that the two experiences of absorbing liquids by sucking and stronger substances by swallowing occur together. But from the start, the two experiences are sharply differentiated; when the infant is suckled, the mother holds it so that its mouth is placed down on the nipple, rather than in the more common fashion in which the nipple is thrust down into a baby's mouth. He learns to draw milk *up* into his mouth. From the very beginning, suckling is a free activity in which the infant is given more freedom of movement than can be the case when the mother thrusts her nipple down into an infant's mouth, and in addition the child is given freedom to determine *when* it shall be suckled.

Exactly the opposite is the case in the method of feeding solids. The mother pre-chews a mixture of rice and banana, and then, either with her lips or her finger, she places a mound of the soft pre-chewed material on the baby's mouth, gradually manipulating more and more of it into its mouth. The infant splutters and chokes, helpless and almost always resistant to the mountain of mush which is being forced on it. Each feeding becomes a sort of attack, in which the baby instead of being free to draw up sweet milk at will, is forced to swallow against its will. Little children, given their meals in shallow coconut shells, may be seen tipping these saucers over their faces, reproducing the smothering situation in which they learned to eat.

All through life, the Balinese have a sensitivity in regard to open mouths, and Balinese betel chewing contains one special element which is congruent with this. After the bit of areca nut and the little roll of pepper leaf and lime or the bit of spice have been chewed and spat, the Balinese takes a great wad of shredded tobacco and places this in his open mouth. This unsightly wad may remain there for hours, protruding from the wedged-open mouth, reminiscent of the pile of mash on the face of the baby, but also serving a second purpose — closing the mouth of the adult against the world. In gesture, too, the same protectiveness of the mouth is often seen. The palm of the hand is placed over the mouth, and sometimes the cloth shawl, worn by men and women in the colder parts of Bali, is also drawn from the chest to cover the mouth, warding off the outside world.

But during late infancy and early childhood, betel is not yet chewed, and there is no wad of tobacco to stop up the alarmingly open space through which strange things may be forced upon one. The baby teethes — and teething is unusually difficult in Bajoeng Gede, perhaps because of mineral deficiencies in the soil — on a large locket shaped like a box, which is hung about its neck on a necklace of small silver medallions. The baby lifts the necklace and thrusts the box into its mouth, teething as it were on a part of itself. Soon the finger replaces the necklace, and the finger is thrust deep into the mouth, avoiding the lips and exploring deeply in the oral cavity. Once in so often the finger is drawn out of the mouth with a slow swish in which the attention is evidently concentrated on the finger and not on the mouth. Even when own finger is thrust into own mouth, it is not the mouth but the finger which is emphasized, and the onlooker gets the impression that the child enjoys a pleasant sensation — located in the finger.

Meanwhile, habits of eating are developed, and eating again falls into two categories; eating solid food as a meal, and the casual swallowing of snacks and tidbits and drinks, which are usually taken standing. So uncomfortable are the Balinese when eating meals that many observers have come away from Bali insisting that the Balinese will never eat in public if they can avoid it, and that if others are present they turn their backs on each other, and toss the food into their mouths as quickly as possible.

Eat together they must, at feasts, at ceremonies, and as members of work groups who are fed by the host, but always there is the turning away, the search for privacy reminiscent of the search for privacy in defecation which contrasts so sharply with the total disregard of privacy for urination. In every house the place of the pigs, the lowest place in the ground plan, is also a latrine, but only for defecation. Adults as well as children urinate casually, in the midst of a conversation, in the open road, where also they buy and consume snacks with no sign of modesty or embarrassment.

Inasmuch as eating solid food is attended with so much unpleasant emotion and the whole process of intake and elimination of food is so sharply divided between that which is liquid, casual, and a matter of choice, and that which is solid, heavily serious, and socially enjoined, it is not surprising to find an astonishing amount of time devoted to the preparation of food. This is the preliminary reduction of foods from large unwieldy masses to symbolically predigested mash. Every feast, every ceremony, is prefaced by group activity in which the meat is chopped into minute bits, sometimes varied by the construction of ornamental *sate*, in which the pig fat or omentum is refashioned into elaborate and fanciful designs. Most preparation of food, which includes also the preparation of offerings (for offerings are merely ornamentally arranged patterns of food and other decorative elements), involves the elimination of the original form of the food and usually the substitution of some new form. The meat paste may be molded into a new shape, or the little sticks on which the paste is smeared may be shaped to a design, or the food may be placed in containers themselves fancifully shaped. Both meat and meal are forced to lend themselves to this endless recombining, this restructuring of food stuffs into forms delightful to the eye and often symbolic of discarded ceremonial usages. The whole roast pig which occurs in a mountain ceremony is likely to be replaced, in the ceremonies of the plains, by a model made of rice meal and elaborately colored.

While the Balinese feel strongly that eating solid food is embarrassing and that defecation should be done in private, their methods of child training are mild and dilatory, and the child learns his excretory manners without extreme pressure being put upon him. The people have little genuine objection to dirt; they bathe a great deal for the pleasure they receive from sitting in an open stream and cooling their skins, but they cheerfully resume their soiled clothing. Infants are carried in clothes which are interchangeably baby slings and shawls, and the infant's excreta are cleaned up by dogs, wherever they happen to fall. A urinating infant is not jerked quickly aside so as to prevent his wetting his mother's sarong, and only slowly do children learn to ask what is the proper place for defecation. The whole childhood attitude was summed up in the behavior of three five-year-olds who solemnly reported to me, "Karsa (aged three) has just defecated over there." "Well, don't you defecate?" "Yes, but never in your yard, *Njonjah*." And I have more than once come upon riotous scenes in which groups of children were dancing in taunting delight around some unhappy child who had been unwary and had stepped in feces.

The attitudes toward eating and defecating contain in fact a large element of conventionality and a failure to conform meets with the sanction of mockery, provoking that acute misery which in Bali follows any lapse from conventional propriety. The component of disgust in these attitudes is, however, more difficult to account for. The toilet training is, as we have seen, not stringent, and to understand fully the nature of their feelings and their extension to both food and feces, it is necessary to see them in a wider cultural setting. We have to bear in mind, simultaneously, the choking with pre-chewed food; the pre-chopping of meals; the Balinese notion that witches eat chicken dung and that luminous saliva drips from their mouths; the scavenging role of the dog; and the Balinese horror of all signs of animality in man or woman.

On the ceremonial level, the elimination of such rubbish as the remains of feasts and offerings has a curious hectic quality, reminiscent of the screams of the small child who is being pursued hopefully by a dog. At the end of ceremonies, the *lis*, a ceremonial broom with which various parts of the paraphernalia and courtyard are sprinkled with water, is thrown away, and special offerings are laid on the ground to be eaten by the dogs, representative of the demons, or are scrambled over by human beings for the pennies which they contain. Human beings so scrambling over ceremonial excreta become animal-like, replacing the dogs, and animality is more abhorrent to a Balinese than any other aspect of humanity. Bestiality is a major crime for which people are banished forever, and the punishment for incest is a ritual in which the partners in crime wear pig yokes over their necks and must crawl to a pig trough and eat with their mouths to the trough as animals do. Any situation which thus likens men to animals by giving them a role in the handling of the unclean, particularly in the handling of corpses, is likely to induce this riotous scrambling and lapse from human quality. A human being stands upright, never crawls, is embarrassed by eating, keeps his right hand for his food.

The institution of the food vendor brings out the other side of the feeling about eating. Food vending is done outside the home, and one's own mother becomes a different person when she takes her little table, set with soft drinks and tidbits, and sits down by the roadside to sell food for pennies. The situation becomes gay and frivolous, people cluster together thinking little of caste or status, except in speech. They eat standing without embarrassment, flirt with the vendor, part of whose stock-in-trade is quick repartee. Eating at the vendor's stall is casual and playful, and it must be compared, not with the baby's forced eating of pre-chewed food, but with the casual and gay suckling. Tiny children, hardly able to talk, are given pennies, wander beyond the confining circle of the home, and turn their pennies into snacks and sweetmeats. The vagrants who wander from village to village, begging a coin here, doing a half-day's work there, may eat almost entirely from these food stalls, living outside all the limitations of citizenship and onerous social participation.

Food eaten standing at a vendor's stall requires no preliminary or final washing of the mouth, but at the end of a real meal each Balinese carefully fills his mouth with water and spews the water forth without swallowing any, thus breaking connection with the food which has just entered his mouth. And it is against this background that the Balinese ceremonial use of water must be understood, whether it is the receiving of holy water, washing one's hair before going to a ceremony, or pouring holy water over a corpse. Water breaks the corrupting tie, not with dirt, but with having had contact with dirt — a very different matter.

It is only when food is actually entering the body that the Balinese feel this way about it. Rice is treated as a god and should be set on a pedestal higher than the seated eater; and there were rules in some villages against speaking to a man who was eating, because it would anger the god that was in him. Food is never laid on the bare ground; when this is done it becomes, psychologically speaking, not food but excreta.

Throughout, the Balinese is preoccupied with the participation of his own body in an act, rather than in a relationship between himself and an outside object. Participation in the act of ingesting and digesting solids is accompanied by repulsion, but the repulsion is not directed toward the food. When the body is seen as a tube through which things pass quickly and relatively unaltered, this idea seems to be pleasant and unembarrassing; while the opposite notion, that substances are taken into the body and there altered, is correspondingly unpleasant and embarrassing.

Autocosmic Play (Plates 38 to 44)

The Balinese treat a baby as something between a toy and a puppet, with a little touch of extra respect if they remember that the baby is recently returned from the other world. Nowhere in all Bali, where people laugh far more readily at a gaff than in response to any direct invocation of their emotions, where tears are disallowed at death and where anger is expressed with greater smoothness of speech, is there anything half as responsive as a baby. The six-month-old baby is carried about continually; if it frets or grows restless there are half a dozen hands stretched out to receive it, and the carrier, piqued at its restlessness, is only too glad to let it go. So a baby passes from hand to hand in a crowd, staying a half-minute in one girl's arms, only to yield to the blandishments of her neighbor with outstretched arms. No one passes a baby without stopping to flick its fingers or flick it under the chin, or utter a teasing, "Where is your mother?" guaranteed to make the baby pucker its lips or to cry outright. A popular baby, from the age of five or six months to a year, is always "wandering about for pleasure" on the hip of some woman or small girl, a relative or a neighbor. Only on the rarest occasions do little girls invent substitute dolls, or play with little carvings, or treat puppies as babies. Most of the time they play with real babies, gay responsive babies, babies which respond to stimulation with tears or laughter as easily as a mechanical doll says "mama" when pressed in the right place. Babies are women's toys, so satisfying as toys that they seldom, even as children, turn to other toys.

Yet there is another side to the attitude toward babies, summed up in the words which are used for them before they are named — "mouse," "caterpillar," "grub" — little crawling things — and significantly some of these terms are also used as scare words to deter a young child from doing anything which his mother doesn't want him to do. These same little creatures occur in paintings of corpses, and a woman who has refused to have children on earth is punished by having to suckle a caterpillar in hell. Mothers of new babies are addressed as "mother of a mouse" or "mother of a caterpillar," and holy persons, priests, and those who have been purified in the hierarchy of Bajoeng Gede must not go near young babies.

What a baby is to a woman — something to play with, to toy with, to titillate and tease, to dawdle over, to carry about, to dress up and undress, to stroke and to tickle — a fighting cock is to a man. Balinese men often carry their own babies about, in the mountains even wearing the baby sling and carrying quite young babies tenderly and skillfully, but for grown men these are always their own children or grandchildren. Carrying babies about is an act of kinship more than a form of amusement. Adolescent boys, not yet sure of themselves as grown men, will often spend time carrying and toying with some young relative, but it is doubtful if any boy who was not constrained to the task by being left with a baby to care for, would ever prefer a baby to a fighting cock. The average Balinese man can find no pleasanter way to pass the time than to walk about with a cock, testing it out against the cocks of other men whom he meets on the road, giving it an onion bath, or putting red pepper on its anus or into its beak. Ruffling it up, smoothing it down, ruffling it up again, sitting among other men who are engaged in similar toying with their cocks — this passes many hours of the long hot afternoons. But if one watches a woman with a baby and a man with a fighting cock, one sees a significant difference: the man is handling the cock as an extension of his own body; the woman is handling the child as something separate, apart from herself, something for which one reaches out and which one seeks to attract. When one man is allowed to handle the cock of another, the men change places rather than the cock changing hands. The newcomer slips into the place behind the cock, and the man who was holding it slips to one side.

Children's first experience of handling live things, which later develops into play with fighting cocks for men and play with babies for girls and women, is provided by baby birds, beetles, grasshoppers, etc., which are tied and given to children as playthings. Baby chicks and puppies are also given to children quite freely as toys. We photographed one scene in which two two-year-old boys were bouncing puppies as if they were rubber balls. The child is taught no identifying attitudes of pity or care toward these live toys on the ends of strings and all his interest is centered on the way in which the small bird flutters and responds to the pull of the string. These living toys have a series of overtones which become part of Balinese symbolism. The children playing with them are at the same time learning to experiment with their own bodies; little girls to flick their pliant fingers as far back as possible, little boys to pull and tug at their genitals. The sense of a body-part symbol which is attached, but by a thread, and which has a life and willfullness of its own, becomes strongly developed. In the shadow-play this idea is further developed. Separable weapons, lances, spears, and arrows shower across the stage, and Towalen, the coarse old servant of the heroes, has a weapon spear-shaped at the point which he uses — until the puppeteer draws a roar of laughter from his audience by turning the leather about to show the phallic butt. The arrows and spears when they are flung, dart across the screen, but Towalen's weapon travels with a slow, wavy, and ponderous motion.

Besides live birds and insects there is a variety of other toys, such as pinwheels, whirligigs, rattles, and clappers which are assimilated to this same picture. One of the most vivid dramatizations of the whole idea of a separable and animated phallus is found in the flocks of pigeons with bells tied to their wings, which circle above the city of Den Pasar; and I once witnessed a telling dramatic improvisation in which our casteless houseboys tied a noisy whirring bumblebee to a string and anchored it in the midst of a spread of clothes which the high-caste girls from the next courtyard had laid on the grass to dry.

This sense that own body parts, particularly the phallus, are very loosely attached and independently animated, is most developed in boys. Girls, although they are occasionally given live birds to play with, usually assimilate such pets to the idea of a baby, so that they become, not parts of the own body, but something live and separate from the self. By the time they are four or five, all little girls have an ample opportunity to play with babies, and more elaborate developments of this preoccupation with an own body which is separate and animated, do not occur. Nevertheless, the attenuated version, which the girls receive from the toys they are given and the models whom they watch, is enough. True, for them the cultural picture lacks the reinforcement which each generation of baby boys must derive from their own bodily sensations. But in later life both sexes, when they watch a dancer at a play, identify not with the character who is being portrayed but with the bodies and movements, skilled or faulty, of the performers.

For the little boy, the handling which he receives from others strongly reinforces the suggestive symbolism of his plaything. A mother dries her baby boy after he has urinated by flicking his genital lightly from side to side, and as he grows older this treatment changes to teasing and ruffling, followed by pulling and stretching. Little boys keep their balance by holding on to their genitals, and learn to stretch the skin as others have stretched it. Against this background of conspicuous attention to the genitals of male children, often with the exclamation "Handsome! Handsome!" — an adjective applicable only to male beauty — the child's body becomes a sort of stage and his body parts the actors on that stage. In many cultures, toys and patterns of adult play with children tend to draw the child's attention away from his own body and into the outside world, but in Bali everything combines to refocus the child's attention back upon himself. His whole body, but especially his genital, is like a toy or a small musical instrument upon which those about him play; they make him toys which tell the same tale and it is not surprising that he develops a bodily consciousness very different from our own.

As children grow older, they withdraw into themselves, away from the overstimulating and unrewarding teasing. Little boys learn to skirt carefully the group of elders who will make casual snatches at their genitals; little girls walk with their abdomens pushed far out in seeming imitation of pregnancy, but they steer clear of the older women who will smack them on their abdomens and ask if they are pregnant, and when the baby they carry will be born. They draw back into themselves, and are thrown back on their own bodies for gratification. The men become narcissistic and uncertain of the power of any woman, no matter how strange and beautiful, to arouse their desire, but the women remain continually receptive to male advances. Strikingly enough, although female homosexuality did occur in the restricted courts of the rajahs among their many guarded wives and sisters, all the records we have indicate that the woman who played the man's role had to fabricate a complete male anatomy. The Balinese find it impossible to imagine a sexual drama which does not include one male, but they do not find it at all difficult to conceive of one male, left alone with his dramatized body, finding satisfaction within himself. In the most exciting scenes, rioting over a corpse, or at the climax of a cockfight, there are always some who stand aside, curved in upon themselves in the postures typical of schizophrenic dreaming.

It is possible to classify play types as autocosmic, when the own body is the stage as well as the principal actor; microcosmic, when a drama is enacted in miniature and the player merely manipulates the pieces, one of which may represent himself; and macrocosmic, when the play themes are lived out in the real world, as when the would-be cowboy does not content himself with riding up and down on a stick shouting (as in autocosmic play), or in playing out the game with toy cowboys and Indians, but instead seizes a large stick and rushes out to beat his father, suddenly seen as an Indian, or plays truant from school under the spell of his fantasy.*

When Balinese children are offered a mechanical mouse, or a doll or a toy koala, they do not construct scenes with these toys as children in many other cultures do. They take one toy at a time, and handle it as part of own body, if they are boys; or they treat the toy as a baby, or more occasionally as a hand, if they are girls. Very occasionally they project their whole bodies into a play world, as when they become cats chasing the mechanical mouse. Balinese children identify themselves in their drawings, rather than merely drawing mythical figures, or realistic portrayals of the people around them.† I have collected children's drawings in seven cultures, but only the Balinese children do this. It is as if the Balinese scarcely discriminate between the feeling for the own body and the sense of dramatic action. This shows up vividly in the dramatic conventions.

In the Balinese theater, the ordinary division into greenroom, stage, and audience is curiously handled. The audience is a hollow square with the stage inside the square, so that the actors are always seen against a backdrop of human faces instead of against an empty screen. The most delicate gestures, which are incredibly lovely when some accident of groundplan makes it possible to see them etched against a temple wall or

---

* These three very useful categories of play are based on E. H. Erikson, "Problems of Infancy and Early Childhood," *Cyclopedia of Medicine, Surgery, and Specialties* (Philadelphia: F. A. Davis Co., 1940), pp. 715–730. We are also indebted to Dr. Erikson for theoretical clarification of the way in which the Balinese audiences' failure to identify with the characters in a play may be described under the autocosmic heading.

† Characteristic of the interpretations given by the Sajan children whose drawings were collected by Jane Belo.

the empty sky, have to be witnessed, as a rule, in the midst of a crowd, so that only kinaesthetic identification with the movement itself makes it possible to realize it. Except in the modern Chinese-influenced *ardja* in which a curtain is strung up in the open between two poles, hiding nothing except about half of a single actor's body, there is no greenroom. Those actors who are not performing sit relaxed, perhaps asleep, headdresses taken off for relief, while the audience sits all about them, interested and unsurprised, waiting for the moment when they will resume their roles. In the shadow-play there is a screen of white cloth against which the shadows are thrown, so that the best effects are seen from the outside. In spite of this, as much as half of the audience, especially children and men who hope someday to be puppeteers, sit behind the screen watching the techniques of creating the illusion, rather than ever surrendering to the illusion itself. Each puppet is painted on both sides with elaborate care, although only a black shadow is thrown on the screen. A Balinese audience at any performance is a group of people who are technically interested; they are uncaught by the plight of the princess lost in the forest, blown away on her silken cobwebs, but they are very deeply concerned with the twist of her little finger.

We think of the tendency of drama to spill over into real life, but in Bali, real life, if the audience of everyday persons standing close packed around the stage can be so called, is always spilling over into the play. When a little dancer's sash has come untied, someone from the village is in pinning it up; or when two unmasked witches are chased down to the brook and ducked by other actors, the whole audience suddenly joins in the chase. The Witch play, begun with carefully marked audience lines and highly stylized dancing, may end with many of the audience in trance, or half of them pursuing the Witch who, tranced herself, rushes blindly through the village. In the theatrical performances, there is continual representation and exaggeration of those emotions which no adult Balinese displays: grief at parting and death; broken hearts; riotous aggression, coupled with a freedom of speech and gesture and an amount of horseplay never seen among adults; birth scenes with vivid dramatization of the fear of witchcraft which surrounds every real birth. The members of the audience, playing out the scenes within their own bodies, are drawn into the play, audience and actor alike preoccupied with their own bodies.

It is particularly revealing to watch the group of Balinese men clustered about an orchestra. They are the other members of the club, who will play when any of those now playing relinquish their instruments. Each member of that group is ready to play an instrument, and is waiting for his chance; they are never a passive audience merely listening to music in which their own bodies have no part. As men change places behind the same cock, so also they slip in and out from behind the different instruments, one player taking up where the other has left off. In one of the modern dance forms the dancer in the center of the circle flirts with the musicians and adds piquancy to this flirtation by taking away the mallet from a leading metallophone player. Occasionally a very small boy, a five- or six-year-old whose musical virtuosity has brought him into the front rows of the metallophone players, will bitterly resent this temporary theft of his tool. He is too much absorbed in musical virtuosity to accept the notion that the hammer is also another toy detachable from his body.

Parents and Children (Plates 45 to 68)

In Bali, the gods are thought of as the *children* of the people, not as august parental figures. Speaking through the lips of those in trance, the gods address the villagers as "papa" and "mama," and the people are said to spoil or indulge their gods, the same term being used as that which is used when spoiling or indulging a child or a monarch. Newborn babies, reincarnated and fresh from heaven, are addressed with honorific terms and the babe about to be born is most politely exhorted by the midwife, "Sir, please condescend to emerge, for we are cold and have no more betel nut. We should like to go home if you, Sir, would only consent to be born." During the early months of its life, before it is quite certain that the child will consent to stay and eat rice with its relatives, a slight aura of the sacred and uncanny surrounds the child; it may not yet put foot to the ground or enter a temple, and its willfullness and its first garbled phrases are taken as inspired. This attitude toward children is carried over and ceremonially expressed in the child trances, in which adolescent boys and grown men take great pleasure in addressing and adorning the little trance dancer, who in turn, possessed by a god, acts as a petted or petulant child. When the music begins, the little trancers begin to dance, rhythmically enacting the familiar scene in which elders attempt to dress a fractious and squirming child.

These scenes are very much enjoyed by everyone. The more pettish and unreasonable the little dancer is, the more amused the audience becomes. For the trancer is at once willful and compliant; she is fussy about the music, rejecting a song by the girl members of the club and insisting upon orchestral music from the boys, but at the same time she responds accurately to her cues. When the words of the song say "Sweep the ground with your fan" she sweeps the ground; or when they say "Give me a flower" she takes a flower from her headdress and hands it to a member of the audience. Tranced, relaxed, puppet-like, sacred and yet completely under control, compliant and yet willful, the *sangiang* dancer is the ideal object for Balinese parental attitudes, and the audience, relaxed and gay, both participates and looks on. The big boys address the little trancers with overdone politeness, "See, your sacred ladyship, it is going to rain and you have not yet stood on my shoulders. Are they not good enough for you?" "Surely, your sacred ladyship is now willing to reascend to heaven, for we are bored with this and would like to go home."

The little dancers are put into trance by incense and singing and, in Bajoeng Gede, by holding on to vibrating sticks connected by a string from which are suspended puppets. The gods first enter the puppets, setting up a violent commotion of the string. The girls then grasp the sticks and are entered by the same gods. Only after the gods have entered them and they are in trance, may the sacred headdresses and sacred bibs be placed upon them. If, in this sacred state, they go from one temple to another, they are carried on men's shoulders, and part of the dance is danced standing on a man's shoulders. If a piece of the headdress falls to the ground, it must be censed before it can be returned to the dancer's head. The girls, especially their heads, are sacred, and yet, if the playful, overpolite exhortations to return to heaven fail, the small girls are finally picked up, summarily and in spite of themselves, the headdresses are taken off their heads, the bibs untied, and the girls are dumped down facing the incense and subjected to the ritual which will bring them out of trance and transform them back into very ordinary little girls again. So babies — and gods — and princes — appear to the Balinese.

But if the *sangiang* dance sums up the general attitude toward the child, an attitude which all adults and older children share, what is the particular affect which binds mother and child together in Bali? The Balinese child is carried either loosely on the hip, as in most of the plains villages, or in a sling, as in Bajoeng Gede, but even where the hand of the mother is substituted for the sling, the child's adaptation is the same, passive, adjusting itself by complete limpness to the movements of the mother's body. It may even sleep with head wobbling to the timing of the mother's rice pestle. The baby receives its cues as to whether the outside world is to be trusted or feared directly from contact with the mother's body, and though the mother may have schooled herself to smile and utter courtesy phrases to the stranger and the high-caste, and may display no timorousness in her artificially grimacing face, the screaming baby in her arms betrays the inward panic. The tendency to take cues directly from the mother's body is increased by the mother's habit of hiding the child's face, placing her hand over its eyes or covering it in her cloth shawl, whenever anything untoward is occurring. Children, surprised in a village lane by strangers, with no time to take to their heels and not even time to turn their faces to the wall, will stand immobile, the backs of their hands pressed firmly against their eyeballs, shutting out the fear stimulus. The Balinese distinguish clearly between fear and the expression of fear, and it becomes a commonplace to hear people say fiercely to cowering or crying children, *"Da takoet"* ("Do not act afraid"), and this is the only reassurance which is ever attempted. Nobody would say, *"Da djerih"* ("Don't *be* afraid"). No one even attempts to furnish enough reassurance so that the child's internal fear may be dispelled.

As the child grows old enough to run away, to get into mischief, to meddle with the belongings of others, or to upset food cooking on the fire, the mother pantomimes the fear which the child has already experienced so often in her arms. Like an old hen clucking in panic to call her chicks back under her wing, the mother of the straying child gives a histrionic fear-laden cry, *"Aroh!"* followed by the mention of any one of a dozen scare symbols, chosen at random and without any concern for their relevance — "Fire!" "Snake!" "Feces!" "Scorpion!" "Witch!" "Elf spirits!" "White man!" "Chinaman!" "Policeman!" "Tiger!" The mother is as likely to exclaim "Fire!" when the baby toddles into a possibly snake-infested banana patch; "Feces!" when it touches the betel basket of a visitor, and "Tiger!" when it crawls under the bed. There is no reality content in the whole performance. The child responds only to the startled fear in his mother's voice, and to the theatrical embrace in which she holds him when he runs back to her. This is almost the only occasion on which the mother meets the child emotionally, giving him her complete, although theatrical, attention. This practice lays the groundwork for the continuation of fear as a major sanction and stimulus in Balinese life. It lays the groundwork for an ambivalent attitude toward fear, an emotion which the Balinese cultivates as well as yields to, and for the open preference for theatricals and theatrical behavior which is so characteristic of the Balinese. Only in the theater is the overt expression of emotion permitted. In real life, the European is often at a loss to tell when two Balinese are quarreling, but on the stage, emotions are so accurately delineated that no mistake is possible.

During our first months in Bali, before I had learned to understand the Balinese preference for theatrical emotions, I was at a loss to explain why my rapport developed so slowly with the people of Bajoeng Gede. Mothers whose babies I had medicated, although they returned for more medicine, remained so unwon that the babies screamed in terror in their arms whenever the mothers saw me. The few days which it takes to win over the women and children in a New Guinea tribe lengthened into months, and still the mothers smiled false anxious smiles, the babies screamed, and dogs barked. Then I had the opportunity to study the behavior of other Europeans who had come to Bali as they might go to the theater, and saw how much more easily the Balinese responded to their exaggerated interest than they did to my affection for individual babies. Readjusting my cues, I gave up depending upon the communication of real emotion, upon which I had depended on all my other field trips, and learned to exaggerate and caricature my friendly attitudes until the Balinese could safely accept them as theatrical rather than real. Mothers who had not loosened one tense muscle when I expressed my real feelings for their babies, relaxed with relief when I cooed and gurgled in tones which no longer had any relation to my real attitudes. Their arms relaxed, the babies stopped screaming, the dogs barked less.

Parallel to the development of fear and its theatrical presentation, the Balinese baby is subjected to a peculiarity of the mother-child relationship which is apparent when the child is only five or six months old and which becomes steadily more definite as the child grows older. This is a series of broken sequences, of unreached climaxes. The mother continually stimulates the child to show emotion — love or desire, jealousy or anger — only to turn away, to break the thread, as the child, in rising passion, makes a demand for some emotional response on her part. When the baby fails to nurse, the mother tickles his lips with her nipple, only to look away uninterested, no slightest nerve attending, as soon as the baby's lips close firmly and it begins to suck. She sets her baby in his bath — after six months this is a round tub — and teasingly thrusts her fingers between his lips, only to look away, disassociated, as the baby bites delightedly at her hand. She hands her baby to another woman, and then threatens to leave him, "I'm off home! You I will leave," but when the baby bursts into tears, her attention has already wandered and she takes him without looking at him, as she comments to her sister on the price of beans in the nearest market.

As the child gets older, from about eighteen months on, the teasing, the stimulus to the never realized climax becomes more patterned and more intense. For the little ruffle at his genital, she substitutes a sudden sharp pull; the little girl who was chucked under the chin or patted lightly on the vulva with a gay "Pretty! Pretty!" is now poked in the abdomen. The mother borrows the babies of others with which to tease her own, by setting the stranger, younger baby over the head of her own, or giving it the breast. But she never plays the scene through. If her own child falls into a tantrum, she suddenly hands him the borrowed baby, but then just as he is ready to throw his arms around her neck, she will take it again or start a conversation with a neighbor. And in turn, the baby plays the role of the borrowed baby, finding itself meaninglessly placed in the center of a scene of which it is not the hero — another unwarranted call upon its emotions.

BALINESE CHARACTER

For the first two to three years of their lives, children respond to these stimuli, although perhaps the increasing strength of the stimulus may be taken as a measure of the increasing resistance which they are developing. The mother, and in line with the mother, the aunt, the sister, and the child nurse tease and tantalize, while the child responds with mounting emotion which is invariably undercut before the climax. Later, the child begins to withdraw. This withdrawal may coincide with weaning, it may precede it, or it may follow it. The intensity of the drama is centered about the mother's breast, and a Balinese baby habitually nurses at one breast and grasps firmly at the other nipple, especially when there are any other children about; but weaning itself is not the high point in the conflict. This is partly to be explained by the fact that a child has been nursed by other women than his mother, and given the breasts of young adolescent girls or the worn breasts of a grandmother where there was no milk, and partly by the fact that even after weaning, the child is permitted to steal back for an occasional sip. For this he will at first be reprimanded, but later after his interest has waned, he would hardly be reprimanded at all. The withdrawal, however, which marks the end of early childhood for a Balinese, and which comes anywhere between the ages of three and six, is a withdrawal of all responsiveness. The mother borrows the neighbor's baby, but her child looks on unmoved. He skirts any group in which he thinks there will be someone to reach out a hand toward him. And once established, his unresponsiveness will last through life.

Most children reach this state by the time they are three or four, vacillating at times, falling into deep sulks or violent tempers, only to resume again their newly acquired imperviousness. For girls this change usually coincides with their taking up the role of child nurse, and starting to carry a baby everywhere with them. For boys, it coincides with the beginning of herding — following older boys to the fields with the oxen in Bajoeng Gede, or with the water buffalo in Batoean. A few children make the adjustment very late; characteristically this means for girls a series of violent temper tantrums, while for boys it means long, almost trancelike sulks and attacks of deep physical dependency when they will lie leaning against some other person or even against some inanimate object. Children manifesting such behavior usually are found to have a combination of deviant temperament and sociotic position in the society. They are the children of a home which broke up with unwonted bitterness, or they have been adopted, or they have been nursed longer than any other child, or they are children of women believed to carry the taint of hereditary witchcraft and so are avoided. In New Guinea, mere deviance of temperament was usually enough to insure maladjustment; in Bali, with the much greater dependence upon fear and the systematic discouragement of inter-personal emotion, temperamental deviance is not enough to bring about maladjustment unless reinforced by some gross distortion in the social framework within which the Balinese individual lives, fearful of the strange but relaxed amid the familiar and the conventional.

While the Balinese child is passing through this first period of responding with passion to his mother's gay, disassociated teasing — teasing which is best illustrated by the audience's treatment of the child trance dancers — he is also the spectator of the drama in which the Balinese express their feeling about such a mother-role. The Witch play, the *Tjalonarang*, the definitive dramatic theme of Balinese parent-child relations, not only expresses the residue in the adults of what they experienced as children, but also is watched by children and shapes their reading of the experiences to which they are subjected daily. It colors the child's appreciation of his mother's behavior, and stylizes his attitude toward her.

The plot of the play, which begins as a simple theatrical performance and usually ends in a series of violent trances with full religious paraphernalia of offerings and ritual, varies in detail from village to village, but is essentially uniform. The Witch is angry at a king because he or his son has rejected her daughter, or married her and then rejected her, or simply because the king has accused her of witchcraft. She summons her disciples — played by the most attractive little girls or by little boys dressed as little girls — and, dressed as an old hag, she schools them in witchcraft. They go forth and spread plague and disaster over the land. People are driven from their homes; babies are born and strangled by the witches and tossed back dead into the parents' laps; corpses fill the land. All of these horrors are in the broadest, slapdash comedy interspersed with exaggerated theatrical emotions. Then the king of the desolated country sends his ambassador, or he may come himself to fight the Witch, now no longer an old and infirm woman, but a masked supernatural being whose tongue is studded with flame, whose nails are many inches long, whose breasts are abhorrently hairy and pendulous, and whose teeth are tusks. Against her the emissary fails. He retires from the stage and is transformed into the Dragon (a two-man mask), who is as friendly and puppyish a beast as the Witch is terrifying. The Dragon confronts the Witch and they hold altercations in ecclesiastical old Javanese. Followers of the Dragon, armed with krisses, enter and approach the Witch ready to attack her. But she waves her magic cloth — the cloth baby sling — and after each attack they crouch down before her, magically cowed. Finally they rush upon her in pairs, stabbing ineffectively at the Witch who has become a half-limp bundle in their tense arms. She is uninvolved and offers no resistance, but one by one they fall on the ground in deep trance, some limp, some rigid. From this trance they are aroused by the Dragon who claps his jaws over them, or by his priest sprinkling his holy water. Now, able to move again but not returned to normal consciousness, they move about in a somnambulistic state, turning their daggers which were powerless against the Witch, against their own breasts, fixing them against a spot which is said to itch unbearably. Thus symbolically they complete the cycle of the childhood trauma — the approach to the mother, the rejection and the turn-in upon the self. Women participate in these scenes but do not attack the Witch. They merely turn their daggers against themselves. The trancers of both sexes writhe and shriek in ecstasy, intermittently pausing for a blank moment, only to begin pressing their krisses against their breasts with an upward movement if they are men, but hurling themselves in a sharp downward gesture on their krisses if they are women. In this violent scene it is rare for anyone to be injured; priests weave their way in and out, sprinkling holy water, and the Dragon, who revives them from their first deep trance, has returned to give them the support and comfort of his presence. Finally they are disarmed, carried into the temple, and brought out of trance with holy water and incense and an occasional offering of a live chick.*

The participants gather in front of the Dragon for a final prayer, the Witch mask is packed up and taken home, only to be brought out soon again for another enactment. In some of the old written versions of this plot, the Witch is killed, but attempts to introduce this form onto the stage have failed.

The most explicit form of the *Tjalonarang*, and a form which is not always given, includes the appearance of the Dragon at the start of the performance to make a magic circle around the stage. At the height of her power, the Witch, alone and pathetic in spite of her mask, stands within the circle and calls to the witches from all the four points of the compass. But the people stay outside the circle and are safe.

The fascination which the figure of the Witch holds for the Balinese imagination can only be explained when it is recognized that the Witch is not only a fear-inspiring figure, but that she is Fear. Her hands with their long menacing fingernails do not clutch and claw at her victims, although children who play at being witches do curl their hands in just such a gesture. But the Witch herself spreads her arms with palms

---

* For an extensive description of Balinese trance, the reader is referred to Jane Belo's forthcoming book on "Trance in Bali" (to be published shortly by Columbia University Press). Trance is a Balinese cultural form accessible to most Balinese but occurring in very different proportions in different communities. There are villages where everyone has been a trancer, villages where no one has been in a trance. There are not, as far as I know, any Balinese who have not witnessed trance often. The trance itself approximates closely to the phenomenon of hypnosis, and comparison of our trance films and records, and those of Miss Belo, with materials on hypnotic subjects in this country, has revealed no discrepancies, except for the substitution of a formalized situation for the hypnotist. Examination of various types of Balinese trancers by a psychiatrist revealed markedly disturbed pupillary reflexes.

out and her fingers flexed backward, in the gesture which the Balinese call *kapar*, a term which they apply to the sudden startled reaction of a man who falls from a tree. The Witch reconstitutes the figure of the mother, not only as the teasing, powerful unsatisfying person who aroused one's emotions only to throw one back upon oneself, but also as the person who cried "Snake!" and "Wildcat!" and so drew the child to her bosom by a display of fear. Only when we see the Witch as herself afraid, as well as frightening, is it possible to explain her appeal, and the pathos which surrounds her as she dances, hairy, forbidding, tusked, and alone, giving her occasional high eerie laugh.

This figure reappears in the dance form which symbolizes the Balinese conception of courtship, the *djoget*. Skilled little girl dancers, especially decked out and trained, are taken from village to village by an accompanying orchestra, and dance in the streets, sometimes with partners who have come with them, but more excitingly with members of the crowd. The little *djoget* coquettes and flirts, follows faithfully in pattern and rhythm the leads given by the villager who dances with her, but always fends him off with her fan, always eludes him, approaches, retreats, denies, in a fitful, unrewarding sequence, tantalizing and remote. Sometimes, in the very midst of such a scene, the tune played by the orchestra changes to the music of *Tjalonarang* (the Witch play), a cloth or a doll appears as if by magic, and the little dancer, still looking her part as the cynosure of all male eyes, suddenly becomes the Witch. She strikes the characteristic attitudes, waves her cloth and dances, balanced on one foot, tentatively threatening to step on the baby doll which she has just flung upon the ground — a pantomimic statement that witches feed on newborn babies. And after the Witch scene, the *djoget* will again return to her role of the desirable and remotely lovely girl. The dance sums up the besetting fear, the final knowledge of each Balinese male that he will, after all, no matter how hard he seeks to find the lovely and unknown beyond the confines of his familiar village, marry the Witch, marry a woman whose attitude toward human relations will be exactly that of his own mother.

There is a conflict which recurs in each generation, in which parents try to force the children of brothers to marry each other, to stay within the same family line and to worship the same ancestral gods, while the young people themselves rebel and, if possible, marry strangers. Fathers and brothers may help a boy to carry off a girl who is not kin, but no male relative of a girl, nor the girl herself, can admit complicity in any such scheme. An elopement (to which, as a matter of fact, the girl agrees) is arranged and staged with every appearance of an abduction, and so strong is the feeling against the complicity of any relative, that there is a special punishment in Hell arranged for men who trade sisters, which is spoken of as "trading human beings." The boy hopes that by marrying outside the family he will find a wife whose charm will not pall and upon whom he can beget many children. He fears that he will not succeed, and this fear is dramatized in the theater in a frequent plot, that of the prince who attempts to abduct a beautiful girl but through accident gets instead her ugly sister, the "Beast" princess, who is always dressed in the distinctive costume worn by mothers and mothers-in-law. It is dramatized again in the marriage ceremonies of Kesatrya princes; the bride whom the bridegroom has never seen is wrapped in white cloth like a corpse, carried to his palace so muffled, and alone with her he cuts the cloth with his kris, seeing for the first time what fate has allotted to him. After one has sat for hours with the ladies of the court, around a bed on which such a bride lies motionless, corpse-like, completely shrouded, one begins to believe that she may indeed look like anything at all, and that beauty is unlikely.

Courtship, either for marriage or for a love affair, is a matter of glances and a few stolen words, and the romantic excitement steadily dies down after the first encounter. Once married, a Balinese husband finds that the girl he has married does indeed act like his mother — for she knows no other pattern of personal relationship — his brief, unreal ardor cools and he counts himself lucky if he begets children. But divorce is a serious matter involving much ritual and trouble, and second wives, although permitted in the plains villages, cause quarreling in the family courtyard for co-wives are by definition jealous. For the most part, only accidents of illness or childlessness cause men, other than the rich, to resort to polygamy. All through life, some excitement may be found in quick, casual extramarital relationships, but when his own daughter is grown the father attempts to marry her inside the family, which she in her turn resists. The stupid, the overcompliant, the unfavored are married by parental arrangement, as are the young daughters of high-caste families in many cases. Other young people observe their case, even less glamorous than their own, and place their hope in marriage with an exciting stranger, or at least with someone outside the family. Girls, especially in the plains, make a great effort to conceal menarche from their parents for fear they will be hustled into marriage. Generation after generation, men continue to dream of the princess and find themselves married to the Witch.

But vis-a-vis the Witch there is always the Dragon, and it is interesting that although I have encountered many Dragons in Bali without a Witch, I have never encountered a Witch mask without a Dragon associated with it. The Dragon represents the chief spirit of the underworld; he represents life and health. His hair will insure a child against bad dreams of the Witch and is sold in the streets for a penny, and when the Dragon roams the village streets, he takes health and safety with him. The sick and unfortunate bring him offerings. When he dances he treats his followers not with the terrorized and terrorizing quality of the Witch, but like a giant, good-natured puppy, he rolls and noses them about. He takes the drum away from the orchestra and playfully beats it with his forelegs (the feet of the man who supports the front end of the animal mask); he riots with the umbrellas which mark the stage entrance. A frenzied trancer has only to rub his face in the Dragon's beard to be calmed. Vis-a-vis the Witch there is always the Dragon; vis-a-vis the teasing, unsatisfying mother, there is the Balinese father, gentle, playful, satisfying.

Though the Balinese mother is always attending to other people's babies, albeit with the desire to tease her own by doing so, a Balinese father attends very little to any children except his own. As we should expect, among a people where neither sex shows any unconscious doubt about sex membership, the father-child ties which are the warmest are father-daughter ties, although both boys and girls may be seen nestled against their fathers' bodies, squirming and wriggling their way back to the relaxation of infancy. When a little baby is fretting, if there is no woman by, the father may give his baby his nipple to suck; and often, in Bajoeng Gede, he carries his very young infant in a sling. Although he shares in the teasing which the mother metes out to a child, plays at frightening the child, at hiding and sudden pouncing games, or threatens it jokingly, *"Djoeka!"* "You will be carried off!" — the joking is mellower and ends in reparation rather than in broken climaxes, temper tantrums, and tears. Little children are taught, as soon as they can toddle, to carry the betel tray to their fathers and to take a handful of tobacco and stuff it in their father's mouth. Later, as adults, they will take food to the Dragon, which the priest will place in the mouth of the mask. In any regressive approach to the mother, the child who has been weaned shows trepidation and is expectant of rejection, but no such double-edged emotion surrounds the relationship to the father. Lying back against his father — and significantly these regressive scenes usually take this form, rather than a face-to-face one — the child may relax with a feeling of utter relief, away from the strain of either responding to the mother's teasing or refusing to respond at all.

The security which the father gives is like the security which the Balinese receives from a known scene, in which the date, the directions, the caste of all present are known to him — the scene which is represented by the village temple, where the smallest babies toddle about alone, even under the feet of visiting dancers. The Dragon circles the village and makes it safe against witches and the disease they bring; he circles the stage three times, and the Witch play, now rigorously confined within safe limits, can go on. If nevertheless, something strange and frightening — and all that is strange and unfamiliar is frightening — enters the life of a Balinese, he takes refuge in relaxation even deeper than that provided when he lies back against his father's body: he goes quietly to sleep. The child who is frightened by the tantrum of his child nurse falls asleep as she shrieks out her unrestrained rage right beside his closed ear. The older child who has lost or broken some valuable thing will be found, when his parents return, not run away, not waiting to confess, but in a deep sleep. Scenes of birth are fearful occasions because newborn babies attract witches. Children learn to be afraid of birth, and if they find themselves in the house — which in Bajoeng Gede means literally in the bed — with a birth, they fall into a deep sleep, and the watching women say, *"Takoet, poeles."* "In a fright, asleep." People on the scene of an accident sit in a paralyzed semi-stupor, not talking, not looking, but nodding; the thief whose case is being tried slowly falls asleep. The sleep is a perfectly natural one; it is possible to arouse people from it as easily as from any deep sleep and they show no special symptoms of catalepsy or rigidity. But tenseness, expectancy, tautness, lead to the Witch, to paroxysm and to trance; whereas relaxation and trust lead to the father, and sleep is one step farther away from tenseness and trouble, whenever the fright is too great to bear.

Siblings (Plates 69 to 74)

The Balinese have definite, stylized ways of treating not only the baby of the family, but the knee baby, and even the child who is third from the bottom. These are so traditional and so much a part of the Balinese attitude toward children that it is relatively unimportant whether a given child has or has not younger siblings. The treatment meted out to him by his own mother, as well as by others, when he is two or three years old, will assume that he is now in the position of knee baby, and later he will be treated as though he were third from the bottom. Occasional children, whose mothers fail to make the transition from one set of attitudes to another, appear seriously maladjusted.

During the first eighteen months of life, the baby is still the center of attention; it is teased, but lightly; it is dressed up; and its birthdays, recurring every 210 days, are occasions for feasting. It is carried most of the time, suckled lavishly, flirted with by older children, and borrowed to tease other children with. If there is an older brother or sister, the elder child is continually admonished to give in to the younger, while the younger is permitted as much aggression and assertiveness as it wishes. Participation in the dramatic jealousy scenes, in the role of the borrowed baby, has taught it a great many things, and a baby of six or seven months nurses with the spare hand on the mother's other breast, ever ready to push off an intruder. As the baby gets older, he grabs and keeps the mother's breast, paying little attention to strange objects, but anything that the older child has attracts his attention and interest, and he will grab at it. And this applies not only to the immediately older sibling or neighbor's child, but even to the five- or six-year-old child nurse.

The more extreme dramatizations of sibling rivalry, staged by the mother to tantalize the knee baby, are never played out with real siblings, but always with borrowed babies. Toward an own younger sibling the knee baby is required to show solicitude, and so the knee baby, at an age when a youngest child would still clutch and push at a borrowed baby at his mother's breast, is often seen showing demonstrative though not unmixed affection for a younger sibling. But two- to three-year-olds, whether they have younger siblings or not, are heavily teased by their mothers, somewhat teased by their fathers, and teased by those around them. They respond with tantrums and with sulks. They slip back into the mother's lap when the younger sibling or the borrowed baby is missing, and they show assertiveness toward the next older child. They habitually try to steal the clothes at the birthday feast of any younger baby, and are forever trying to pull off their mother's baby sling or to hide their faces in part of it. It is at this period that little boys spend most time anxiously feeling their genitals and little girls walk with pronounced "pregnant" postures.

The knee baby is too old to carry easily and walks, while the smallest child is carried and the next older child is carrying a baby. The knee baby vacillates between father and mother as the mother's overstimulation becomes more and more acute and the father takes more and more care of him. The child often sleeps with the father; and this is the age when the father-child tie is the strongest.

Traditionally American culture only recognizes two positions — those of the new baby and the baby "whose nose is out of joint." But in Bali, for the "third from the bottom" age there is also a stylized position, a formal expectation. This third-place child has passed into the stage of unresponsiveness, of skirting groups and ignoring cues which would have called for tantrums a year ago. Only extreme provocation will make the average child of third-place age cry, although a great increase in crying may occur in the period when the child is moving, either because of age or because of the birth of a new baby, from the knee-baby to the third-place position. Almost all physical contact with the parents ceases. A mother seldom touches her third-place child except to louse her, an act which is performed between adults as much as between adults and children. The knee baby is given his food carefully by the mother, but the third-place child is in an in-between position, half expected to be caring for the younger children, half too young to fend for herself. I say "herself" because this third-place position is more heavily stylized for girls than for boys, and is, in fact, the child-nurse position. Little boys, who need not carry small siblings, start to follow their fathers earlier to the fields, and if they are bolder and more fearless than most they may *"bani ke tegal,"* "dare to go to the fields alone," at four rather than at six. Their mothers no longer dress them up for temple feasts, but for the most part they still center their lives at home with their mothers, rather than out in the fields with older boys. They still watch for a chance to creep back, to lie with head against the father's or mother's back, when one of the younger children is away. The death of a child means that the older child, who has been in third place, will slip back into the knee-baby role at once, clinging, hanging on to the mother, reclaiming the physical attention which has been lost.

The third-place period ends when the girl becomes a willing child nurse — she may have been an unwilling one before — and when the boy leaves the family group for the whole day and sometimes at night, going out to herd the oxen or the water buffaloes. Today in the plains this change also coincides with going to school. Such a child no longer makes any physical claims on the parents; he or she is absorbed into a children's group and the ties to younger children now imitate the parental ties; the older boy teaches his younger brother and tumbles him about; the older girl carries the babies, teasing and stimulating them as her mother has done. This transition from the third-place position, still primarily oriented to the parents in a distant, nostalgic fashion, to the position of fourth or more from the bottom where all children are grouped together, is one of which the Balinese are articulately conscious. They regard with concern the little girl of six or seven who still has temper tantrums when her mother won't take her to market and who still wants to snuggle up, and the little boy of the same age who prefers home to the fields. One father in Bajoeng Gede refused to renew permission to a vendor to keep a food stall in front of the house because he thought it encouraged his six-year-old son to stay around the house rather than go out to the fields.

There are frequent lapses from these stylized patterns. One sees four-year-olds carried in slings, three-year-olds unweaned, and five-year-olds who cling like three-year-olds; but always in the behavior of the parents and the onlookers there is the recognition that the behavior is aberrant. In America, although a mother may keep her four-year-old boy in curls, she and her neighbors all know that this is unusual and vaguely improper behavior. In Bali, the stylization of child age is as definite as is our stylization of sex, and the same sort of self-consciousness on the part of the parent and the child accompanies any inappropriate behavior. Each stage is underlined for the developing child, whether its parent follows the pattern or consciously deviates from it, and whether the child itself moves smoothly from one role to the next or resists the transition. In spite of deviance and lapses, there remain three distinct and highly patterned levels of emotional development before the Balinese child enters latency.

Stages of Child Development (Plates 75 to 83)

Latency, that period when a child has finally given up any hope of an immediately complete relationship to its parents, and has settled down into a period of waiting to grow up in company with other children, is very marked for boys in Bali, and much less marked for girls. Boys become members of ragamuffin gangs, playing group games away from their elders, rioting about in tussles which look violent but in which all attack is really shadow boxing, consisting of feints which never become blows. When they play with girls, it is with girls either younger or older than themselves; otherwise they tend to play alone. They spend most of their time away from the village with their oxen — each ox is tended by a separate small boy — and come into the village for food and occasionally for feasts. They have very slight religious duties to perform, such as carrying the pig at a wedding in Bajoeng Gede, or dancing in certain temple feasts. They hang about men's skilled activities — making puppets out of dead leaves while a craftsman is cutting new puppets, drawing in the sand while an artist paints a picture, hanging about the edges of orchestral rehearsals and often becoming skilled players at seven or eight. They may also be found in gambling groups, scrambling for pennies in discarded offerings, and helping to dismantle a cremation tower. But their relationships with women are very slight, and the occasional boy who is much with his mother does the things which his sister, if he had one, would do — he helps care for a baby or gathers flowers for the offerings. So sure is the Balinese sense of own sex that such boys do not as a rule develop any feminine traits.

For a high-caste boy, marriage may coincide with puberty, but for most Balinese boys there is no special puberty ceremonial. Sometime between puberty and young-manhood his teeth will probably be filed, and this is said to be essential for completeness; parents are said to be in debt to their children until their teeth are filed. If he lives in Bajoeng Gede and he is the eldest son at home, the village will "ask for him," and he will become a member of the young unmarried men's group, owing definite ceremonial duties to the village. He will spend a little less time out in the field, spend less time in groups and more with one or two friends who will help him arrange rendezvous and watch while he takes the risk of climbing into his sweetheart's courtyard. Finally, at twenty or so he will settle down, perhaps with a wife, perhaps with the help of a mother or sister to make up a complete household, a full unit in the village community. In the plains villages, if he is unmarried and has an unmarried sister, the two may share a house in the paternal courtyard. In Bajoeng Gede, he and his sister would have a household of their own. Adulthood is not definitely associated with marriage, which is probably another reason why occasional women as well as men fail to marry in Bali — a condition unusual in a society which permits polygamy.

Girls, during this period, are torn between two systems of behavior, that of grown women and that of the little boys who are their age mates. Patterning their behavior on that of grown women, they spend a great deal of their time taking care of babies, making offerings, carrying offerings, going for wood and water, and going about in mixed age groups which contain old women and small girls. Because of the ceremonial position of virgins, little girls and older girls spend a great deal of their time with older women who, purified from marriage and past the child-bearing period, can also approach closer to sacred things. Patterned also upon older girls is a sex consciousness, a giggling response to anything male, which has no counterpart in the behavior of boys of their own age.

But running through this imitative acceptance of an adult feminine role there is a streak of rowdyism, strongest in the little girls who are just entering latency, but cropping up periodically all through this period. Sometimes the roughhousing lasts into adolescence for the girl whose many sex affairs begin also in a quick roughhouse exchange with boys near her own age. This behavior seems to be not a rejection of femininity but a rejection of adulthood, an escape from a staid and controlled demeanor and from endless concern with babies and offerings in favor of splashing in the mud, throwing coconut shells of water at other children, or rushing shouting through the village. The rowdiest of such little girls will be found, however, making up or trying to conceal their cropped heads under wigs of grass, practicing, with little bits of leaf instead of fans, the dances which their older sisters dance. Much earlier than the boys, sometimes at eight or nine, the eldest daughter at home will take on ceremonial duties: in Bajoeng Gede she will become a dancer or maker of offerings for the village; in the plains she will perform a hundred small duties in connection with the offerings which are made every day in the house temple, at the gate, and at the water jar.

For a high-caste girl, menarche is marked by a ceremony with many offerings. Before the ceremony, she is kept in a special house and finally she is dressed with the same care as a bride and is specially blessed by a Brahman priest; and even if she has not been betrothed before, she will be married soon after. The low-caste girl may be married by an elopement phrased as an abduction — even before puberty.

Rites de Passage (Plates 84 to 100)

Each Balinese goes through the stages which we have discussed — he is a baby, a knee baby, a third-place child, a latency child, an adolescent, finally an adult who, aging surprisingly little, lives to a beautiful old age, with delicate, lined features and feet that are often still willing to dance. The different periods of life are held together by the thread of consistent personality; Balinese are said to be either "serious" or "naughty" and this dichotomy extends from babyhood to old age; it cuts across sex, caste, and hierarchical lines. Remarkably consistent, the "naughty" old intellectual temple priest will be found to be *au courant* with every love affair in the village, every gambling debt, every scandal, but the very pretty "serious" girl of sixteen will know nothing of such doings. Other personality characteristics are presumed to be just as stable; they are attributed early and continually reinforced by the expectation of the community. Some people are "daring," "poised before those of higher status," "bold" to touch unclean things like corpses or women past menarche; others are "fearful," "shy," "tongue-tied in the face of status," "timorous" in face of the aura of ceremonial uncleanliness surrounding birth and death. Some people are "show-offs" seeking the limelight, acting as if they thought "they had lights on the tops of their heads"; others are "embarrassed ones," unwilling to ask a favor, although the Balinese say that "if you want to receive, you must be willing to ask." Some people have a "shining" quality of high birth or special beauty and spirit; they are said to *mebawa,* to glitter, and with this may be joined a high temper, which will make them comparable to a sharp sword whose touch is death. Some love to go among crowds, to watch and participate; others go among crowds only as much as their affairs demand. All such differences are accepted as innate and are recognized early in life. People comment upon them continually, as we might say, "She has blue eyes," or "She is going to be tall." Parents make no attempt to modify such behavior, and sometimes say articulately, "Oh, the one who is incarnated in you must be a great gambler."

For Balinese life is a series of never-ending circles, half of which are spent in life between birth and death, and half in the supernatural world between death and rebirth. Generation after generation, souls are reborn into their great-grandchildren, direct or collateral. They are greeted with respect as having come from the other world, and pass through the series of ceremonies which bind them more and more to this life. They receive holy water, are sprinkled with sacred meal, and pray as human beings to the ancestors. They set foot on the ground and have their hair cut, have their teeth filed, elope, go through a marriage ceremony, and finally pass out of this body to wait in the next world until the third generation brings them back again, perhaps to a better "turn," perhaps to a worse one, for everyone "takes turns" in having sometimes a good fate, sometimes a poor one. People say philosophically, "I am having bad luck this incarnation." Each of the ceremonies is endlessly like the last; for every new element distinctive of a three-month birthday as compared with a six-month, of a wedding as compared with a tooth-filing, there are a hundred which are similar. Every ceremony stresses the timelessness, the solidity of the ritual frame in which people and gods are caught.

Except death. Death, necessary as it is to the theory of reincarnation, presents a stumbling block to the Balinese of quite a different order from that which we have to face. Among them, parting with loved ones is never emphasized and tears are inappropriate except for a small baby who might as well not have come at all — it stayed such a short while and shared so little food. Individual immortality, both past and future, is affirmed to the point of monotony. A child knows who he is, and a man spends much time trying to stem or avert misfortune by paying up the ceremonial debts which his soul contracted, either during an earlier incarnation or in heaven. When a guilty man drinks the magic water which is used to discover which member of a group is a thief, he calls down leprosy and other horrible deaths upon his own head for a thousand generations. The sense of personal uniqueness in Bali is slight and people are shy at mentioning their own names or the names of others, but each has an impersonal individuality which is completely tough and incontrovertible.

The trouble with death is the body; it is the problem of how to get rid of that body which is of such enormous importance to every Balinese. The body is the stage on which his emotions are played out in isolation, cut off from all close inter-personal ties, endlessly guarded against some disaster which will declare him cut off from the full society of men. The most terrible swearword in Bali is *"Sakit Gede,"* the "Great Sickness" — leprosy — and high-caste Balinese in a group will turn cold and sick beyond all possibility of breeding to hide their feelings, if one mentions that there is said to be a Brahman priest in the leper colony. They dare not think how many people are living whose birth-feasts and marriages and burials were desecrated by holy water which that priest consecrated after he was contaminated. The problem is impossible of solution; the body cannot finally be separated from the soul, nor can they finally be united. The decaying body, as it falls to bits and is eaten by worms, typifies the Balinese major fear of witches who eat corpses and young babies; but the souls must be tenderly ushered out of life into heaven. Cremation, a Hindoo importation still not followed in Bajoeng Gede, is not a solution; one finds in the mountains and in the plains the same tendency — to re-create the body of the dead, to dispose of it, to re-create it, to dispose of it, to re-create it again. Cremation, as a means of disposal of the original corpse and of its subsequent surrogates, is dramatic, but it is not a final solution.

Significantly, the Balinese show intense emotion — a riotous, hysterical gaiety — at the burials of other people. When their own relatives and spouses die, they are merely subdued; but when a new corpse which has been kept in the house about ten days is to be carried to the graveyard for cremation, all the repulsion toward the fact of death crops up. Men overcompensate, plunge their arms into the rotting corpse and boast that their skin crawled with maggots; or they suddenly stop dead in the midst of the scene, staring unseeing, only to plunge back into the melee which characterizes the carrying of bodies to be buried, of corpses to be cremated, or of towers which contain bones only.

The first funeral is a comparatively quiet and orderly affair. Neighbors bring food to be cooked for all the guests, offerings are prepared, and the body is washed and adorned with various magical devices to insure beauty in the next incarnation. It is dressed and undressed several times, carried to the cemetery amid a mild amount of rioting — sometimes with none — and buried. The village or caste group, or ward in a large city, is *sebel* (ceremonially unclean) for three days, the household for a longer period, after which the tie with death is ceremonially cut. The spirit is ordered to go away but still invited to watch over the household, and life is resumed. This misleading simplicity, in which a death is treated with no more ritual or fuss than a big birthday or a marriage, belies the real feeling about death, which is expressed in the later ceremonies in which the body is re-created — out of the actual bones in the plains villages, or with rice in a basket in Bajoeng Gede — only to be laboriously disposed of again; and again re-created, and again disposed of.

When there is to be a great cremation in which many casteless people will share in the great ceremonials for a Brahman priest or a member of the prince's household, people prepare for weeks, making thousands of prescribed offerings and selling everything that they have in order to spend more on the ceremony. Because of the great number of guests who come to cremations, it is impossible to predict the cost, and this weight of rising and unguessable expenditures adds to the anxiety. Cremations are regarded as work by those whose responsibility they are, but they provide a festival for the surrounding villages.

The weeks of laborious preparation culminate in three days of ceremonial. The graves are first dressed in human clothes, then opened, and the bones are dug up and assembled. They are dressed again and laid out in a little town built in the cemetery. Delicate little dolls which represent the souls of the dead are carried home from the cemetery to the houses where they lived on earth, there to receive food and drink, to pray to the ancestors, and finally to ask leave to depart. These little "souls" are then carried back to the cemetery and placed inside the bundles of dressed-up bones. Thus the person is again re-created. On the next day, a new set of "souls" is taken to the priest's house and blessed, and the "bones" are later given a second laying-out as if they were corpses. On the third day the bones are burned in coffins shaped like animals appropriate to each caste, but the cremation fires are no sooner out than the people are poking among the ashes, gathering the small bits of specified bones and again re-creating a body upon which the little cornucopia-shaped prayer leaves are laid, so as to define again all the sacred anatomical points. Representative samples of this re-created body are then ground to dust in a mortar, each close relative taking a hand at the grinding, and the dust is placed in still another human replica and finally carried to the sea. It is thrown into the sea, but only to be re-created again in a new replica at stated periods thereafter. When someone dies, people may insure themselves by buying a special holy water, which permits them to wait twenty-five years before undertaking this elaborate, expensive, and demanding ritual. After each phase in the death ceremonial — after the real death, after the cremation, after the disposal of later re-creations of the body of the dead — comes the ceremony of *mepegat,* in which the souls, carried in the arms of members of the family like the babies which they will again become, ceremonially break the tie which binds them to the living — but only for a little while.

Conclusion

In these various contexts of life the Balinese character is revealed. It is a character based upon fear which, because it is learned in the mother's arms, is a value as well as a threat. It is a character curiously cut off from inter-personal relationships, existing in a state of dreamy-relaxed disassociation, with occasional intervals of non-personal concentration — in trance, in gambling, and in the practice of the arts. The Balinese carries the memory of his mother's intense theatrical exclamation of fear, "*Aroh,*" to deter him from ever venturing on an untrodden path; but he carries also the equally strong memory of his father's protective arm as long as he stays on a trodden one. Fear and absolute confusion will arise if he does not know the day, the directions, and the caste of those whom he addresses, but he has such sureness of movement within a known place that his acts require only a tithe of his attention. He is vulnerable, but deft and gay, and usually content. Always a little frightened of some undefined unknown, always driven to fill the hours, so empty of inter-personal relations, with a rhythmic unattended industriousness, he follows the routines laid down by calendars and the revelations of those in trance, relaxed at the center of any world of which he knows the outlines. No appeal has ever been made to him to achieve in order to validate his humanity, for that is taken as given. From each according to his status — from the poor and the unfortunate the gods expect but small offerings; from the rich and the well-placed they expect much. If a man follows the prescribed forms, he may expect safety — and if that safety is still meager, there will be a different turn to come in another incarnation. Life is without climax, and not the ultimate goal but rather the first impact of experience, the initial ping of startle, is the only stimulus that has real power to arouse one's interest. And there is always the danger that one may not be aroused at all. Between the Death which is symbolized by the Witch's claws and the graveyard orgies, and the death which is sleep into which one retires when frightened, life is a rhythmic, patterned unreality of pleasant, significant movement, centered in one's own body to which all emotion long ago withdrew.

M. M.

NOTES ON THE PHOTOGRAPHS AND CAPTIONS

Taking the Photographs

Of the 759 photographs reproduced in this book, eight can fairly be said to have been "posed," in the sense that the postures of the subjects were directly influenced by the knowledge that a picture was being taken. Of these eight, four (Pl. 27, fig. 5; Pl. 46, figs. 1, 2, and 3) are reproduced here to show the subject's behavior in a frightening or embarrassing context; two (Pl. 4, fig. 7 and Pl. 97, fig. 6) are reproduced for the sake of objects which the people are holding; and the other two are Pl. 82, fig. 6 and Pl. 83, fig. 8.

We tried to use the still and the moving-picture cameras to get a record of Balinese behavior, and this is a very different matter from the preparation of "documentary" film or photographs. We tried to shoot what happened normally and spontaneously, rather than to decide upon the norms and then get Balinese to go through these behaviors in suitable lighting. We treated the cameras in the field as recording instruments, not as devices for illustrating our theses.

Four factors may be mentioned which contributed to diminish camera consciousness in our subjects:

A. The very large number of photographs taken. In two years we took about 25,000 Leica stills and about 22,000 feet of 16 mm. film, and it is almost impossible to maintain camera consciousness after the first dozen shots.

B. The fact that we never asked to take pictures, but just took them as a matter of routine, wearing or carrying the two cameras day in and day out, so that the photographer himself ceased to be camera conscious.

C. We habitually directed attention to our photographing of small babies, and the parents overlooked the fact that they also were included in the pictures (as even American parents will, in similar circumstances).

D. We occasionally used an angular view finder for shots when the subject might be expected to dislike being photographed at that particular moment (e.g., Pl. 29).

We usually worked together, Margaret Mead keeping verbal notes on the behavior and Gregory Bateson moving around in and out of the scene with the two cameras. The verbal record included frequent notes on the time and occasional notes on the photographer's movements, such as the direction from which he was working and which instrument he was using. Whenever a new roll of film was inserted in the camera, the date and time of insertion were scribbled on the leader; and when the film was removed, the date and time were again recorded, so that the film could be accurately fitted to the notes.

For work of this sort it is essential to have at least two workers in close cooperation. The photographic sequence is almost valueless without a verbal account of what occurred, and it is not possible to take full notes while manipulating cameras. The photographer, with his eye glued to a view finder and moving about, gets a very imperfect view of what is actually happening, and Margaret Mead (who is able to write with only an occasional glance at her notebook) had a much fuller view of the scene than Gregory Bateson. She was able to do some very necessary directing of the photography, calling the photographer's attention to one or another child or to some special play which was beginning on the other side of the yard. Occasionally, when we were working on family scenes, we were accompanied by our native secretary, I Made Kaler. He would engage in ethnographic interviews with the parents, or take verbatim notes on the conversations.

In a great many instances, we created the *context* in which the notes and photographs were taken, e.g., by paying for the dance, or asking a mother to delay the bathing of her child until the sun was high, but this is very different from posing the photographs. Payment for theatrical performances is the economic base upon which the Balinese theater depends, and the extra emphasis given to the baby served to diminish the mother's awareness that she was to be photographed. A visit "to photograph the baby being bathed" would last from fifteen minutes to two hours, and the greater part of the time after the bathing would be spent watching the family in a large variety of types of play and other behavior. In such a setting, a roll of Leica film (about 40 exposures) lasted from five to fifteen minutes.

Selection of Photographs

Selection of data must occur in any scientific recording and exposition, but it is important that the principles of selection be stated. In the field, we were guided first by certain major assumptions, e.g., that parent-child relationships and relationships between siblings are likely to be more rewarding than agricultural techniques. We therefore selected especially contexts and sequences of this sort. We recorded as fully as possible what happened while we were in the houseyard, and it is so hard to predict behavior that it was scarcely possible to select particular postures or gestures for photographic recording. In general, we found that any attempt to select for special details was fatal, and that the best results were obtained when the photography was most rapid and almost random. Pls. 71 and 72 illustrate this; the photographer assumed that the context was interesting and photographed as far as possible every move that the subjects made, without wondering which moves might be most significant.

One rather curious type of selection did occur. We were compelled to economize on motion-picture film, and disregarding the future difficulties of exposition, we assumed that the still photography and the motion-picture film *together* would constitute our record of behavior. We therefore reserved the motion-picture camera for the more active and interesting moments, and recorded the slower and less significant behaviors with the still camera. The present book is illustrated solely by photographs

BALINESE CHARACTER

taken with the latter, and as a result, the book contains no photograph of a father suckling his child at the nipple, and the series of kris dancers (Pls. 57 and 58) leaves much to be desired.

After taking the photographs, a further selection occurred. On returning to America, we had the entire collection of 25,000 frames printed as diapositives on strips of positive film, and in planning this book we made a list of categories which we intended to illustrate — a list similar to, but not identical with, the grouping of the plates in the table of Contents. We then projected all the diapositives, one by one, and wrote category cards for those which seemed to merit further consideration for inclusion in the book. We thus obtained a list of about 6,000 frames. Of these, we enlarged approximately the first 4,000 in chronological order, desisting at this point because time was short. From these 4,000, the majority of the prints reproduced here were selected, and we only drew upon the later negatives for a few special points which were not represented in the earlier series. The book thus contains a disproportionate number of photographs taken in the first three-quarters of our time in Bali.

The final choice of photographs for each plate was in terms of relevance, photographic quality, and size. In a number of cases, relevance to a problem is necessarily two-sided; there would be some photographs making one half of a psychological generalization, and others making a converse or obverse point. In these cases, we have tried to arrange the photographs so that most of the plate is occupied with the more typical aspect, while a statement of the obverse is given by one or two photographs at the bottom (usually in the right-hand corner) of the plate (cf. Pls. 22, 27, 45, etc.). In other cases, it has seemed worth-while to devote two plates to the contrasting aspects of the same generalization (cf. Pls. 6 and 7; Pls. 45 and 98).

Conflict between scientific relevance and photographic merit has usually been easily settled in favor of the former, and a large number of pictures have been included in spite of photographic faults. Selection by size was more distressing. Each plate was to be reproduced as a unit and therefore we had the task of preparing prints which would fit together in laying out the plate. Working with this large collection of negatives, it was not possible to plan the lay-out in advance, and therefore, in the case of the more important photographs, two prints of different sizes were prepared. Even with this precaution, the purely physical problems of space and composition on the plate have eliminated a few photographs which we would have liked to include.

Retouching

We have to thank Mr. Karsten Stapelfeldt for skillful work which he very kindly performed in spotting out blemishes in the prints. In this work, he scrupulously respected the scientific conventions, removing faults which confused the picture, but adding nothing without consulting us. After such consultation, he made the following additions involving draftsmanship: on Pl. 31, fig. 5, he painted in the strip of background, which was obscured by lichen and erosion; and in Pl. 62, fig. 4, he painted over the hand and forearm of the man inside the Dragon.

In a large number of cases, some shading was done in the process of enlarging the photographs, but this adds no drawing to the photograph, only making it possible for the paper to give a more complete rendering of what is present in the negative.

Technical Notes

All the photographs were taken with the Leica camera, and the majority were taken with an Elmar 50 mm. lens. A Weston exposure meter was used constantly (with both the Leica and the moving-picture camera) but the exposures were not recorded except for occasional test strips, none of which are reproduced here. After exposure, the films were stored in an airtight box with calcium chloride, until there was a sufficient accumulation to warrant our devoting an evening to developing them. We used Eastman D 76 developer in a 100-ft. Correx tank, and usually developed two batches (between 30 and 40 films) in an evening. The enlarging was done in the American Museum of Natural History and in a summer camp in New Hampshire. The paper used was Kodabromide F.

The stock used was mostly Eastman Panatomic, but a number of other types of stock were used at various times — partly in order to have greater speed in recording banana fiber; on Pl. 49, fig. 5, he increased the contrast between the baby and the scenes of extreme activity, and partly owing to the difficulty of obtaining film in bulk in the East Indies. The first 30 or 40 rolls were of Agfa Superpan commercially cut, and Agfa Superpan in bulk was used for all photographs taken in 1939. Eastman Supersensitive Panchromatic was used for a period in 1937, and Eastman Super-X was used for some scenes which included dancing figures.

In April 1937, the photographic equipment was increased by the addition of a Scnoo Rapid Winder, a Telyt 200 mm. telephoto lens, and an Elmar 35 mm. wide-angle lens. The rapid winder was in constant use from then on, except for a period when the silk tape wore out. The telephoto lens was used very often, especially for recording ceremonials (Pl. 8; Pl. 68, figs. 3 to 6), theatricals (Pl. 22, figs. 1 and 2), and the behavior of audiences (Pl. 5, fig. 6). The photographs taken with the telephoto lens can easily be recognized by the unusual perspective (Pl. 15, figs. 1, 2, and 3; Pl. 17, fig. 7; Pl. 24, fig. 1; etc.). The telephoto lens was also used for all the reproductions of Balinese drawings and shadow-play puppets. The wide-angle lens was rarely used (Pl. 1, figs. 4, 6, and 7).

In 1939, the 50 mm. lens was replaced with a Hector 73 mm. f/1.9, which was used for all the photographs taken in that year (Pls. 48 and 64). This lens enabled the photographer to work at somewhat greater distance from his subjects, and especially its longer focal length made it more nearly equivalent to the 25 mm. lens on the 16 mm. Movikon. It was, therefore, easier to use the two instruments together.

BALINESE CHARACTER

Notes on the Captions

Each plate is accompanied by a general statement telling the reader about the contextual setting in which the photographs were taken, and defining the theoretical points which we think the plate conveys. Each photograph, or each series of photographs, is then described separately. The penultimate paragraph of this description gives the names and relationships of the principal people in the photographs, and the last paragraph gives the name of the locality in which the photograph was taken, the date of taking, and the frame number of the negative.

The reader is thus provided with scientific statements of a number of different degrees of objectivity and generality. Each single photograph may be regarded as almost purely objective, but juxtaposition of two different or contrasting photographs is already a step toward scientific generalization (e.g., Pl. 5, figs. 4 and 5, or Pl. 20, figs. 4 and 6). The introductory statement on each plate provides, in many cases, an extreme of generality, whereas the detailed captions contain a blending of objective description and scientific generalization. We have assumed that the objectivity of the photographs themselves justifies some freedom in the writing of the captions. We have not hesitated, therefore, to select for emphasis those features of the photograph which seemed most revealing, and to describe those features in words and syntax which might convey a sense of the emphases of Balinese culture as we understand it.

Cross references from one photograph to another and from one plate to another have been inserted often, and such insertions often carry implicit generalizations like those implicit in the juxtapositions. To enable the reader to explore the plates for himself, a random supply of cross references is given in the Glossary and Index of Native Words and Persons. As far as possible, native words have been kept within parentheses. They are provided for the use of readers already familiar with Balinese language and custom, and the ordinary reader need pay no attention to them unless he wishes to set side-by-side the various photographs connected with one ceremony or native concept, in which case the Index and Glossary will enable him to do this. Similarly, it is possible from the names of identified persons to obtain an over-all view of some of the most photographed individuals, such as I Karba, I Karsa, I Gata, and their respective parents.

Frame Numbers

These refer to our catalogue of the negative collection, but even without consulting the collection something can be read from the numbers. The films were arranged in chronological order in groups of 26. Each successive group of 26 films was given an initial number, and the 26 films in the group were given letters from A to Z. Finally, each frame was identified by its ordinal position in the film. A film usually contains between 35 and 42 frames. Thus, the frame numbers "12 M 7, 8, 9, 15; 12 N 1" would mean: These are five photographs from a sequence. The first three photographs were consecutive frames and may have followed each other at as little as two-second intervals. There was an interval between the third and fourth photographs while five other photographs were taken, which are not reproduced here. There was another interval between the fourth and fifth photographs, in which the remainder of film 12 M was exposed and a new film was inserted in the camera. The fifth photograph was on the beginning of a new roll, and therefore the fact that no other photographs in this sequence are reproduced was *not* due to there being no film in the camera. (It takes about one minute to insert a new film.)

G. B.

BALINESE CHARACTER

PHOTOGRAPHIC ANALYSIS

By Gregory Bateson

Plates 1 to 100

Plate 1
BAJOENG GEDE: VILLAGE AND TEMPLES

There are conspicuous differences between the communities of poor peasants in the mountain regions of Bali and those richer, more loosely organized communities in the plains. Bajoeng Gede is a typical mountain village and conforms closely in its plan to the ideal pattern. The village is built about a crossroads with dwelling houses in three of the quadrants. The fourth quadrant, toward the northeast (*kadja-kangin,* literally the "inland-east"; cf. Pl. 10, fig. 2), the most sacred direction, is occupied by the main village temple (Poera Desa) and by the temple of origin (Poera Poeseh). Each household is walled off from the others with mud walls, and within these enclosures the buildings are precisely laid out with a special area on the northern or eastern side for shrines of ancestral and other gods.

Bajoeng Gede is also like the majority of Balinese mountain communities in the very poor development of arts and crafts and the very rich development of communal ceremonial with emphasis on the rights and duties of citizenship.

1. View of Bajoeng Gede, looking south from the crossroads at dawn. The wide street with dwelling houses on either side leads down to the ceremonially lowest gate, and beyond that to the cemetery in the forest.
Bajoeng Gede. July 4, 1936.   1 W 24.

2. The village slit-gong at the crossroads. This is kept in a house raised on a platform between four trees. The gong is used to summon the villagers to meetings and as a tocsin in case of thefts.
Bajoeng Gede. March 5, 1938.   22 M 20.

3. A smaller street in Bajoeng Gede, showing mud walls, and gates to houseyards. The two entrances to left and right nearest the camera are to minor temples (Poera di Panti and Poera di Eboene); beyond these are entrances to houses.
Bajoeng Gede. July 16, 1937.   12 U 28.

4. The citizens' ceremonial meeting house (*bale agòeng*) in the front court of the village temple.
Bajoeng Gede. March 5, 1938.   22 J 27.

5. The interior of men's ceremonial meeting house (fig. 4) with feast laid out for the annual ceremony (*neleb*) of dividing the temple land (cf. Pl. 2, fig. 1). A long mountain of cooked rice extends the whole length of the building, with supplies of highly seasoned foods on each side. The men are beginning to gather for the feast. The senior citizens will sit in order of seniority at the far (north) end.
Nang Goenoeng in right foreground.
Bajoeng Gede. April 27, 1937.   7 L 15.

6. The family shrines in the houseyard of Djero Baoe Tekek. This man, though no longer a full citizen (since his youngest child was married) was an important religious functionary and keeper of the village calendar. His house shrines are somewhat more elaborate than most.
Bajoeng Gede. Nov. 24, 1937.   19 F 22.

7. Djero Baoe Tekek's houseyard. A little to the right of the center is the main house in which he and his wife sleep. To the left of the center is the small shelter where water is stored in jars. All water is carried to Bajoeng Gede from a stream about a mile away. On the extreme right is the rice barn.
Bajoeng Gede. Nov. 24, 1937.   19 F 3.

1

2

3

4

5

6

7

1

2

3

4

5

6

Plate 2

BAJOENG GEDE: AGRICULTURE

In the mountains, rice is grown in dry fields and the crop is small. Rice is, however, the food with maximum prestige for feasts and the mountain people continue to grow it, though maize and root crops provide a great part of the diet.

In addition to the house (*oemah*) in the village, almost all families have a second house (*pondok*) out in the fields, and always one or more members of the family are there to look after the oxen and pigs.

Land tenure is of three major sorts: *laba* is a share in temple land which is re-allotted each year; *ajahàn* is a share in village land which is allotted for life in recognition of regular services to the village; *soegihan* is land privately owned by purchase or by inheritance from those who originally cleared it.

1. Temple land (*laba*) belonging to the village temple of Peloedoe, an outlying suburb of Bajoeng Gede with a social system similar to that of Bajoeng but less complete and less strict. Most of the inhabitants are people who have not yet attained citizenship in Bajoeng or who have lost citizenship through non-conformity with the stringent rules. This field is about a thousand yards in length (from left to right in the picture) and is subdivided every year with ploughed grooves marking off each citizen's share.
Peloedoe. May 31, 1937.   10 B 34.

2. Farm (*pondok*) belonging to Nang Oera, a citizen of Bajoeng Gede. Like the house in the village, the *pondok* is carefully enclosed. But here the yard is cultivated and, in general, life is pleasanter away from the restrictions of the village.
Lod Oemah (Bajoeng Gede). Aug. 6, 1936.   2 D 37.

3. Unidentified woman weeding dry rice growing in Bajoeng Gede temple land. She is probably a casual laborer from another community working temporarily for some citizen of the village.
Bajoeng Gede. Oct. 12, 1937.   17 N 35.

4. A ploughing bee (*metadjoek*) in the fields of Nang Roni of Bajoeng Gede. In the ploughing season, a man will invite his neighbors to come together and in one day plough his piece of land. He gives a small feast with special foods but no ceremony. The occasion is made more "crowded" (*rame*, cf. Pl. 5) by the sound of heavy wooden bells around the necks of the oxen, and by decorating the oxen with elaborate leather headdresses (fig. 6).
Bajoeng Gede. Aug. 19, 1937.   13 X 26.

5. A scene on Nang Oera's farm showing the oxen in shelter, and carefully fenced lanes.
Lod Oemah (Bajoeng Gede). Aug. 6, 1936.   2 D 21.

6. Oxen at a ploughing bee (cf. fig. 4) wearing bells and leather headdresses.
Bajoeng Gede. July 26, 1936.   2 C 8.

Plate 3

COMMUNITIES WITH IRRIGATION

Wherever it is possible to terrace and irrigate the land, we find a way of life very different from that of Bajoeng Gede. In place of the rigid formal communities and almost undecorated temples of the mountains, we find big sprawling villages and towns where family ties become more important than citizenship; where the decorative arts and music and dancing flourish; and where a man will spend his day in working up to his waist in the mud of his fields, and his evening in the local orchestra.

But in spite of these very conspicuous superficial differences and in spite of the many differences in custom, the basic psychological emphases of Balinese culture are the same both in Bajoeng Gede and in the plains. The treatment of children is virtually the same and the basic ethos is the same. In the plates which follow we shall treat the cultures of the mountains and the plains as a single psychological unit.

1. A courtyard gate in the old palace of the former Rajah (*Anak Agoeng*) of Bangli. The same topological frame, the rectangular houseyard with its gate, the same orientation to the Balinese cardinal points, the same orientation in time by means of the cyclic calendar are common to the mountain peasant and the rajahs of the plains (cf. Pls. 1 and 2).
Bangli. July 29, 1937.   12 Z 16.

2. Main gate to the village temple in Sanoer (South Bali) on a feast day. The gate is decorated with pendants on high bamboos and the statues are clothed. Note that Balinese art style swings very easily from the effective simplicity of fig. 1 to the overdecoration of fig. 2 (cf. Pl. 30, fig. 5).
Sanoer. Dec. 13, 1937.   19 Y 33.

3. A man flattening the mud in his flooded fields, after ploughing and before sowing. He weighs down with his foot on a board which is set at a slight angle to the ground and drawn by a pair of water buffaloes. (In the foreground, a bench mark of the Government Survey.)
Near Boeleleng. Dec. 27, 1936.   3 Y 5.

4. Terraced and flooded rice fields with the rice growing in the water.
Iseh (Karangasem). Aug. 9, 1937.   13 I 31.

5. Small boy bringing his water buffalo back from washing it in the stream. The care of the oxen and buffaloes is an important duty of the small boys.
Batoean. Feb. 21, 1939.   36 N 16.

6. Woman carrying home sheaves of rice from the fields at harvest. Men do not carry on the head. They would carry a load of this kind by suspending the sheaves on the ends of a pole balanced on the shoulder.
Karangasem District. Feb. 23, 1939.   36 S 24.

1

3

2

4

5

6

1
2
3
4
5
6
7
8

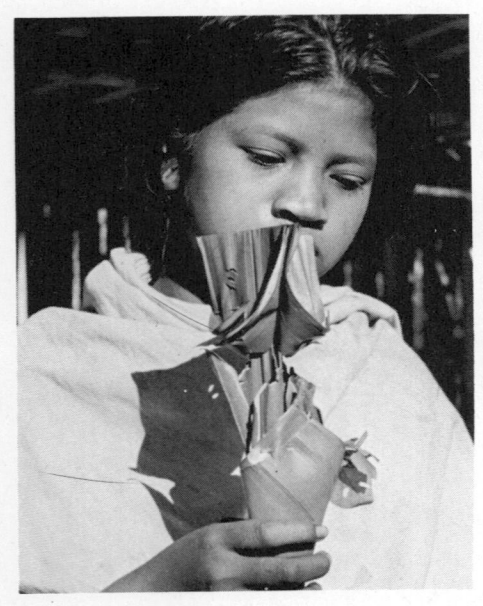

Plate 4
ANTHROPOMORPHIC OFFERINGS

In Balinese ceremonials most of the important offerings, including the sprinkler (*lis*) which is used for scattering holy water, are representations of gods, spirits, souls, or bodies of the dead (cf. Pls. 97 and 98). In *rites de passage*, it is common to find offerings representing the soul or body of the candidate.

1. An offering (*tjanang rebong*) made principally of flowers supported on a central core of banana stem and supported on a stand (*doelang*). This offering is carried whenever the gods move about from one temple to another or go for purification to the sea shore or to some special spring. This specimen was made for a *ngaskara* ceremony in the cremation sequence (cf. Pl. 98). The only recognizable anthropomorphism is the fan-shaped headdress (*tjili*) which is characteristic of representations of gods and souls of the dead.
   Batoean. Aug. 23, 1937.   14 V 1.

2. A figure (*reregek*) made from the base of a palm leaf with a roughly incised human face. The figure wears a sarong and a sash. Such figures are carried in procession in various *rites de passage*. This specimen was used at the 105-day birthday (*neloeboelanin*) of a baby in Boeleleng, and represents *Dadong Badjang* (literally, "old-maid grandmother"), an imaginary nurse (*ngempoe*) for the baby.
   Boeleleng. Nov. 8, 1936.   3 F 13.

3. An offering with very complete human form, made for the periodic festival in the temple on the island of Sakenan near the town of Denpasar. Every temple has its special day (in the 210-day cycle) when the gods are called down and offerings are made to them. This particular ceremony is perhaps more crowded than most because the trip out to the island provides a small excursion for the townspeople of Denpasar. The offering is made of fruit fixed to a central core of banana stem; the face is a female dancer's mask with a dancer's headdress of the type used in modern secular dances (*djanger*).
   Sakenan (Denpasar). Oct. 18, 1936.   2 Y 1.

4. An offering called *Nini* (Mother) representing the Rice Goddess (*Betara Sri*) at ceremonies of harvest-home. The figure is built up on a cylindrical basket or *wakoel*. The *wakoel* is covered with a sarong, a sash, and a bib. The torso and fan-shaped headdress are made of lontar-palm leaf. Around the neck is suspended 100 cash. The *wakoel* contains 1 coconut, 1 egg, uncooked rice, bananas, fruit, a combination of special leaves (*alas-alasan*) and a packet of betel-chewing ingredients (*gegantoesan*). This last item is usually itself anthropomorphic.
   Batoean. Oct. 5, 1937.   16 N 4.

5. A *Nini* in Bajoeng Gede. This is the simpler mountain analogue of the elaborate representation of the Rice Goddess in the plains. It consists only of a few heads of rice tied together. It is made of the first heads which are cut in the harvest and is later put in the rice barn when the harvest is brought home.
   Bajoeng Gede. April 6, 1937.   6 Q 22.

6. A number of *wakoel* offerings. For every important village ceremony, each of the 16 senior citizens of Bajoeng Gede sends his *wakoel*. The word *wakoel* is etymologically related to the words *awak* (body) and *wakil* (a person who acts as a substitute for another). Each *wakoel* contains a knife with the point turned down and a coconut, rice, fruit, etc. The smaller baskets are called *toegoe* and are sent by the giver of the feast and by visitors.
   Ceremony (*sampi gelis*) of presenting an ox to the village herd.
   Bajoeng Gede. July 16, 1936.   2 A 37.

7. *Toegoe loeh-moani*, a small double container made of palm leaf and used in the ceremony (*meteboes*) of tying newly married couples. The two parts of the top of the *toegoe* are incised with rough human faces, back to back like Siamese twins. The *toegoe* contains a piece of string. The bride provides one *toegoe* and the groom another. The string from the bride's *toegoe* is tied around the groom's wrist and a piece of it is put behind his ear. The string from the groom's *toegoe* is tied on the bride.
   Toegoe held by I Tjibloek at I Moedri's marriage.
   Bajoeng Gede. June 26, 1937.   12 D 8.

8. A portion of the sash (*sapoet*) from a high offering (cf. Pl. 11, fig. 3) at a high-caste (Kesatrya) temple feast. It is made by stringing together small slats of green sugar cane on which the shadow-play figures are scratched with great care. The object dries up and spoils in a few days. It illustrates the Balinese habit of playing with extreme detail and is an example of anthropomorphism added to an already anthropomorphic object, the high offering (cf. *gegantoesan* in fig. 4 above).
   Bangli. Nov. 16, 1936.   3 G 20.

Plate 5

CROWDS (*RAME*)

The Balinese enjoy very much the gay impersonal atmosphere of crowded occasions. Bodily contact with friend or stranger is pleasant to them and a Balinese crowd will pack almost solid, without any of those spaces which we try to preserve around ourselves. Such occasions are made "more crowded" (*ramean*) and still more enjoyable by the addition of firecrackers, orchestras, and the like.

Balinese offerings consist of "what is necessary" (*sane perloe*) and other ingredients (*roentoetan*) which are added to make the offering "more crowded" and more decorative.

1. A great procession of perhaps a thousand people follow the ashes to the sea. This was the end of a very elaborate and costly post-cremation ceremony (*meligija*) performed by the Rajah of Karangasem for the deification of his father. An image of the father was cremated in a repeat of the original cremation ceremony.
Karangasem. Aug. 9, 1937. 13 J 9.

2. Women and girls of Bajoeng Gede carrying home offerings from a festival in the Poera Doekoeh, a temple out in the fields.
Bajoeng Gede. Dec. 16, 1936. 3 U 31.

3. The procession in fig. 1 reaches the beach. Men carrying lances and swords and wearing a uniform of ceremonial checkered cloth (*poleng*).
Karangasem. Aug. 9, 1937. 13 J 30.

4. Crowd on the beach for the ceremony which drives the mice and grasshoppers across the sea to the Island of Lombok. The ceremony was held by order of the Rajah, and people came from as far as two days away bringing special offerings.
Lebih (Gianjar). Dec. 3, 1937. 19 P 5.

5. A scene at a marriage ceremony, while the assembled relatives are waiting for the arrival of the village officials. This shows *rame* at the family level. A mother with two of her own children and a sister's child (with cloth on neck) in a scuffle on her lap. An unrelated child watches and the mother's sister sits laughing. A photograph taken a few seconds later shows the sister's child back with her own mother and clutching hard at her breast and jacket; the mother looking vacantly away, her son still in her lap looking off into space; her daughter has slipped down from the breast.
Men Karma (with headcloth); Gata, her son, in center on her lap; Kenjoen, her baby daughter, to the right; Men Lintar behind Men Karma; Meres, Men Lintar's daughter, with cloth on her neck and shoulders; I Sepoeng, unrelated little girl, standing to the left.
Bajoeng Gede. June 25, 1937. 12 C 18.

6. Four girls and the village priestess in the audience watching a comedy fear scene (cf. Pl. 46, fig. 8) performed by a visiting theatrical troupe. (For other cases of covering the mouth with cloth, cf. Pl. 53, fig. 3; Pl. 60, fig. 5; Pl. 67, figs. 1 and 2; etc.).
In front, left to right: I Sepoeng; I Raksi; I Karni; I Rinjen; and behind I Sepoeng, Djero Balian Soekoeh.
Bajoeng Gede. May 30, 1937. 10 B 2.

1

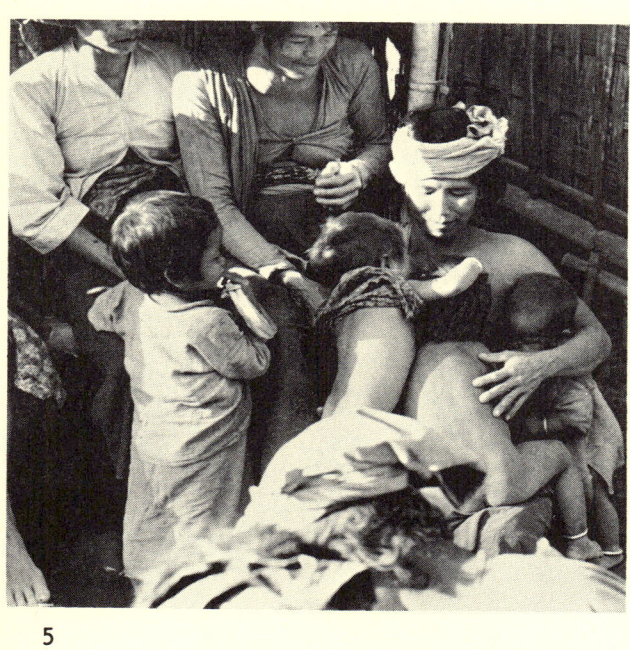

2

3

4

5

6

1

2

3

4

5

6

7

8

Plate 6
INDUSTRIALIZATION

Closely connected with the Balinese love of crowded scenes is the tendency to reduce all tasks to separate stages with a definite sequence of bodily movements necessary at each stage. The movements are then performed smoothly and fast, laughing and singing, with a minimum of conscious attention to the task. There is also a tendency to arrange matters so that a maximum number of items can be accomplished simultaneously. Thus the Balinese habit of muscular rote behavior (cf. Pls. 15 and 16) combines with their love of busy and active crowds to give something which we might call "mass production" methods. Their "mass production" differs, however, from our own in lacking any emphasis on efficiency. There are always many more people present, e.g., at the cooking for a feast, than are necessary; and people enter and leave the working group constantly and casually.

1. A Brahman priest (*pedanda brahmana boda*) making holy water (*toja pengentas*) for cremation ceremonies. He sits with several dozen pots of water in front of him, going through his prayers. He prepares one pot of special holy water, which then is diluted into all the pots.
   Batoean. Aug. 24, 1937.   14 V 16.

2. Preparing offerings for a ceremony (*metjaroe*) to purify the houseyard. First a large number of little leaf trays are folded and stitched; then the trays are laid out; then each tray is filled (as in photograph) from mass stores of each appropriate object. One woman puts a special kind of cake in each tray; another distributes little puddings; another betel; and another flowers, etc.
   Men Minab and Men Lemek in foreground; I Maring looking up; I Rendoet behind I Maring.
   Bajoeng Gede. July 14, 1937.   12 P 13.

3. Men preparing bamboo pegs for marking out the land in the annual sharing of the temple land.
   Left to right: Nang Singin; Nang Soni; Nang Ringin; Djero Keneh in background.
   Bajoeng Gede. April 27, 1937.   7 K 3.

4. Three carvings of a man with a duck in one hand and a flag for herding ducks in the other. This subject was for a time very popular with Balinese carvers working for the tourist market. These three specimens were all made by the same artist. It is usual to make such carvings in parallel stages. First, the carver collects a number of suitable pieces of wood; then he roughly carves all of them; next, he finishes the carving on all; and finally polishes them.
   Carved in Pajangan.
   Bajoeng Gede. June 9, 1937.   11 O 28.

5 and 6. Scenes at a post-mortuary ceremony (*metoeoen*) in which the dead speak through the mouth of the village priestess (*Djero Balian*) in trance. Women prepare piles of banana leaf plates, each with a little cooked rice and a stick of *sate* (cf. fig. 8). One woman holds the plates; another adds the rice; another, the *sate*; and when each pile of plates is complete it is passed up to the priestess who holds it a moment and speaks as a particular ghost. After the priestess has spoken, the pile is broken up; all the rice is put together in a basket, the *sate* in another basket, and the leaf plates are passed back to the beginning of the workline to be stacked again with more rice and *sate*. Each pile must have the correct number of layers according to the number of deaths in that household since the ceremony was last held (3 plates for one death; 5 for two; 7 or 9 for three; 11 for four deaths, etc.). The work involves rapid mechanical movements in co-operation and is accompanied all the time by counting. A European participating is rapidly reduced to a slightly dissociated state.
   Bajoeng Gede. July 10, 1937.   12 G 26, 13.

7. Girls shredding tree fern leaves for cooking at a wedding. The leaflets must be stripped from the stalks.
   I Gedir; I Njantel; and I Renoe.
   Bajoeng Gede. Aug. 18, 1937.   13 P 30.

8. Mass production of *sate* for a tooth-filing ceremony. *Sate* are small sticks on which meat is spiked or pulped food is smeared. Here several hundred such sticks of food are being cooked simultaneously over a long narrow charcoal fire. They are held in place by sticking them into a banana stem. They must be turned from time to time. Note the folded posture of the boy pausing in this task.
   On the extreme right, I Tompelos; others not identified.
   Batoean. Sept. 30, 1937.   16 G 3.

Plate 7
AWAYNESS

An obverse of the Balinese love of crowded scenes is their habit of withdrawal into vacancy — letting themselves suddenly slip into a state of mind where they are, for the moment, no longer subject to the impact of inter-personal relations. This withdrawal occurs in a large variety of contexts, but is perhaps especially common in parent-child and teacher-pupil relationships, and following some rather definite activity of work or play. The face of mother or child, or both, will become vacant immediately after unusually active play; or the face of an artist will be similarly unresponsive after he has just finished a carving.

1. Mother and son during a lapse of inter-personal contact. She is selling food in the road near their house and sits with face vacant. He has his mouth full of food and is, perhaps, a little sulky (cf. postures of the same mother and child in temper, Pls. 52 and 53).
Men Singin and her son, I Karsa.
Bajoeng Gede. May 2, 1937. 7 X 35.

2. Mother and daughter visiting our house. They are somewhat shy or disoriented by being in a strange place, and this perhaps brings them into closer physical proximity (cf. Pl. 46). There is close parallelism in posture between mother and daughter in the angles of the knees and relaxed straightness of the left arms, but in spite of this parallelism and their close contact, they are emotionally apart. Each is turned away from the other, and the mother has covered her mouth.
Men Koeboe and her daughter, I Rendoet.
Bajoeng Gede. Sept. 29, 1936. 2 S 23.

3. A psychopathic vagrant sitting in our yard. This man was unable to remain in communication with other people for more than a few seconds, after which he would wander away muttering or singing. He spent a great part of his time sitting like this alone. He would also devote a great deal of labor to making ornamental headdresses for himself. These he would wear for a short time, and then would leave them hanging on the trees. He was an experienced draftsman, doing conventional drawings of scroll designs and shadow-play characters. His carving was crude and idiosyncratic (cf. Pl. 27, fig. 3).
I Tjoengkoeh, said to have been born in Sebatoe.
Bajoeng Gede. April 6, 1937. 6 P 30.

4. The organizer of a dance club sits while his club performs. This man was one of the most assertive people in the village, and was also the priest and organizer of the *sangiang* club (cf. Pls. 18 and 19). He was somewhat too assertive for the very rigid equalitarian ethos of Bajoeng Gede, and this dance club finally broke up because of mild dissatisfaction with their leader.
Nang Karma; I Sadia; I Moedri.
Bajoeng Gede. Aug. 16, 1936. 2 G 11.

5. A small boy at the 210-day birthday ceremony (*otonin*) of his younger sibling. He is sitting with the old woman who performed the ceremony. This picture closely resembles fig. 2 above, showing the same seeking for close physical contact and the same complete lack of emotional contact. (See the same in Pl. 39, fig. 5.)
Men Gangsar and I Soewaka at the *otonin* of I Gae.
Bajoeng Gede. March 29, 1937. 6 J 23.

6. A carver after the completion of his representation of a dancer, which had taken him several days. Verbal record says, "He leant back utterly empty and spent. Asked if he would have made the carving any differently, he says 'no' and poses gaily to show how he would make another carving. He begins to work on another carving, saying that he has (to get money) to build a house." These periods of awayness are not followed by manifestations of fatigue, and are usually terminated by a sudden resumption of activity.
I Made Keloepoes of Bedoeloe (Gianjar).
Bajoeng Gede. July 9, 1936. 1 Z 31.

1

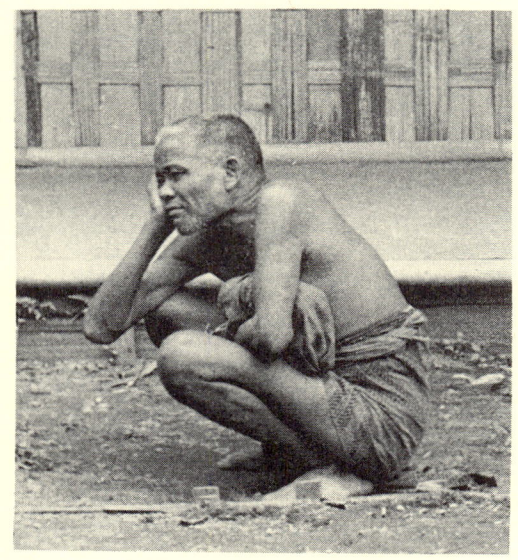

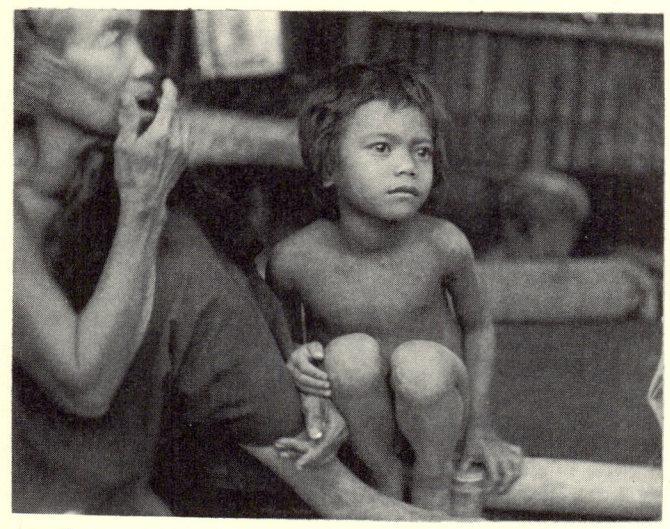

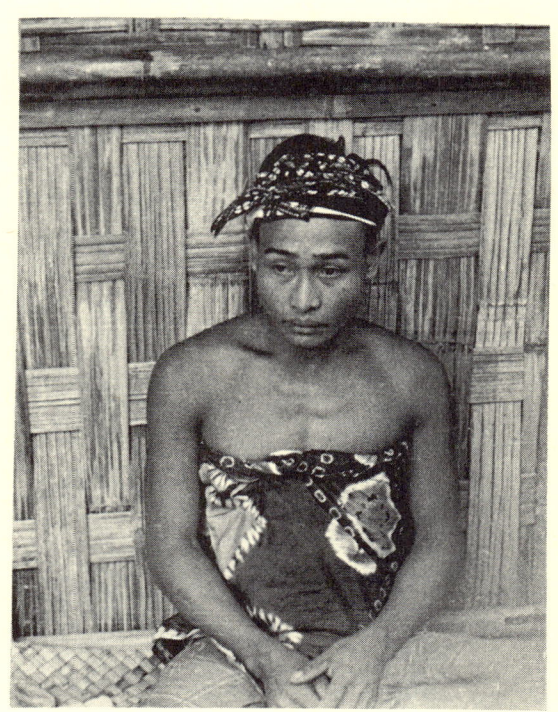

2

3

4

5

6

1 2 3
4 5 6
7 8 9

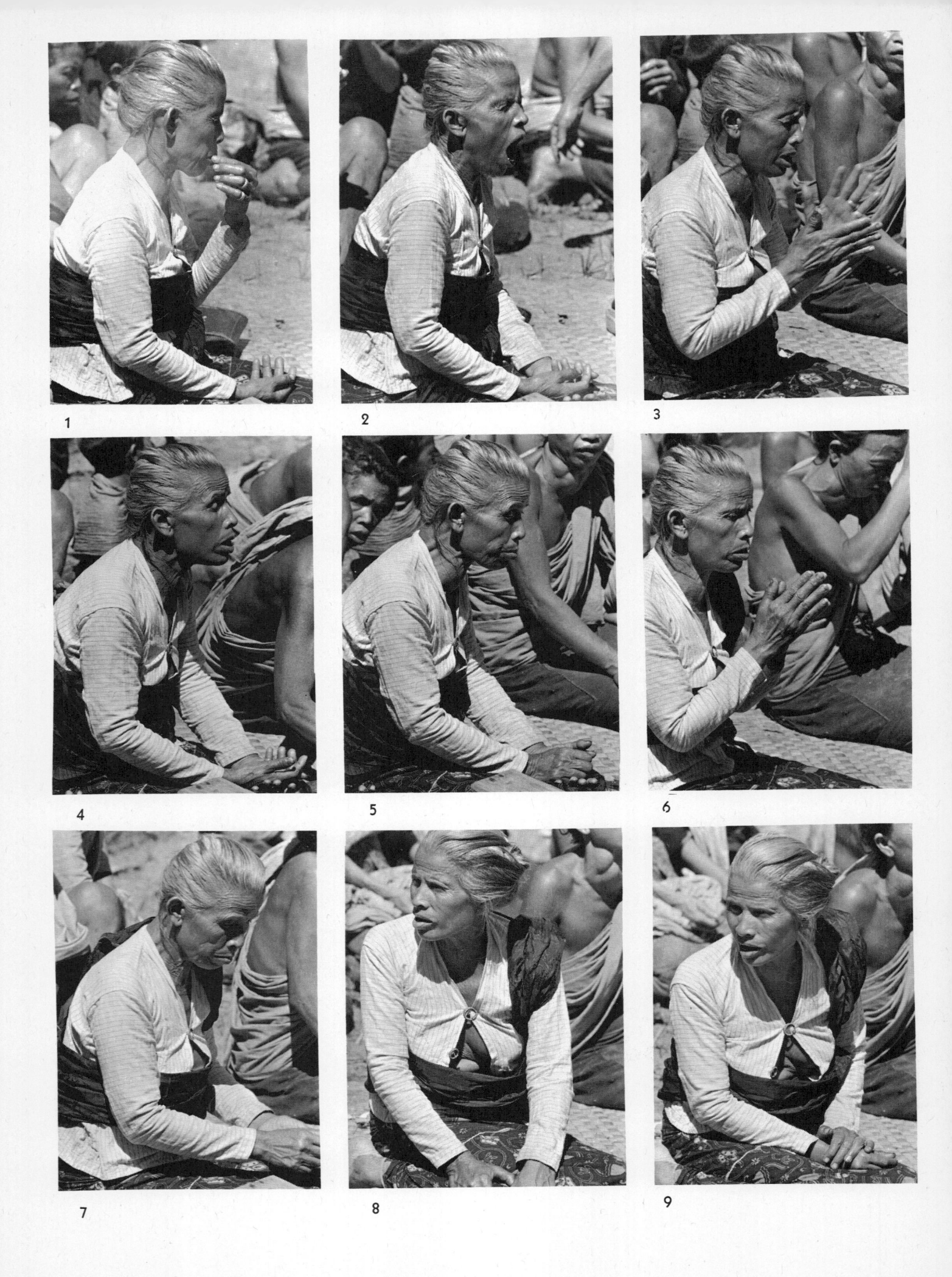

Plate 8

OFFICIAL TRANCE

In most Balinese villages trance plays a special role in the social organization. Bajoeng Gede has its councils of assembled citizens (cf. Pl. 9) but these groups are concerned with maintaining a well-known *status quo,* and in their deliberations, both the citizens and their leaders shrink from any sort of assertive behavior or innovation. Characteristically the function of innovation or initiating new ceremonial sequences — e.g., the decision to renovate an old disused temple — is left to the gods, and is performed by the village priestess (*Djero Balian*) in trance when she speaks as a god and is not personally involved in what she says.

At almost all village ceremonies, *Djero Balian* goes into trance twice, but usually, as on the occasion shown here, the god's utterances are confined to formal greetings to the village and acknowledgment of the offerings in a singsong voice.

Figures 1 and 2 show characteristic behavior before going into trance; figs. 3, 4, 5, behavior in trance; and figs. 6, 7, 8, and 9 show recovery from trance.

1. *Djero Balian* inhaling smoke from the burning chips of wood in the incense brazier (*pasepan*). She removes tobacco from her mouth before going into trance. Smoke is used in Bali both to induce trance and to induce recovery from trance.

2. *Djero Balian* yawns. This was her regular habit before going into trance. On this occasion, the photographic record shows that she yawned at least three times.

3. *Djero Balian* rubs her hands together. She habitually marks the moment of going into trance by suddenly plunging her hands into the embers of the incense brazier (not shown in the sequence of photographs). Immediately after this she rubs her hands together as shown. She has already taken on the facial expression usual in her trances, an expression of mixed agony and ecstasy with the eyebrows drawn together, forehead wrinkled, and corners of the mouth drawn down.

4. *Djero Balian* in trance. Her hands have returned to the passive position in which they were while she was waiting for the trance, but her head is lifted momentarily while she speaks. She emphasizes her speech by rhythmic raising of the head followed by nodding. These gestures probably do *not* coincide with the punctuation or sense of her speech but the recording was not precise enough to demonstrate this.

5. She pauses before coming out of trance.

6. Praying immediately after coming out of trance. She habitually marks the end of her trance by two sudden shrugs, first a shrugging of one shoulder and then of the other. After this she prays.

7. *Djero Balian* relapses for a moment into trance. Formally she is now completely normal, and the god has left her, but she reverts for a moment to her trance expression.

8. *Djero Balian* starts to look around her, but is apparently still not fully oriented.

9. *Djero Balian,* apparently fully oriented with her characteristic shrewd and bright facial expression.

Djero Balian Soekoeh.

Bajoeng Gede. June 23, 1937. 11 Y 34, 35; 11 Z 3, 9, 12, 14, 18, 21, 26.

(Note: the sequence is incomplete, having a gap of nearly a minute between fig. 2 and fig. 3 when the camera had to be reloaded.)

Plate 9

SHARING AND SOCIAL ORGANIZATION

A great deal of care is devoted to the accurate sharing of ceremonial food, which is laid out in patterns according to the hierarchical structure of the contributing groups.

There are two principal patterns of sharing in Bajoeng Gede:

Kawes (figs. 2 and 3). The members of some group (e.g., the citizens of the village, or the members of a smaller temple club) contribute whatever food is conventionally necessary (rice, coconuts, and pig or chicken) for the calendric feast. This food is laid out on banana leaf platters in rows, with extra shares at the top end for special senior members of the group. The members take their shares and either eat them on the spot or carry them home, according to the conventions of that particular occasion.

Loengsoeran (literally, "things which are asked back"). These are shares of food which has been offered to the gods. Every member must contribute a measured amount of rice and coconuts, which the group, communally, offers to the gods at temple festivals. The ceremonies recur at regular calendric intervals, and each member in rotation must provide more valuable items such as pig or chicken. Other members, also in rotation, have the duty of reminding the man whose duty it is to provide the chicken. After the food has been made up into elaborate decorated offerings and offered to the gods, it is carefully sorted, shared back to the original contributors and given to them informally.

1. Four senior members (*doeloe*, literally "heads") of a temple club (Dadia di Panti) sit in the courtyard of their small temple (Poera di Panti) in the early morning of the day of their temple festival (*odalan*) discussing the arrangements.

Djero Koebajan Poepoe, with elbows on knees; Nang Karma, the priest of the club, facing the camera.

Bajoeng Gede. July 8, 1936. 1 W 25.

2. *Kawes* spread for the New Moon (*tilem*) meeting of full citizens (*kerama desa*). The two long parallel lines of platters are for the ordinary citizens. The two outside shares on each end of the cross line are for the four men (*saja*) who provided the food this month. The two center shares in the cross row are for the two senior citizens (*koebajan*). The senior *koebajan*'s share is on the left (inland-east). The third and fourth citizens (*baoe*) receive the first platters at the top of the long parallel lines. The remaining two platters in the top line are shared between the first and third, and the second and fourth citizens respectively. The other objects laid out are the coconut shells and shovels which are used in measuring and arranging the food.

Bajoeng Gede. April 11, 1937. 6 Q 29.

3. The men (*saja*), who prepare and provide the food, laying out *kawes* for the 210-day festival in a minor temple (Poera di Panti).

Bajoeng Gede. July 8, 1936. 1 X 29.

4. A feast meal spread for relatives at a marriage ceremony (cf. Pl. 29, fig. 1).

Bajoeng Gede. April 21, 1937. 7 D last.

5. Feast spread for people of Katoeng by the people of Bajoeng Gede. This was an important occasion, when, under divine instructions delivered in trance, the gods of the village of Katoeng were ceremonially brought to visit related gods in Bajoeng Gede. The feast is spread in the main court of the village temple of Bajoeng Gede.

Bajoeng Gede. March 25, 1937. 6 F 2.

6 and 7. *Loengsoeran*, one person's share from the communal offerings at a 210-day temple festival in one of the smaller temples (Poera Pemetelan). In fig. 7, this *loengsoeran* is opened and spread out. In the sharing, it is necessary to subdivide most of the cakes and puddings so that, except for the banana, most of the food which is received back is in the form of small pieces of pudding, cake, etc.

Bajoeng Gede. April 24, 1937. 7 E 21, 22.

1

2

3

4

5

6

7

1

2

3

4

5

6

Plate 10
ELEVATION AND RESPECT I

This and the four following plates illustrate the Balinese systems of hierarchy and respect. In addition to the system already noted, according to which the inland-east (*kadja-kangin*) is the most honored direction, a great deal of attention is paid to elevation, and the head is ceremonially the most sacred part of the body. Respect is expressed by lowering the self or elevating the respected person.

Every Balinese, in all his personal relations, continually orients himself in terms of the cardinal points and the relative elevation of the various persons.

1. A man looking at an aeroplane. In looking up at this strange and surprising object, he has, from habit, put his hands in a posture of ceremonial respect (cf. fig. 5).
I Wajan Keloepeos, of Bedoeloe.
Bajoeng Gede. July 3, 1936.   1 T 14.

2. The Goenoeng Agoeng, the central mountain of Bali. This mountain is regarded as an abode of gods, and links together the system of cardinal points and the system of elevation. The cardinal points differ from ours in that, though east (*kangin*) and west (*kaoeh*) are determined by the rising and setting of the sun, the other two directions (*kadja* and *kelod*) are determined by reference to the central mountain. In Bajoeng Gede and South Bali generally, *kadja* coincides with the European "north" and has been so translated in this book. In North Bali, however, *kadja* coincides with the European south, and *kadja kangin*, the most honored direction, is southeast. The translation "inland-east" is applicable in both cases.
Photograph from near Bajoeng Gede.
June 17, 1937.   11 R 27.

3. Trance dancer (*sangiang*) on a man's shoulders. The two little girls who dance in trance (cf. Pls. 18, 19 and 38) are to some extent sacred in ordinary daily life and they must avoid going under aqueducts or suspended chicken roosts. In trance, when they are "possessed" by angels (*dedari*), they become much more sacred; their commands are obeyed and they dance, not only on the ground but also elevated on men's shoulders. Most men normally avoid carrying a grown woman, and women's clothes must not be put on top of men's clothes. *Sangiang* dancers cannot dance after puberty, and the reason given for this rule is that men would not "dare" to carry them on their shoulders.
I Misi on shoulders of I Lasia.
Bajoeng Gede. May 26, 1937.   9 O 32.

4. Painting of a *sangiang* dancer being carried. Here the respect is expressed not only by elevation but also by the use of umbrellas.
Painting by I. B. Kt. Diding, Batoean; bought Feb. 24, 1938. Reduced x ⅓ linear. Picture 119.

5. Comic servant (*kertala*, cf. Pl. 13) in Balinese drama, in position of respect (*soembah*), waiting for the entry of his prince.
Dendjalan. May 26, 1936.   1 I 13.

6. The dream of a Brahman artist. The dictated text of the dream is as follows:
"Another time I dreamt of burning a body. The dead man had never once helped (others). Lazy so to speak, and he died. And no citizens went to visit (*medelokin*) there. I carried (him) to the cemetery and came to the cemetery; and, when I got there, there were all the citizens, all together; and I was stared at by the citizens. They would not lift the firewood for the burning. And so I alone, I burnt him. And while it was burning, I mumbled to myself. The citizens were still there, far off. That's how — when alive, too lazy to help the neighbors, and now stared at by the citizens."

Note that the artist has represented himself as lower than the assembled citizens, and that in the dream he is both the "lazy" man and the man who does the burning. This painter was unusually preoccupied with caste, because he had broken a serious caste rule in stealing the wife of another Brahman.
Painting by I. B. M. Togog of Batoean; bought Aug. 26, 1938. Reduced x ¼ linear.

Plate 11

ELEVATION AND RESPECT II

On Plate 4, we showed that the "offerings" in Balinese religion are in most cases representations of gods, spirits, souls, and the like. It is, therefore, natural that offerings should be elevated on high shrines to the high gods. (Certain offerings to low demons and to the dead are placed on the ground, and here the upright anthropomorphic form is replaced by flat figures on top of which the food is placed, cf. Pl. 30, fig. 6.)

1. High shrine for offerings at a girl's puberty ceremony. Note that the shrine is here treated anthropomorphically, and is dressed in a long bib (*lamak*) with a decorative cut-out design of sewn leaves (cf. Pl. 93, fig. 4, for the whole decorated house of the pubescent girl, and for other cases in which the shrine or house is equated with the immanent sacred object).
Batoean. Dec. 8, 1937. 19 U 29.

2. Altar or shrine to the Sun (Betara Soeria) at a great post-mortuary ceremony (*meligijah*). It stands open to the sky, outside the great hall which was specially constructed for the ceremony (cf. Pl. 5, fig. 1 for the procession terminating this ceremony).
Karangasem. Aug. 5, 1937. 13 G 18.

3. High offering carried in procession by a man. Every year the people of a large number of villages attend a great ceremony at Batoer Kalanganjar to receive there a special kind of holy water (*banjoen tjokor*). A series of these very high offerings was carried in procession at this ceremony. They were carried by men, being too heavy for women. The decorative top is made of cut palm leaf, and the facing of the base is of cake attached to a central wooden frame.
Batoer Kalanganjar. April 25, 1937. 7 E 27.

4 and 5. Ceremony to install a god in a house shrine. This god (Betara Doekoeh) had formerly been kept (*ngamong*) by the Lasia family in their house temple but the shrine had broken and the god had gone back to his temple (Poera Doekoeh) in the fields north of Bajoeng Gede. In fig. 4, the village priestess accompanies Men Lasia to meet (*memendak*) the god out in the fields. The priestess prays, while Men Lasia does her hair. The god is represented by his substitute (*wakoel*), the black basket offering on the mat. Fig. 5 shows the *wakoel*, i.e., the god, installed in his shrine in the house temple of the Lasia family. The *wakoel* and its contents will be *loengsoeranga* ("asked back") next morning and the contents will be eaten like any other offering.
Bajoeng Gede. July 14, 1937. 12 P 14, 24.

6. High cremation towers (*wadah*) being carried to the cemetery. The relative height and the construction of these are correlated with the caste and wealth of the deceased. Rajahs have high cremation towers with multiple roofs, but the tower of a Brahman high priest who is still higher in caste, is carried in an open structure similar to the sun shrine shown in fig. 2.
Blahbatoe. May 28, 1936. 1 L 5.

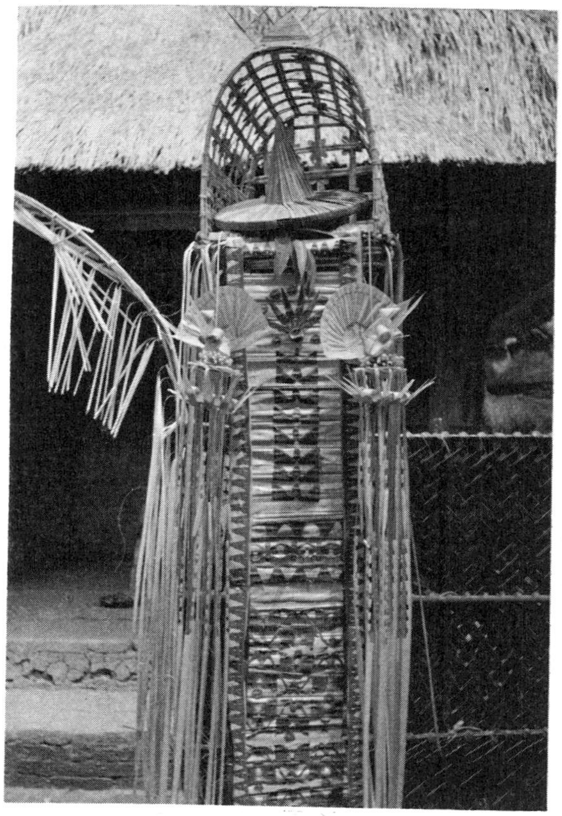

1

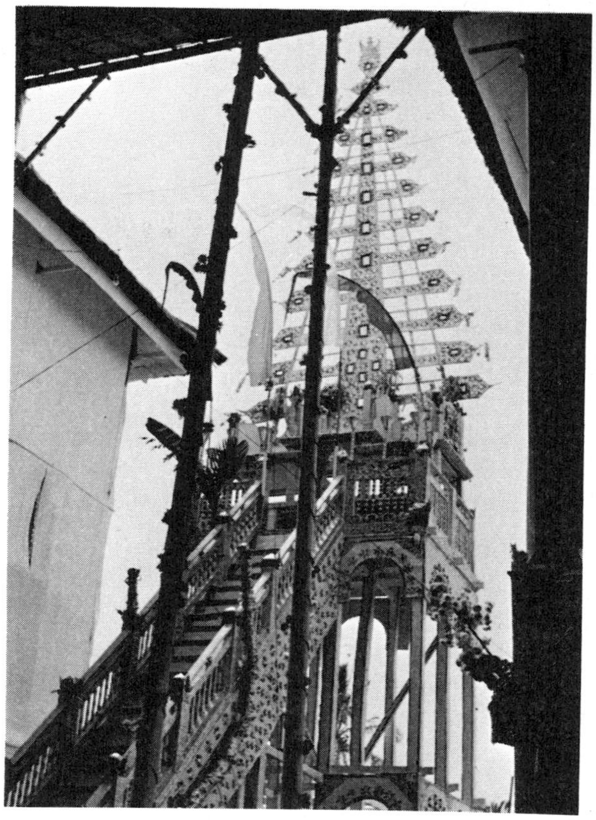

2

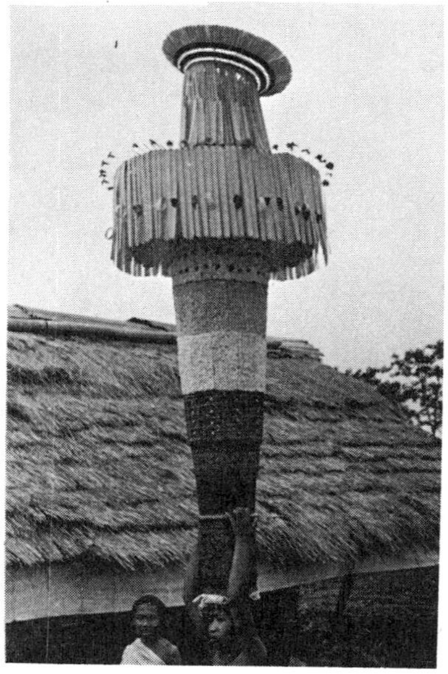

3

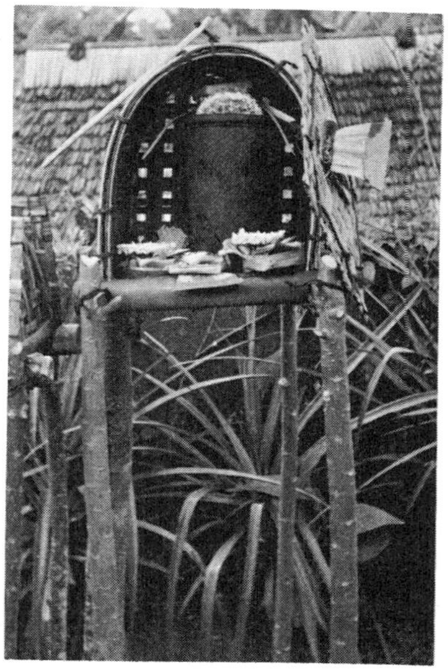

5

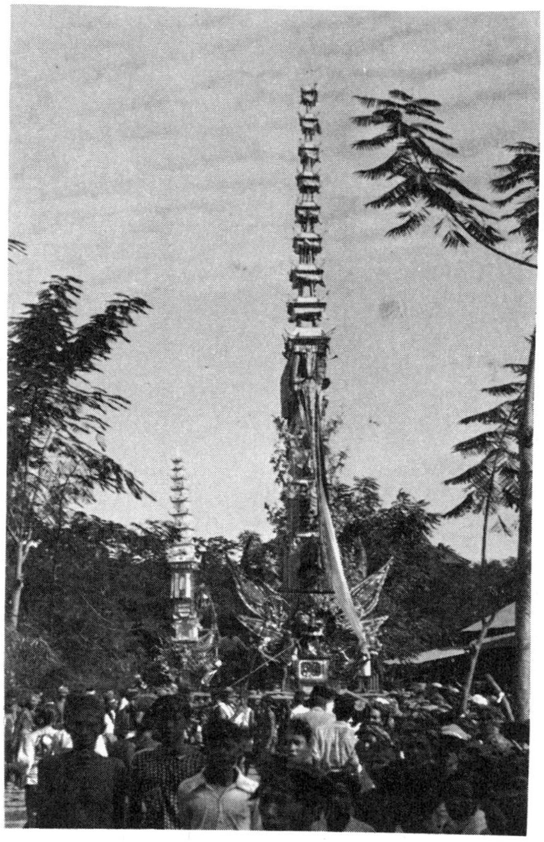

6

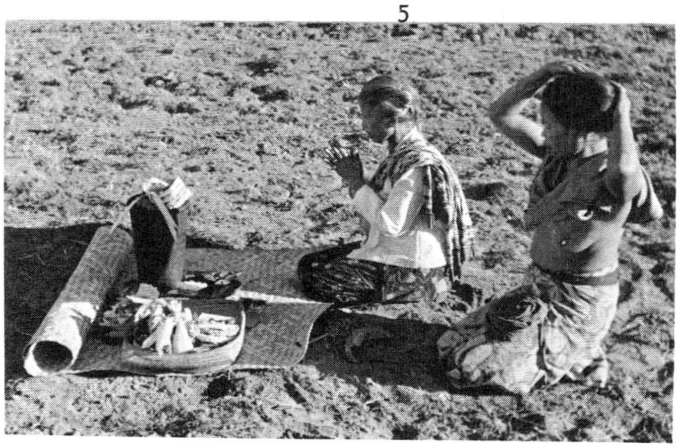

4

1

2

3

4

5

6

Plate 12

ELEVATION AND RESPECT III

There is an important contrast between the Balinese orientation to the cardinal points and their orientation to levels. Except for amusement when some person forgets where "north" is or is confused in his orientation after crossing the island, the cardinal points are rarely a subject for joking. Levels, on the other hand, continually provide matter for joking and mockery. The cardinal points are an essential, "matter of course" element in the everyday life; but levels and the respect associated with levels are a less essential theme about which there is enough constant anxiety so that it is amusing to embroider upon possible reversals. A baby learns the cardinal points in the very early stages of speech, and his orientation becomes automatic. But relative levels and the variations of language which go with respect and caste never become automatic and are regarded even by the most expert adults as difficult. They are a source of continual anxiety and continual amusement.

1. A village official witnesses a marriage. This is done by one of the lower "heads" (*doeloe*) of the village, but not by one of the first four. He sits on a platform (*bale*) while the relatives of the bride and groom sit on the ground. He asks rather sharply and formally about the type of marriage contract, and underlines his superior position more than would be done by one of the senior four.
   Nang Polih.
   Bajoeng Gede. June 25, 1937.   12 C 7.

2. One of the relatives at the same marriage ceremony. He sits on the ground, and further lowers himself by bending his back and thrusting his head forward. The posture of the hands is also a conventional gesture of respect.
   Unidentified man, a relative of the bride from another village.
   Bajoeng Gede. June 25, 1937.   12 C 5.

3. A mother plays upon the system of levels. The play shown in this picture is an unusual variant of the play shown in fig. 5. This was the warmest and least teasing mother in the village. She has borrowed a younger baby and allows her own son (wearing necklace) to be above it and to play with its head. The play in this case involves no reversal of the respect system. The mother of the borrowed baby protested a little against this play. She said, "Won't he be cruel? I Bawa (another baby) was cruel."
   Men Degeng; her son, I Sepek with necklace, aged 276 days; I Koewat, the borrowed baby, wearing clothes, aged 30 days; I Njawa, elder sister of the borrowed baby behind her mother, Men Njawi.
   Bajoeng Gede. April 30, 1937.   7 V 1.

4. A *djanger* dance. This is performed by boys and girls who form an open square sitting on the ground. In one of the figures of this dance, the boys form pyramids as shown in the picture. In some cases the girls go in procession through the arch, but little trance dancers (*sangiang*, cf. Pl. 10, fig. 3) and high castes cannot do this (cf. Pl. 83, figs. 3 and 4 for play with levels among boys).
   An itinerant *djanger* troupe from Sanding.
   Bajoeng Gede. Oct. 25, 1936.   3 A 31.

5. A mother teases her child by putting a younger borrowed baby on his head. This play takes various forms, and its point is the reversal of the respect system. The head of an elder brother is sacred, and typically a mother puts her own youngest child on the head of the next older. In this case there was no younger child, and she has borrowed a neighbor's child to fill out the pattern. After this teasing, the verbal record states: "Men Goenoeng gives up Tongos (the borrowed baby) — flicks Raoeh's (her own child's) penis with paper to quiet him."
   I Pindet, mother of borrowed baby on the left; Men Goenoeng, center, holding up I Tongos; Men Goenoeng's youngest son, I Raoeh, sitting on ground.
   Bajoeng Gede. June 25, 1937.   12 B 35.

6. A painting of two well-known folk characters of Balinese drama and shadow play. They are I Tjoepak, the gross, boastful and cowardly elder brother, and I Gerantang, the refined and brave younger brother (cf. Pl. 70, fig. 2). The picture shows I Gerantang, beautifully dressed and exquisite, but acting as servant in washing Tjoepak's hands, and the meal of sucking pig on which Tjoepak will gorge himself. In the story they go out to kill a demon (represented by a Witch mask). I Gerantang climbs down a rope into the demon's hole and kills the demon. I Tjoepak takes away the rope and goes home and claims the credit, leaving I Gerantang to starve in the hole (cf. Pl. 20, fig. 7). He escapes by making a ladder out of the demon's bones. He becomes a baby and is cared for by a fisherman's wife. Finally he returns to expose Tjoepak.
   The story gives the elder brother wish-fulfillment — the younger is left in the hole — but the wish-fulfillment is followed by self-contempt and punishment.
   Painting by I Goesti Kobot of Oeboed.
   Reduced x ¼ linear. Cat. No. 043.

Plate 13

ELEVATION AND RESPECT IV

In the relationship between a Balinese rajah and his servants, the paternalism is almost all on the servant's side, and the master is "spoiled" (*sajanganga,* see Glossary) by the servant (cf. Pl. 45). Both parties in this relationship play exhibitionistic roles, but whereas in Western culture the servant dresses up in a vicarious exhibition of his master's greatness, in Bali the servant dresses in his shabbiest clothes acting as a foil to the master. Similarly it is a point of virtuosity among servants to exaggerate their manifestations of respect to the point of mockery.

In the Balinese theater the servants are the clowns and a great part of the comedy is extemporized around the relationships between master and servants and between elder and younger brothers, both of whom are servants. These photographs are all from theatrical performances.

1. A prince (*mantri*) and his two servants. The prince stands in an aloof posture which shows off his beautiful clothes, while his face is averted and his left arm is held stiff in a posture which separates him from the servants to whom he is talking. The elder brother servant (*poenta,* with his back to the camera) kneels in stiff exaggeration of respect. The younger brother servant (*kertala*) in sleeveless ragged garments roars with exaggerated laughter.
Itinerant troupe of *ardja* dancers from Tiga.
Bajoeng Gede. May 12, 1937.   8 P 17.

2. A princess (*galoeh*) and her servant (*tjondong*). The servant of the princess in Balinese theater is typically older than the princess, and represents a nurse. The part is often acted by a man (cf. Pl. 22, figs. 1 and 2). The princess adopts an aloof posture very closely resembling that adopted by the prince in fig. 1.
Itinerant troupe of *ardja* dancers from Tiga.
Bajoeng Gede. May 12, 1937.   8 N 30.

3. Elder and younger brother servants kneeling, waiting for the entry of their prince. The painted moustache of the younger brother servant, the awkward position of his dagger (*kris*) and his stiffly splayed fingers are all clownish exaggerations of his role.
Itinerant troupe of *Tjalonarang* dancers from Tatag.
Bajoeng Gede. May 29, 1937.   9 V 15.

4. The same younger brother servant in posture of prayer to his prince. In the normal Balinese prayer position, the fingers are straight, but side by side, instead of being splayed out (cf. mock prayer position in Pl. 88, fig. 3).
Bajoeng Gede. May 29, 1937.   9 V 17.

5. Elder and younger brother servants (Towalen and Moerdah) in dramatized shadow-play (*wajang wong*). This theatrical form is a version of a Javanese theatrical form. The angular dancing conventions of the shadow-play have been adapted to living dancers. Here the two servants are stylized along lines somewhat different from those followed in other Balinese theatrical performances, but the basic motif of contrast between brothers persists. The elder brother is big and black and his jokes are lusty and coarse, while the younger brother is represented as very much younger and speaks in a childish falsetto.

In this particular performance, the elder brother was danced with very limp postures while the younger brother had quick lively movements and tense muscles.

In all these pairs of brothers, the comedy is worked out on contrasts between the elder and the younger, but the actual distribution of the roles may vary greatly. In one troupe, the elder brother will be short and fat while the younger is tall and thin; in another troupe, this contrast may be reversed; and in yet another troupe the contrast may be played in terms of age (cf. fig. 2 above, where the normal age contrast between nurse and princess is reversed).
Itinerant *wajang wong* troupe from Kedoewi.
Bajoeng Gede. May 13, 1937.   8 V 19.

6. A younger brother servant (*kertala*) approaching his prince. The general physique and posturing of this younger brother servant were like those of the younger brother servant (Moerdah) in *wajang wong* (fig. 5).
Witch play in Dendjalan.
Dendjalan. May 26, 1936.   1 I 24.

1

2

3

4

5

6

1

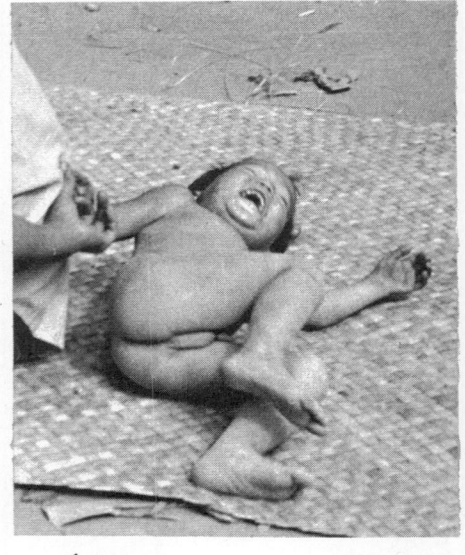

2

3

4

5 6 7

Plate 14

ELEVATION AND RESPECT V

The head is the highest part of the body, and this theme also becomes a base for comedy. This plate shows the body inverted, and the pubes turned into the head (cf. Pl. 20, fig. 4). This inversion is probably linked with the general notion that, in witchcraft, ritual is reversed, as in the "widdershins" of European witchcraft.

1, 2, and 3. A sequence from a witch drama (*Tjalonarang*, cf. Pls. 55 to 58 for details of the plot). In the version here shown, the minor witches (*lejak*) who have caused pestilence are finally exposed by a seer who, with his assistant, lectures them (fig. 1). In this picture, the two witches are reduced to squatting on the ground. After this, the seer and his assistant "cut off the heads" of the witches, removing the masks. The witches then perform half a somersault forward, arriving back to back against the papaya tree (fig. 2). The orchestra starts to play, and the witches begin to dance with their legs in the air. The masks are then placed on the witches' pubes (fig. 3), while they continue to dance, posturing with their legs, as though their legs were arms. Finally the masks are taken off them and they then stand up normally; the masks are given back to them and they run off.

Tjalonarang dance by itinerant troupe from Tanggan.
Bajoeng Gede. June 2, 1937.   11 C last; 11 D 1, 9.

4, 5, 6, and 7. A small boy trying to stand on his head. His mother had been intermittently teasing him and he had been playing at being a dragon (*barong*, cf. Pl. 67, fig. 7), while she tried to make his cousin (I Karba) frightened of him. In the beginning of the sequence (fig. 4), he poses to attract his mother's attention, with right arm and left leg extended and back flexed. He then stands on his head, falls roaring, and tries again.

This sequence occurred before the dancers did their upside-down dance in the village. After the little boys in Bajoeng had seen the witch dance (which was new to them), there was a great deal of this sort of play, attempting to imitate the dancers.

I Karsa.
Bajoeng Gede. May 25, 1937.   9 K 19, 20, 21, 22.

Plate 15

VISUAL AND KINAESTHETIC LEARNING   I

An individual's character structure, his attitudes toward himself and his interpretations of experience are conditioned not only by what he learns, but also by the methods of his learning. If he is brought up in habits of rote learning, his character will be profoundly different from what would result from habits of learning by insight.

Among the Balinese, learning is very rarely dependent upon verbal teaching. Instead, the methods of learning are visual and kinaesthetic. The pupil either watches some other individual perform the act or he is made to perform the act by the teacher who holds his limbs and moves them correctly. During this process the pupil is entirely limp and appears to exhibit no resistant muscular tensions. A Balinese hand, if you hold it and manipulate the fingers, is perfectly limp like the hand of a monkey or of a corpse.

1, 2, and 3. Learning to carry on the head. These three photographs were all taken on the same occasion and show a girl (fig. 2) preparing to go home from a temple feast, carrying on her head the offerings which her family sent to the ceremony. Figs. 1 and 3 show two smaller girls imitating her and so beginning to participate in the ceremonial life of the village.

Fig. 1, I Djani; fig. 2, I Maderi (unrelated); fig. 3, I Djana (younger sister of I Djani).

Bajoeng Gede. June 23, 1937.   11 Z 30, 26, 33.

4 and 5. A father teaches his son to dance, humming a tune and posturing with his hand. In the first picture, the father shapes his facial expression to a typical dance smile and the son looks at the raised hand. In the second picture, the son tries to grasp the arm, and the father's expression becomes inter-personal instead of stylized.

Nang Oera, the father; I Karba, the son, aged 265 days.

Bajoeng Gede. Oct. 1, 1936.   2 U 30, 31.

6. The same father teaches his son to play the xylophone.

Nang Oera; I Karba, aged 393 days.

Bajoeng Gede. Feb. 5, 1937.   4 S 1.

7. A child nurse teaches the same baby to walk. She holds the baby by the upper part of the arms. There was no baby in her household and she spent a great part of her time looking after her father's step-brother's child. This photograph of learning to walk was taken five months later than the photographs of the same child learning to dance.

I Djeben teaching I Karba, aged 414 days.

Bajoeng Gede. March 26, 1937.   6 F 15.

8. Small high-caste boys learning to draw in the sand. The boy in the center was the most skilled and the others stopped their own drawing to watch him. All three boys show the typical Balinese high kinaesthetic awareness in the hands, and this is heightened by their using very small twigs for their drawing.

I. B. Saboeh; I Dewa Moeklen; I Dewa Loepiah.

Batoean. Oct. 5, 1937.   16 M 2.

1

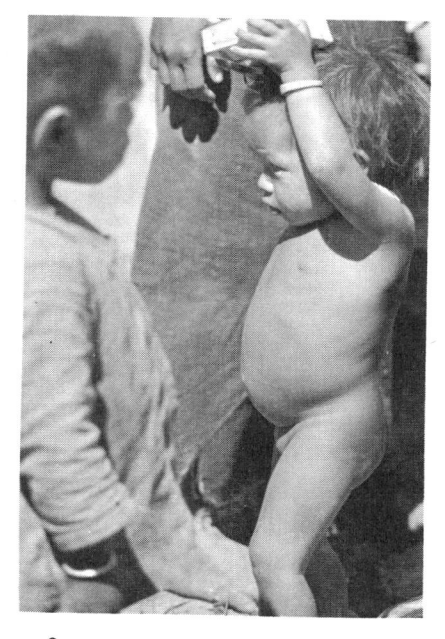

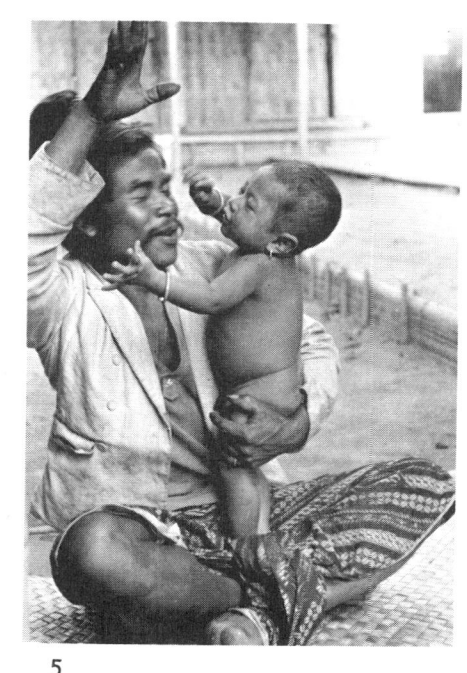

2

3

4

5

6

7

8

1
2
3
4
5
6
7
8

Plate 16

VISUAL AND KINAESTHETIC LEARNING II

Teaching by muscular rote in which the pupil is made to perform the correct movements is most strikingly developed in the dancing lesson.

Mario of Tabanan, the teacher in this sequence, is the dancer chiefly responsible for the evolution of the *kebiar* dance which has become very popular in Bali in the last twenty years. The dance is performed sitting in a square space surrounded by the instruments of the orchestra, but though the principal emphasis is upon the head and hands, the dance involves the whole body, and Mario has introduced a great deal of virtuosity into the difficult feat of rapid locomotion without rising from the sitting position. The chief faults in the pupil's dancing are that he dances only with his head and arms, and does not show the disharmonic tensions characteristic of the dance.

This sequence of photographs illustrates two essential points in Balinese character formation. From his dancing lesson, the pupil learns passivity, and he acquires a separate awareness in the different parts of the body (cf. Pl. 20, fig. 4).

1. The pupil dances alone while Mario watches in the background. Note the imperfect development of the pupil's finger posture.

2. Mario comes forward to show the pupil how it should be danced.

3. Mario urges the pupil to straighten up the small of his back. Note that this instruction is given by gesture rather than by words.

4. Mario's hand position and facial expression while demonstrating (cf. Pl. 22).

5. Mario takes the pupil by the wrists and swings him across the dancing space.

6. Mario makes his pupil dance correctly by holding his hands and forcing him to move as he should. Note that Mario is actually dancing in this photograph, and that he postures with his fingers even while holding the pupil's hands. The position of Mario's left elbow in these photographs is characteristic of the tensions developed in this dance.

7. Mario even assumes the conventional sweet impersonal smile of the dancer while he moves the pupil's arms and holds the pupil tightly between his knees to correct his tendency to bend the small of his back.

8. Mario again tries to correct the pupil's tendency to bend his back.

I Mario of Tabanan teaching I Dewa P. Djaja of Kedere.

Tabanan. Dec. 1, 1936. 3 O 11, 13, 14, 17, 21, 22, 23, 25.

Plate 17

BALANCE

Plates 14, 15, and 16 taken together give us indications about the Balinese body image. We have, on the one hand, the fantasy of the inverted body with its head on the pubes; and on the other, the Balinese methods of learning through their muscles, the discrepant muscular tensions which are characteristic of their dancing, and the independent movement and posturing of the separate fingers in dance. We have, in fact, a double series of motifs — indications that the body is a single unit as perfectly integrated as any single organ, and contrasting indications that the body is made up of separate parts, each of which is as perfectly integrated as the whole.

This plate illustrates the motif of the perfectly integrated body image, while Plates 18, 19, and 20 illustrate the fantasy that the body is made up of separate parts and may fall to pieces (*beroek*).

1 and 2. A small boy learns to stand and walk. His father has set up for him in the houseyard a horizontal bamboo supported on two posts (*penegtegan*). The boy learns to walk by using this as a support.

The topology of this arrangement is the precise opposite of that of the play-pen of Western culture. The Western child is confined within restricting limits and would like to escape from them; the Balinese child is supported within a central area and is frightened of departure from this support.

In fig. 2, when unsure of his balance, he holds onto his penis. This method of reassurance is common in Balinese baby boys.

I Karba, aged 414 days; I Kenjoen, his cousin, aged 317 days, behind him.
Bajoeng Gede. March 26, 1937. 6 F 20, 21.

3. A baby girl unsure of her balance. She clasps her hands in front of her abdomen.
I Kangoen.
Bajoeng Gede. April 21, 1937. 7 A 15.

4. A child nurse picks a baby from the ground. Note the straightness of the small of the back and the resulting emphasis on the buttocks.
I Njantel picks up I Karba; I Dani watches.
Bajoeng Gede. May 13, 1937. 8 U 30.

5. A girl stoops to pick up part of an offering. The flexibility of the body and the emphasis on the buttocks continue into later life, and occur even in those who are unusually heavily built.
I Teboes; I Tjerita behind her.
Bajoeng Gede. April 26, 1937. 7 H 18.

6. Decorative panel on a temple wall. This figure stands as one of a series of representations of transformed witches (*lejak*) and graveyard spirits (*tangan-tangan, njapoepoe*, etc., cf. Pl. 20, fig. 5).
Poera Dalem, Bangli. Nov. 23, 1936. 3 J 5.

7. A small boy scratches his leg. He was waiting in the road, uncertain whether his playmate was following. His natural movement is to raise his leg, rather than to stoop.
Bajoeng Gede. April 19, 1937. 6 W 19.

8 and 9. Paintings of a woman transforming herself into a witch (*anak mereh*). She goes out alone at night, sets up a little shrine and makes offerings on the ground to the demons (cf. Pl. 33, figs. 2, 3, and 4). She dances before the shrine with her left foot on a fowl, and becomes transformed into supernatural size and shape. The fantasy that the body is as integrated as a single organ is here danced out in grotesque balance, and leads to a nightmare transformation or ecstatic dissociation of the personality. The drawings illustrate the close association between grotesque posture and the ecstasy of witchcraft (cf. figs. 6 and 7).
Paintings by I. B. Nj. Tjeta of Batoean.
Purchased Feb. 2, 1938. Reduced x ⅓ linear. Cat. Nos. 545 and 548.

1

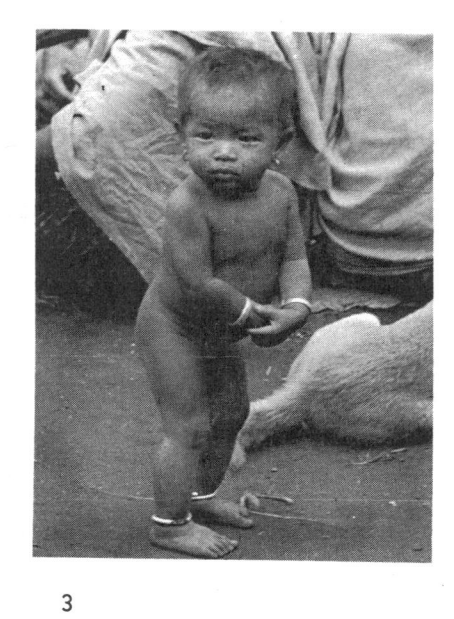

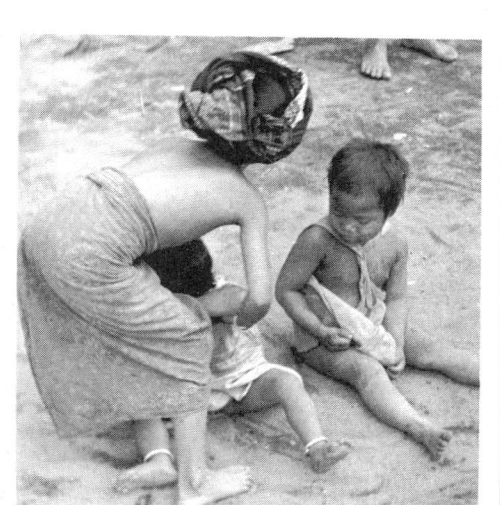

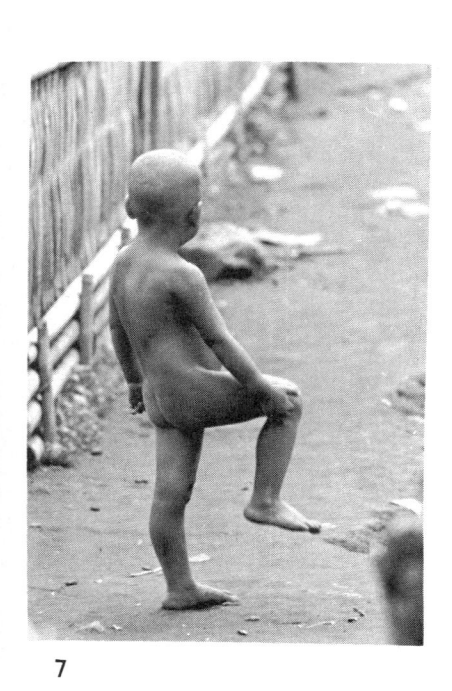

2

3

4

5

6

7

8

9

1

2

3

4

5

6

Plate 18

TRANCE AND *BEROEK* I

The word *beroek* is used by the Balinese to describe a corpse which is falling to pieces with decay. It is here used to epitomize the fantasy of the body as made of separate independent parts. This fantasy takes many forms, among others the notion that the body is like a puppet, just pinned together at the joints, and, as already noted (Pl. 17, figs. 8 and 9), the same fantasy is closely linked with phenomena of ecstasy and trance.

This and the following plate show various stages in the trance performance of the *sangiang* dancers (cf. Pl. 10, fig. 3; Pl. 38, figs. 1, 3 and 4). These are a pair of little girls who go into trance possessed by gods, and who dance in the trance state. They are sacred, and though the performance is given chiefly for entertainment, the *sangiang* dancers may also give special holy water, which is used for medicinal purposes. They must not dance after menarche.

1. The puppets on a string. The performance begins with a dance by the gods, who are represented by two dolls. They are threaded on a string which is tied at the ends to the tops of two sticks (*patokan*) to which bells are attached. Each stick is held by a man whose arm is slightly flexed at the elbow. After a few minutes, trembling or changes in tension of the string set up clonic contractions in the arms of the two men, and the dolls begin to "dance." They are said to be "possessed" (*kerawoehan*) by the gods. While waiting for the clonus, the man who holds the stick pays very little attention and often looks away, as in this picture. The native introspective account is that the man does not make the dolls dance — "they dance of themselves and the men cannot stop them."

Rhythmic clonic contraction is an example of a part of the body taking on its own independent integration. (Among the Iatmul of New Guinea, trance is preceded by ankle clonus.)

I Lasia holding the *patokan*.
Bajoeng Gede. May 26, 1937. 9 M 38.

2. The stick (*patokan*) and back view of the puppet. The puppet is weighted with bells at the lower end, so that it will stay in a more or less upright position while dancing.
Bajoeng Gede. Aug. 18, 1937. 13 U 19.

3. When the puppets are dancing and the sticks moving with sufficient violence, the two little girls, I Renoe and I Misi, come and sit beside the men with the sticks. They hold the lower end of the sticks tightly with both hands and are thus shaken by the movements of the sticks. Each child sits in the lap of an older girl who is ready to catch her when she falls into trance.

I Lasia holding left-hand stick; I Renoe holding the base of this stick and sitting in lap of I Wadi; Nang Ngetis holding the right-hand stick; I Misi holding its base and sitting in the lap of I Rinjin; Nang Karma, the priest of the club, in the right foreground.
Bajoeng Gede. May 26, 1937. 9 N 28.

4 and 5. I Misi falls into trance. The people sing while the little girls hold the sticks, and the girls begin to sway sideways. This swaying becomes more and more violent but later diminishes, and the girls begin to beat with the sticks on the supporting stands. They impose the rhythm of the song on the sticks which are moving with the clonic rhythms of the two men. Finally I Misi gives a stronger beat with the stick to coincide with a final beat of the song, and collapses limp in the lap of the woman who holds her (cf. Pl. 68 for discussion of falling backward and sleep as forms of regression toward the father).

I Misi in trance, in lap of I Rinjin; Nang Karma, in foreground; I Gati (daughter of Nang Karma) holding the baby, I Kenjoen.
Bajoeng Gede. May 26, 1937. 9 N 30, 32.

6. I Renoe not yet in trance. She is still holding the base of the stick and beating in time to the song.

The man who holds the stick has closed his eyes and appears to be on the verge of trance. He is not known to have gone into trance on this occasion, but there was one boy (I Malih, Pl. 21, fig. 1) in Bajoeng Gede, who several times went into trance while holding the stick. Such trance was discouraged, and he was finally told that he could not hold the stick any more unless he gave up going into trance. He was able to give it up.

Same people as in fig. 3 above.
Bajoeng Gede. May 26, 1937. 9 N 33.

Plate 19

TRANCE AND *BEROEK* II

The little girls are now possessed by the gods which had possessed the puppets. They sit limp while headdresses and aprons of gilded leather-work are fixed on them, and then they are carried to a clear space where they stand waiting for the orchestra to begin. Sometimes (for a joke) the orchestra begins to play before the girls are ready. They automatically begin to dance in the arms of whoever is holding them and the orchestra must be stopped before the dressing can proceed.

As is the case with all Balinese dancers, their costumes and especially their sashes are very loosely fixed and constantly come undone during the dance. Members of the audience go out onto the dancing space and do the necessary repairs (cf. Pl. 45, figs. 3 and 4; and Pl. 61, fig. 2).

1. I Renoe waiting for the orchestra to begin. She stands limp and with her eyes shut. Of these two dancers, I Renoe rather often opened her eyes but I Misi was never observed to do this.

A woman in Boeleleng, North Bali, who used to be a *sangiang* dancer in her childhood states that she used to be unconscious while she was being put into trance and unconscious again while she was being taken out of trance, but that she was conscious during the middle period while she was dancing. It was not possible to get any introspective account from I Renoe and I Misi, since the whole trance period is nominally lost in amnesia.

I Renoe; Men Soni leaning forward behind her.
Bajoeng Gede. Feb. 11, 1939.   36 A 7.

2. A masked dancer representing a wounded warrior. This photograph is given for comparison with fig. 3.

From a series of *topeng* masks made by Pedanda Made of Sanoer.
Sanoer. Dec. 13, 1938.   19 X 23.

3. I Renoe dancing. This photograph shows the extreme limpness which is characteristic of the dance. In spite of this, it is a quick dance.

I Renoe; I Lasia, on the right, behind her.
Bajoeng Gede. May 26, 1937.   9 O 37.

4. A *legong* dancer. The *legong* is a dance very similar to that of the little trance dancers (*sangiang*), but the *legong* performers are not in trance. Comparison between this photograph and the others on this plate shows the very great difference in muscular tension in the two dances. In addition, the *legong* dancers are carefully trained, while the priest of the *sangiang* club boasts that his little girls are entirely untrained and enabled to dance by the gods. It was noticeable that after *legong* dancers had performed in the village, the *sangiang* dancers added to their repertoire new steps which they had copied from the *legong*.

Itinerant *legong* dancers from Tiga.
Bajoeng Gede. Nov. 3, 1936.   3 E 23.

5. A figure in the trance dance in which the dancers, facing each other, take quick sideways steps (*segseg*) in opposite directions. A number of the figures and steps in the dances are dictated by the songs. The song says that the dancers *segseg* and they *segseg*; or, the song tells them to pick a flower out of their headdresses, and they pick out a flower and give it to the audience. (In certain trance dances in the Karangasem District, this pattern is carried to extreme lengths, the singers giving various grotesque and obscene orders to the young men who are dancing in trance, so that the whole performance becomes reminiscent of the psychopathology of *latah*, the imitation hysteria, which also occurs in Bali.)

I Misi, with back to camera; I Renoe, facing camera.
Bajoeng Gede. Feb. 11, 1939.   36 A 15.

6. "Sweeping the ground with her fan." This is another movement which is enjoined on the dancer by the words of the song.

I Misi.
Bajoeng Gede. May 26, 1937.   9 O 20.

7. Waiting to be taken out of trance. At the end of the dance — when either the audience or the dancers so decide — the little girls are picked up and carried to the mats. Their headdresses are removed, and they are smoked with incense from a brazier, while the audience sings special songs.

I Made Kaler (our secretary) with head band; I Lasia, sitting with his back to the camera; I Misi in lap of I Soka.
Bajoeng Gede. Feb. 11, 1939.   36 B 29.

1
2
3
4
5
6
7

1

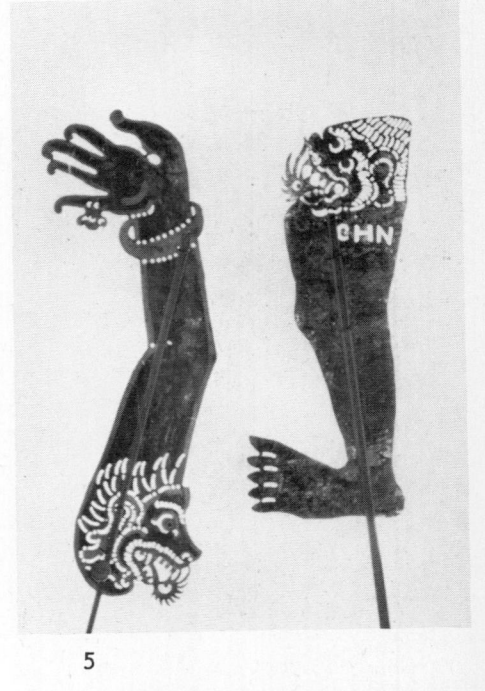

2

3

4

5

6

7

8

Plate 20
TRANCE AND *BEROEK* III

The puppets of the shadow play illustrate many aspects of the Balinese attitudes toward the body and their fantasies about it.

1. Two dancers (*legong*, cf. Pl. 19, fig. 4). These puppets are built on a single stand, and they are made to dance in exact unison by means of a stiff forked wire which goes to their heads. These puppets are unusually flexible in their bodies, being made of three parts — head, torso, and legs — so that they can lean over backward till their heads touch the ground. All shadow-play puppets are painted on both sides. The majority of the audience sees only the silhouettes but many, especially small boys, prefer to sit on the puppeteer's side of the screen.
Modern North Balinese puppets made by I Made Oka of Boeleleng.
Cat. No. 291.

2. Puppets representing three of the five Pendawa. These five brothers are the heroes of the epic, Berata Joeda. The puppeteer either takes his plots from the epic, or more often makes up his own plots using the stock characters. The three brothers here shown are (from left to right): I Darma, the eldest, a wise and quiet character; I Bima, the second, a jovial man of great strength and violence and one of the favorite characters; I Redjoena, the third, an exquisite and perfect warrior. The other two, not shown here, are twins, I Nahoela and I Sahadewa, who are comparatively unimportant. The puppet of I Redjoena might also be used to represent I Garantang, in the story of Tjoepak (cf. Pl. 12, fig. 6).
All these puppets were made by I Wara of Negara, who copied them from models which he obtained in Kloengkoeng. (Puppets are usually made by tracing from an old puppet.)
American Museum of Natural History, Nos. 70.0–8223, 8194, and 8199.

3. Shadow-play puppet of a graveyard spirit (*lawean*). This is a personified headless figure. The two projections, where the base of the neck should be, are characteristic of decapitated figures in the shadow play. They show that this is not a figure whose head has contracted into the chest but a personified headless trunk.
Made by Dalang Sebeng of Sebatoe. He stated that he had invented (*ngeragrag*) this figure.
A.M.N.H., No. 70.0–8043.

4. Line drawing of a protective spirit. This spiritual being is a compound of body parts, each of which is personified. The text under the drawing reads as follows:
"This is named Bala Serijoet [literally "Multiple Soldier" or "Multiple Army"] with golden menstrual cloth. Used as a *toembal* (magical object) for the country. Bury it in the middle of the village. Bala Moeka [literally "Face Soldier"] is his name. Used as a powerful *djimat* (magical object). Great is his power who uses this." (For assistance in translating this archaic text, we have to thank the Javanese scholar, Raden A. K. Widjojoatmodjo.)
Painting by I Goesti Nj. Lempad.
Purchased Nov. 28, 1936. Cat. No. 16.

5. Shadow-play puppets of two graveyard spirits. One is a personified hand (*tangan-tangan*), the other a personified foot (*batis-batis* or *njapoepoe*). The letters cut on the *batis-batis* are put there to make the figure more terrifying.
Made by Dalang Sebeng of Sebatoe.
Cat. Nos. 31 and 41.

6. Shadow-play puppet of Sangiang Tjintjia. This deity typifies extreme unity. He has no shrines or observances, but he is central to the whole pantheon. He is entirely aloof and self-contained but he is "god of gods" (*dewaning dewa*). The pantheon contains several other figures who claim the same distinction, who are represented in the same way; that is, enclosed in their own effulgence. Of these, one of the most important is Betara Soeria (the Sun); another is Betara Toenggal ("Unit God").
Made by Dalang Sebeng of Sebatoe.
A.M.N.H., No. 70.0–8021.

7. Shadow-play puppet of I Gerantang. This represents the exquisite and brave younger brother of I Tjoepak (cf. Pl. 12, fig. 6), after he has been starved in the demon's hole, and has become an "unfortunate" (*sasaran*). The figure is flexible at the neck and at the insertions of the limbs, and the limbs hang limp from any position in which the body is held.
It can be shown from other Balinese artistic products that a fear of animality is closely linked to the notion that the body may be *beroek*.
Made by Dalang Lana of Sebatoe.
A.M.N.H., No. 70.0–7965.

8. Shadow-play puppet of the wife of I Delem (comic elder brother servant opposed to I Towalen; cf. Pl. 13, fig. 5). This figure combines limpness with the oral overresponsiveness which is to the Balinese both disgusting and comic (cf. Pl. 27, fig. 6). The coarseness of this figure is emphasized by the elegant finger-postures.
Made by Dalang Sebeng of Sebatoe.
A.M.N.H., No. 70.0–7980.

Plate 21

HAND POSTURES IN DAILY LIFE

Related to the Balinese fantasy of the body as made of separable parts, and also to the habit of learning by muscular rote, we find that Balinese hand postures, whether in activity or at rest, differ markedly from those usual in Western cultures. We commonly place our hands in positions of regular flexion, e.g., with the fingers either equally flexed or progressively more flexed from one side of the hand to the other. The hands of the Balinese are more usually in positions which appear to us to be irregular, and, in particular, the Balinese hand postures tend to emphasize the sensory functions of the finger tips.

1. A boy tying up the dolls after they have been used to put the dancers in trance (cf. Pls. 18 and 19). With his left hand he holds the dolls, chiefly with the tips of his fingers, while the tip of his left index finger is on the first loop of the string. With his right hand he places the other end of the string around the dolls. The tip of his right thumb is against the string, while the index and little fingers are more extended than the two middle fingers.
I Malih.
Bajoeng Gede. Aug. 18, 1937.   13 W 9.

2. A carver strikes a pose to show the posture he intends for his carving representing the leader (*dag*) of a modern dance (*djanger*).
I Wajan Keloepoes of Bedoeloe.
Bajoeng Gede. July 9, 1936.   1 Z 32.

3. A mother, after bathing her baby, sits watching him play with another baby. Her arms are lightly crossed over her knees and her hands, while completely relaxed, still show the characteristic emphasis on sensory function. Her baby sits with his left hand on his knee and his finger tips raised.
Men Sama, the mother; I Sami, her son, aged 233 days; I Karba, aged 450 days.
Bajoeng Gede. April 30, 1937.   7 O 7.

4. A boy playing with the same baby. After rolling him about on his lap for some time, he pauses with relaxed hands. (For other cases of regression into the lap of an older male, cf. Pls. 63 and 65.)
I Sambeh of Selat holding I Sami, aged 233 days.
Bajoeng Gede. April 30, 1937.   7 P 10.

5 and 6. Using the hand as a measure of length. These two pictures show the men measuring the strips of rattan which were used to mark out the citizens' shares of temple land (cf. Pl. 1, fig. 5 and Pl. 2, fig. 1). In our culture we have several units of length based upon parts of the body — the inch, the foot, the cubit, etc. In Bali, this system is very highly developed, and the vocabulary contains dozens of these terms. It is probable that this large development is related to the Balinese fantasy of separable body parts.

Curiously, the ceremonially prescribed dimensions for houseyards, doorposts, etc., are usually given in this form: "The post should be twenty spans (*rai*) made alive (*maoerip*) with one middle-finger inch (*agoeli lindjong*)," i.e., 20 spans *plus* 1 inch.
Bajoeng Gede. April 27, 1937.   7 K 21, 26.

7 and 8. A father holding his baby. The fingers of his right hand are flexed, so that the baby is supported on the heel of the hand and the finger tips.
I Sama holding I Ngendon, aged 42 days.
Bajoeng Gede. Dec. 20, 1936.   3 V 9, 12.

1

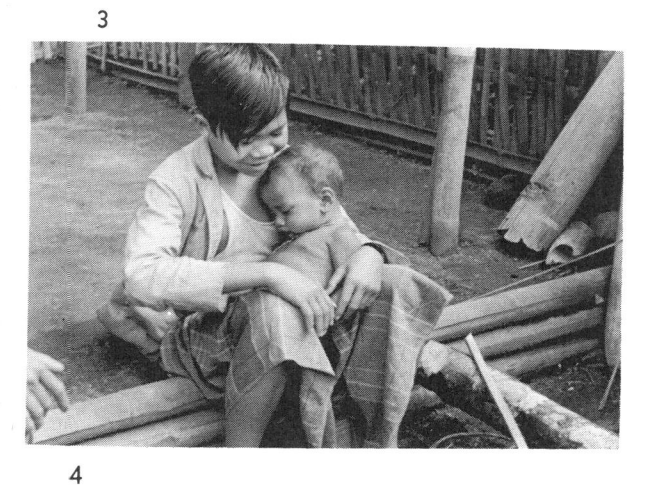

2

3

4

5

6

7

8

1

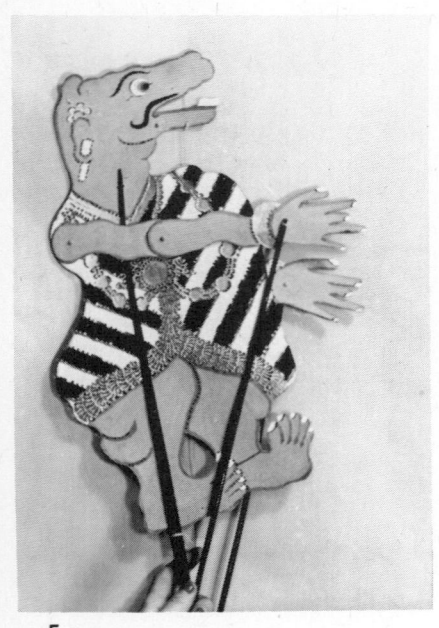

2

3

4

5

6

7

Plate 22

HAND POSTURES IN DANCE

The hands, and especially the fingers, are important in all Balinese dances, and provide an effective means of expressing the elegant, the diabolical, the stupid and the aloof.

Almost all Balinese are able to bend their fingers backward from the base and also at the joint between the first and second phalanges. Children constantly fidget with their fingers, bending them back.

1 and 2. A man dancing as I Raroeng, the Witch's Daughter. Female roles are frequently danced by men or boys, and the Balinese much enjoy the fine points of these sex reversals. In comedy parts, it is not uncommon for a female dancer to play a female role as it would be played by a male dancer.
 Itinerant troupe of *Tjalonarang* players from Tatag.
 Bajoeng Gede. May 29, 1937. 9 U 26, 19.

3. A courtship dance (*djoget*, cf. Pls. 59, 60, and 61). The girl is a trained dancer who came to the village with an itinerant orchestra. She begins to dance, and men come out of the audience to dance to her, while she responds to them with an aloof coquetry. She fends the man off with gestures of her left hand (as in this picture) or with her fan, while the man momentarily emphasizes his intense perception of her with his hand over his eyes and his fingers extended.
 Itinerant *djoget* from Pelaktiing; Nang Moespa dancing with her.
 Bajoeng Gede. May 12, 1937. 8 R 12.

4. Another girl in the same type of dance (*djoget*) expressing untouchable aloofness with fan and left hand.
 I Tiroe, itinerant *djoget* from Pangsoet, Bangli.
 Bajoeng Gede. May 28, 1937. 9 R 25.

5. Comic shadow-play puppet of human figure with horse's head (*dangdang bang*). Here the coarseness and ineptitude of the figure are stressed by making the fingers perfectly straight, shortening the middle finger and representing the toes of the left foot as awkwardly bent.
 Made by I Made Oka of Boeleleng.
 A.M.N.H., No. 70.0–8248.

6. Shadow-play puppet of the Witch (*Rangda*). This shows her in her supernatural form with flames coming from her head and joints. This posture with the arms raised, which is characteristic of *Rangda*, is called *kapar* (cf. Pl. 60, fig. 2). On the stage, when the Witch assumes this posture, her fingers are straight and limp. This picture is of a puppet whose fingers cannot be moved. (The left hand of this puppet was used for the design on the cover of this book.)
 Bought in Bangli.
 Cat. No. 243.

7. The female servant (*tjondong*) in a theatrical performance (cf. Pl. 13, fig. 2, for another photograph of this girl). She is kneeling before her princess.
 Itinerant *ardja* troupe from Tiga.
 Bajoeng Gede. May 12, 1937. 8 N 35.

Plate 23

HAND POSTURES IN ARTS AND TRANCE

The emphasis on the separateness of the fingers and on the sensory function of their tips is very evident in the hand postures of artists at work. Remarkably, where Occidental artists accentuate the sensory function in the right or active hand, it appears from the photographs that the Balinese artist accentuates this in the *left* hand. The same appears to be true of the dance postures. The photographs illustrating the more elaborate hand positions show mostly the *left* hand in these positions. (Unfortunately this point was not noticed in the field and therefore cannot be stated definitely or backed up by native statements.)

For the Balinese, there is a very profound difference between left and right. The left hand should be used for unclean things — the genitals, feces, etc. — while the right hand should be used for eating and for giving or receiving gifts. The apparent emphasis on the sensory or perhaps exploratory function of the left hand may be connected with this differentiation.

1, 2, and 3. A Brahman artist works on the pencil drawing for a picture. In fig. 1, he smiles at the photographer. His right hand is inactive while his left is in an apparently sensory position, touching but not pressing down the edge of the paper. In fig. 2, he rules the lines marking off the margin of the paper. In fig. 3, he is drawing, and again his left hand takes a position which emphasizes the sensory function of the finger tips.

I. B. Made Djatisoera of Batoean.
Batoean. Oct. 4, and Oct. 6, 1937.   16 K 9, 22; 16 O 15.

4. A carver shaves the surface of the head of his carving with an oblique-edged scalpel. In this action the carving is held in the left hand, and the pressure of the left thumb on the back of the scalpel is the major force used. The right hand serves chiefly to guide the scalpel.

I Made Keloepoes of Bedoeloe.
Bajoeng Gede. July 1, 1936.   1 Oa 11.

5. The same carver polishing his carving with sandpaper. Here the fingers of the left hand which holds the figure are in an irregular posture.

I Made Keloepoes of Bedoeloe.
Bajoeng Gede. July 4, 1936.   1 W 10.

6. A carver incising lines on his figure. His left hand, with fingers irregularly spread, holds the head of the figure, while the base of the figure is supported against the carver's abdomen. The right hand, holding the scalpel, is unsupported.

I Wajan Gangsar of Bedoeloe.
Bajoeng Gede. July 4, 1936.   1 W 12.

7 and 8. A man recovering from trance looks at his hands which are still "in trance." He looks first at one hand, then at the other. These pictures illustrate another aspect of the notion that the body is made up of separable parts. In the District of Karangasem, there is a considerable variety of trance dances, in some of which only the arm of the performer is in trance. (J. Belo, unpublished researches.)

M. M.'s verbal record describing the performance of the Witch drama in which this trance occurred contains the following passages:

"11:55 A.M. Rangda (the Witch) goes off and Barong (the Dragon) appears out of the temple. Barong, apparently in trance, dashes about snapping, and attacks orchestra. Man in orchestra rises and beats drum into the mouth of the Barong, holding the drum so that the Barong's mask rests upon it, and the man in trance inside the Barong can get no farther into the orchestra.

"11:58 A.M. Someone has replaced the front man in the Barong. He lies 'out' (i.e., in trance) in a little group of men. The Barong stands over the man in trance (cf. Pl. 66, fig. 6).

"11:59 A.M. Priest (*pemangkoe*) with holy water comes out of temple. He flicks the dish of holy water under the Barong's beard. Sprinkles man in trance. Feeds him holy water. Men on each side of the man in trance have their hands caught in his *rigor*. His hands are sprinkled and massaged to loosen grip. He sits up, arms still rigid, and gives a series of convulsive jerks and looks dazedly about him. The jerks are similar to those which *Djero Balian* gives (cf. Pl. 8, fig. 6), but involve whole arm.

"12:00 M. Shoulders jerk convulsively. The Barong mask is covered with cloth. Man who was in trance now out of trance, moves over to orchestra group and is handed a bundle of his clothes."

Dancer in itinerant *Tjalonarang* troupe from Pengelijangan.
Bajoeng Gede. May 17, 1937.   9 A 18, 19.

1

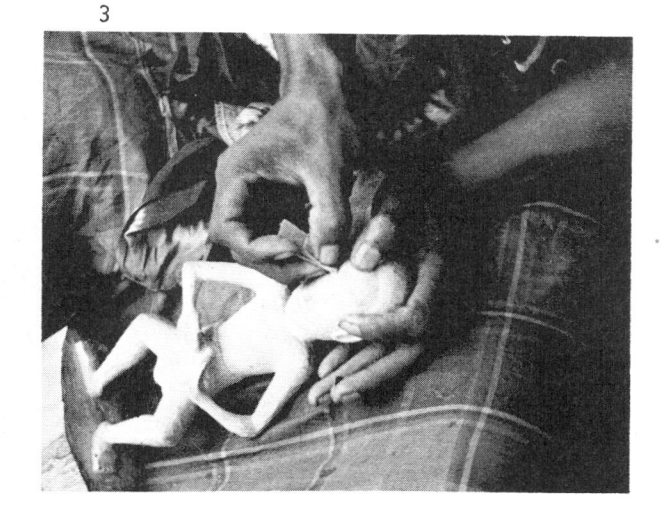

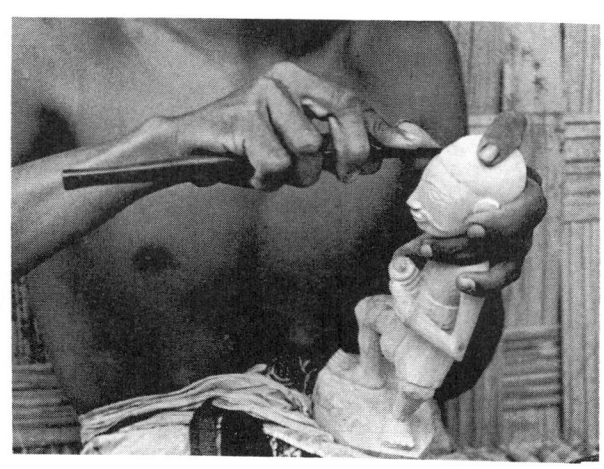

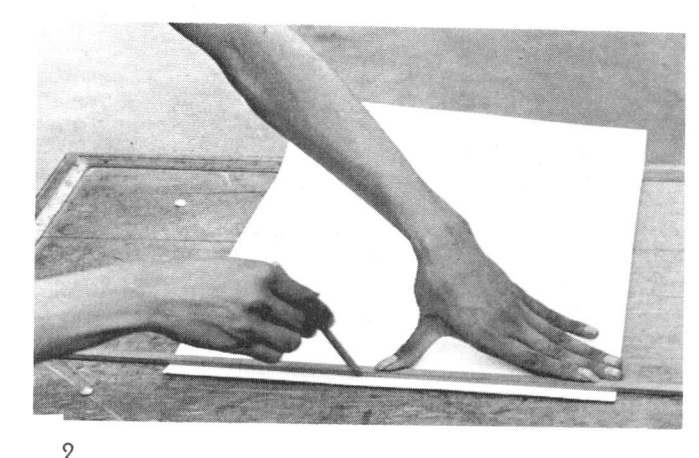

2

3

4

6

7

8

1

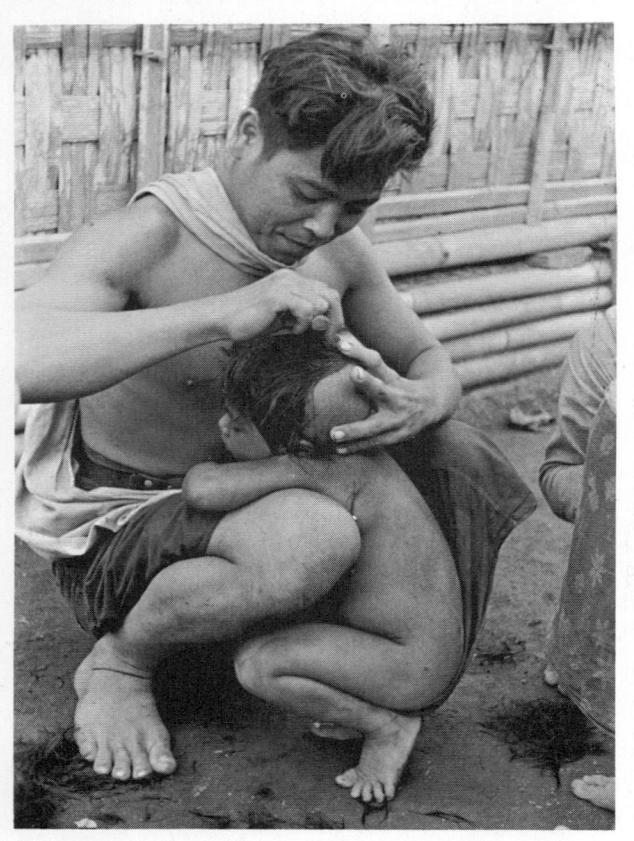

2

3

4

5

6

7

Plate 24

THE SURFACE OF THE BODY

Linked with the emphasis on the sensory function of the finger tips and the fantasy of separable body parts is a common habit of titivating the skin and adjusting the hair and clothes.

The Balinese are continually feeling with their finger tips for small irregularities of the body surface (fig. 2). The fixing of Balinese costume is very unstable and needs continual readjustment (cf. Pl. 45, figs. 3 and 4), and similarly the hair style of the women, in which the chignon is suspended in a wisp of hair, is constantly falling to pieces and being readjusted (cf. Pl. 11, fig. 4).

1. An old man sitting, after shaving his face. He supports his chin on his hand, and his fifth finger is separated so that it covers his nose.
Nang Gentos, a dependent relative (*roban*) of Nang Karma.
Bajoeng Gede. April 19, 1937.   2 K 24.

2. Brahman artist pausing before he begins to draw. The tip of his left index finger, and probably the tips of the fingers of his right hand, touch his face (cf. Pl. 23, figs. 1, 2, and 3).
I. B. Made Djatisoera.
Batoean. Oct. 6, 1937.   16 O 24.

3. Women lousing at a wedding. At weddings, funerals and the like, when a number of relatives and neighbors come together, it is not unusual for a group of women to fill in periods of waiting by lousing each other. This activity fits in with the Balinese interest in perfection of the skin, their enjoyment of fine sensitive use of the fingers and their love of the mild inter-personal contact provided by crowds (cf. Pl. 5).
I Modoh, looking at camera; I Gedir, lousing, in left center; Men Reta lousing Men Lintar in right center; Men Adjan, lower right corner.
Bajoeng Gede. March 1, 1937.   5 B 22.

4 and 5. Man shaving with a soft-iron knife. This mildly pathological man lived as a dependent (*roban*) in the house of Nang Djeben, taking no part in social life, but working at whatever he was told to do. He spent almost the whole of his spare time shaving his face and head, and it was said that he shaved his pubic hair every two or three days. In fact, he carried the cultural interest in the perfection of the skin to pathological exaggeration.
Nang Rentet, place of birth unknown.
Bajoeng Gede. Feb. 1, 1937.   3 Y 25, 26.

6. Haircutting at a child's 210-day birthday. After the proper child had its head shaved, the man who performed the operation went on and cut the hair of this older child.
I Kanggo cutting hair of I Asa, unrelated, at *otonin* of I Mirib, I Kanggo's brother's child.
Bajoeng Gede. April 14, 1937.   6 T 10.

7. Painting of a mother shaving her child's head while the father and older sibling watch. Haircutting is delayed until the 210-day birthday (*otonin*, cf. Pls. 84 and 85). In this painting, the operation is seen as an aggressive act, and the size of the mother is exaggerated as compared with that of the other figures. The emphasis upon the mother's right elbow, which appears to be an essential part of the aggression, is, however, almost naturalistic (cf. Pl. 85, fig. 7).
Painting by I. B. Kt. Diding of Batoean.
Purchased Sept. 23, 1937. Cat. No. 111. Reduced x ¼ linear.

Plate 25

HANDS, SKIN AND MOUTH

A central focus of the sensory titivation and fidgeting with the hands is the area of the mouth (cf. Pl. 28) and nose. The commonest positions of rest in this fidgeting are those in which the mouth is covered by the hand or fingers, but a great variety of exploratory positions also occurs.

1 to 8. A small girl sitting in the audience at a theatrical performance. She goes through a whole series of different forms of fidgeting with her hand to her mouth and nose.

She covers her mouth with her hand while her finger tips press on her nose (figs. 1 and 2). She opens her fingers and pinches her nostrils between index and third fingers while bending the tip of her thumb in against her cheek (fig. 3). Her thumb reaches in toward the corner of her mouth, while her index finger reaches out across the thumb toward her cheek (fig. 4). She explores the edges of her teeth with her thumb, while extending all her fingers (fig. 5). She turns the whole hand and flexes the fingers, while her thumb remains in her mouth (fig. 6). She removes her hand from her mouth and looks down, with the tip of her tongue in the corner of her lips and her fingers lightly flexed in a sensitive position (fig. 7). She returns her hand to her mouth, hooking her index and middle fingers over the lower incisors (fig. 8).

I Moespa, center; I Dira, left foreground.

Bajoeng Gede. May 28, 1937. 9 R 12, 13, 15, 16, 17, 18, 20, 21.

9, 10, and 11. A girl watches a woman with a baby. She covers her mouth with three fingers, pressing on the tip of her nose with the tip of her middle finger (fig. 9). She removes her fingers from her mouth and rests her cheek on them (fig. 10). She flexes the fingers, and the little finger comes back to the side of the nose (fig. 11).

I Wandri watching Men Resi with I Resi, her daughter.

Bajoeng Gede. Nov. 25, 1937. 19 L 37, 38, 39.

1 2 3 4

5 6 7 8

9 10 11

1

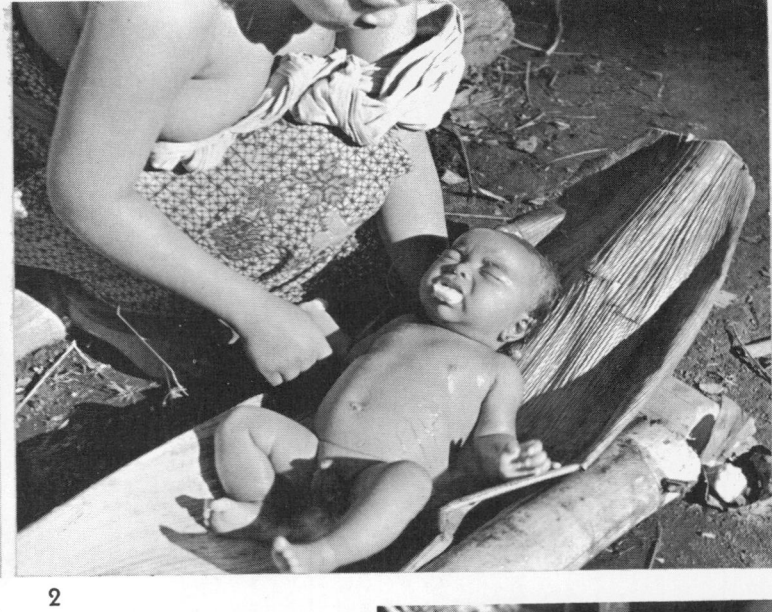

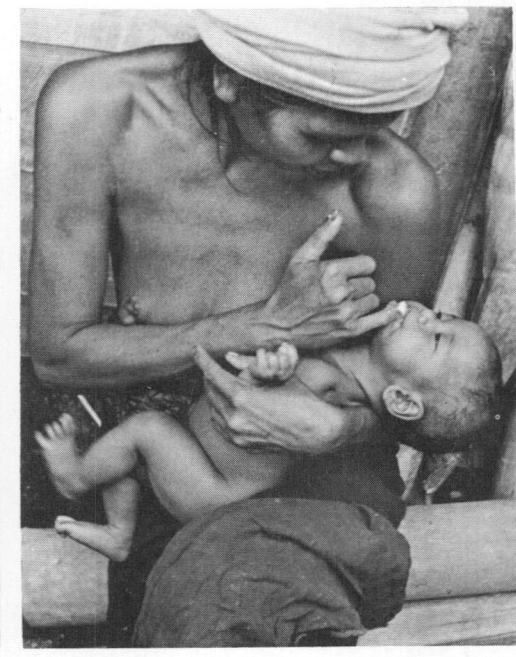

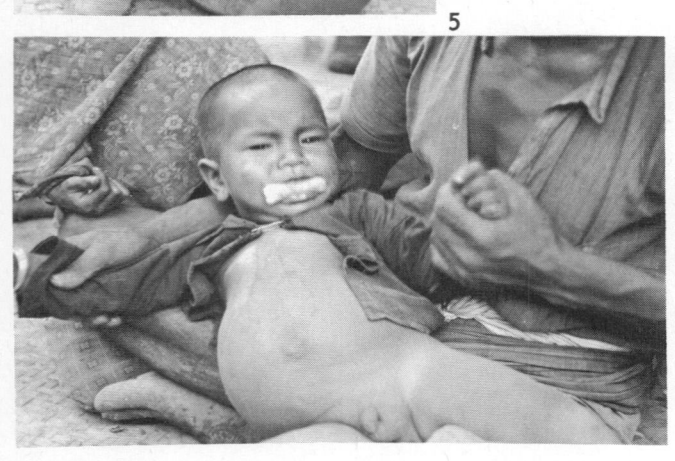

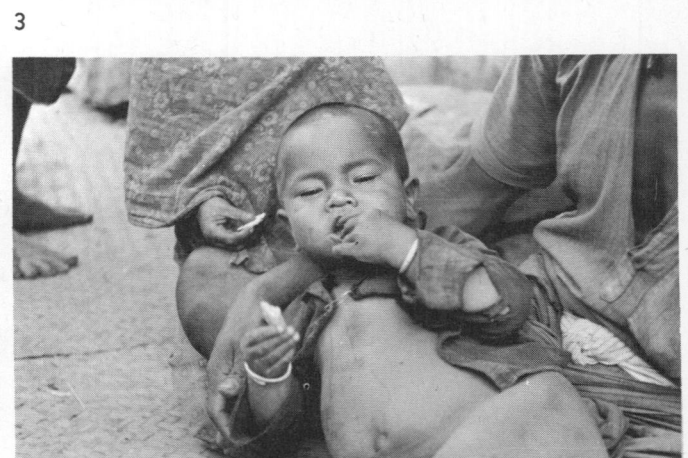

2

5

3

4

6

7

Plate 26

ATTACK ON THE MOUTH

Plates 26 to 37 are concerned with the mouth and the anus, and with the various psychological modes which are related to these orifices — eating, drinking, excretion, elimination, purification, etc. From Balinese behavior and symbolism, it appears that in describing their culture it is necessary to divide this whole field into two contrasting categories. The eating of meals and defecation are both invested with considerable shame and form one category, as contrasted with drinking, urination, and the eating of snacks, all of which are performed casually and without shame.

This great dichotomy is evident in the feeding of the very young baby, who receives two sorts of food: he is casually suckled at the mother's breast and at stated intervals (usually when he is in his bath) his mouth is stuffed with a pre-chewed mixture of rice and banana. As the child grows older, the eating of meals becomes more important, and it is our thesis that the eating of pre-chewed food is the prototype for the eating of meals, while the suckling is the prototype for the eating of snacks and for drinking.

1 and 2. A baby is fed in his bath. He lies on his back, while his mother chews a mixture of rice and banana. She places a large bolus of this mixture on his mouth. During this process the baby usually cries (perhaps because the water of the bath is cold or because his mouth is overfilled or because he feels helpless). While he cries, his mother readjusts the mountain of food on his mouth, so that it shall not fall off, and she sometimes pokes the food downward into his mouth with her finger.

Men Ngendon feeding her son, I Ngendon, aged 71 days.
Bajoeng Gede. Jan. 19, 1937.   4 F 5, 7.

3. A mother adjusting the bolus of food on her baby's mouth. She holds the baby tightly so that it is powerless, and adjusts the food with the tip of her little finger, with her hand in characteristically Balinese position.

M. Sama feeding I Sami, aged 117 days.
Bajoeng Gede. Jan. 21, 1937.   4 H 25.

4. A small boy eating. He stands with his head thrown back licking the last grains of rice out of the coconut shell. The eating of meals is usually done with the head bent back, so that the food is thrown *downward* into the mouth (cf. Pl. 29). This supports the thesis that this type of eating is modelled on the earlier eating of boluses of pre-chewed food when lying on the back.

I Leket.
Bajoeng Gede. July 13, 1937.   12 L 12.

5, 6, and 7. This sequence shows a father cleaning his son's nose and the son's subsequent regressive behavior with food. In fig. 5, the father holds the boy pinioned and pokes at the mucus with his fingers. His posture has many elements in common with that of the mother in fig. 3. In figs. 6 and 7, the son sprawls on the ground with a sausage-shaped lump of rice paste in his mouth.

M. M.'s verbal record states:

"I Gata (the son) has a leaf-roll of rice cake which he slowly opens. He offers his father the long 'sausage' of rice paste, which he gets out of the leaf. Father merely nods.

"I Gata drops the leaf and puts the cake 'sausage' crosswise in his mouth, which amuses everyone.

"I Gata sings loudly.

"His father wipes I Gata's nose (again) and sticks his finger up each nostril."

Whether the regression is connected with the first attack on the nose is not perfectly clear. It is recorded that a few moments earlier his father had been playing with I Gata's penis, and that I Gata touched his penis anxiously after the resulting erection had subsided.

I Gata, with his father, Nang Karma.
Bajoeng Gede. Sept. 30, 1936.   2 U 17, 18, 19.

Plate 27

DEFENSE OF THE MOUTH

Related to the almost forcible feeding of the baby with heaps of pre-chewed food placed on the mouth and to the general overstimulation of the baby (cf. Pl. 47), we find a development of unresponsiveness, which is commonly expressed by plugging the mouth or by tight closure of the lips. Both plugging and tight closure are modes with anal as well as oral significance.

1 and 2. A man plugging his mouth with tobacco. In Bali, after chewing betel, people wipe out the insides of their mouths with tobacco and then place the tobacco in their mouths where it protrudes, held loosely between the lips. This plug is not removed for conversation, but serves somewhat to isolate the individual while he is talking. (High-caste people and young women usually content themselves with wiping the mouth with tobacco and do not keep the plug in their lips.)

I Ampiag.
Bajoeng Gede. Sept. 30, 1936.   2 T 32, 33.

3. Carving by a psychotic vagrant (cf. portrait and character sketch, Pl. 7, fig. 3). In this carving the mouth is plugged with a piece of silver paper, and the intestines (or vulva?) are represented by a snakelike spiral.

Carving by I Tjoengkoeh, said to have been born in Sebatoe.
Bajoeng Gede. June 21, 1937.   11 X 3.

4. Tooth-filing. This is an important *rite de passage* which takes place in late adolescence or at marriage (cf. Pl. 86 for general account of the ceremony; and especially Pl. 86, fig. 5, for the facial expressions of spectators). The filing is very painful and is felt to be an attack on the mouth (cf. Pl. 24, fig. 7 for the corresponding notion that haircutting is aggressive).

I. B. Made Katji filing teeth of I Keteg.
Batoean. Sept. 30, 1937.   16 H 6.

5. Unresponsiveness in an adolescent girl. She was asked to stand for a portrait but was not posed in any way. Her reaction is extreme withdrawal, with head bent, lips pursed, eyes downcast, and arms folded under her blanket.

I Geloeh, with Men Goenoeng holding I Raoeh in the background.
Bajoeng Gede. June 30, 1936.   1 N 14.

6. A psychopathic vagrant begs tobacco. The man on the right is of a type rather common in Bali. In place of the normal Balinese unresponsiveness, these individuals have an over-responsiveness which is chiefly expressed in the loose, constantly smiling mouth (cf. Pl. 20, fig. 6 for a Balinese caricature of this type). The man from whom he is begging permits the vagrant to take betel from his basket, but he preserves aloofness with a tightened, unsmiling mouth.

I Pageh, vagrant from Kintamani, begging from an unidentified man.
Bajoeng Gede. Jan. 13, 1937.   11 Q 23.

7. Roast sucking pig in the offerings at a baby's 210-day birthday ceremony. A cone of rice (*toempeng*) protrudes from the anus of the pig.

On another occasion, at which a similar roast pig was prepared, an old woman noticed that the pig's anus was empty. She told them that they had put the rice cone at the "wrong end." There was a great deal of laughter about this and the mistake was corrected. That such a mistake could occur indicates that the plugging motif is ambiguous and may have either oral or anal overtones.

Offerings at *otonin* prepared according to Selat (Bangli) style.
Bajoeng Gede. April 30, 1937.   7 W last.

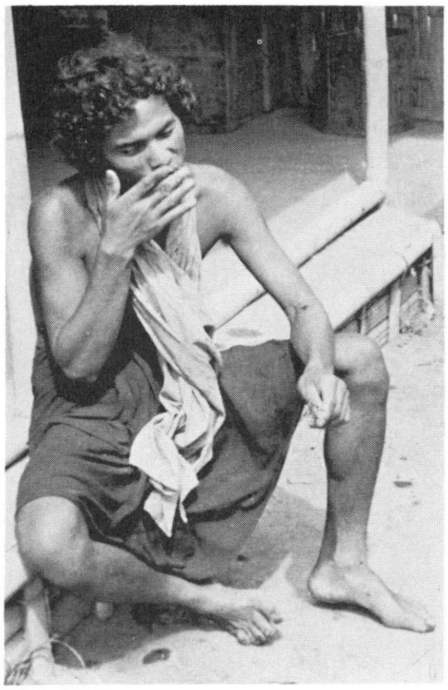

1

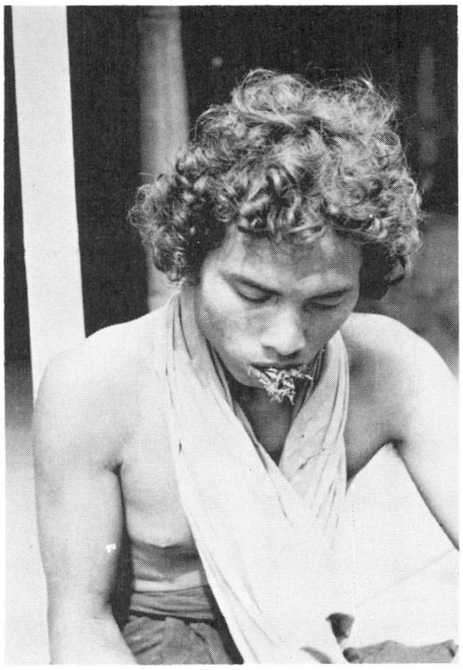

2

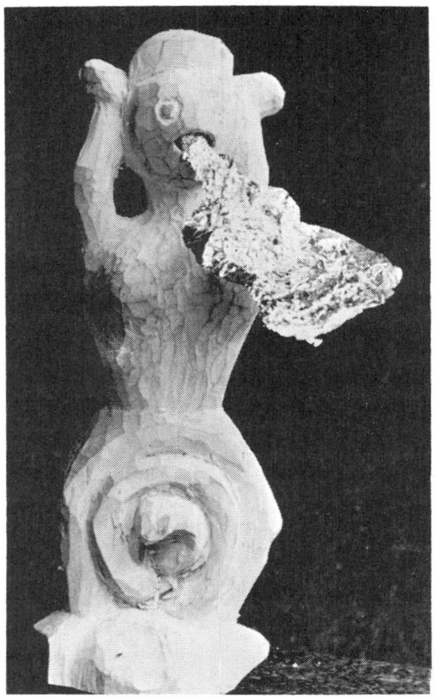

3

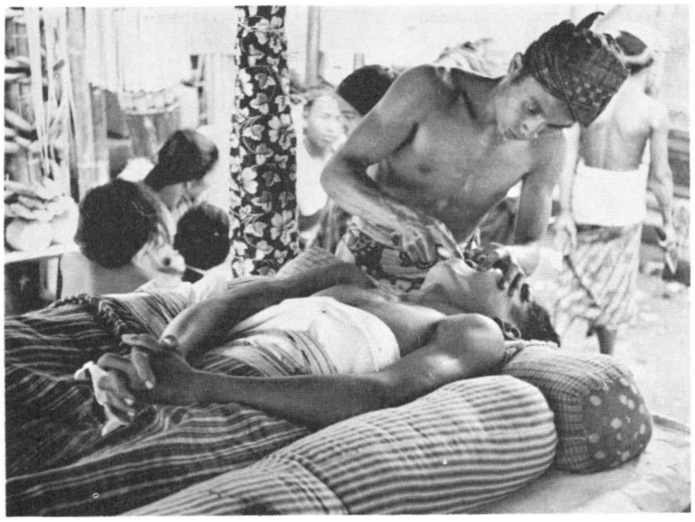

4

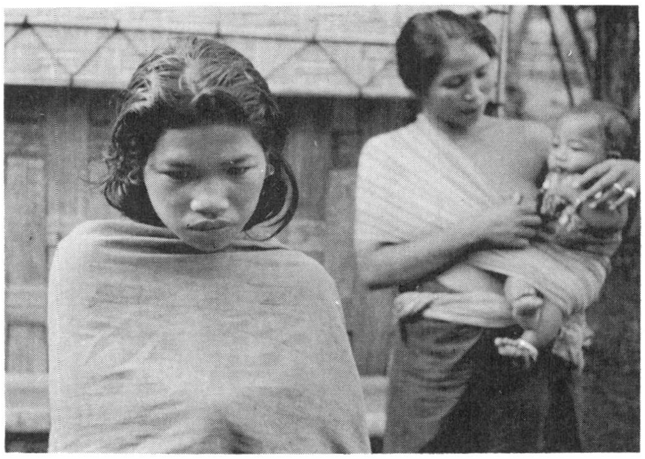

5

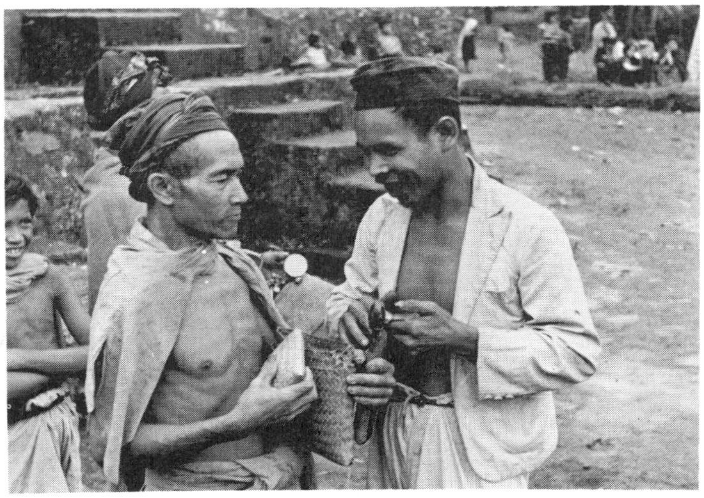

6

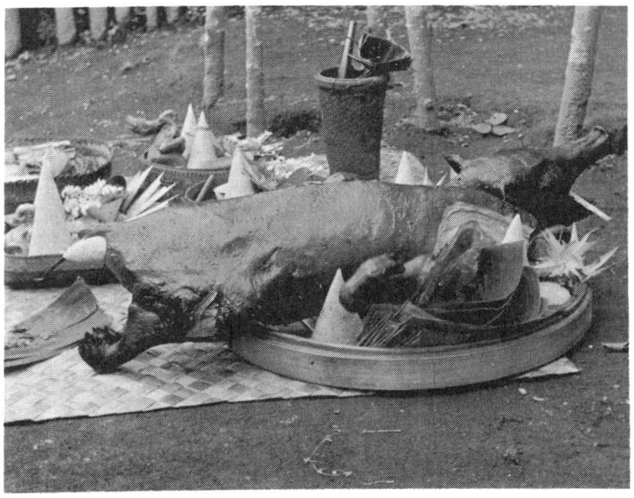

7

1
2
3
4
5
6
7
8
9

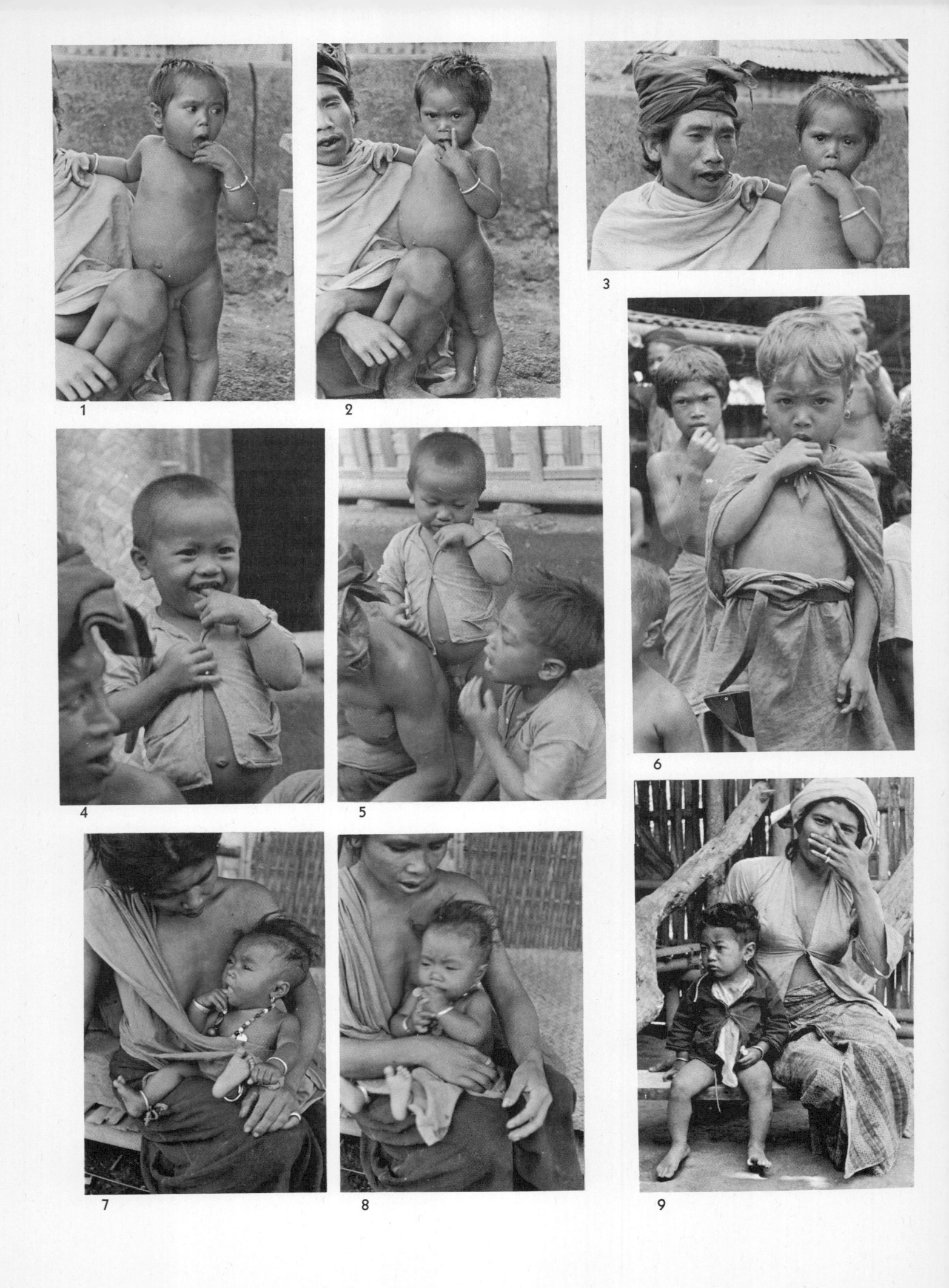

Plate 28

FINGERS IN MOUTH

Thumb-sucking of the European type, in which the sensory pleasure is located chiefly in the mouth, is not characteristic of Balinese children. Instead we find oral manipulation in which the sensory emphasis is on the hand or fingers. The lips of a European child shape themselves in response to the presence of the thumb; those of the Balinese child typically do not respond in this way (fig. 6 shows a trace of response in the lip). Several types of this behavior can be observed; the fingers may be hooked over the incisors, or they may be thrust deep into the mouth in what appears to be exploratory activity or they may serve as a plug blocking oral responsiveness. These behaviors are not reproved, except in the presence of superiors, but they normally disappear with the onset of latency.

1, 2, and 3. A small boy with his fingers in his mouth. He stands beside his father with his abdomen pressed against his father's knee. His left hand takes a series of positions in his mouth.

In fig. 1, he feels inside his lips with his index finger.

In fig. 2, he has lowered his hand and placed the third finger in his mouth, while the index finger touches his face near the nostril.

In fig. 3, he thrusts both index and third finger deep into his mouth.

I Bontok with his father, Nang Rimpen.

Bajoeng Gede. Dec. 7, 1936.   3 S 19, 21, 22.

4 and 5. A small boy with his finger in his mouth while he laughs. His finger reaches in, probably sideways toward the premolars. His lips are unresponsive to the presence of his finger, and his smiling expression is unmodified.

He stands just behind his uncle and elder brother, and fig. 5 shows the uncle with his mouth plugged with tobacco and the elder brother with his hand raised toward his mouth.

I Degeng; his father's brother, Nang Leket, and his elder brother I Leket, who has been adopted by Nang Leket.

Bajoeng Gede. April 30, 1937.   7 R 23, 24.

6. A boy with his finger in mouth. This boy was somewhat retarded in his development. He was the youngest surviving child of three, but a still younger child had died (cf. Pl. 35, fig. 8 for a case of regression to childish role after death of younger child). Behind him is another boy with his hand to his mouth.

I Karia; I Lintar behind him.

Bajoeng Gede. Mar. 1, 1937.   4 Z 23.

7 and 8. A baby with hands to mouth. In fig. 7 she feels her lips, and in fig. 8 she puts her fist to her lips. At this age, the sensory pleasure appears to be in the lips rather than in the hand.

Men Rimpen holding I Mesom (younger sister of I Bontok who is shown in figs. 1 to 3).

Bajoeng Gede. Dec. 7, 1936.   3 S 15, 17.

9. A mother with her sick son. On the day before this photograph was taken, I Karba, the son, had been sick enough for his father to be seriously worried, and on this day his behavior was very changeable. His mother tried several times to stimulate him and to make him respond to our presence, and he actually had several moments of normal high spirits. He rapidly reverted, however, to the mood shown in this photograph. Here he is seen with sulky withdrawn expression. His mother has given up trying to stimulate him and has her hand to her mouth, probably biting at some small callus.

Men Oera with her son, I Karba, aged 561 days.

Bajoeng Gede. Aug. 19, 1937.   14 B 10.

Plate 29

EATING MEALS

The eating of meals is accompanied by considerable shame. Those who are eating usually turn their backs toward anybody who may be present, and hunch themselves over their food. It is not polite to speak to anybody who is eating. The same shame shows itself in the quick movements of eating. The food is picked up in the fingers, passed back into the palm of the hand and then pushed or thrown into the mouth in a single quick gesture, while the mouth is opened very wide under cover of the hand, and the eyes are almost closed — a method which appears very coarse to the European observer. There is also a more polite method of eating, in which the food is put into the mouth with the fingers (fig. 8), but this refinement is almost never seen in the mountain villages, although the shame attached to eating is as clearly developed there as in the plains. (Contrast this plate with Pl. 36 which shows the eating of snacks.)

1. A ceremonial feast. This feast was given at post-mortuary ceremonies (*metoeoen*, cf. Pl. 6, figs. 5 and 6). The food is spread on a long line of bamboo or pandanus matting, and the assembled relatives and neighbors sit in two rows, facing in opposite directions. They sit sideways so that each man's right hand (the correct hand for food) is toward the food, while his back is toward his neighbor.
Bajoeng Gede. July 10, 1937.   12 G 22.

2. A girl eating. She is in the act of pushing the food into her mouth with the palm of her hand.
I Maderi; Nang Djani in the background.
Bajoeng Gede. Jan. 15, 1937.   4 C 22.

3, 4, and 5. Men eating a small feast after helping in the work of housebuilding. This was a much less formal occasion than that shown in fig. 1, and the men have not turned their backs on each other.
In fig. 3, the man on the right is just putting food into his mouth with the base of his fingers. (This is probably a little more polite than using the palm of the hand.)
In fig. 4, the same man is about to put another handful of food into his mouth. His next motion will be to throw back his head with his hand over his mouth.
In fig. 5, the young man on the left is putting food into his mouth with the lower part of his palm.
Throughout this series, there is no appearance of inter-personal communication during eating.
Clockwise: Nang Saboeh (eating in fig. 3); I Sadia; I Wajang (with pencil in ear); Nang Roni. I Wajang is a stranger from Karangasem; the others are all of Bajoeng Gede.
Bajoeng Gede. April 14, 1937.   6 T 22, 23, 26.

6. Children about to eat at a post-mortuary ceremony (the same occasion as that shown in fig. 1). Note the sulky uneasiness while waiting to eat.
I Asin holding her feet; I Mondel holding scarf.
Bajoeng Gede. July 10, 1937.   12 G 19.

7. Children eating. This scene occurred during the preparations for a large birthday ceremony (*otonin*), which was to be held the same afternoon. Perhaps the presence of numbers of visitors in the houseyard makes the children somewhat more self-conscious than usual. They have withdrawn to a corner of the yard, and all have their backs turned.
I Reta; I Degeng behind him; and a strange little girl from Abang.
Bajoeng Gede. June 2, 1937.   11 G 2.

8. The village priestess with offerings and paraphernalia laid out in front of her, putting betel in her mouth during a pause in ceremonial. Her gesture illustrates the more polite method of eating in which the food is placed in the mouth with the fingers. (Actually betel chewing has a psychological value somewhat different from that of eating meals. It is done almost without shame and the emphasis is on plugging the mouth rather than on absorption, cf. Pl. 26.)
Djero Balian Soekoeh.
Bajoeng Gede. April 24, 1937.   7 E 12.

1
2
3
4
5
6
7
8

1

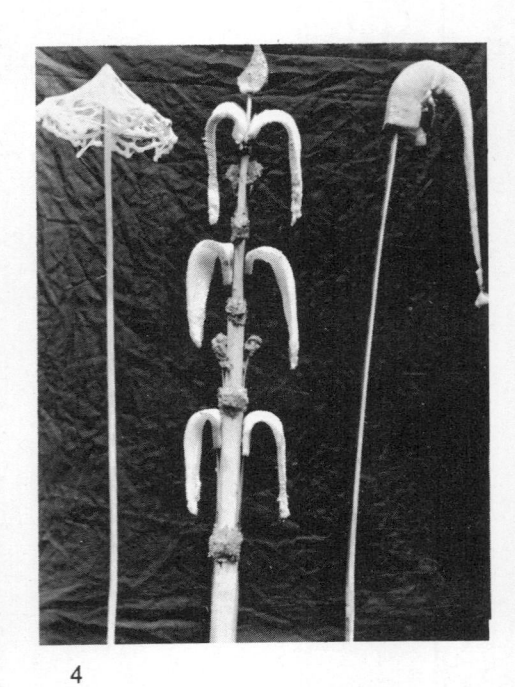

2

3

4

5

6

7

Plate 30

PRE-CHOPPED FOOD

In line with the early feeding of pre-chewed food (Pl. 26) and the shame which is associated both with eating and defecation, the preparation of food is usually referred to as "chopping" (*ngebat*), and in fact the majority of foods for feasts and meals are chopped in this way. In many cases, the chopped foods are fixed on sticks and then cooked to make what are called *"sate."* The simplest *sate* are made by spiking a number of small pieces of meat on small sticks and then roasting over a small fire (cf. Pl. 6, fig. 8) but very much more elaborate types are made out of raw pig's fat, built up into pendant scrolls and tree-like structures. These forms are not cooked; they are decorative elements in offerings.

1. Chopping meat for a village feast (*saba dalem*). The men are gathered around a trough similar to those used in feeding animals but containing meat. They take pieces of meat out of the trough and chop them, using their heavy knives on the wooden edge and letting the chopped pieces fall back into the trough.
Bonjoh (near Bajoeng Gede). Oct. 6, 1936. 1 M 31.

2. Making sausages for a village feast (*metjaroe*, cf. Pl. 33, fig. 1). These sausages are made of chopped meat stuffed into pig's intestine. They are not twisted off into short lengths as in Europe. The whole long spiral is cooked in boiling water and afterward cut up.
Bajoeng Gede. April 3, 1937. 6 O 28.

3. Tree-like *sate*. This structure is about six feet high. Its central core is a banana trunk, and into this the various separate *sate*, each made of raw pig's fat, are inserted. It was one of the offerings at a tooth-filing ceremony.
Batoean. Sept. 30, 1937. 16 I 6.

4. Three separate *sate*. A single structure, such as that shown in fig. 3, may contain twenty or more different types of individual *sate*, all of which are named. In the total structure, the details of the separate *sate* are completely lost. The three *sate* shown here are (from left to right): *sate padjeng* ("umbrella") made from the pig's omentum; *sate kaijonan* ("tree"); *sate oembel-oembel* ("pennant," cf. Pl. 40, fig. 4).
Bajoeng Gede. June 4, 1937. 11 G 24.

5. Carving on a temple gate. Balinese carving and painting are often overburdened with scroll designs (*oekiran*), and in this case the central figure, a mythological bird (*garoeda*) with a snake in its mouth, is almost entirely obscured by the scroll work. This type of decoration is not associated with the same sort of compulsive anxiety which we associate with analogous motifs in Europe. The Balinese craftsman draws his scrolls with very great facility and ease and we must think of them as an efflorescence of muscular rote (cf. Pls. 6 and 15) rather than of carefulness and concentrated effort. They are associated with automatic functioning of the body rather than with tense control.
Bangli. Nov. 27, 1937. 19 M 8.

6. Figure of plaited coconut leaf with food laid on it. This object was a part of the lay-out of offerings for a great ceremony (*desa mesakapan*, a more elaborate form of *metjaroe*), which was performed to purify the village after a case of incest. The offerings were laid on the ground (cf. Pl. 33) on five figures of this sort, corresponding to the "five directions" (four cardinal points and the center). The photograph shows *sate* laid on the figure's chest, and a heap of cooked rice on its belly. In the foreground is a bamboo container for palm beer (*toeak*). Other offerings are visible in the background.
Bajoeng Gede. Feb. 23, 1937. 4 W 32.

7. Drying chopped sweet potato (*késela*). In the mountains, the very poor rice crop is supplemented with this root crop of starchy tubers. The tubers are chopped up into pieces a little larger than rice grains, and these are dried in the sun to provide a sort of substitute rice (*tjatjah*).
Bajoeng Gede. Aug. 6, 1936. 2 D 24.

Plate 31

THE BODY AS A TUBE

This plate shows a form of play made possible by culture contact which has provided the sweater and the ball manufactured in Japan. The play is, however, perfectly consonant with the Balinese cultural emphases which classify eating with defecation, and defecation with birth.

1 to 9. A small boy plays with a ball inside his sweater. He first wraps the ball in a leaf, then holds it to his abdomen by bending over it; later, he puts it inside his sweater from the top, and works it down till it comes out at the bottom. Finally, he puts it in from the bottom and works it up to the top.

M. M.'s verbal notes on this behavior contain the following details:

"Men Singin (the boy's mother) came to our house with Karba (her sister's son, whose foot is visible in the top left corner of fig. 8) in a sling. Karba has been taken back into favor since Karsa (the boy with the sweater) weaned himself. Karsa was also with her.

"I gave Karsa a large parti-coloured ball, the same kind Karba had had yesterday, only larger. The minute Karba saw it he gave a desirous cry.

"Karsa took it, and danced with it, hitting it with his hands.

"Karsa then put the ball inside his sweater, and let it bulge out, and stroked the bulge.

"Karsa then let the ball fall out of sweater, picked it up and passed it up and down in front of himself.

"Karsa went over to the banana plants, carefully holding ball, which fell once and was immediately retrieved; broke off a piece of banana leaf and wrapped the ball in this.

"I called G. B., who photographed the remainder of sequence.

"Karsa turns the ball around on his chest — around and around (fig. 1).

"He drops it, runs after it (fig. 2).

"He stands and hits it.

"He picks up the piece of banana leaf, which he had thrown down, and wraps the ball in it (fig. 3).

"He scrubs the ball with the leaf, and tears off a long piece of banana fiber.

"He puts ball between his legs, as he twists the fiber (fig. 4).

"He puts ball under arm, and twists fiber (fig. 5).

"He puts ball in the top of his sweater (fig. 6). It falls out.

"He puts ball in the bottom of his sweater and pulls it up toward the top (figs. 7 and 8)."

Later he goes off and squats by his mother (fig. 9).

Throughout the sequence, his mother is close by (her sarong is visible in figs. 4 to 8) and is holding his rival cousin, I Karba. It is probable that the ball acquired extra symbolic value as something that his rival, I Karba, wanted; and this would give shape to the notion of the ball as "food" — something to be wrapped in a leaf, and something to be passed through the symbolic tube of his sweater. In the final picture, when they sit, his mother is still completely unresponsive to him, and he squats with a sulky expression.

I Karsa; Men Singin, his mother; I Karba, Men Singin's sister's son, aged 527 days.

Bajoeng Gede. July 16, 1937.   12 Q 12, 13, 16, 17, 18, 19, 20, 22, 24.

1 2 3
4 5 6
7 8 9

1

2

3

4

5

6

7

8

Plate 32

BODY PRODUCTS

For the Balinese, the two products of bodily excretion, urine and feces, have very different psychological value. Feces are regarded with disgust, while urine is unimportant and the act of urination is performed very casually and without conspicuous modesty.

1 to 5. A baby (I Karba) sweeps up the remains of an orange after his aunt has just swept up his feces. His treatment of the orange illustrates the intensity of his repudiation of the feces.

Extracts from M. M.'s verbal record:

"Karba squats on the steps of G. B.'s veranda, urinates, then defecates.

"Men Singin (his mother's sister) exclaims (because it is very wrong to defecate in somebody else's houseyard).

"Men Singin picks him up and sets him down on the ground. From there he watches his feces and, at once climbs back on the veranda.

"Men Singin tells a little girl (I Kesir) to pick up a piece of brown paper from back of me. She is afraid but another girl (I Ridjek) gets it and gives it to Men Singin, who lifts off the feces.

"Men Singin then gets a broom and sweeps the step and stands broom against the wall.

"Karba goes and gets the broom and begins to sweep. He sweeps the ground, not the step (fig. 1).

"He takes the pierced orange which he had in his hand, throws it on the ground (fig. 2).

"He stamps on it (figs. 3 and 4).

"He sweeps again in a circle (fig. 5).

"He picks up the dirty orange; rolls it in his hands and throws it down again and stamps on it.

"He squats, picks up the orange again; stamps it into the ground again.

"He gets broom and begins to sweep it away.

"He sees the cine camera and starts to walk towards G. B.

"Men Singin exclaims, 'The white man is called by I Karba.'

"She raises her hands above her head, rocking in witch style, wriggling her fingers.

"She shouts, points at Karba.

"He begins to cry."

I Karba, aged 499 days. He cannot talk yet.

Bajoeng Gede. June 18, 1937.   11 R 33, 34, 36, 37, 39.

6 and 7. A small boy gets off his mother's lap to urinate. His mother smiles while he is getting down and looks at him inattentively. While he is on the ground, she laughs but evidently at something else. His elder sister idly watches him getting down, and then leans forward to watch him urinate, but she does this with no reproof or tension. He gets down smiling (fig. 6) and sits squatting on the ground, playing with his fingers after he has urinated (fig. 7).

I Karmi (elder sister); Men Karma (mother); I Gata.

Bajoeng Gede. Nov. 23, 1937.   19 D 20, 21.

8. Children sweeping the houseyard at a harvest-home ceremony (*mantenin padi*). The girl has a rake and the boy carries a broom in one hand and a coconut inflorescence in the other. This is a purely ceremonial cleaning of the yard in which the children go around the yard pretending to sweep.

Two children of I. B. P. Sentoelan.

Batoean. Oct. 5, 1937.   16 N 26.

Plate 33

SCAVENGERS, FOOD, AND FECES

This plate illustrates three symbolic equations: the identification of food with feces; the identification of dogs with the lower spirits; and the identification of people with lower spirits.

For ceremonial purification, offerings made of food are laid out on the ground for the lower spirits and demons (*boeta, kala,* etc.). These offerings are normally eaten by dogs. In some ceremonies, these offerings take the form of a feast eaten by people sitting on the ground.

1. Annual feast (*metjaroe desa*) for the lower spirits. This feast is held in the road leading to the ceremonially lowest (coastal-west) gate of the village. The gate is visible in the background. The food is laid out on trays on the ground, and the whole village sits on the ground to eat, the men in one group, the small boys in another and the women and children in another. The eating was accompanied by a lot of shouting and gay scrambling to find places, and everybody ate very fast. There was some rowdyism reminiscent of behavior (*ngarap,* cf. Pl. 95) in handling a corpse. Later, small packets of food were hung on the trees at the west gate and small boys scrambled for these.

Offerings to demons are usually considered unfit to eat.

Bajoeng Gede. April 3, 1937. 6 P 16.

2. A painting of a low demon (Sang Kala Ngadang) eating offerings (*segehan*) at the crossroads. The offerings are of the same type as those shown in fig. 4.

Painting by I. B. Made Bala of Batoean.
Purchased Feb. 10, 1938. Cat. No. 27.

3. A low-caste priest (*pemangkoe*) makes offerings (*segehan*) to the lower spirits on the ground, and a dog comes up to eat the offerings.

Dendjalan. May 26, 1936. 1 H 20.

4. Offerings (*segehan*) spread on the ground for the lower spirits. They consist of: a ring of five small leaf trays containing rice; two burning coconut shells, one on top of the other; and two trays (*tjanang genten*) containing betel-chewing ingredients, tobacco, and ornamental leaf cut-outs.

This type of spread occurs in almost all ceremonies in addition to the raised offerings for the high gods. The circular form, the fire, and the position on the ground are characteristic of offerings to the demons.

Batoean. Dec. 1, 1937. 19 M 21.

5 and 6. A baby defecates while crawling in the houseyard, and a dog at once comes up to eat the feces. The baby is resentful and helpless, and crawls as fast as possible across the yard to where the other children are. The dog follows, and the other children pay no attention.

I Sepek, the baby, aged 276 days; I Leket walking; I Degeng leaning against the wall.

Bajoeng Gede. April 30, 1937. 7 U 10, 14.

7 and 8. A small boy (Gata) pours out his food for a dog. This incident occurred immediately after we entered the house, and there is therefore no record of the antecedent events. M. M.'s verbal record is as follows:

"3:50 P.M. Kenjoen (the baby girl) eating out of basket; Gata standing about (fig. 7).

"3:51 P.M. Gata overturns his rice (fig. 8).

"Their mother shouts ''ti! 'ti!' (calling to Gati, the older sister), as a dog gets at the rice. She rushes down and rescues the top layer and takes it into the house.

"Gata sits and cries.

"Gati picks up the scraps mixed with earth and puts them in a tin of pig food.

"3:56 P.M. Gata cries for money, and is given a *cash* (worth about a fourteenth of an American cent)."

I Kenjoen, baby girl; I Gati, elder sister; I Gata, brother.

Bajoeng Gede. Aug. 19, 1937. 14 I 4, 5.

1
2
3
4
5
6
7
8

1

2

3

5

6

4

7

Plate 34
ELIMINATION BY SCRAMBLING

Closely related to the nexus of ideas illustrated in the last plate is the notion that scrambling for money is a means of eliminating the unclean. We noted that the silence of eating gives way to rowdyism when the people are eating unclean offerings to the lower demons (Pl. 33, fig. 1), and later we shall note the rowdyism which occurs in the handling of corpses. In part, this rowdyism in face of the unclean can be regarded as over-compensation for an underlying disgust and fear, and men will even boast of their insensitivity to unclean stimuli, claiming to be *"sapta"* (cf. Pl. 95). But, in addition, the role of the dog as a scavenger provides a sort of logic, in terms of which rowdy searching and scrambling for money becomes naturally a method of purification.

1 to 4. Scrambling for money in a ceremony (*mepegat*) in which relations are "cut off" between the living and the dead. This ritual is performed at the conclusion of any sequence of mortuary ceremonies, e.g., after burial or after cremation; and in some communities it is also performed at marriages, as a statement of finality. The ceremony consists essentially in walking through a thread suspended between two sticks, the breaking of the thread being the symbolic statement of the broken-off relationship.

In the photographs, the ceremony is being held after a funeral, and the sister of the dead woman, standing on the left in fig. 1 and holding a doll representing the dead, will walk through the string. Her laughter is conventional behavior in the face of death.

The participants in the ritual are high-caste Brahmans, who are scrambling for Chinese cash concealed in the offerings. In fig. 4, two men are searching inside an offering for cash.

Mepegat ceremony, following the death of I. B. Nj. Sasak's wife.
Batoean. Sept. 29, 1937. 16 F 11, 18, 19, 22.

5. An old woman looking for cash in discarded offerings. This scene occurred at a ceremony to consecrate a new house-temple in a rich low-caste household. An elaborate broom-like sprinkler (*pring*, a sort of *lis*) was used to scatter holy water, and after use this sprinkler was thrown out into the road as unclean. The woman is searching for cash in this object and in offerings which were thrown out after they had been offered to demons.
Batoean. Oct. 6, 1937. 16 S 18.

6. A funeral procession in the mountains. The procession, carrying the dead from the village to the cemetery, goes at a fast excited pace, almost at a run. There is a pause in the last field to wash the dead, before going on to the cemetery in the forest. At this point, the women drop out of the procession, so that only men are present at the final burying. The women throw cash after the departing group of men, who are here seen with their blankets spread to catch the cash.

After the body has been buried, further parting gifts (*bekel*) of cash are presented to the dead. The cash is thrown onto the men who are smoothing the grave. They scramble violently for the cash and the mound over the body is thereby stamped down. The men return to the village and gamble with the cash which they acquired at the funeral.
Funeral of Djero Balian Dapet.
Bajoeng Gede. Sept. 8, 1936. 2 M 10.

7. Children searching for cash in the grass where a funeral procession has just passed.
I Reta; I Degeng, at the funeral of Dong Merada.
Bajoeng Gede. Oct. 9, 1937. 16 Z 9.

Plate 35

SUCKLING

In introducing Plate 26, we noted that in Balinese culture the gamut of activities having to do with the bodily orifices falls into two categories — eating of meals and defecation, which are accompanied by shame; and eating of snacks, drinking, and urination which are performed casually and without shame. Plates 26 to 34 illustrate the first half of this dichotomy. Plates 35 to 37 illustrate the second half.

Suckling differs from the eating of pre-chewed food in that: it is performed casually, at no fixed times; it is performed in such a position that the food comes *upward* into the mouth, instead of *downward* as it does in the absorption of pre-chewed food and in the eating of meals; and — perhaps more significant than any of these differences — the baby is unconstrained and has the initiative in free access to the breast.

1. A mother suckles her baby. Note the position of the baby's hands and the extreme abduction of the left little finger.
    Men Karma suckling I Kenjoen, aged 152 days.
    Bajoeng Gede. Aug. 22, 1936. 2 H 25.

2. A mother suckles her baby. This photograph shows the extreme development of the postures which place the baby above the breast.
    Unidentified woman from Sekardadi.
    Bajoeng Gede. Aug. 22, 1936. 2 H 27.

3. A mother offering her baby the breast. The act of offering consists in turning the nipple *upward*.
    Men Njawi with her son, I Koewat, aged 42 days.
    Bajoeng Gede. April 14, 1937. 6 U 13.

4. A mother suckles her baby. This case is peculiar in that the mother had been advised by her husband's European employer to keep the baby on a schedule. Unfortunately, it was not possible to follow this baby's development in detail, but it is worth noting that the people of the village commented on the baby's extreme quietness and on the great amount of time which it spent asleep. We were able to observe this baby asleep even in its bath. The child is dressed up for its 42-day birthday, wearing a golden fontanelle ornament and a flower in the hair.
    Wife of I Made Tantra, with her child, aged 42 days.
    Klandis, Denpasar. Feb. 28, 1939. 36 T 3.

5. A baby suckled at a dry breast. The woman in this picture was an old maid who had never had a baby.
    I Neka suckling I Gae (a neighbor's baby).
    Bajoeng Gede. Mar. 29, 1937. 6 J 13.

6. A baby plays with the right breast while he is sucking at the left. This behavior is accentuated in presence of rival babies (cf. Pl. 70), but occurs constantly even without this extra stimulus. (This photograph is extracted from the series shown on Pl. 47.)
    Men Goenoeng suckling I Raoeh, aged 580 days.
    Bajoeng Gede. Aug. 19, 1937. 14 G 30.

7. Statue in a temple, representing a mother suckling her baby. This photograph shows the habit of playing with the other breast, naturalistically represented in Balinese art.
    Poera Medoewe Karang, Koeboe Tambahan, North Bali.
    Nov. 8, 1936. 3 F 26.

8. A baby refuses the breast, sucking his hand instead. This baby was suffering from very severe scabies, and his mother was sluttish and treated him casually and with evident dislike. He died a few days later, and his elder brother who had been weaned was allowed to return to the breast.
    Men Reta, with her unnamed son, aged approximately 100 days.
    Bajoeng Gede. June 20, 1936. 1 N 2.

1

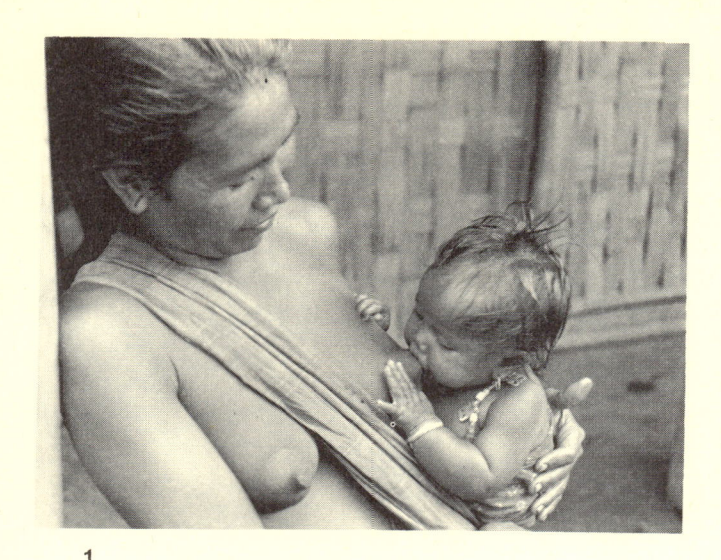

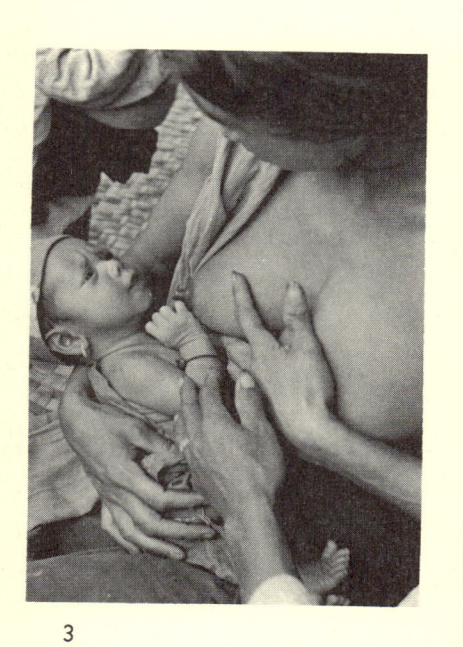

2

3

4

5

6

7

8

1
2
3
4
5
6
7

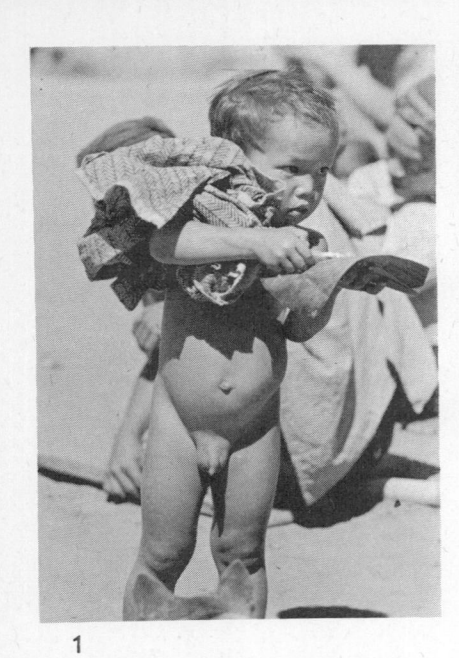

Plate 36
EATING SNACKS

Long before he is weaned, a Balinese baby is given cash which he spends on snacks. On some days his own mother will make up a tray of drinks, cakes, and peanuts, and sit selling them on the side of the street. He will then be able to get his small refreshments free. On other days it will be an aunt or a neighbor who is selling, and his one or two cash will buy him a supply of peanuts. In early life, the vendor is in this sense a mother-substitute. For adolescents and adults, the group which forms around the seller's table is a setting for mild flirtation and many sellers cultivate their skill in repartee.

Most of the foods which are eaten in this way are not pre-chopped, but are solid units, like cakes or sausages, out of which the eater can take a bite, instead of throwing the food downward into his mouth as he does at meals.

1, 2, and 3. A small boy, not yet weaned, eating rice got from a seller's table. He eats it horizontally. In this case, the seller was his own mother (cf. figs. 6 and 7).
I Karsa.
Bajoeng Gede. May 24, 1937. 9 F 4, 5, 6.

4. A high-caste woman eating casually after a child's 210-day birthday ceremony. She holds her youngest child in her arms, and puts rice into her mouth horizontally, from a plate which was handed to her after the ceremony.
Wife of I. B. Wajan Gede and her child.
Batoean. Aug. 4, 1937. 13 C 34.

5. A group of vendors with their tables at a big ceremony. Whenever crowds come together for theatricals, dances, gambling, ceremonial, etc., many sellers set up their tables on the outskirts of the crowd. On this occasion, several hundred people had come together from outlying villages bringing their gods to the sea (*melis*). Most of the sellers were down with the crowd on the beach, but this group set up their tables in the shade of a temple close by.
Saba, South Bali. April 22, 1936. 1 A 25.

6. A group of children around a vendor in the village temple. There is a rule in Bajoeng Gede against eating in the village temple while standing up; but this rule only applies to the eating of meals and shares of feasts. It does not apply to the eating of cakes and peanuts got from the vendors.

In the photograph, the seller is visible on the left, holding a plate. In front of her are two jars of cakes bought from a Chinaman at the nearest market; and gathered around are children who have come to the temple to watch theatricals.
Men Singin, the vendor; three children of Nang Moespa beside her; I Gati with cigarette; I Renoe, with black sarong, looking down at I Rendoet; I Nampah with outstretched hand.
Bajoeng Gede. Oct. 10, 1936. 2 X 15.

7. Two women selling drinks and peanuts on the side of the village street. The son of the woman on the left squats in the foreground.
Men Singin and I Radin selling; I Karsa squatting.
Bajoeng Gede. May 2, 1937. 7 X last.

Plate 37

WATER AND DRINKING

Drinking, like the eating of snacks, is done casually and without shame. Water is, in fact, actually regarded as purifying. Before eating, a Balinese washes his hands and his mouth; after eating, he usually washes his mouth again and then drinks.

At the springs where people go to wash, a little gutter is installed so that the water comes out in a jet, and there are many special bathing places in temples, where pools are constructed under such gushing jets (*pantjoran*).

1. A man drinking after a meal. He holds a coconut shell above his mouth and pours the water so that a free stream runs into his mouth, without his lips touching the shell. In the plains villages, special pottery containers, with a spout out of which the water comes in a stream, are used for drinking.
Nang Saboeh drinking; Nang Roni beside him (cf. Pl. 29, figs. 3, 4, and 5 for other pictures in this sequence).
Bajoeng Gede. April 14, 1937.   6 T 31.

2. Boys bathing in a temple pool. Bathing in Bali is a sensory pleasure rather than an effort to get clean. In general, the Balinese are not a compulsively clean people. They like the smell of people (cf. *rame*, Pl. 5), and, though they bathe often, their clothes are usually dirty. They are especially fond of the sensation of cool water running over the skin, and will sit for hours in a flowing stream or under a jet of water. After bathing, they say that the body is *"tis,"* neither too hot nor too cold. They use the same word to describe the sensation after a bout of malaria.
Tampaksiring. Photograph by Jane Belo.

3. Girls receiving holy water on a calendric holiday (*Galoengan*). This is a day on which people make elaborate offerings for their home temples, wear their best clothes and visit each other. The Brahmans shown in this and the next photograph start the day by receiving holy water from a priestess. They drink some, and sprinkle the remainder on their hair and bodies.
Batoean. Dec. 1, 1937.   19 N 16.

4. High-caste Brahman men receiving holy water on the same occasion.
Batoean. Dec. 1, 1937.   19 N 6.

5. The water pot of an adolescent girl. This photograph is taken from outside the houseyard and shows the corner where the people go for defecation. The pot contains the special water supply for the toilet of a high-caste girl at menarche. It stands on the wall which bounds her specially decorated house (cf. Pl. 93 for discussion of the symbolic relation between the house and the body).
Batoean. Dec. 5, 1937.   19 U 30.

6 and 7. Bathing at a mountain spring. These scenes occurred at an annual ceremony (*saban jeh*) at which offerings were made to the gods of the springs from which the village gets its water. The main part of the ceremony was conducted in the village temple, but a priest and two girls were sent with a few offerings to the springs. On arriving there they offered to the gods, and then took the opportunity of bathing.
Djero Baoe Kentel at the jet; I Pinti doing her hair.
Bajoeng Gede. Nov. 25, 1937.   19 G 36, 37.

8. Washing a corpse. The pouring of holy water over the dead is an essential feature of Balinese mortuary ceremonial. This photograph shows the funeral procession clustered around the body while holy water from a special spring is poured over it. The water is contained in a long bamboo (cf. Pl. 89, figs. 4 and 6, and Pl. 99, fig. 3).
Nang Mebet holding the bamboo at the funeral of Dong Merada.
Bajoeng Gede. Oct. 9, 1937.   16 Z 9.

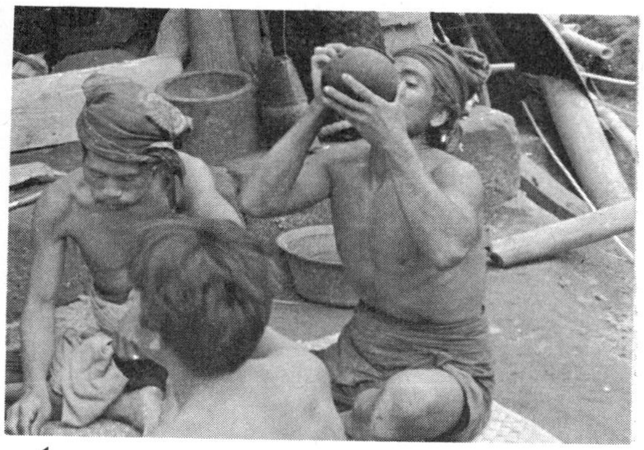

1

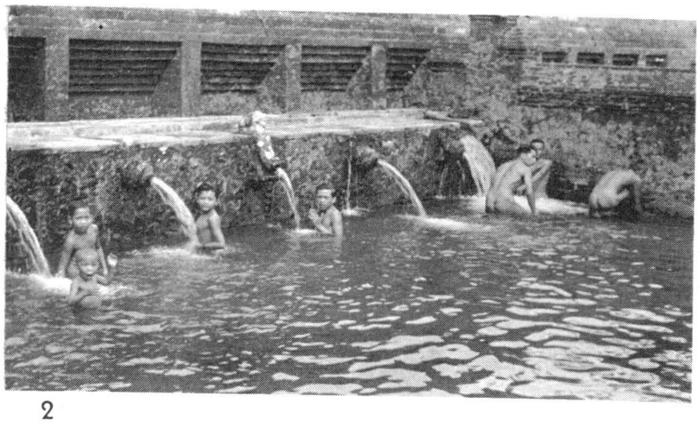

2

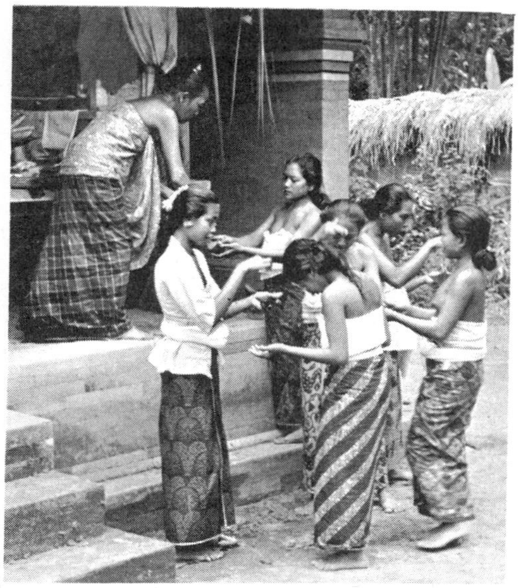

3

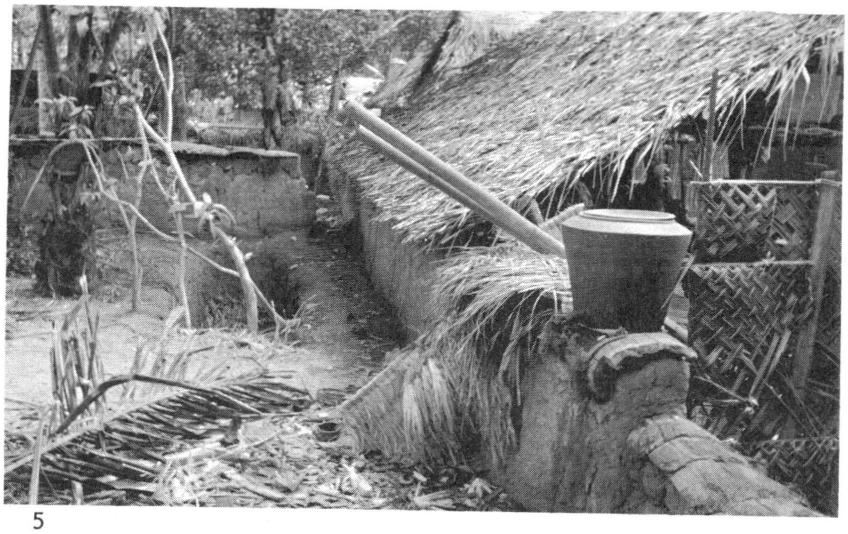

5

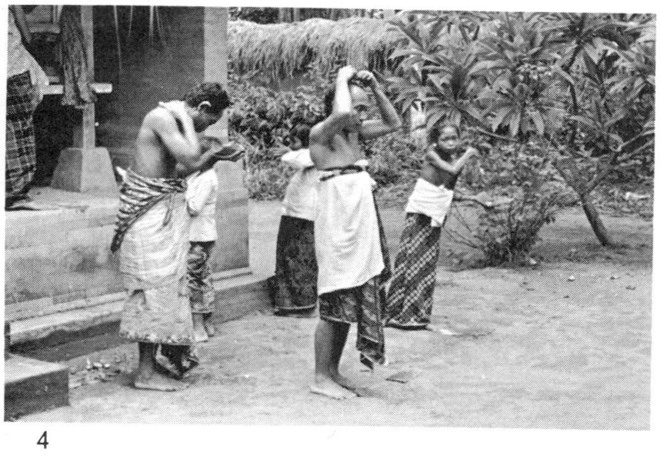

4

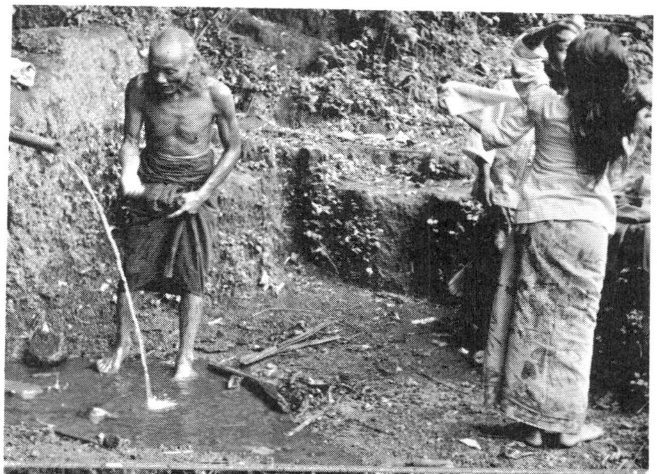

6

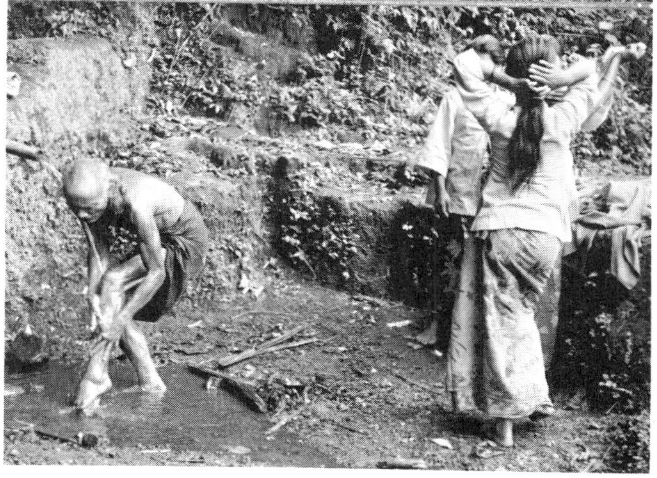

7

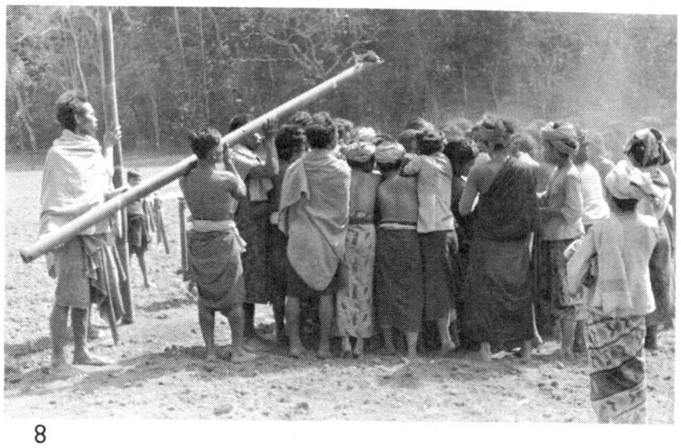

8

1

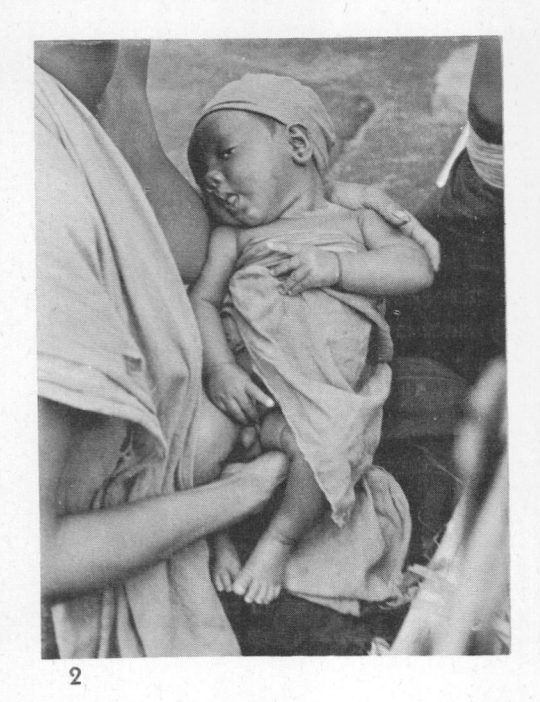

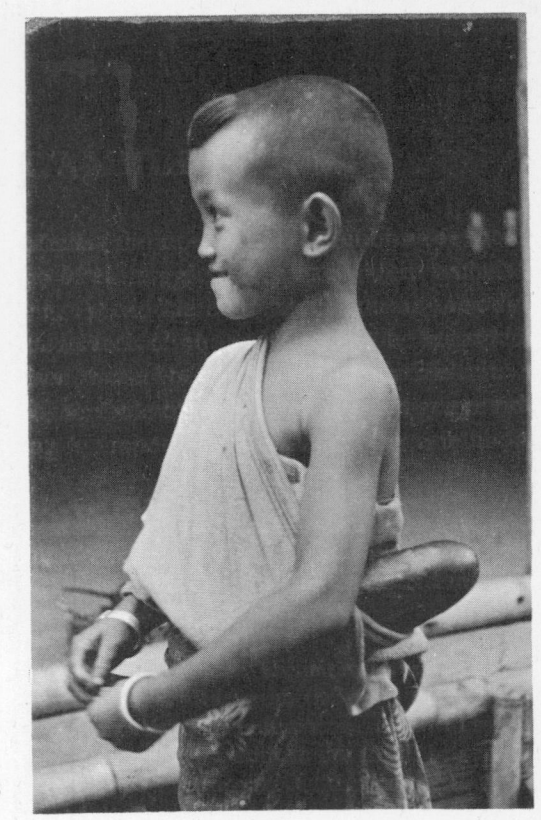

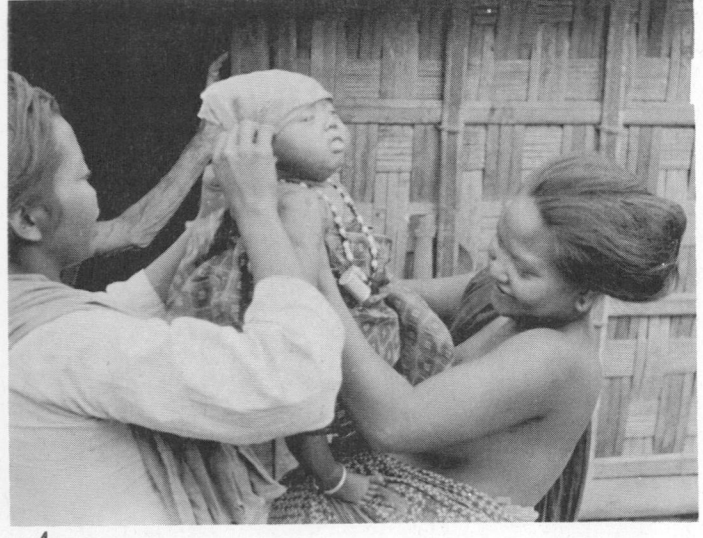

2

3

4

5

6

7

Plate 38

AUTOCOSMIC SYMBOLS: THE BABY

Plates 38 to 42 are concerned with autocosmic genital symbolism. It is not enough to state that a given object is a genital symbol, because such symbolism is probably universal in human cultures. Some more specific statement is necessary in order to throw light on character structure. We need to know what sort of things are symbolic in this sense, so that we may know what psychological role the genital organs themselves play in the character; and we need to know of any given item whether it is a symbolic extension of own body or represents something apart from the self, some power to which the self must bow.

Balinese genital symbolism is almost entirely of the autocosmic type; i.e., some object in the outside world is identified as an extension of own body. The vast majority of these symbols, so far as we have observed, represent the male genital, and these are all alike in that the symbol is in some sense responsive to manipulation.

Of such symbols, the most important is the baby. Balinese adults avoid over-responsiveness in inter-personal relations, but they can obtain responses by applying either pleasant or unpleasant stimuli to babies who have not yet learned the unresponsive habit.

1. Drawing of a father who has a child who has a flower. This drawing (whatever may have been its meaning to the artist) provides us with a diagrammatic statement of the inter-personal patterns which follow from the role of the child as an autocosmic genital symbol. The child is in the middle of a series; he is treated as an extension of his father's personality and he learns to collect analogous extensions of himself.

The father in this drawing carries a rake and has a sickle-shaped knife in his belt.

Painting by I Taweng of Batoean.
Purchased Aug. 28, 1937. Cat. No. 499.

2. Genital manipulation of the baby. This takes several forms; commonly the mother grasps the penis and gives it a quick tug while letting it slip through the fingers, as if "pulling it off." In other cases, the mother passes her hand repeatedly upward over the pubes and abdomen in such a way that the penis is pressed upward by each passage of the hand; or she may ruffle the penis upward with repeated little flicks, using almost the exact gesture that a man uses when he ruffles up the hackle feathers of his fighting cock to make it angry (cf. Pl. 43, fig. 4). These behaviors are all play; they are not motivated by the desire to quiet the child, but by the desire to see the child respond.

Men Njawi holding I Koewat, aged 30 days.
Bajoeng Gede. April 30, 1937. 7 V 4.

3. A little girl with a cucumber doll. She carries it in a sling like a baby. Play with dolls is comparatively rare, since most of the girls have real babies which they must look after and with which they can play (cf. Pl. 78, for another baby-substitute).

I Nampah.
Bajoeng Gede. Oct. 2, 1936. 2 U 32.

4. Dressing a baby for his 105-day birthday. The woman on the right is in advanced pregnancy (her baby was born five weeks later), and she holds the baby up at an angle, supporting his feet on her abdomen. The girl on the right is fixing the baby's headcloth.

I Tatah; I Sepek, aged 105 days; I Maring.
Bajoeng Gede. Oct. 2, 1936. 2 V 3.

5. A mother squeezing mucus out of her daughter's nose. This is done to babies more frequently than is necessary, and, like the pulling of the genitals, it is done with a sudden sharp motion, letting the nose slip through the fingers. An older woman watches, laughing.

Men Kesir; I Meres; Men Nami.
Bajoeng Gede. April 14, 1937. 6 V 25.

6. A mother washing her baby's head before putting her in the basin. She holds the baby so that the baby's head projects forward over the basin of water (cf. fig. 4 above).

Men Singin washing I Djantoek.
Bajoeng Gede. Feb. 12, 1939. 36 H 27.

7. A traditional punishment in hell. "Had a woman one child only and this child came to die and herewith the woman followed her child by sorrow to the land of the dead, then she got to carry a very large catepilar on her chest. How the woman tried to repudiate this animal from herself, it stayed hanging on her chest." (Extract from an essay on "The Cremation in Baly" written by I Made Kaler of Boeleleng, while he was learning English.)

Painting sketched by I Djata and finished by I. B. P. Boen, of Batoean.
Purchased Sept. 6, 1937. Cat. No. 346. Reduced x ⅓ linear.

Plate 39

GENITAL MANIPULATION

Parallel with the treatment of the child as an autocosmic genital symbol, we find that manipulative play with the genital is permitted to the child. Further, either as a defense against the continual demand for response or as a natural extension from the pleasure of this introvert play, we find later, in children and adults, many postural habits of withdrawal. The most extreme of these is a sitting position in which the head is bent down over the knees.

1, 2, and 3. A small boy in his father's lap.

In fig. 1, the father is asking M. M. for a jacket for his son, while the son plays with his penis.

In fig. 2, the father's attention has shifted away from the son, and the son's hands have come together on his chest.

In fig. 3, the son's hands move up to his face and the right hand starts to play with his lip.

(This child was left-handed. The ordinary Balinese rule is that the right hand must not be used for handling the genitals, and this child was constantly corrected. Later they will probably decide that he ought to follow the reverse of the ordinary rule and reserve his left hand for gifts and food and use his right for unclean things.)

Nang Karma, the father; I Gata, the son.
Bajoeng Gede. June 18, 1937. 11 S 2, 3, 4.

4. A male dancer after his dance. He had just given an exhibition dance with his sister whom he had trained as a courtship dancer (*djoget*, cf. Pl. 59, figs. 1 and 3, for photographs of his dancing). He now sits folded in on himself.

I Daweg of Selat, Bangli.
Bajoeng Gede. May 28, 1937. 9 Q 1.

5. Two small boys watching a procession. They are sitting in the outside porch of the village temple, watching a stream of villagers and strangers carrying gods and offerings into the temple. The procession is passing within a few feet of the boys. In this exposed position, one boy sits looking up from a posture in which he was folded in on himself; the other squats with his hands under his thighs, pulling his penis sideways.

I Soewaka; I Karsa (unrelated boys).
Bajoeng Gede. March 24, 1937. 6 E 34.

6. A low-caste boy from another village in a group of smaller high-caste boys who are drawing in the sand. The stranger turns his back on the others and draws by himself. Our secretary (low caste, age about 21) guessed that this behavior was shyness in the presence of an adult high-caste artist (not visible in the photograph). The boy himself said that it was because of the "little ones"; that he did not want them to see his drawing (which was more skillful than theirs). The photograph illustrates withdrawal in an embarrassing setting, where age and caste give conflicting cues.

I Sambeh of Selat, top left; I. B. P. Tendo of Batoean, center.
Batoean. Oct. 5, 1937. 16 L 34.

7. A high-caste boy withdraws after he has been drawing in the sand with the others. This is the same boy shown in the center of fig. 6, but the photograph was taken on another day.

I. B. P. Tendo.
Batoean. Oct. 7, 1937. 16 V 3.

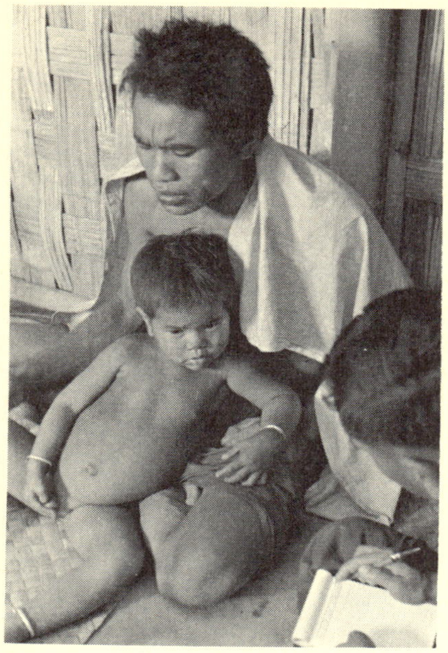

1

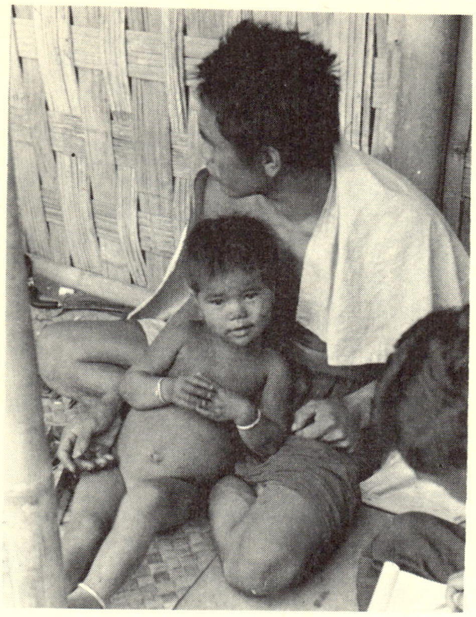

2

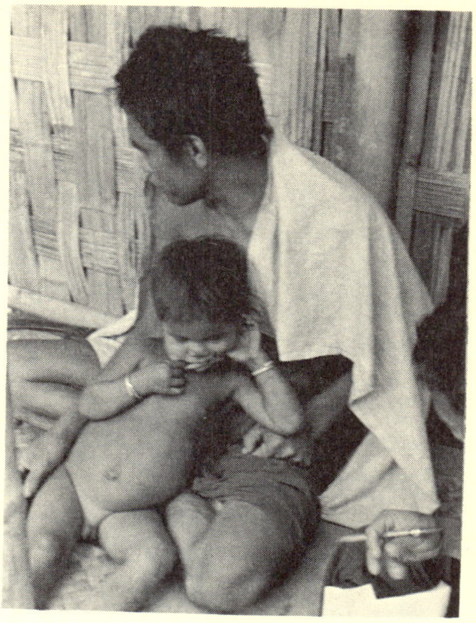

3

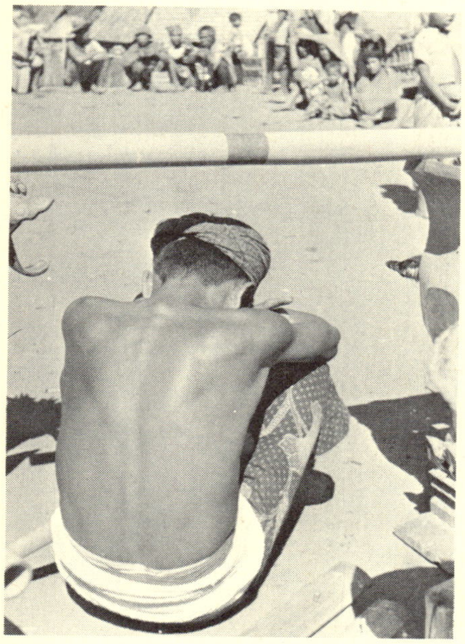

4

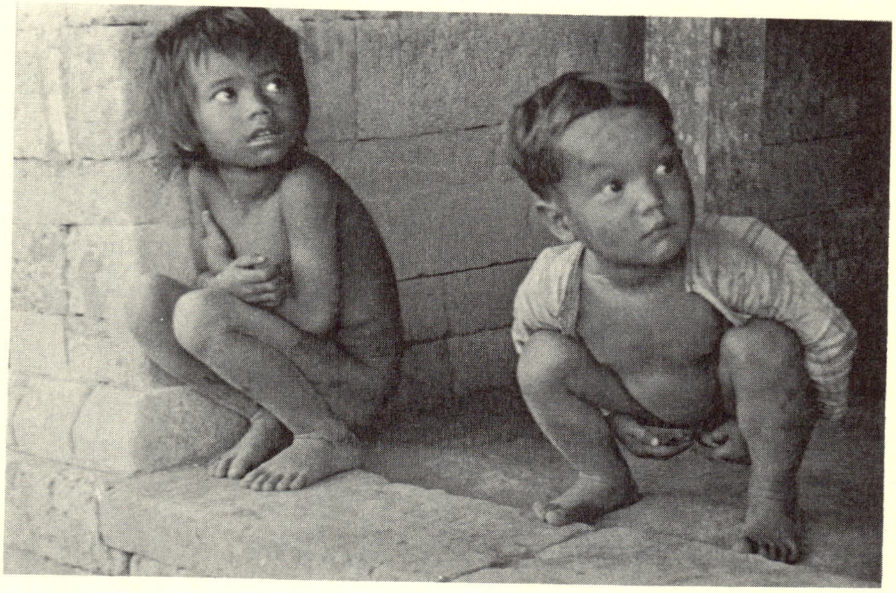

5

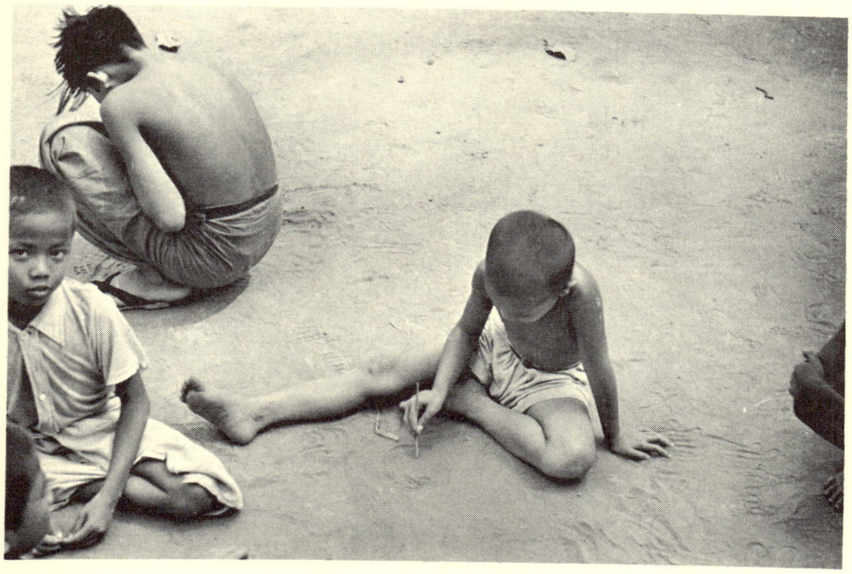

6

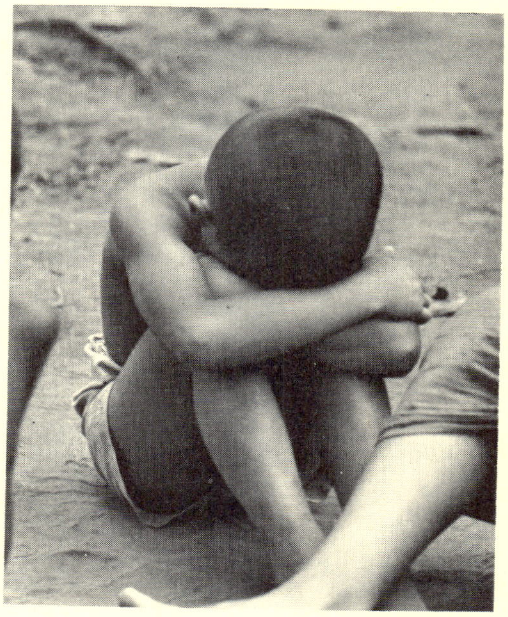

7

1

2

3

4

5

6

7

8

Plate 40
AUTOCOSMIC TOYS

A very large variety of objects fall into this category, and their identification as genital symbols can be supported from the extensive North Balinese slang vocabulary of metaphors for the penis ("puppy"; "child"; "kris"; "spear"; "leg"; "short leg"; "tail"; "walking-stick"; "Dragon"; etc.).

It will be noted that many of the objects shown on this and following plates combine autonomous movement with responsiveness. Many of them are alive (babies, puppies, fighting cocks, crickets, etc.), and even those which are not alive are capable of movement (top-heavy pennants which bend in the wind, kites, pinwheels, etc.).

1 and 2. A small boy with a chopper (*belakas*). This boy strutted around for several minutes with this chopper held at various angles.

In fig. 1, the chopper is pointing directly at the camera, and the boy is in the act of turning with a swinging movement.

In fig. 2, he stands still for a moment with his shoulders thrown back and his feet turned in.
  I Karsa.
  Bajoeng Gede. Dec. 12, 1936. 3 X 22, 23.

3. A spear dance (*baris toembak*). These mountain dances are performed by a number of men dancing in unison. They are slow dances and usually performed with very little kinaesthetic verve. In the photograph, the dancer stands holding his spear at a raised angle. His grip on the spear is limited to the tips of the fingers of his *left* hand.
  I Wandera.
  Bajoeng Gede. Nov. 25, 1937. 19 I 32.

4. A high pennant (*oembel-oembel*) which is carried in processions with the gods. This specimen has a mythological serpent (*naga*) painted on the cloth.
  South Bali (village of origin not recorded).
  Saba. April 22, 1936. 1 B 9.

5. A woman giving a pinwheel to a small girl. Pinwheels and propellers are very common in Bali. They are set up on the housetops and in the fields and are usually arranged so that they make a noise in the wind.
  Low-caste woman with a Brahman girl.
  Batoean. Oct. 5, 1937. 16 N 20.

6. A painting of boys flying kites. This sport is a form of vicarious conflict, like cockfighting and cricket-fighting. Two boys "fight" with their kites, each trying to make the string of his kite cut the string of the other's (cf. Pls. 41 and 42, for autocosmic symbols on strings).
  Painting by I. B. Kt. Baroe of Batoean.
  Purchased Nov. 1937. Cat. No. 57. Reduced x ¼ linear.

7. A painting of cricket-fighting. The men have their crickets in small bamboo cages. To make the crickets angry, they are teased with brushes. When they are sufficiently angry, two crickets are put together by placing their cages end to end and removing the partition. The men bet on the result of the conflict.

The artist stated that he drew the large cricket in the foreground of the picture as a "sign" (*tjiri*) of what the picture represented.
  Painting by I. B. Made Togog of Batoean.
  Purchased Feb. 13, 1937. Cat. No. 640A.

8. Two high-caste boys teasing a cricket. One boy tickles the cricket with a grass stem, while the other watches. Compare these facial expressions with those on Pl. 44.
  I. B. Mari; I. B. M. Saboeh.
  Batoean. Feb. 8, 1938. 21 E 6.

Plate 41

AUTOCOSMIC SYMBOLS ON STRINGS

An ideal combination of spontaneous movement with responsiveness is provided by those toys which consist of a living animal on a string. The list of animals which are treated in this way is considerable (bees, centipedes, babies, birds, puppies, etc.), and several sorts of inanimate objects are treated in the same way (kites, banana flowers, etc.).

Identification of these toys as genital symbols can be had not only from the behavior of the children in their play with them, but also from the jingling rhymes which the children sing. Such rhymes typically consist of two paired couplets. The first couplet is superficially meaningless, e.g.,

"A starling on a string,
A duckling in a basket";

while the second elaborates on the sexual theme implicit in the first.

The Balinese habit of attaching such symbols to strings instead of holding them directly is perhaps related to their fantasy that the body is made of separable autonomous parts, and to their habit of giving a sudden tug at the baby's penis.

1 and 2. A man ties two babies together. In fig. 1, he is tying a string to his son's wrist. For a while he played with him on the string like a bird. Then he tied both wrists, remarking "like someone punished for stealing." Men Singin (I Karsa's mother) suggested that he tie Karba to Karsa and Karba would then "be an ox" (i.e., yoked).

Fig. 2 shows the two children tied together.

Nang Oera; I Karba, his son, aged 503 days; I Karsa, cousin of I Karba.

Bajoeng Gede. June 22, 1937.   11 X 6, 12.

3, 4, 5, and 6. A boy with a small parrot on a perch. He is leaning over the low barrier which prevents the pigs from entering the houseyard. In fig. 3, he looks down the road, ignoring the bird.

In fig. 4, he lifts the bird and gazes at it, while his right arm, which holds the perch, also caresses his cheek.

In fig. 5, he lifts the perch high with both hands and looks up at the bird through the arch made by his arms.

In fig. 6, the bird has turned round on its perch and starts to flap its wings at him.

I Karsa.

Bajoeng Gede. Aug. 18, 1937.   13 X 17, 20, 21, 22.

7, 8, and 9. A small boy with a banana flower on a bamboo thong. The toy was made for the child by his parents. He went off with it alone, and became completely absorbed in slowly posturing with it.

In fig. 7, he has the thong over his head and is slowly patting the thong with a rhythmic movement. Later he patted his head in the same way.

In fig. 8, he has turned toward the camera. He holds both hands to his head and looks out from between his arms.

In fig. 9, he has returned to his complete absorption, and now has the thong bent over in a graceful curve passing between his legs to the banana bud which is behind him. The "handle" end of the thong is against his chest.

The unopened banana bud (*poeseoh*, literally, "heart") is used in Balinese symbolism in place of the lotus bud of Indian Hindooism. It appears as a surrogate for the child in ceremonials. (We collected a carving of a princess cradling such a bud in her arms.)

I Gata.

Bajoeng Gede. Jan. 19, 1937.   4 G 6, 8, 9.

1

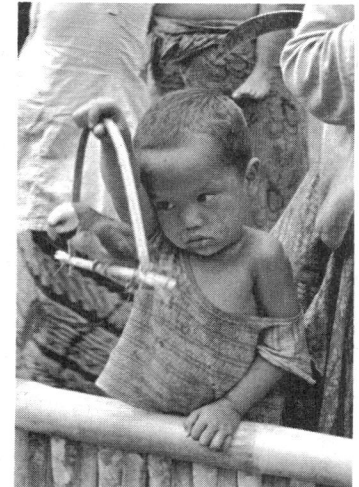

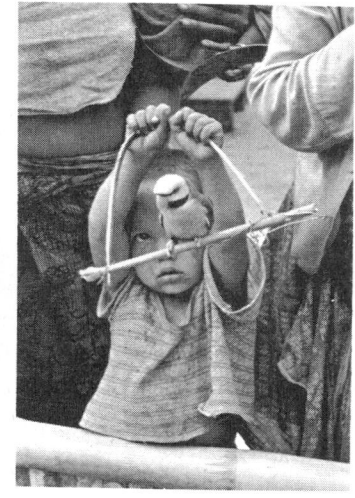

2

3

4

5

6

7

8

9

1 2 3
4 5 6
7 8 9
10 11 12

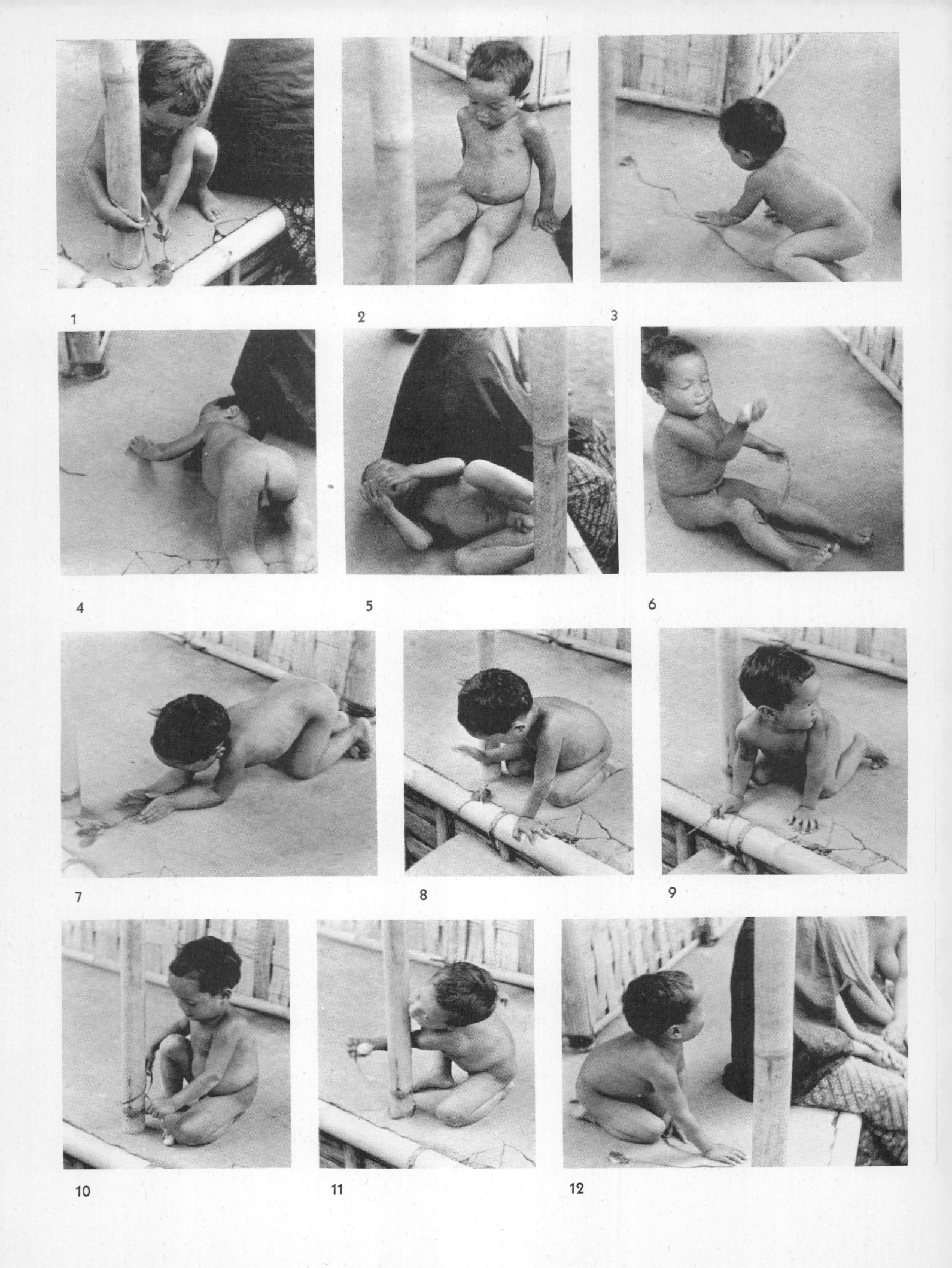

Plate 42

A BIRD ON A STRING

This sequence illustrates the variety of behavioral patterns which a single child exhibits in playing with an autocosmic genital symbol. The whole sequence, as recorded in M. M.'s notes, lasted about 15 minutes, but of this period only about 7 minutes was recorded with the camera. At this point the film in the still camera finished, and the remainder of the sequence was recorded with the motion-picture camera.

Extracts from M. M.'s notes:

"Suddenly, while looking at carvings (brought by a seller), I noticed that I Karsa had a tiny bird on a bark string, which he was dragging about — dropping the end of the string so that it fluttered away — dragging it about again. Karsa took the bird over to his father, asked some questions about it and tried to hide it in his father's blanket (cf. Pl. 64, fig. 2).

"Karsa drops the string. Watches the bird flutter.

"He falls on it — feet locked together. Mutters over it with his mouth right over it. Curls over it.

"He crawls with it in his fingers toward mother. Drops it. Says 'It's dead.' He climbs up on his mother's back, rollicks, kicks his heels up, on his mother's back.

"Another woman asks him some question about the bird. Karsa says 'I'll tie it up.' Comes over to the corner post (of our veranda) and fastens the bird with two twists round the post (fig. 1). (At this point, Karsa sat back away from the bird and looked at it, while extending his legs on each side of the post. This behavior is shown in fig. 2, but was not recorded in the verbal account.)

"Karsa loosens string, and the bird, freed, flutters across the floor. Karsa hurts his finger as he goes after it (figs. 3 and 4).

"Karsa cries — rolls over, crying (fig. 5).

"I say 'Where's the bird?' Made Kaler (our secretary) says 'Is the bird lost?' Karsa goes and gets the bird again.

"He holds it up loose in his upraised hand and lets it flutter down (fig. 6).

"Repeats this. The bird cries.

"Karsa holds the bird over the step" (figs. 7, 8, and 9).

During this episode M. M. could not see what Karsa was doing. In fig. 7, he has the bird on the floor and holds his hands in an open V. In fig. 8, he has the bird on the edge of the veranda and is slowly patting at it with his right hand (cf. Pl. 41, fig. 7). In fig. 9, he has let the bird fall down over the edge, where it hangs while he looks back at his mother.

"Karsa ties the bird to another post (figs. 10 and 11). (Apparently he first tied it by twisting the free end of the string around the post in fig. 10, and then varied this by carrying the bird itself round the post in fig. 11.)

"Karsa feints at pouncing on the bird with both hands cupped.

"He says 'Oh! It's dead' and holds it out to his mother. He beats at his mother with his hand. She says 'No. It's alive'" (fig. 12).

In the second half of the sequence, he again ties the bird to a post; and again plays with the notion that his mother is responsible for the bird's "death." In addition to these repeats, he starts a new type of play by putting the bird between his legs, leaving it for a moment behind his back pretending to have forgotten it (cf. Pl. 41, fig. 3). Then he suddenly turned and "found" it, as if surprised. After this play with the bird between his legs, he held the bird in the opening of his mouth, letting it flutter against his lips.

I Karsa.

Bajoeng Gede. March 4, 1937. 5 G 2, 5, 7, 8, 9, 11, 13, 14, 15, 16, 18, 20.

Plate 43

COCKFIGHTING

Of the large variety of autocosmic toys of childhood, one of the most important of those which persist into adult life is the fighting cock. Cockfighting, in Bali, is a gambling sport which is indulged in by a very large proportion of the male population. There are certain individuals, however, who are particularly addicted to it, who keep many fighting cocks, go constantly to cockfights, and bet more than they can afford. Men whose citizenship is incomplete or who have been disappointed in some way "take to" cockfighting, as men in our civilization take to drink.

The evidence for regarding the fighting cock as a genital symbol comes from the postures of men holding cocks, the sex slang and sex jingles, and from Balinese carvings of men with fighting cocks. The postures imagined by the carver are even more diagnostic than those of the living men.

1. Watching a cockfight. The men in the front rank of the audience, and especially those whose cocks are fighting, usually squat in this way with their arms supported on the knees at a point just above the elbows. The man on the right had lost his citizenship in the village because his only child had been a girl. He was an addict of cockfighting. M. M. observed that when he was excited watching his cock in battle, he moved his hands as if he were identifying with the conflict rather than with his own cock. In his hand movements, it appeared that one hand represented one cock while the other hand represented the other.

Unidentified man in left foreground; I Kari on the right.
Bajoeng Gede. Jan. 21, 1937.   4 Ga 37.

2. Watching a cockfight. The man on the left is squatting in the typical position, and has his fingers extended so that they just touch the ground.
Nang Oera; Nang Salib.
Bajoeng Gede. Feb. 2, 1937.   4 K 20.

3. Matching the cocks and making them angry. First the cocks are tried one against another to find two which will fight. This is done by holding them so that they face each other, while their owners pluck at their combs, flutter their hackle feathers and make the cocks peck at each other (as in this photograph). The first bet is placed by the owners, and this bet is always even. (Later bets are placed by both owners and spectators and various odds may be given.) Before the fight each man holds the other man's cock, so that he can feel the enemy cock's strength and make sure that it is not much stronger than his own. When the cocks are matched and angry, they are separated and a long steel spur is carefully bound onto the lower surface of each cock's left foot. The cocks are again brought together and after further teasing are freed to fight each other. The rounds are regulated by an umpire with a water-clock.
Batoean. Oct. 5, 1937.   16 R 33.

4. Matching the cocks and making them angry. The man facing the camera is ruffling up the hackle feathers under the cock's neck with quick upward-patting movements (cf. Pl. 38, fig. 2).
Nang Oera facing the camera; Nang Salib behind him.
Bajoeng Gede. Feb. 2, 1937.   4 K 16.

5. Man holding a cock. He is rising from a squatting position. Many men spend hours sitting, playing with their cocks.
Nang Karma.
Bajoeng Gede. Jan. 17, 1937.   4 C 5.

6. Man examining the legs of a cock. Every fighting cock has an elaborate toilet every day including a bath (like that of a baby) with water containing onions and various leaves.
I Lanoes, vagrant worker and habitual clown.
Bajoeng Gede. Oct. 24, 1936.   3 A 22.

1

2

3

4

5

6

1
2
3
4
5
6
7

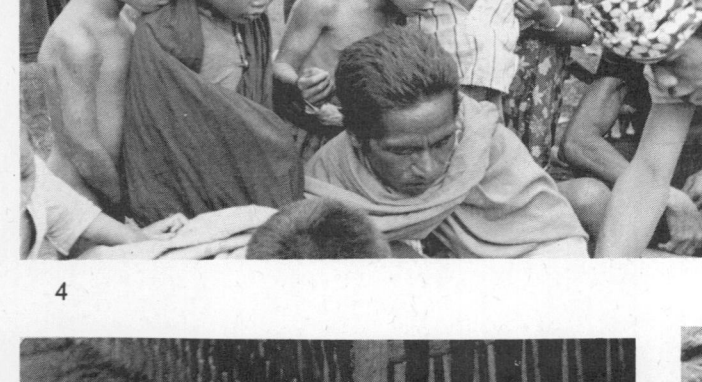

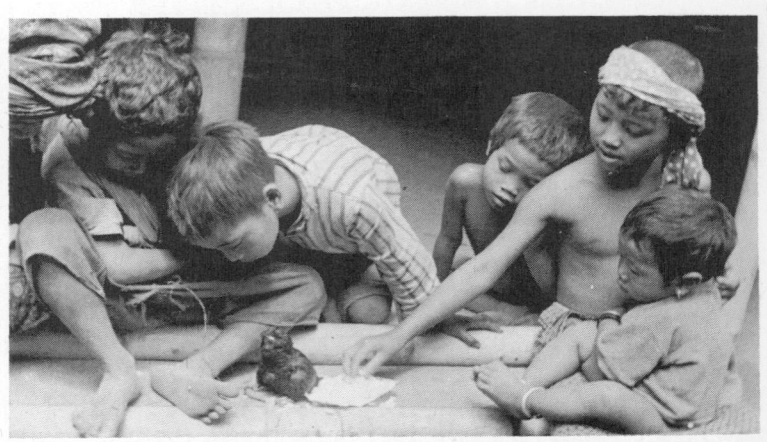

Plate 44

AUDIENCES AND AUTOCOSMIC SYMBOLS

Plates 38 to 43 have shown a series of the facial expressions and bodily postures which occur in the handling of autocosmic genital symbols. This plate shows the same expressions and postures in a variety of contexts. The habit of regarding external, and especially living, objects as symbolic extensions of own body recurs constantly, and can even be recognized in the behavior of the audience at a theatrical performance. The spectators are not interested in the plot and never identify with the characters portrayed in the play; but, as technicians, they are interested in the acting, and their identification is with the actors as extensions or kinaesthetic replicas of their own bodies.

This generalization adds a new facet to the Balinese pleasure in crowded occasions (cf. Pl. 5, *rame*). When the individual's attention is fixed on the play of autocosmic symbols (actors, firecrackers, cockfights, processions, etc.) he becomes orally responsive to the symbol, and the need for inter-personal distance diminishes or is forgotten. The way is open, then, for sensuous pleasure in skin contacts either with other people or with own limbs (cf. figs. 4, 5, 6, and 7 on this plate; Pl. 5, fig. 6; Pl. 38, fig. 5; Pl. 40, fig. 8; Pl. 41, figs. 4 and 5; Pl. 42, fig. 11; Pl. 47, fig. 1). Conversely, close inter-personal skin contact may set off autocosmic play (cf. Pl. 39, figs. 1, 2, and 3; Pl. 64, figs. 3 and 5).

1, 2, and 3. A dicing group at a cockfight. In the intervals of the cockfighting, many of the men go and gamble with dice or play other games for money. The dice are spun with the hand. Such groups are very noisy, the men roaring at the dice to make them fall as they wish, and roaring at the fall when it is revealed. In fig. 2, the man in the center is just about to throw the dice and in fig. 3, he has just thrown. (Compare the facial expressions in fig. 1 with Pl. 38, fig. 5; and the hand postures in fig. 3 with Pl. 43, figs. 1 and 2.)

I Kaler in center, figs. 2 and 3; I Omong to the right of I Kaler; the others are strangers who came to the cockfight from other villages.

Bajoeng Gede. Jan. 21, 1937.   4 Ga 10, 12, 13.

4. Children watching the butchering of an ox. The carcass is on the ground and the intestines are being removed. All the children show their attention by slight protrusion of the lips (cf. figs. 2 and 3). The two children on the left are in close physical contact, as also are the three on the right.

The children (from left to right) — I Goewet; I Gelis; I Karta; I Badera; and one stranger to the village. Nang Goenoeng is in the center of the foreground and Nang Loka bending forward on the right.

Bajoeng Gede. Sept. 1, 1936.   2 J 12.

5. Girls looking at a doll which M. M. has just unpacked. The two girls who are attending to the doll show marked oral responsiveness to it and are standing in close physical contact with each other. After this initial reaction to the strange object, they approached it tentatively, and touched only its hair.

I Ngembat; I Modoh; I Moegloek; I Gangsar in bottom left.

Bajoeng Gede. Oct. 9, 1937.   16 X 32.

6. Three small boys with a mechanical mouse. They pretended to be cats and jumped about on all fours, but never touched the mouse. Finally I Nandoer, the leader of the group (farthest from camera) pounced not on the mouse but on I Gelis (nearest to camera).

I Gelis nearest to camera; I Doeroes in the middle; I Nandoer farthest from camera.

Bajoeng Gede. May 18, 1937.   9 D 9.

7. Children playing with a baby crow. The girl on the right is trying to make it eat some rice on a leaf. The children are in two groups with close physical contact inside each group, and the two children on the right show oral responsiveness to the bird.

In the course of play with the bird, I Gelis (with curly hair), the owner of the bird, chewed up some rice for it and over-filled the bird's mouth with this material (cf. Pl. 26, figs. 1 and 2). Later he opened the bird's mouth and spat into it as a man does who is medicating his cock.

I Gelis; I Nandoer; I Goewet; I Djeben; I Karba in lap of I Djeben.

Bajoeng Gede. May 4, 1937.   7 Z 26.

Plate 45

THE CHILD AS A GOD

Children are treated not only as autocosmic symbols, but also as gods (cf. Pl. 98 for the converse proposition that gods are treated as children). This motif is strongest at birth. Before and immediately after delivery, the child is addressed in the most courteous (*aloes*) language and is accorded the title "sir" (*djerone*), which is otherwise reserved for village functionaries and strangers.

The same motif persists through infancy and is expressed by elevating the baby and dressing it up. In later childhood (Pl. 83) the normal child loses these attributes but they are retained, and indeed exaggerated, in the little girls who dance as gods in trance (cf. Pl. 10). Even when not in trance, these girls are sacred and must protect their sanctity by not walking under aqueducts or hen roosts. In trance, the girls are willful, and an important part of the audience's enjoyment comes from the conventional "spoiling" of the little girls (cf. Pl. 13, for the conventional treatment of princes, in which they are "spoilt" — like children).

1. A trance dancer falls into the audience and the flowers in her headdress are repaired. One of the willful tricks of the dancers is falling suddenly into the audience, an act which is greeted with great amusement. The little dancers also exhibit pettishness, stamping their feet and making impatient movements with their fans when they want to dance to the orchestra instead of to the songs sung by the audience.

I Dampoek repairing I Misi's headdress; I Modoh (face half covered by fan); I Soka; I Djeben; I Nampah; I Tamboen with mouth open, behind I Nampah.

Bajoeng Gede. Feb. 11, 1939. 36 B 6.

2. A baby at its 105-day birthday. The mother holds the baby girl up in her arms, while two little girls (cousins of the baby) look at it. Compare the facial expressions in this picture with the expressions of the same girls in the bottom right-hand corner of fig. 1.

I Nampah holding I Karba; I Lenjad holding I Resi, aged 105 days; I Djeben.

Bajoeng Gede. July 11, 1937. 12 Ha 22.

3 and 4. A man repairing the costume of a girl trance dancer. This man was unmarried and was a very devoted attendant of the little girls at their trance performances. It was on his shoulders that they preferred to dance (cf. Pl. 10, fig. 3). He also expressed his devotion by fixing their headdresses for them and repairing their sashes when they came undone in the dance.

I Lasia fixing I Misi's sash.
Bajoeng Gede. Feb. 11, 1939. 36 B 16, 17.

5. A high-caste baby at its 840-day birthday. The baby girl is being held high by an old woman. The baby wears silver bracelets and a gold ornament on her fontanelle.

Dajoe Gambar held by a relative of her father.
Batoean. Aug. 4, 1937. 13 D 6.

6. A baby boy decorated. This headdress is made of stitched and cut out palm leaves, by the same technique as that used in making offerings. The baby was with a group of women who were making offerings, and playfully they made this headdress for him.

Orphan Brahman boy adopted by I. B. P. Sentoelan.
Batoean. Aug. 23, 1937. 14 U 23.

7. A mother holding up her baby. The baby wears the elaborate necklace on which he cuts his teeth.

Men Njawi holding I Koewat, aged 129 days.
Bajoeng Gede. Aug. 20, 1937. 14 K 26.

8. A painting of the birth of the elephant god, Ganesha (called "Betara Gana" in Bali). The hideous baby god lies on the ground with its four-lobed placenta (the *kandampat* or "four brothers") while its mother dances. This picture illustrates the extreme opposite of the theme of this plate. The baby in this case actually is a god but the mother's reaction to it is narcissistic aversion (cf. Pl. 48). According to the artist's description the mother of Ganesha is Giri Poetri. This goddess is the wife of Shiva, and she exists in two forms, one beautiful as in this drawing, the other witchlike.

Painting by I Goesti Kobot of Oeboed.
Purchased from Pita Maha, artists' club.

1

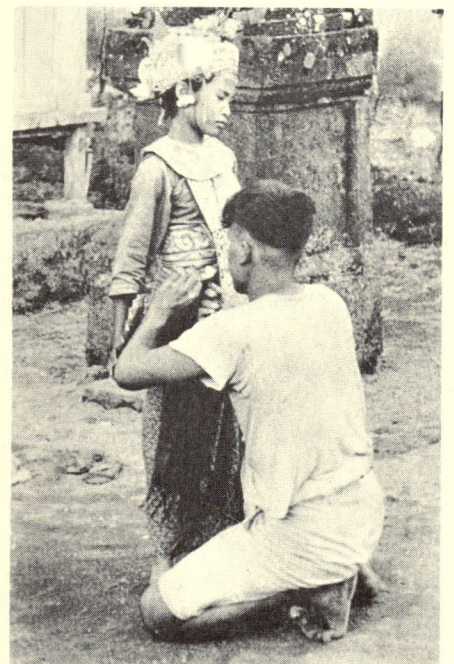

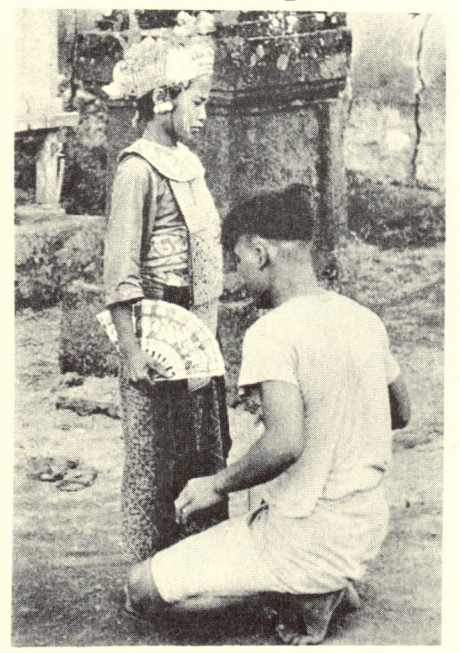

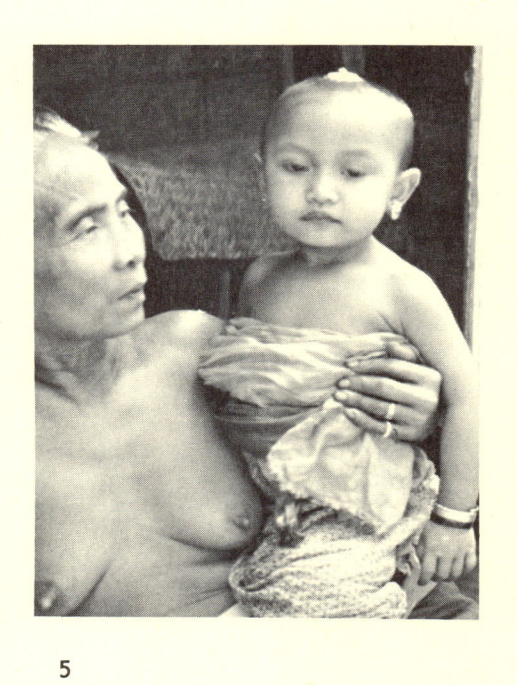

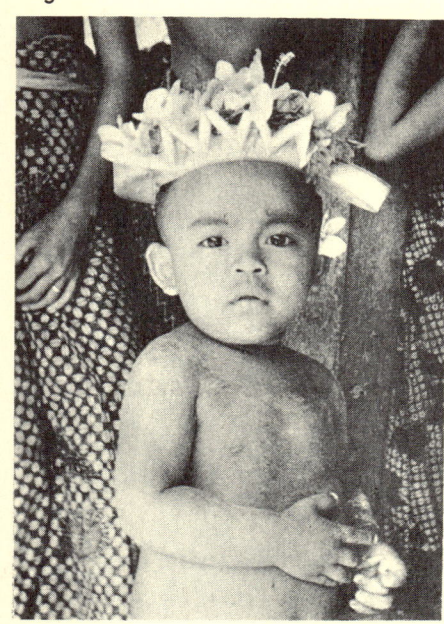

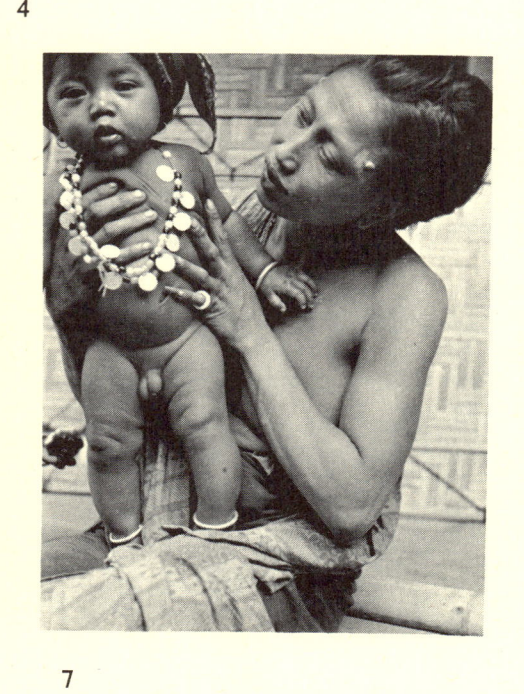

2

3

4

5

6

7

8

1
2
3

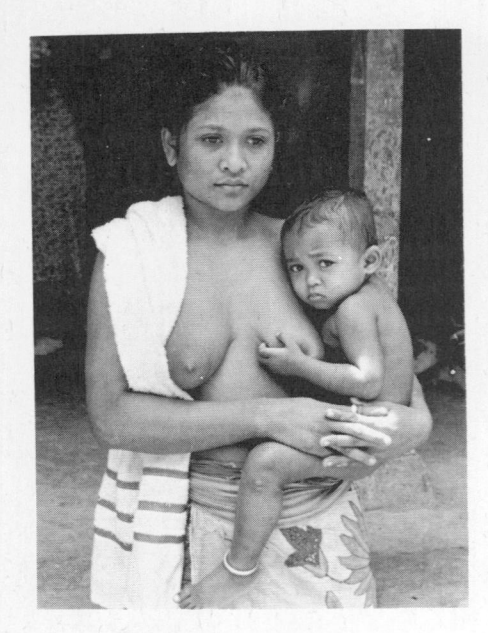

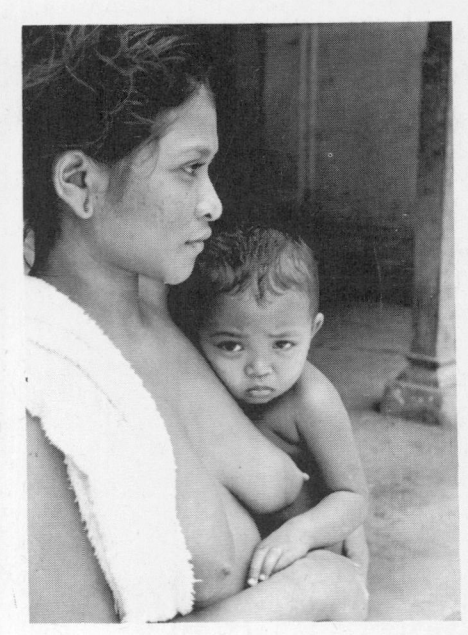

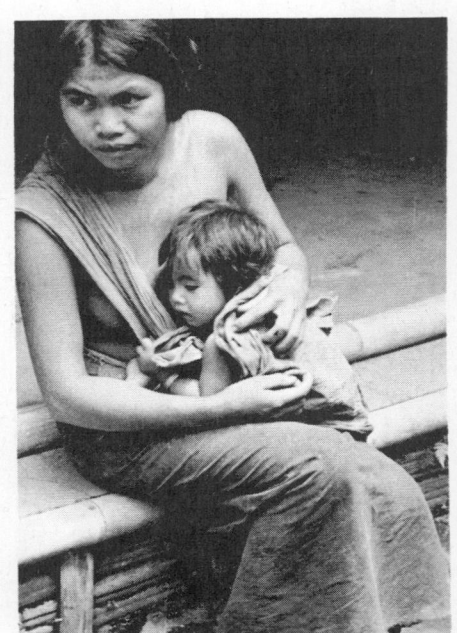

4
5
6

7
8

Plate 46

THE MOTHER: FEAR

Plates 46 to 61 are concerned with the relationship between the Balinese mother and her child, and with the symbolic re-statements of this relationship in ritual and courtship.

Fear plays a very important part in this relationship, but fear *with* the mother rather than fear of her. Whenever the child wanders and she wants to recall him, she suddenly exclaims in simulated fear, "Aroh! Wildcat!" or "Aroh! Caterpillar!" or she may invoke snakes, tigers, policemen, white men — and this when the child is still too young to attach specific meaning to her words. The child responds, however, to her tone and so she succeeds, as a hen does, in recalling her chicks by her own simulated fear.

This method of controlling the child is related to three important themes in Balinese character:

A. Fear of many sorts becomes a pleasant emotion, since in childhood shared fear brought mother and child together.

B. The Balinese develop a nameless and unpleasant fear in face of the unfamiliar or of any context involving initiative. The known conventions of the culture are reassuring rather than restricting (cf. the topology described in Pl. 17, fig. 1).

C. In Balinese social organization, instead of dominance-submission based on fear *of* the superior individual, we find what may be described as *startle* systems in which the behavior of the superior is characterized by suddenness in speech and gesture. He clips the premonitory syllables off his words while the inferior individual indulges in long smooth periphrases.

1, 2, and 3. Mother and child afraid. In this sequence, the mother was afraid of the photographer. She communicates her fear to the child by the tenseness of her muscles.

In fig. 1, though she appears outwardly relaxed, she has already communicated her fear.

In fig. 2, her act of readjusting the child on her hip is probably rendered awkward both by her own fear and by her response to the child's fear.

In fig. 3, she has begun to recover, but the child is still afraid and watches the photographer while still huddling close to the mother.

Ni Gedjer, aged 21 years, with her child.
Sajan (Gianjar). March 3, 1939. 36 V 15, 16, 17.

4 and 5. Mother and child afraid. They were visiting at our house and were frightened of the photographer and of the strange situation. In fig. 5, the child is apparently recovering and finds himself brought by fear closer to his mother.

Men Saoe with her child, I Mirib, aged 221 days.
Bajoeng Gede. April 3, 1937. 6 O 31, 32.

6. Mother and child in the forest. The mother's right arm is raised and she goes on tiptoe with bent knees, a posture characteristic of fear and witchcraft (cf. Pl. 61, fig. 3; Pl. 45, fig. 8; Pl. 60, figs. 2 and 8).

The outline for this picture was drawn by I Ngendon; the finishing was done by I. B. P. Moeda; both of Batoean.

Purchased Oct. 7, 1937. Cat. No. 363.

7. Fear simulated by a comic dancer. The pleasant emotion which we are here calling "fear" or "startle" enters into a great many contexts where there is nothing of which to be afraid. Especially in the theater, the Balinese constantly portray a quick, heightened awareness which has in it something of fear. This high-caste actor is performing a solo dance in which he portrays a man going out to catch frogs. The dance begins rather slowly in a sitting position and works up with sudden rhythmic rising movements till the man is almost erect. At the end of the dance, he subsides, limp.

Brahman dancer, name unknown.
Batoean. April 29, 1936. 1 B 26.

8. Two boys dancing as mischievous and frightened spirits (*memedi*). In their dance, they chase each other all over the dancing space and into the audience, stealing from each other the various items (a rag, a housefly, etc.) which they have inherited from their father.

Itinerant troupe of *ketantrian* dancers from Taro.
Bajoeng Gede. June 1, 1937. 10 B 6.

Plate 47
STIMULATION AND FRUSTRATION

We have already noted (Pl. 38) that the child's responsiveness is played upon by the mother. In practice, this means that the give-and-take of stimulus and response between mother and child lacks the sort of climax structure which is characteristic of love and hate in our own culture. The Balinese mother stimulates her child, but when he responds, she is unresponsive and never allows the flirtation to end in any sort of affectionate climax.

1 to 9. About two minutes of inter-personal behavior between mother and child. Extracts from M. M.'s verbal record:

"12:20 P.M. Men Goenoeng (the mother) calls I Raoeh (her son) over to her. He goes to her, and holds her breast; holds his penis; holds his knee, and begins to fret.

"Men Goenoeng bumps her head against him (figs. 1 and 2).

"Men Goenoeng settles I Raoeh astride her lap and I Raoeh plays with both nipples (fig. 3).

"I Raoeh sucks (fig. 4) and holds the other breast (figs. 5 and 6).

"Men Goenoeng pats his back rhythmically, and I Raoeh screws the right breast way over to the center of the body.

"Men Goenoeng traces a pattern on the side of her foot with her own hand (figs. 7 and 8).

"I Raoeh holds the other breast in a tight grip.

"12:22 P.M. I Raoeh looks around; hand still on breast" (fig. 9).

In this sequence, the mother's gesture in figs. 1 and 2 was in response to the child's fretting, but when he responds with affection her attention is away. Immediately after her advance, her face goes completely blank (fig. 3) and later she laughs at some unrecorded outside stimulus (fig. 4). It is probable that the "rhythmic patting of his back" recorded in the notes was performed without paying any attention to the child. In fig. 7, the camera records her with her hand in a caressing gesture on the child's head, while she looks up, laughing at something else (cf. Pl. 44 for the connection between spectatorship and sensuous skin contacts).

At the end of the sequence, both mother and child appear bored (fig. 9).

Men Goenoeng and her son I Raoeh, aged 580 days.
Bajoeng Gede. Aug. 19, 1937. 14 G 22, 23, 27, 28, 29, 30, 31, 33, last.

1

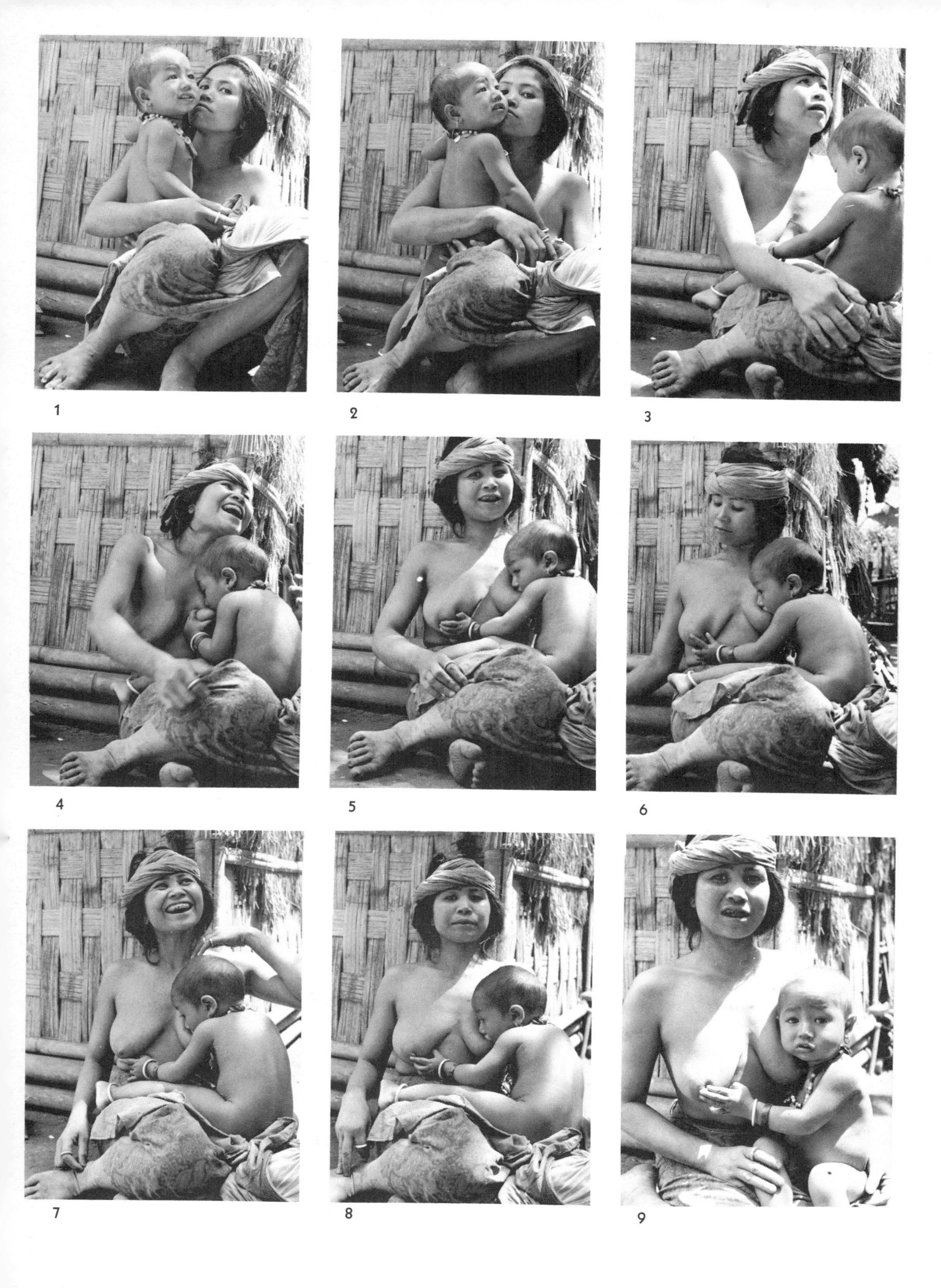

2

3

4

5

6

7

8

9

1

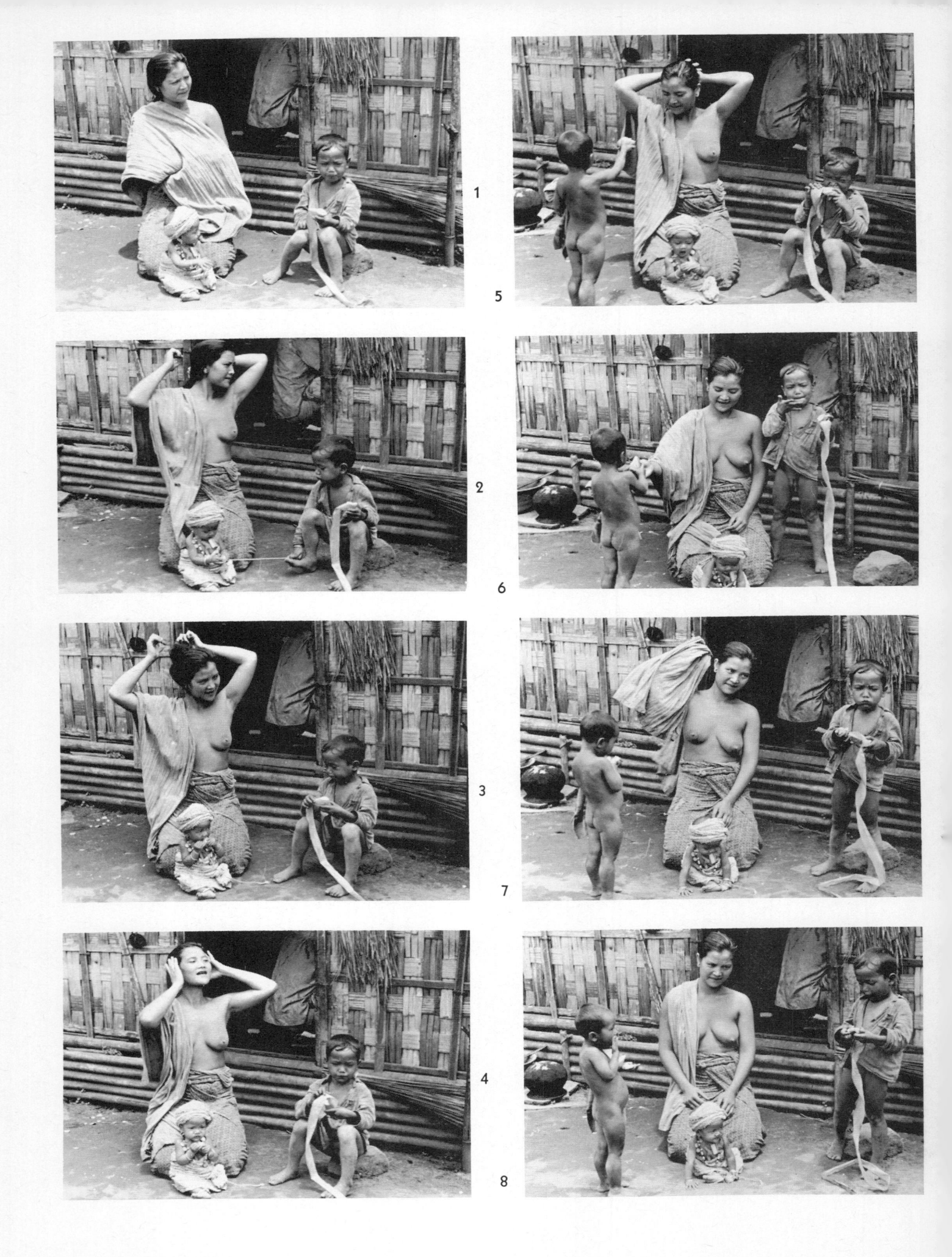

2

3

4

5

6

7

8

Plate 48

THE MOTHER: NARCISSISM

We have noted the Balinese habit of feeling and titivating the skin with the tips of the fingers (Pls. 24 and 25), their habit of introversion (Pl. 39), their fantasy of the body as made of separable parts (Pl. 20) and their avoidance of inter-personal climax (Pl. 47). These themes together make up a personality which we can describe as "narcissistic." This quality in the mother is apparently frustrating to the child who has not yet learned the drawbacks of responsiveness and the satisfactions of Balinese gaiety.

1 to 8. About one minute of maternal behavior, in which the mother does her hair and adjusts her sling (*anteng*). This piece of cloth is carried by almost all women and girls regardless of whether they have babies; it is used as a sling in which the baby is supported on the hip (cf. Pl. 79) or as a ceremonial sash (cf. Pl. 82, fig. 6). The witch's cloth is also called "*anteng*" (cf. Pl. 56, fig. 3).

In fig. 1, Men Singin kneels with her sling across her breast and covering her hands, while she looks over toward the entrance of the houseyard. I Karsa, her son, sits rather sulky on a stone on the right. He is slowly unwrapping the long strip of palm leaf in which a cake (*bantal*) of rice paste is wrapped. Her baby daughter (age about 8 months) sits on the ground at the mother's knees. This baby has a string made from the Dragon's hair tied to her right wrist (cf. Pl. 67, fig. 9).

In fig. 2, Men Singin takes her hands out from under the sling and starts to adjust her hair. I Karsa gives an experimental tug at the string on the baby's wrist.

In figs. 3 and 4, the mother continues doing her hair, and I Karsa goes on unwrapping his cake.

In fig. 5, a small girl (a first cousin of the other two children) comes in with food in her hand. She holds the food up to Men Singin who smiles at it while still doing her hair. I Karsa takes a large bite out of his cake.

In fig. 6, Men Singin has dropped her left hand to her lap, and refuses the food, pushing it back toward the little cousin with her right hand. I Karsa has stood up and moved over toward his mother. He is finishing his mouthful of cake and has apparently just licked some crumbs off his fingers. The sulky expression has disappeared from his face.

In fig. 7, Men Singin adjusts her sling which had fallen down toward her wrist; she swings it up onto her shoulder, while looking over toward I Karsa. He has moved away from his mother and the sulky expression has returned to his face. In fig. 6, he was standing erect and happy, with his legs straight and his feet well planted, but in fig. 7 he has begun to lose this bold stance, and his feet are beginning to turn inward.

In fig. 8 (about 20 seconds later than fig. 7), Men Singin's face has lost its bright expression and she sits with her hands limp in her lap, and her eyes fixed vacantly on I Karsa. His attention has returned to his cake, his facial expression is sulky and his feet are turned inward as they were in fig. 1. The little cousin has started to eat.

Men Singin; I Karsa, her son; I Djantoek, her daughter, aged about 8 months; I Marti, Men Singin's husband's brother's daughter, aged 929 days.

Bajoeng Gede. Feb. 12, 1939.   36 G 7, 8, 9, 12, 16, 30, 32, 34.

Plate 49

BORROWED BABIES

One of the commonest ways in which a mother stimulates her child to active response is by borrowing and nursing some other woman's baby in the presence of her own. This is a game which is played constantly and which is often concluded by giving the borrowed baby to the jealous child to hold for a few seconds.

1. A mother nurses her own baby while holding a borrowed baby on her knees. The mother is watching her own baby who is responding to the presence of the intruder by more passionate sucking. The girl on the extreme left is the elder sister who was acting as child nurse to the borrowed baby, and from whom the mother borrowed it. She is inattentive to the scene.

I Karmi, elder sister of I Kenjoen; Men Oera; I Karba, Men Oera's son, aged 240 days; I Kenjoen, I Karba's cousin, aged 138 days.

Bajoeng Gede. Aug. 6, 1936.   2 I 38.

2. An adoptive mother borrows a baby. Men Leket, the woman on the right, has adopted the boy, I Leket. In this picture, Men Leket has borrowed the youngest of the children belonging to her sister (who sits on the left) and plays with it, while I Leket stands on the ground at her knees. The aunt watches I Leket's reaction, but he is beginning to learn unresponsiveness and stands with his face vacant, exploring his mouth with his finger.

The two little girls sit with vacant faces and with their hands covered inside their slings (*anteng*). The younger child has even covered her mouth. Men Leket is looking at these two children.

Men Njawi; I Njawi; I Njawa; Men Leket holding I Koewat, aged 122 days; I Leket standing.

Bajoeng Gede. July 13, 1937.   12 M 6.

3 and 4. A woman with two of her sister's children. Men Leket (the woman on the right in fig. 2) standing with I Njawi and I Njawa, the two daughters of her sister. The sister is sitting on the right, outside the picture with her new baby, I Koewat.

In fig. 3, Men Leket gazes straight ahead, holding I Njawa by the elbows. I Njawa holds onto Men Leket's sash and bends over backward while her eyes are directed to the extreme right, looking at her mother and the new baby. I Njawi hides behind Men Leket (cf. Pl. 73, fig. 5).

In fig. 4, Men Leket louses I Njawi (cf. Pl. 73, fig. 4), while I Njawa has turned her head to look directly at her mother and the new baby.

It is probable that the intensity of feeling shown by the two girls in figs. 2, 3, and 4, is enhanced by the fact that the occasion was the celebration of the baby's 105-day birthday.

Men Leket; with her nieces, I Njawa (with white blanket) and I Njawi.

Bajoeng Gede. July 13, 1937.   12 N 19, 21.

5. A statue of the Witch (*Rangda*) with a baby. She holds the baby by one arm and one leg, while its head hangs down to the right. Compare this suspension of the baby in the arms of a hostile mother symbol with the postures in figs. 3 and 4 and with Pl. 50, fig. 9. It seems that the fantasy is not merely a nightmare, but that the children also play out the postural roles which equate the mother with the Witch.

Belabatoeh. May 28, 1936.   1 L 14.

6, 7, and 8. A temper tantrum stimulated by borrowing a baby. Men Singin has her nephew on her hip and she laughs gaily as her own son comes up crying and strikes at her. Men Singin avoids his blows by casually holding him off (fig. 6). This behavior is typical of Balinese mothers. The child's temper tantrums evoke no relevant response from the mother, so that the climaxes of anger are frustrated like those of affection.

In fig. 8, Men Singin has picked her son up in her arms while he writhes and kicks, now refusing the attention for which he was fighting. Men Singin laughs at him, and he covers his eyes in withdrawal (cf. Pl. 67).

Men Singin carrying her nephew, I Karba, aged 207 days, on her hip; I Karsa, her son, in temper tantrum.

Bajoeng Gede. Aug. 30, 1936.   2 I 34, 35, 36.

1
2
3
4
5
6
7
8

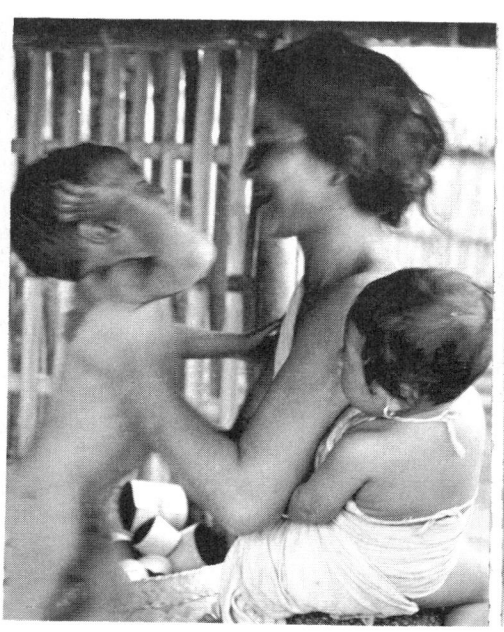

1

2

3

4

5

6

9 8 7

Plate 50

SULKS

Many young Balinese children develop one or the other of two patterns of reaction to their repeated frustration in inter-personal sequences. Some children learn to sulk, while others have temper tantrums. Both sexes show both patterns, but it seems that the more directly assertive children of both sexes develop tantrum behavior while the more passive of both sexes develop sulks. Both these patterns normally disappear in early latency, but they persist in a few children whose development has been delayed.

Adults usually do not respond to either the sulks or the tantrums of their children, but a younger child will often attempt to stimulate a sulking older child.

1. A small boy sulking, alone in the houseyard. This photograph was taken immediately after the temper tantrum of this boy's elder sister (Pl. 65, figs. 1 and 2), and the withdrawal into sulks was probably his response to her tantrum.
I Gata.
Bajoeng Gede. July 31, 1936. 2 C 36.

2. A small boy sulks and a baby tries to stimulate him. I Karba, the sulking child in this photograph, had been the center of attention while his mother bathed him and flirted with him. Later I Sami, the baby in this picture, was bathed and attention focussed on him. I Karba played at bathing I Sami for a little while, and imitated the sharpness of his mother's gestures (motion-picture record). After this, he went off and lay down alone. I Sami made two or three attempts to stimulate him but he only lifted his head for a moment and stared at the interruption.
I Karba, aged 550 days, sulking; I Sami, aged 256 days.
Bajoeng Gede. April 30, 1937. 7 P 36.

3. A witch's granddaughter sulks. This girl's mother's mother was suspected of being an hereditary witch, and witchcraft is supposed to be passed down in the female line. As a result, the mother of this girl was already avoided by other people in the village and the children were to some extent ostracized. They went to theatrical shows and ceremonies, but usually stayed together and did not mix with the other children. This girl in particular was very suspicious, and though she often came to our house, she was always afraid we would swindle her in some way, e.g., by not giving her some present which had been promised.

She is already rather old to be indulging in sulks, and her delayed adjustment to latency is probably a result of her not being accepted into the children's group.
I Rimpen sulking; I Mesom, her younger sister, trying to stimulate her.
Bajoeng Gede. Aug. 19, 1937. 14 D 37.

4 to 9. A boy sulks and then shows regressive behavior. This sulking was apparently precipitated by the amount of attention given to I Karba, the younger child in figs. 4 and 5. The older boy, I Gelis, went and leaned over a wooden rice mortar for about five minutes, moving his legs from time to time, but remaining with his head down on the mortar. I Karba went to him and attempted to rouse him (fig. 4) but went away again (fig. 5).

In fig. 6, I Gelis starts to rouse himself from his sulk and looks up toward the photographer.

In fig. 7, he walks over to two older boys who are leaning against the fence of the houseyard.

In fig. 8, he attracts the attention of one of the boys who is leaning over the fence from the other side.

In fig. 9, about 20 seconds later, he stands with his arms up and his hands held by the older boy toward whom his back is turned. This posture is probably regressive and related to the postures shown in Pl. 49, figs. 3, 4, and 5.
I Gelis sulking; I Karba trying to rouse him; I Misi (male) on far side of fence; I Moedri with his back to the camera in fig. 8.
Bajoeng Gede. Oct. 9, 1937. 16 X 8, 12, 14, 15, 16, 25.

Plate 51

BOYS' TANTRUMS

Many children develop tantrum behavior instead of sulks, and we may regard these tantrums as a last attempt on the part of the child to introduce some sort of climax into the sequences of everyday inter-personal behavior. Tantrum behavior disappears with the successful change into latency, and in later life, behavior sequences with a clear climax structure occur only in very special contexts such as trance (cf. Pls. 55 to 58, and Pl. 46, fig. 7).

1 to 4. A small boy in a state intermediate between tantrum and sulks. At this stage it was not clear whether I Karsa would show tantrum or sulky behavior, and in this sequence he first struggles against his mother in figs. 1 and 2, and then goes limp in fig. 3. His mother's response is unconcerned, especially in fig. 3. In fig. 4, she picks him up and (probably laughing) covers his head in her sling (cf. Pl. 60; Pl. 67, fig. 2; Pl. 52, fig. 4).

Men Singin with her son, I Karsa.

Bajoeng Gede. Dec. 14, 1936.   3 U 2, 3, 4, 7.

5 to 8. The same small boy, five and a half months later, in typical tantrum behavior. His mother (not visible in the photographs) is sitting nearby at her little table selling food and paying no attention to I Karsa's behavior. The tantrum started when I Made Kaler (our secretary) refused to give I Karsa a pencil, but this was perhaps only a final precipitating cause, and it is probably more significant that he has chosen for his tantrum a spot on the ground at the feet of his uncle who is playing with his baby daughter.

In fig. 5, Karsa has his head down on his arms and is kicking his heels in the air with a scissors motion. I Marti, his baby cousin, reaches forward with her foot toward his head (cf. Pl. 12, fig. 5; Pl. 61, fig. 6). Her father watches her and helps her to balance in this position.

In fig. 6, I Karsa is quiet for a moment and looks up at his uncle, but his uncle is looking at the camera, and the baby cousin is looking away.

In fig. 7, I Karsa turns away from his uncle and again starts to cry with his legs widespread. The baby cousin looks at him but withdraws toward her father, who attends to her and not to I Karsa.

In fig. 8, I Karsa rolls over on his back in a paroxysm of crying, with his head and legs bent back so that his body is arched backward in this climax. His cousin has turned toward her father who attends to her and not to I Karsa.

After this tantrum, another pencil was offered to I Karsa, but he refused it. This final refusal of the thing which was desired before the tantrum is common in Bali and the individual who behaves in this way is described as *kimbul*.

I Karsa in tantrum; Nang Marti with his daughter I Marti, aged 406 days.

Bajoeng Gede. May 25, 1937.   9 H 5, 17, 18, 23.

9, 10, and 11. A boy crying. This boy has passed the age at which tantrum behavior is common, but he is the youngest child in a family of six children and has been adopted by two old people (Djero Baoe Tekek and his wife). His adoptive mother, who is childless, sentimental, and whining, treats him in a way very unusual in Bali, fussing over him and indulging him.

In the present instance, he is crying over a small hurt to his foot, and in fig. 9, two other children come up and look at it.

In fig. 10, he has stopped crying and gazes at the foot.

In fig. 11, he again starts to cry; probably his behavior is due to intermittent rage rather than to pain.

I Nandoer.

Bajoeng Gede. June 4, 1937.   11 D 18, 19, 20.

1 2 3 4

5

6

7

8

9

10 11

1
2
3
4
5
6
7
8

Plate 52

MEN SINGIN AND HER SON I

The sequence of behavior shown on this and the next plate lasted for about six minutes and occurred at a wedding. Men Singin and her son were among the numerous relatives and neighbors who gathered in the houseyard of the bridegroom's parents.

At the beginning of the sequence, mother and son are flirting happily, until she picks up another baby. Her son, I Karsa, shows jealousy when she suckles this other baby, and as the sequence continues, his behavior alternates between impotent misery and rage. His mother remains for a long time completely unresponsive to him and even starts again to flirt with the other baby. At the end of the sequence, Men Singin picks him up while he struggles against her, and his struggling subsides when she gets a plate of food.

1 to 8. In fig. 1, Men Singin and her son, I Karsa, are on the left of the picture and he is flirting with her, leaning against her knees. His elbows are in her lap and his face close to hers.

In fig. 2, about 90 seconds later (after the camera had been reloaded), Men Singin stoops forward to pick up her niece, I Meres, who has tumbled forward on the ground. At this moment I Karsa is behind Men Singin reaching forward into her lap. His facial expression is still happy.

In fig. 3, Men Singin has picked up I Meres, who is crying and holding Men Singin's breast. I Karsa apparently starts a sort of game, reaching forward stealthily under his mother's arm and toward her breast.

In fig. 4, Men Singin has lifted I Meres and pushed her sling aside preparatory to giving her the breast. I Karsa still continues his game but is now frustrated by I Meres' leg and Men Singin's arm.

In fig. 5, Men Singin suckles I Meres, and her son begins to show jealousy. He has drawn away from his mother, and his facial expression, with the lips turned outward, shows that he is on the verge of crying. His right hand is raised to strike at his mother. On this occasion he struck at her several times, but the posture in which the camera has caught him is common in Balinese children, and they sometimes remain in this position for several seconds, not striking but standing impotent.

In fig. 6, Men Singin has lost interest in the baby, I Meres, and she sits unresponsive to I Karsa. She gazes vacantly at the camera while her mouth is blocked with betel or tobacco. She remains in this state until after fig. 2 on the next plate, only altering the direction of her gaze and the position of her hands.

I Karsa, in fig. 6, stands awkwardly behind his mother, sulky and inactive.

In figs. 7 and 8, I Karsa moves around till he is almost on his mother's line of vision and there he postures with his hands raised to his head. These movements may be abortive preparations to strike his mother or they may be gestures toward shutting off his awareness of her (cf. figs. 3 and 4 on the next plate). Men Singin has given the baby back to its child nurse, but her vacant stare continues unbroken.

Men Singin; I Karsa, her son; I Meres, her niece, about a year and a half old.

Bajoeng Gede. March 1, 1937.   4 Z 25; 5 A 2, 4, 5, 7, 8, 9, 10.

Plate 53

MEN SINGIN AND HER SON II

The photographs on this plate conclude the behavior sequence begun on Pl. 52.

1 to 8. In figs. 1 and 2, Men Singin remains vacant and aloof, with her mouth full of betel, while her son postures in impotent anger. His posture in fig. 2 is almost a mirror image of that in fig. 1; he has turned but still retains the same stance with legs slightly bent and trunk thrust forward. His head is still at the same awkward angle, though now he looks toward his mother over his right shoulder instead of his left.

In fig. 3, Men Singin has moved over to the wall and is now looking at I Karsa — her first response to him since she picked up the other baby in fig. 2 of the previous plate. Even now she holds her sling cloth over her mouth, thus reducing the value of her response. I Karsa, on the other hand, has ceased to look at her and stands with his feet turned inward and his hands clasped over his head. This position of the hands is probably a form of withdrawal (cf. Pl. 41, figs. 7, 8, and 9).

In fig. 4, I Karsa has turned toward his mother, covering his ears with his hands. She, on the other hand, has now turned again toward the baby, I Meres, toward whom she extends her hands in a gesture of invitation.

In fig. 5, the little girl carrying I Meres has gone over to Men Singin and now stands between her and her son. I Karsa still has his hands over his ears, but is now looking out through the gate.

In fig. 6, Men Singin again looks at I Karsa, but she reduces her response by holding her hand up in front of her face.

In fig. 7 (after an interval during which five photographs of another group were taken), Men Singin has picked up I Karsa and fixed him in her sling. He resists and pushes her face away from him.

In fig. 8, Men Singin holds a plate of food passed to her by one of the women in the group in the lower right-hand corner of the picture, and I Karsa has become quiet, looking at the food.

Men Singin; I Karsa, her son; I Meres, the baby in figs. 4, 5, and 6; I Ngembon carrying I Meres.

Bajoeng Gede. March 1, 1937.   5 A 11, 12, 16, 18, 19, 20, 26, 28.

1

2

3

4

5

6

7

8

1 2 3 4

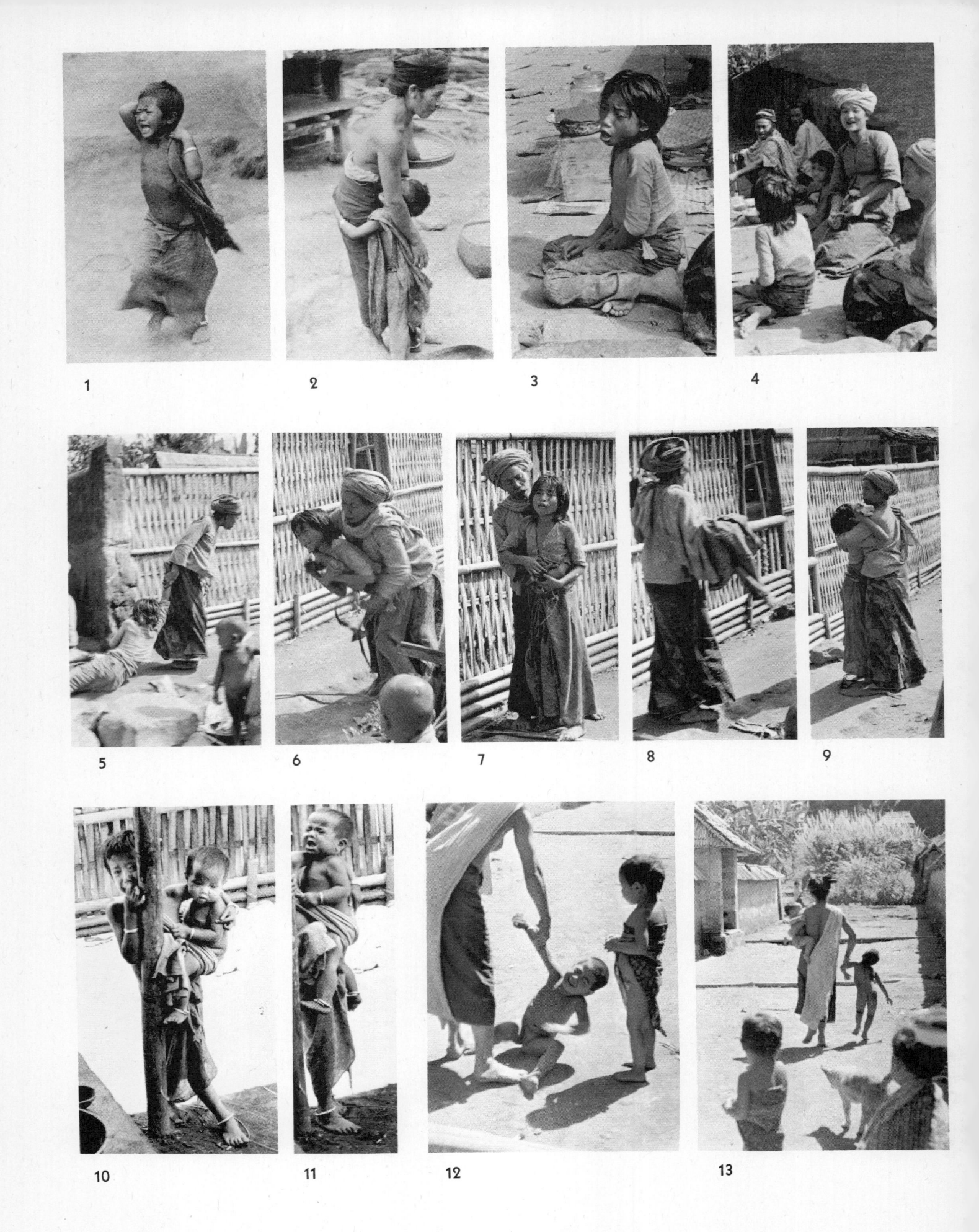

5 6 7 8 9

10 11 12 13

Plate 54

GIRLS' TANTRUMS

We did not detect any positive differences between the tantrum postures of the two sexes, although such differences are to be expected from the difference which occurs in the postures of climactic trance (cf. Pl. 56, fig. 8). It is perhaps significant that we have no clear case of a girl in tantrum bending her trunk backward (cf. Pl. 57, fig. 8).

1 and 2. A tantrum in the road.

In fig. 1, the girl is shown screaming, with her hands raised to her head in a posture closely related to those of the boy in Pl. 53.

In fig. 2, she has run to her mother and clings to her mother's legs. The mother's response to this is negligent and relaxed. She leans forward with her arm scarcely in contact with the girl's sling cloth. This picture, in 1936, gave us the first clue for the formulation that the Balinese mother avoids adequate response to the climaxes of her child's anger and love.

Men Karma and her daughter, I Gati.

Bajoeng Gede. July 31, 1936.   2 C 34, 35.

3 to 9. A great-aunt responds to anger with anger. The normal behavior of adults, as stated above, is avoidance of response to the child's tantrums. Occasionally, however, a woman will lose her temper with her child in a sudden explosive manner. In such cases, the conventional act of the adult is to put chewed betel or mashed red pepper on the child's eyes. M. M. saw Men Singin do this to her son after he had been whining for a long time. The mother showed no preliminary anger, but with a single quick movement took betel from her mouth and struck with it at the child's eyes. We believe that the explosive suddenness of this incident is typical of the rare occasions on which Balinese mothers use the red pepper sanction.

A similar suddenness is characteristic of the excessively rare occasions on which adults resort to physical violence. Only two such cases occurred among the five hundred people of Bajoeng Gede in the two years that we were there. Both of these were sudden outbursts over the ownership of knives and one of the participants in one of these outbursts had once before lost his temper in the same sudden way over the ownership of another knife.

The sequence of photographs shown here is abnormal for Bali, in that the woman was unusually bad-tempered, the red pepper was suggested and provided by a bystander, and further, the girl was exceptionally high-spirited and maladjusted as a result of her father's deviance and his remarriage.

M. M.'s record states that the whole incident took about 8 minutes. I Karni came running up the road yelling and was stopped by the small group which was gathered around Men Singin selling food on the side of the road. Men Endeh, Karni's great-aunt, came up in a rage, chasing I Karni to make her go and work on offerings for a big ceremony at Men Endeh's house. She took hold of Karni's hands and Karni resisted, screaming and writhing. Men Endeh let out a long stream of invective, scolding her and talking to the audience who gave Karni no sympathy.

While Men Endeh scolded, Karni sat on the ground (figs. 3 and 4).

Karni took a piece of banana leaf and held it tight across her upper lip and then dropped it.

Men Endeh, who is sitting on the extreme right in fig. 4, got up and started to drag Karni down the road (fig. 5).

At this point, Men Singin (who is seen laughing in fig. 4) smilingly offered a plate of red pepper paste to Men Endeh, who took some and rubbed it in Karni's face while she struggled (this must have occurred just before fig. 6).

There ensued a pause, and Karni changed the tempo of her crying (fig. 7).

Men Endeh again tried to drag Karni, and then tried to carry her (fig. 8), but put her down after a few steps (fig. 9).

Men Singin offered more red pepper, but Men Endeh and Karni were now some way down the road. Finally Karni walked off with Men Endeh.

Men Endeh; I Karni (half adopted by her grandmother, who is Men Endeh's sister); Men Singin (unrelated).

Bajoeng Gede. May 25, 1937.   9 I 8; 15; 20; 24; 29; 31, 32.

10 and 11. A child nurse in a temper. In fig. 10, the baby pays no apparent attention, but in fig. 11, she has started to cry.

I Gati carrying her younger sister, I Kenjoen.

Bajoeng Gede. Jan. 19, 1937.   4 F 21, 22.

12 and 13. A mother drags her daughter home. She is carrying her youngest baby on her left hip, and in fig. 12, she stoops down to pick up the next older girl, who is having a tantrum.

In fig. 13, she walks off, holding the child by the elbow.

Men Doeroes; I Karti, her daughter; I Karta, her baby boy.

Bajoeng Gede. May 24, 1937.   9 E 16, 17.

Plate 55

TRANCE: THE SETTING

This and the following three plates deal with successive phases in the performance of the Witch play (*Tjalonarang*). This drama throws more light on Balinese character structure than any other, and it differs from the others in that the plot centers around two sacred and symbolic figures, the Witch (*Rangda*, literally "widow," also called *Tjalonarang*) and the Dragon (*Barong*).

This drama is examined here, at the end of the series of plates dealing with the mother-child relationship, because the relationship between the Witch and the men who attack her resembles in many ways the relationship between mother and child. (The resemblance between the Witch-Dragon relationship and the father-mother relationship is illustrated on Pl. 62, and the role of the Dragon is compared with that of the father on Pls. 66 and 67.)

The photographs are arranged in plot order, but to show all the necessary phases of the plot, it has been necessary to use photographs taken on different occasions and in various villages. The performances were ordered and paid for by us and were given in the daytime. Balinese theatricals are usually on a commercial basis, somebody (an individual or a temple club) paying the dance club to give its performance — partly as an offering to the gods and partly to embellish some religious festival (cf. *rame*, Pl. 5). Large performances of this sort are usually, but not always, given at night.

1. The Dragon dances. This is the formal opening of the drama. In some villages it is omitted; in others the Dragon circles the dancing ground three times to mark off a boundary which no witch (*lejak*) can cross. He is a mixture of fierceness and comical puppyish behavior, and his completely flexible body enables him to turn around upon himself.
Pagoetan. Feb. 8, 1939. 35 G 9.

2. The Witch's disciples (*sisia*). The plot begins with one to three hours of dancing by these little girls. In the village of Pagoetan they dance in pairs, each pair dancing for about 30 minutes. When one pair of girls have finished their dance, they sit on a mat at the edge of the stage, and their place is taken by another pair. This continues until all the disciples are sitting and waiting for the Witch.
Their dance closely resembles that of *legong* or *sangiang dedari* (Pl. 19).
Pagoetan. Feb. 8, 1939. 35 H 7.

3. The Witch instructs her disciples. The part of the Witch is played by a man who hobbles across the stage aided by a staff. At this stage of the drama, the Witch is "unripe" (*matah*) — not yet transformed into her supernatural form — and she therefore wears no mask.
The Witch is angry with the king of the country. The reasons for her anger vary with different versions of the myth. The king's son has refused to marry her daughter; the king has married her and cast her off because of her witchcraft; or she took to witchcraft because she was cast off. The Witch approaches her disciples and, in archaic religious language, gives them instructions. They are to transform themselves into little witches and cause plague and pestilence in the land. They answer her speech in long-drawn-out falsetto.
Pagoetan. Dec. 16, 1937. 20 F 12.

(After this, there are several scenes of pestilence, birth and death. These macabre subjects are treated with uproarious clowning, shown in Pls. 14 and 88, and end with the exposure of the minor witches who have been playing pranks on the people smitten with pestilence.)

4. The Witch appears, transformed. She is now wearing a mask with enormous teeth and pendent tongue. She stands in the temple gate and is attacked by the king. In the photograph she lies on the temple steps, momentarily "killed" by the king. She covers her face with her white cloth.
Pagoetan. Feb. 8, 1939. 35 J 13.

5. The Witch dances. She rises from the steps and dances solo. She calls out to other witches to come from the east and from the west, and the north and the south, and she laughs and roars as she waves her cloth.
Pagoetan. Dec. 16, 1937. 20 H 17.

6. The Witch addresses her disciples. Both she and they are now in supernatural form and again she lectures them as she did in fig. 3. (This episode is omitted in most performances, and we saw it only in Pagoetan, perhaps because only the Pagoetan dance club had enough masks to stage this scene.)
Pagoetan. Dec. 16, 1937. 20 H 26.

1

2

3

4

5

6

1

2

3

4

5

6

7

8

Plate 56

TRANCE: ATTACK ON THE WITCH

In some versions of the myth, the king is transformed into the Dragon; in any case, with or without this rationalization, the next scene in the drama is a conflict between the Witch and the Dragon (cf. Pl. 62, fig. 4). This conflict is a brief scolding match conducted in archaic language. Neither side is victorious, but the Dragon withdraws and his place is taken by his "followers," young men armed with krisses.

1. The Dragon's followers ready to attack the Witch. They squat in ballet formation in two lines, holding their krisses ready to rush forward. The Witch is behind the camera at the other end of the dancing ground.
Pagoetan. Dec. 16, 1937.   20 I 4.

2. The Dragon's followers at the end of their rush. As they reach the Witch, she turns upon them and they subside backward into half-squatting postures, cringing backward before her. She laughs and roars and waves her cloth, and then runs between the two lines and down to the other end of the dancing ground.
Pagoetan. Dec. 16, 1937.   20 I 10.

3. Two of the Dragon's followers lie on the ground, powerless against the Witch's white cloth (*anteng*, literally, the "sling" in which a mother carries her baby). The Witch stands threatening them with the cloth.
Pagoetan. Feb. 8, 1939.   35 J 25.

4. Two more of the Dragon's followers attack the Witch. After a series of massed rushes against the Witch, the young men with krisses come running up to her two at a time, and attempt to stab her. She does not resist, but reels with her arms limp at her sides, like a rag doll (or like a Balinese mother refusing to respond to her son's tantrum). They are powerless against her and collapse on the ground, either limp or rigid, but unconscious.
Pagoetan. Dec. 16, 1937.   20 I 19.

5. The collapse of two of the Dragon's followers. The Witch is reeling off and will shortly be attacked by another pair of young men, while the two who have just attempted to stab her lie on the ground. Other members of the dance club come to pick them up. The man on the extreme right gingerly takes hold of the unconscious man's kris.
(The black mark over the foot of the unconscious man is a blemish in the photograph.)
Pagoetan. Dec. 16, 1937.   20 I 13.

6. Lifting the man shown in fig. 5. He is apparently limp, but his left arm retains its position against the pull of gravity.
Pagoetan. Dec. 16, 1937.   20 I 15.

7. The unconscious men laid out neatly in two rows. They lie, still holding their krisses, some of them giving spasmodic twitches. A priest walks between the two rows, sprinkling holy water over them, and in the background the Dragon is visible. He is clapping his jaws over the end man on the left, and as he does this, the man rises to his feet. In this way all the men are revived into activity and they run off stage, still unconscious, but in some sort of somnambulistic state.
Pagoetan. Dec. 16, 1937.   20 I 23.

8. Women enter with krisses. We had seen women dance with krisses at temple festivals at night and had observed that their dancing, though nominally the same as that of the men, was fundamentally different (cf. Pl. 57). We wanted to get a motion-picture record of the women's dancing, and therefore suggested to the dancing club of Pagoetan, in 1937, that they should include in their performance some women with krisses. This they did without any hesitation, and by 1939 the women were an established part of the performance.
The women come on stage in two lines as here shown, and after several ballet maneuvers they go into trance and turn their krisses on themselves without any attack on the Witch or complete preliminary collapse.
Pagoetan. Feb. 8, 1939.   35 J last.

Plate 57

TRANCE: ATTACK ON THE SELF

The men return, still in a somnambulistic state, and after a few simple ballet maneuvers, they strut about singly. Suddenly, first one and then another gives a loud yell and turns upon his own chest the kris with which he attacked the Witch. This in-turned aggression is accompanied by a roaring noise and posturing in which the body is suddenly and repeatedly bent backward with a rising movement of the arms (fig. 3). In this action, the accent is on the upward motion of the arms and on the forward thrust of the pubis. After a few seconds of this activity, the man will start strutting again, tense and silent, only to revert, with another loud yell, to his spasmodic posturing. Some men actually fall backward onto the ground with an extreme backward bending of the trunk, and lie on the ground writhing in some sort of orgasmic climax.

Meanwhile the women have also turned their krisses on themselves. But their behavior differs from that of the men in that they accent the *downward* bending movement, while the upward and backward movement, which is accented by the men, is, in the women, only a recovery or preparation for another downward movement of the hands, a forward bending of the trunk and a withdrawal of the pubis. This difference and the writhing behavior of the men indicate a close relation between this trance behavior and sexual climax. We have noted that the tendency of children to look for climaxes of affection and anger is frustrated and probably in some sense repressed. It is probable, therefore, that this conventionalized trance behavior is a return to patterns of behavior which have been extinguished or inhibited.

1. Native painting showing the stages of going into trance. The man standing to the left of the Witch is attacking her with a kris in his hand; the man on the ground has presumably just fallen from the attempt to stab her; and the man on the right holds two krisses and has turned them on himself. The Witch herself is apparently preening her hair with her right hand while she waves her cloth with the left.
Painting by I Goesti Njoman Lempad of Oeboed.
Dated by the artist "March, 1938."

2. Portrait of a man *before* the attack on the Witch. He is taking part in the preliminary ballet and holds a kris raised high in his right hand. Note that the pursing of the lips at this stage has an extrovert or aggressive appearance sharply contrasting with the apparent introversion on the faces of men actually in trance.
Dendjalan. May 26, 1936.   1 J 22.

3, 4, 5, and 6. A series of postures of a man in trance.
Fig. 3 shows the high point of his krissing movement. His back is bent far back; the point of his kris is against his chest; and he holds the handle of the kris with both hands high above his head. In dancing in this way with the kris, there is, so far as we could observe, very little flexor tension in the biceps. Instead there is a strong pronator tension in both arms, which holds the point of the kris against the man's chest. If the man's body were not there, the point of the kris would move downward in an arc with the center in the man's hands. In the background of fig. 3 is a second man jumping in the air and yelling at the moment of transition from strutting to krissing himself.

In figs. 4 and 5, the man struts with his kris held against his upper arm by the cramped supination of the forearm.
In fig. 6, he is jumping. This man performed a series of consecutive jumps in this posture.
Dendjalan. Nov. 23, 1936.   3 I 14, 18, 25, 28.

7. A man krissing himself. In contrast with the high degree of tension shown in fig. 3, a number of men kris themselves in this very "offhand" manner, using only one hand. Some of the obscene carvings show postures very closely related to this. In the background, the priest, who was looking after the men in trance and giving them holy water, has himself gone into trance and is being supported by two club members who are not in trance.
Dendjalan. May 26, 1936.   1 K 2.

8. A small boy in a tantrum. This photograph illustrates the relationship between krissing behavior and tantrum behavior. In both we find the extreme backward bending of the body and the climax.
Men Goenoeng holding I Raoeh.
Bajoeng Gede. Oct. 12, 1937.   17 N 37.

9. Men krissing themselves on the ground. This photograph was taken at a religious ceremony (the so-called "*perang dewa*" or "fight of the gods"), but the trance behavior is nominally the same as in the Witch drama. It appears that in this village, the conventional climax position on the ground is lying on the belly, instead of on the back as in Pagoetan (cf. Pl. 51).
Paksebali. Oct. 17, 1936.   2 Y 13.

1

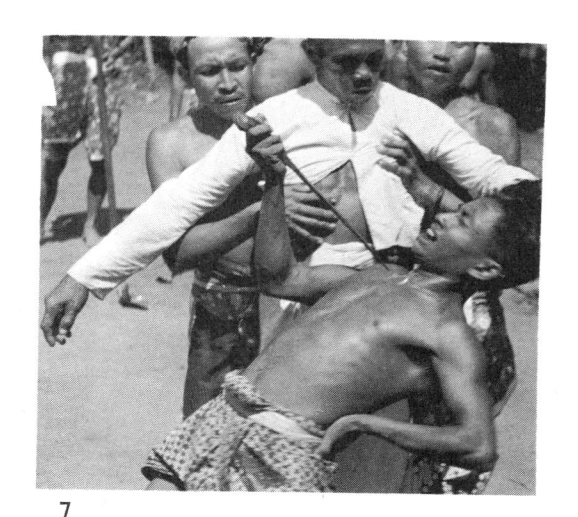

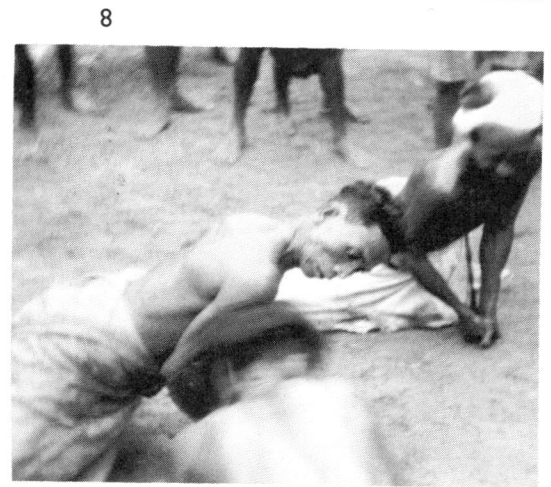

2

3

4

5

6

7

8

9

1

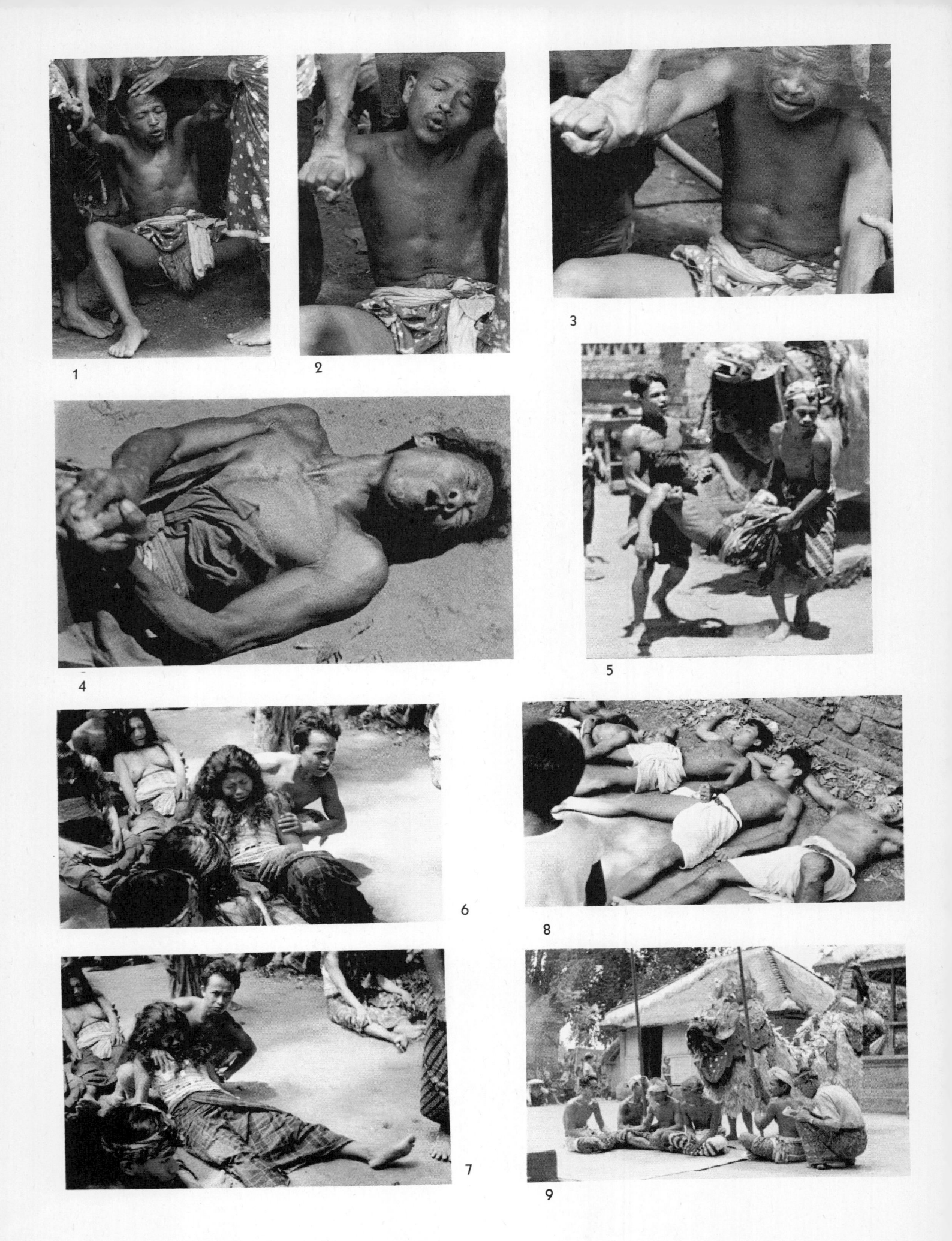

2

3

4

5

6

8

7

9

Plate 58
TRANCE: ECSTASY AND RECOVERY

The climax of trance is a mixture of agony and ecstasy similar to that which we have already noted in the less dramatic trance of the village priestess (Pl. 8). Either just before or during this stage, the men are disarmed by other club members who watch to see that they shall not hurt themselves; and when disarmed, they are carried off either limp or rigid into the temple to be brought back to normality. They are laid out in the temple, and are given holy water and smoked with incense. Some individuals recover much more rapidly than others, and the rate of recovery depends to some extent upon status. The more important individuals who are supposedly possessed by named deities, instead of by the nameless minor demons (*boeta, kala*) who possess the majority of the young men, resist recovery until special offerings (*segeh,* cf. Pl. 33, fig. 4) have been made to their deities.

A few of these special individuals gather for this ceremony, which is conducted by the priest of the club, while the Dragon stands over them. The Dragon thus appears in the final scene, as he did in the opening of the performance.

1, 2, and 3. Agony and ecstasy in a man without a kris. This man went into trance too soon, while still sitting with the other young men who were going to act as "followers of the Dragon." The theatrical part of the performance was not yet over, and the young men were in the audience. It seems that the appearance of the Witch on the stage was sufficient stimulus to send this man into trance.

The others held him, as is shown in these photographs, until the proper time came for all to kris themselves; then he was given a kris and performed with the others.

These photographs show two quite distinct facial expressions: one, which the Balinese call "*boedjoeh,*" in which the lips are pushed forward into an O shape, while the man roars; and another in which the mouth is elongated and the forehead wrinkled, while the man sobs.

Dendjalan. May 26, 1936. 1 J 11, 12, 14.

4. A man lying on the ground, roaring and krissing himself. This photograph shows that it is the flat and not the point of the kris which presses on the skin.

Dendjalan. May 26, 1936. 1 J last.

5. A man being carried into the temple. His arms hang limp. Some men are rigid at this stage.

Dendjalan. Nov. 23, 1936. 3 Ha 29.

6 and 7. Inside the temple, a woman waiting to be brought out of trance. In fig. 6, she sits sobbing; in fig. 7, she has collapsed backward and extended her legs until she is approximately in the posture of the young men in fig. 8.

Pagoetan. Dec. 16, 1937. 20 J 2, 3.

8. Young men in trance laid out in the temple to wait for holy water.

Pagoetan. Dec. 16, 1937. 20 I 42.

9. The final ceremony in front of the Dragon. The man in striped trousers has danced as the front legs of the Dragon. He had gone into trance and was replaced in the Dragon.

Pagoetan. Dec. 16, 1937. 20 J 13.

Plate 59

COURTSHIP DANCERS

In any culture, the behavior patterns which the man adopts toward the opposite sex in courtship are necessarily related to those which he learned as a child to adopt toward his mother; the girl's must be related to her experience of her earlier relationship to her father. Further, there must be some mutual relevance between the boy's and the girl's behavior patterns if courtship is to progress. Unfortunately it is not possible to demonstrate these relationships with photographs of actual courtship, but it is possible to demonstrate them with pictures of those dances which are a stylized representation of courtship.

The *djoget* dancer is a preadolescent girl who is carefully trained in this dance. She is one of the members of an itinerant dance club who go from village to village carrying their musical instruments and giving performances wherever they are paid to do so.

The performance begins with the *djoget* dancing alone, but soon a man joins her and they dance to each other. The man may be either a regular partner of hers who accompanies the club, or he may be a member of the audience whom she has never met before, and a part of her virtuosity consists in fitting her dancing to his figures. She must never relax her polished style, and she must try to avoid giggling when, as often happens, her partner decides to skit his courtship role.

1. A *djoget* dancer dances with her brother. This girl had been trained by him, and together they gave the best performances of this sort that we witnessed. This photograph shows them at a moment when their bodies are facing each other, while their faces are turned away. Face-to-face moments are brief, and the dance may be said to consist very largely of the *interruption* of courtship. The partners continually break away from each other, pirouetting off in opposite directions, until they arrive at another momentary face-to-face encounter (cf. Pl. 22, fig. 3 for a face-to-face encounter). In speaking of real courtship, the Balinese liken the behavior of boy and girl to that of two cocks straining toward each other with their heads down and their hackle feathers up (cf. Pl. 43, fig. 3).

I Daweg with his sister, I Tiroe, itinerant dancers from Selat, Bangli.
Bajoeng Gede. May 29, 1937. 9 Y 15.

2. A comic partner. This man left the audience to fetch a mask from our collection. He put it on while hiding in the audience and then suddenly stepped out into the dancing ground to confront the *djoget* dancer.
Nang Oera wearing a mask from Sebatoe.
Bajoeng Gede. June 9, 1937. 11 O 2.

3. A conventional facial expression in courtship dancing. This is the same man as in fig. 1, and he wears a simpering narcissistic expression which is commonly adopted by male dancers (cf. Pl. 16). His bodily posture may be compared with that of the man (Pl. 46, fig. 7) who, dancing solo, worked up to a climax and then collapsed.
I Daweg of Pangsoed (dancing to I Tiroe).
Bajoeng Gede. May 28, 1937. 9 R 4.

4. A *djoget* dancer coquetting while fending off her partner with her hand. This photograph was obtained by entering the stage and dancing to the *djoget*, camera in hand, as if photographing were a courtship act.
Djoget dancer from Selat, Bangli.
Bajoeng Gede. June 5, 1937. 11 J 29.

5. A *djoget* dancer dancing solo, and showing her virtuosity by bending backward.
Djoget dancer from Malet.
Bajoeng Gede. June 9, 1937. 1 M 23.

6. A *djoget* dancer at the end of the dance. She stands limp and withdrawn waiting for the music to start again (cf. Pl. 7, fig. 6).
Djoget dancer from Pelaktiing.
Bajoeng Gede. May 12, 1937. 8 S 21.

1

2

3

4

5

6

1

2

3

4

5

6

7

8

9

Plate 60

COURTSHIP AND THE WITCH'S CLOTH

We have already noted (Pl. 56, fig. 3) that a great part of the Witch's power is symbolized in her white cloth, and that this cloth is called *"anteng,"* i.e., by the same term as the mother's sling in which she carries the baby on her hip. This plate shows in more detail how this weapon is handled.

The plate also shows a *djoget* dancer impersonating the Witch. This is one of the special solo dances which these little girls perform. That the beautiful and desirable girl who chiefly plays a courtship role should also play the role of Witch fits with our assumptions that the Witch is comparable to the mother, and that courtship patterns are necessarily related to parent-child patterns. There are two sorts of women who may be witches according to the conventions of Balinese drama — those who are either very old and very ugly or those who are very young and very beautiful (cf. the Witch's disciples, Pl. 55, fig. 2 and Pl. 61, figs. 1 and 2). Such dramas commonly have for plot some story in which a prince abducts what he thought was a beautiful girl; later he looks behind him and finds that he has made a mistake and abducted an ugly woman — whose part is usually acted by a man.

1 to 4. The Witch dancing with her cloth. In fig. 1, she is chasing one of the comic servants (cf. Pl. 13, fig. 5).

In fig. 2, with the cloth in her right hand, she raises both arms high above her head. This posture, which the Witch frequently adopts and may retain for several seconds, is called *kapar* — a word also used for the posture suddenly assumed by a man when he falls out of a coconut palm or when he sees a snake. We interpret this as an indication that the Witch is not merely a frightening figure, but is a personification of fear or of startle in the sense that she herself is *afraid*. Such an interpretation fits with our analysis of the relation between Witch and mother, and our analysis of the role which shared fear plays in the mother-child relationship (Pl. 46). In general, one would not guess that the Witch is acting fear, but we once saw a performance at night in which the actor gave to this part a curiously pathetic and lonely quality.

In fig. 3, she stoops forward at the end of a down stroke with her cloth.

In fig. 4, she stands with cloth raised in one hand, as she would when challenging the Dragon. (The exact context of this photograph was not recorded.)

Itinerant troupe of *Wajang wong* dancers from Kedoewi.

Bajoeng Gede. May 13, 1937.   8 V 36, 37, 38, 39.

5. The Witch covers her face with her cloth. This photograph was taken immediately after Pl. 55, fig. 4 in which she is shown lying on the temple steps, "killed" by the king. Here she rises with her face hidden. This is a common gesture of the Witch, and it is most usually done when she first comes on the stage. It is, we presume, related to the motif of fear though its precise significance is not clear. On the one hand, we have the recurrent mythological theme of the prince who does not at first see his bride and later discovers that she is hideous; and the actual ceremonial of royal weddings in which the bride is delivered to the groom entirely wrapped in white cloth and previously unseen. On the other hand, we must compare this gesture of the Witch with the mother's habit of covering her face (especially her mouth) to break inter-personal contact with her child (cf. Pl. 53, fig. 3), and with the children's habit of covering the eyes in fear (Pl. 67).

Pagoetan. Feb. 8, 1939.   35 J 18.

6 and 7. An unfinished sketch of the Witch and the Dragon. Fig. 7 is an enlarged photograph of the Witch's hand and cloth in this drawing. In this quick freehand sketch the cloth, the Witch's weapon, appears limp and cylindrical.

One informant (Nang Oera, born in Malet, living in Bajoeng Gede) told us that a man, when he is frightened, may reduce his fear by taking off his sarong and shaking it out. He said that he himself had done this on one occasion when he was scared of witches at night.

Unfinished drawing by I. B. Nj. Tjeta. Not purchased.

Batoean. Aug. 22, 1937.   14 U 20, 21.

8 and 9. A courtship dancer (*djoget*) impersonating the Witch. In fig. 8, she stands in the *kapar* position discussed above (fig. 2); while in fig. 9, she stands hunched forward with her wrist flexed and her forearm sloping downward after a weak downward stroke of her cloth.

I Tiroe of Pangsoed.

Bajoeng Gede. May 29, 1937.   9 Y 11, 12.

Plate 61

LITTLE WITCHES

This plate gives further illustrations of the postures and roles of the little girls who act as witches and of their transformations.

1. The Witch's disciples dancing with raised knees. This posture is very common in carvings and paintings of such figures (cf. Pl. 17, figs. 8 and 9). In the theater, minor transformed witches playing a comic role sometimes hop about the stage with one knee raised. Here the little girls show this posture in their dancing before their transformation into hideous witches.
Pagoetan. Dec. 16, 1937. 20 E 20.

2. Repairing the costume of one of the Witch's disciples. Here we see the little girl who is, theatrically speaking, a baby witch, receiving the same sort of respect and solicitude which is lavished on the girl who is possessed by a god (cf. Pl. 45, figs. 3 and 4).
Pagoetan. Dec. 16, 1937. 20 E 12.

3. A minor witch in the shape of a monkey. This boy, with his face painted and his tail, was one of the transformed witches in the Pagoetan play. He ran around with his arms and legs and fingers in these very disharmonic postures and played various pranks on the human beings in the play — stealing the baby from the comic birth scene, tossing it in the air, and returning it dead.
Pagoetan. Dec. 16, 1937. 20 F 32.

4. A courtship dancer impersonating the Witch with a baby. The Witch is imagined to eat and tear babies (Pl. 49, fig. 5), and when this is represented on the stage, the relationship between Witch and baby (represented by a doll) has a curious cat-and-mouse quality; she holds the baby up and admires it, swings it downward (as in this picture) and again holds it up and admires it. Finally she flings it from her and dances over it.
Djoget dancer from Malet.
Bajoeng Gede. June 24, 1937. 12 A 10.

5. A transformed witch. Various types of grotesque masks may be used for witches (heads with a single large eye, etc.). This was one of the most effective that we saw. She has brilliant black and white coloring so that her sharp teeth are accented, and her eyes appear to flash.
Wajang wong performance in Sanoer.
Sanoer. May 20, 1936. 1 G 11.

6 and 7. A courtship dancer with a doll representing a baby. (This is the same dancer as in fig. 4, but the photographs were taken on the following day.) In fig. 6, she has flung the baby on the ground and dances with her knee raised and her foot over it, in the witch posture shown in fig. 1.
In fig. 7, she has moved and stands away from the baby with open rejecting hands.
Bajoeng Gede. June 25, 1937. 12 B 16, 17.

8. A witch unmasked. The part of the transformed witch was played by a young man, and after the various comic scenes in which he plays pranks on the mortals, he is unmasked by a soothsayer (*balian*). In the photograph, he sits laughing, with his mask on the ground beside him. He is handcuffed by tying his hands to a string which passes through a tube of bamboo.
Dendjalan. May 26, 1936. 1 I 12.

1

2

3

4

5

6

7

8

1

2

3

4

5

6

Plate 62

PARENTS: WITCH AND DRAGON

This plate illustrates the contrast between the father's and mother's relationships to the child, the analogous contrast between Dragon and Witch, and the mythological conflict between the two figures.

1. A mother playing with her son on his 105-day birthday. She holds him up above her head, admiring him with her lips drawn back from her teeth (cf. Pl. 61, fig. 4).
Boeleleng. Nov. 6, 1936.   3 F 21.

2. A father holds his son while his foot is medicated. The baby had a slight scabies on his foot, and in the treatment it is necessary to remove the scabs. The father holds his child in an embracing way, enclosing the baby's body in his own. His face is in contact with that of the baby and he attends to the baby's facial expression while holding the foot firmly in his hand. The baby, slightly frightened, has his eyes shut.
Nang Oera holding I Karba, aged 242 days.
Bajoeng Gede. Oct. 4, 1936.   2 V 15.

3 and 4. The conflict between king and Witch. In fig. 3, the king's representative (*pepatih*) accuses the Witch's daughter of witchcraft. He holds a kris in his outstretched right hand pointing at her. This pose is suddenly assumed, retained for one or two seconds, and suddenly terminated by a quick turn of the wrist which lifts the kris off its aim. This is a momentary gesture of extreme intensity and is usually performed without a kris, using instead the extended index and middle fingers to point for a moment at the offending person. The timing of the gesture is comparable to the timing which we noted in the courtship dances. The sudden establishment of intense face-to-face relationship, which is held for a moment and then as suddenly broken off, is characteristic both of theatrical courtship and of theatrical anger. (So far as we know the gesture occurs only in theatricals, though we heard of one European lady who used it against her cook and thereby disorganized her kitchen staff.)

After this encounter between king's representative and Witch's daughter in human form, the latter left the stage. Her place was taken by her transformation, the Witch in full costume, and there followed a conflict between the Witch and the king's representative, in which the Witch was "killed" and laid out on a mat. The king's representative then left the stage, and his place was taken by the Dragon, into which he had transformed himself. The Witch, meanwhile, revived.

In fig. 4, we see the conflict between Dragon and Witch which consists of a scolding match in archaic language (*Kawi*). The gestures typical of this conflict are clearly shown — the Dragon expressing anger by sudden forward thrusts of his head, and the Witch stretching out her arm with all five fingers splayed and rigid, a gesture not of physical attack but rather oriented to make the opponent powerless.
Itinerant troupe of *Tjalonarang* dancers from Tatag.
Bajoeng Gede. May 29, 1937.   9 W 26, 36.

5. The Witch. This photograph shows her coming onto the stage. Her cloth, which she holds in her right hand, is draped across her left forearm, as though it were a baby. The photograph also shows her teeth and tongue and her enormous fingernails. (She wears gloves, to which the fingernails are attached.) It appears from her behavior that the function of these fingernails is not to suggest scratching or physical aggression. It is true that small children, playing at being the Witch, often hook their fingers to give an impression of claws (cf. Pl. 74, fig. 6), but this is not true of the real Witch in costume or of adults, without costume, but "possessed" by the Witch. The Witch's fingers are more often splayed out straight, as in the left hand in this photograph, and the effect of the fingernails is to give emphasis to such gestures as that shown in fig. 4, and to the *kapar* gesture (cf. Pl. 60, figs. 2 and 8).
Dendjalan. May 26, 1936.   1 J 7.

6. The Dragon with a man in trance. One of the significant features of the Dragon's structure is the enormous gaping hole in the front of his chest, through which the man inside the front of the mask is able to manipulate the head. This hole and the Dragon's beard have the curious property of reducing the violence of trance, and trance dancers sometimes push their heads into this cavity. In this photograph, a trance dancer is being held in front of the hole while the Dragon lifts his head high (cf. the child's attempts to get inside the father, Pl. 61, and the father's attempts to encompass the child, fig. 2, above).
Dendjalan. Nov. 23, 1936.   3 I 27.

Plate 63

THE FATHER-CHILD RELATIONSHIP

This relationship is characterized by three very conspicuous themes: (a) the child tries to get inside the father or the father tries to encompass the child; (b) the father romps with the child, mixing roughness with friendliness; and (c) the child feeds the father.

This plate illustrates the first of these themes. In general, it seems that the attempt to "get inside" the father is made facing away from him and leaning backward.

1 to 6. Nang Marti and his daughter, I Marti. This father had an exceptionally close and warm relationship with his baby daughter. The mother, Men Marti, had had a quarrel with Nang Marti's brother's wife (Men Singin) before I Marti was born, and Nang Marti spent a great deal of time with his brothers. The mother would not go anywhere where she was likely to meet Men Singin, and therefore Nang Marti went alone with the baby.

In fig. 1, he carries I Marti, aged 126 days, enclosing her in the blanket which is around his own shoulders.

In figs. 2 to 5, Nang Marti is sitting, playing with I Marti, aged 341 days. In fig. 2, she lies on her back in his lap, slightly kicking and pulling down the collar of his singlet. In fig. 3 (four photographs — perhaps ten seconds — later), she has contracted her legs till she becomes a ball, except for her right hand which is extended. The position of the father's head altered in the intervening photographs, but in fig. 3 he has returned to the same attentive angle that appeared in fig. 2. In fig. 4, the father leans down to touch her face with his nose or lips, while she gazes up at him with her head back and her arm abducted. In fig. 5, he has arranged her in his lap, inside his arms and stooping chest, so that only part of her face shows.

In fig. 6, I Marti, aged 493 days, stands between her father's knees while he squats. His arms come forward around her knees and his wrists are flexed toward closing her in.

Nang Marti; I Marti. (For a sequence of the same father and daughter 18 months later, see next plate.)

Bajoeng Gede. Aug. 18, 1936.   2 G 22 (fig. 1).
               Mar. 21, 1937.   6 D 16, 20, 26, 33 (figs. 2, 3, 4, 5).
               Aug. 20, 1937.   14 L 5 (fig. 6).

7 and 8. A father with his daughter and younger son. The daughter's foot is being treated with potassium permanganate, and the father holds her foot on the edge of the basin of solution (cf. Pl. 62, fig. 2). His attention goes chiefly to his son who comes and leans back against him, laughing. The two pictures show the son in different flirtatious or regressive postures, the second of which may be compared with Pl. 49, figs. 3 and 4, where a girl is shown with her ventral surface turned toward her aunt.

Nang Loka; I Loka, his daughter, on the right; I Dana, his son, on the left.

Bajoeng Gede. May 2, 1937.   7 Y 6, 7.

9, 10, and 11. A father with his youngest daughter. In fig. 9, she reaches up to borrow his cigarette, wriggling her hand in under his to reach the base of the cigarette. Intervening photographs (not reproduced) show her smoking the cigarette.

Fig. 10 shows her still seated on her father's lap between his knees and drinking a very burning peppery drink (*oeroedjah*) out of a coconut shell which her father holds for her. She spluttered a little over it.

At this point, her father sent her to get his basket (*kompek*) in which he carries his tobacco and betel, and fig. 11 shows her teasing to get at the contents of this basket, which her father is opening, with his arm around her.

Nang Maderi; I Marsi, his daughter.

Bajoeng Gede. Mar. 30, 1937.   6 K 15, 18, 19.

1
2
3
4
5
6
7
8
9
10
11

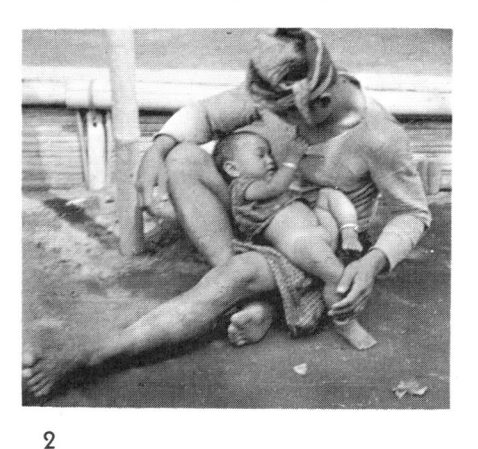

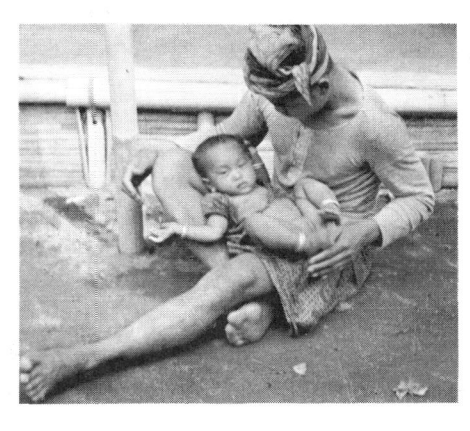

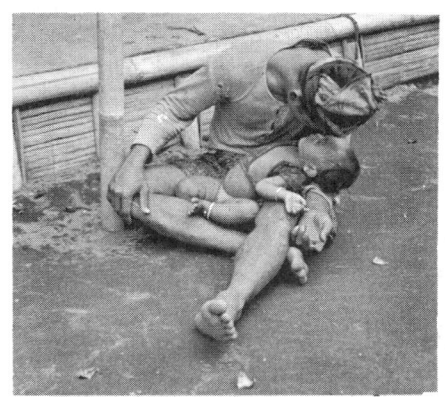

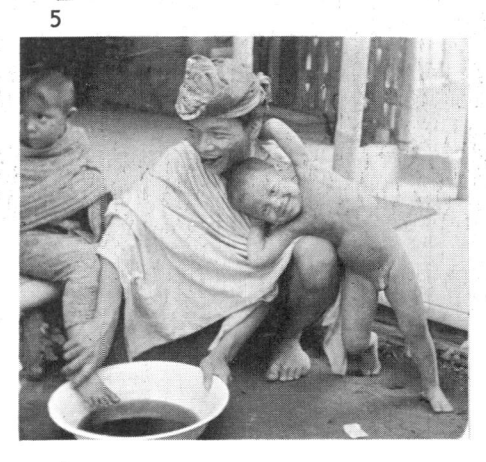

1

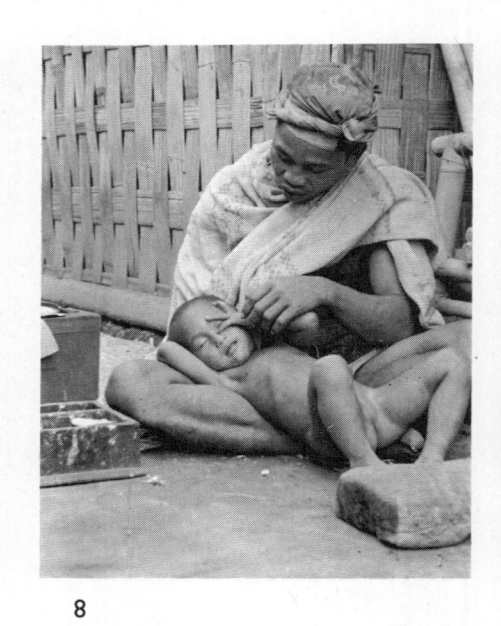

2

3

4

5

6

7

8

9

Plate 64

A FATHER AND HIS DAUGHTER

This plate shows the behavioral themes which were outlined in the previous plate — "getting inside the father," and feeding the father. And, at the end of the sequence, there is an interesting break in the regressive behavior after the father attempts to pull away his daughter's hand, with which she was covering her eye.

The photographs are selected from a series of 40, covering about five minutes; they fall naturally into groups and are therefore so handled in the detailed captions.

1, 2, and 3. Previous frames show the father leaning forward over the tray on the left of the picture, preparing a betel nut for chewing. In fig. 1, he has given the prepared mouthful to his daughter, and she is putting it into his mouth.

In fig. 2, she has got under his blanket, and he encourages her in this by holding the edge of the blanket in his left hand and stretching it over her.

In fig. 3, she has come out from under the blanket and sits with her legs widespread. Her father has his left hand on her thigh, while he adjusts the betel in his mouth with his right hand.

4, 5, and 6. This series is almost a repeat of the first. The father, in the photographs which intervene between figs. 3 and 4, has prepared the wad of tobacco with which he will wipe out his mouth after the betel, and in fig. 4, his daughter puts this tobacco into his mouth, holding it in her cupped hand.

In fig. 5, the father adjusts the tobacco between his lips, while his daughter covers her abdomen with her spread hands. In fig. 6, she again tries to get under his blanket. It is probable that the notion of putting food into her father's mouth is, psychologically, closely akin to the notion of getting "inside the father" — putting her own body inside his.

7. The daughter sits in her father's lap, leaning backward with her legs spread and her arms raised and flexed. Her eyes are shut.

8 and 9. The daughter has now sprawled forward, still lying on her back but cushioning her head on her right arm while she covers her left eye with her hand — probably to keep out the intense sunshine. Her father, teasing, pulls at her wrist, trying to uncover her eye. This annoys her, and in fig. 9, she is sitting up, away from her father with a slightly sulky expression, while he sits looking at her.

Nang Marti with his daughter, I Marti, aged 2 years, 9 months.

Bajoeng Gede. Feb. 12, 1939.   36 L 9, 11, 13, 18, 19, 20, 25, 37, 40.

Plate 65

THE FATHER: FRIENDLY ROUGHNESS

This plate illustrates the third theme in the father-child relationship — that of rough, friendly play. Fathers vary in the degree to which they show this behavior, and perhaps none show it so markedly as it appears in the second sequence of pictures, where the "father-substitute" is a postadolescent boy.

The first sequence is inserted here to mark a parallel between the child's plasticity in face of the father's roughness and the pupil's plasticity in the hands of the dancing teacher (Pl. 16). In both relationships, the child is relaxed with his back toward the senior (cf. also Pl. 66, figs. 6, 7, and 8; Pl. 39, fig. 1).

1 to 4. A father with his son.

In fig. 1, the son lies half asleep with his head pillowed on his father's knee. The father apparently decided to wake him and make him sit up.

In fig. 2, the father jerks the boy forward with a brusque movement, holding him by the upper part of the right arm. The next frame (not reproduced) shows the father and son stationary, in postures similar to those in fig. 2, except that the father is leaning farther forward and the son shows a tendency to fall back into the position from which he was aroused.

In fig. 3, the father has shifted his grasp to the boy's left arm, in order more effectively to make the boy sit up.

In fig. 4, the father has withdrawn his arm and is no longer looking at his son, but the son's arm stays up in almost the precise position in which it was set by his father.

Nang Karma, with his son, I Gata.

Bajoeng Gede. June 20, 1937.   11 V 4, 6, 8, 9.

5 to 8. Romping play with a small boy. Earlier frames in this series show that the pattern is recurrent. The postadolescent boy first lies back on top of I Karsa, the small boy, and then sits up; I Karsa then teases to make him lie back again.

In fig. 5, I Karsa has his arms around the boy's neck, pulling at him. The bigger boy pretends to pay no attention.

In fig. 6, the boy lies back on top of I Karsa, who is almost completely covered. One of his legs shows on the side towards the camera.

In fig. 7, the boy sits up again, and I Karsa still lies on his back — sulking now because the boy's attention is away from him.

In fig. 8, the boy again leans back, and I Karsa cries out in agonized joy (cf. Pl. 59, fig. 4).

I Karsa, with I Repen (orphan from Malet, partly adopted by Nang Oera, who is Karsa's father's brother).

Bajoeng Gede. May 25, 1937.   9 K 32, 33, 34, 35.

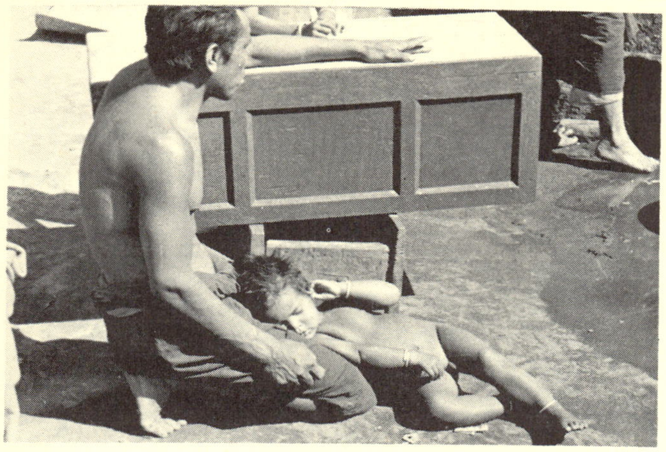
1

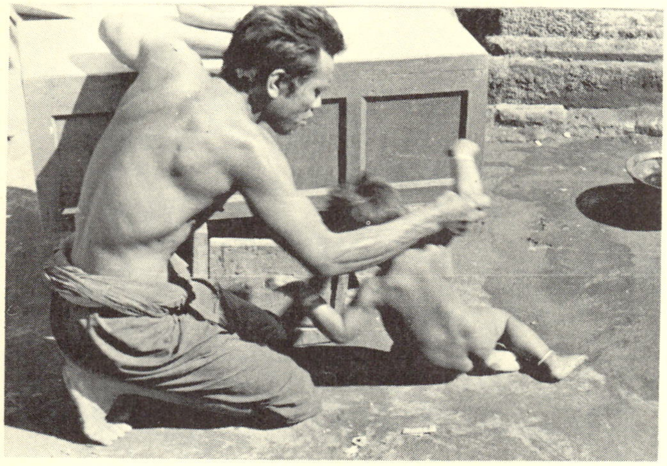
2

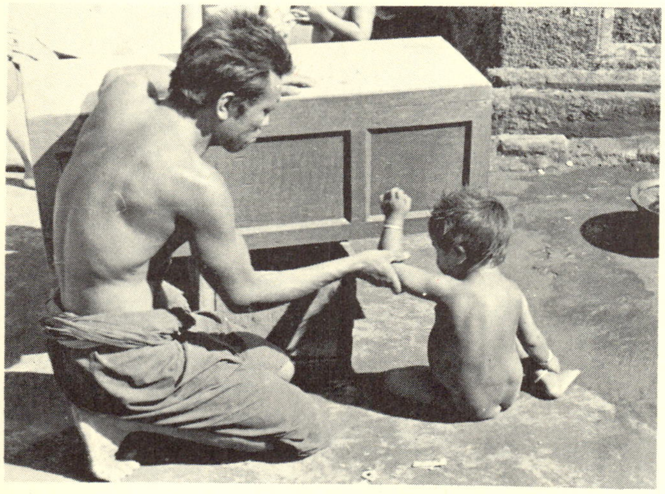
3

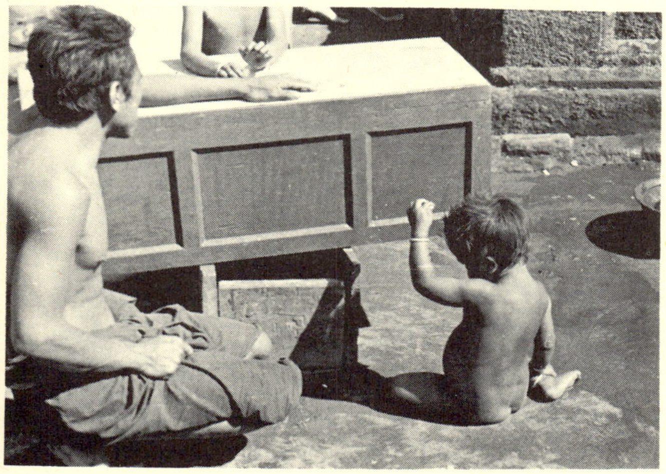
4

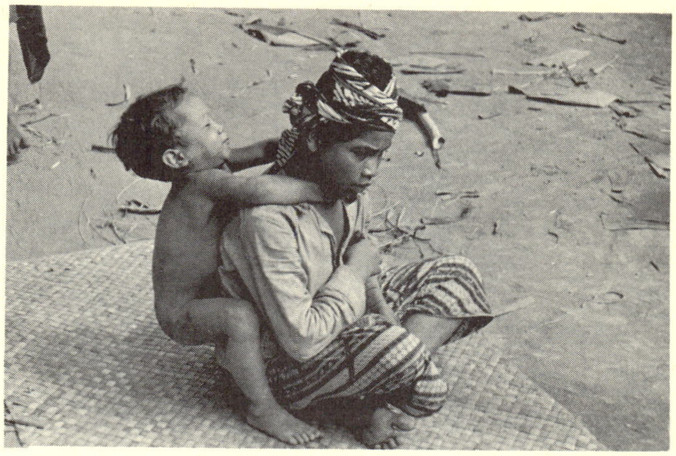
5

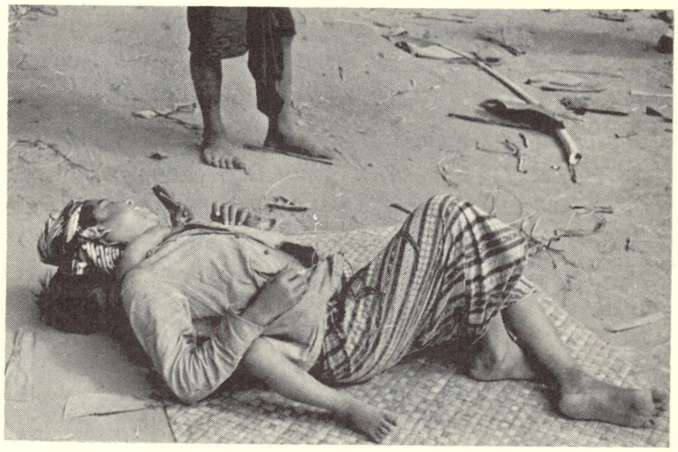
6

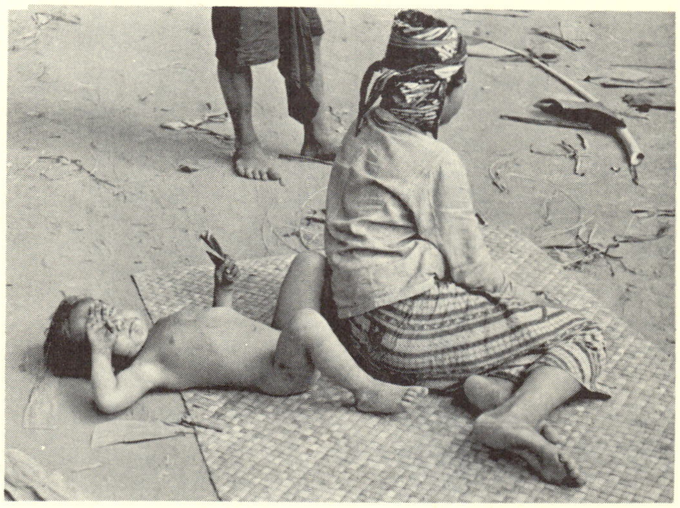
7

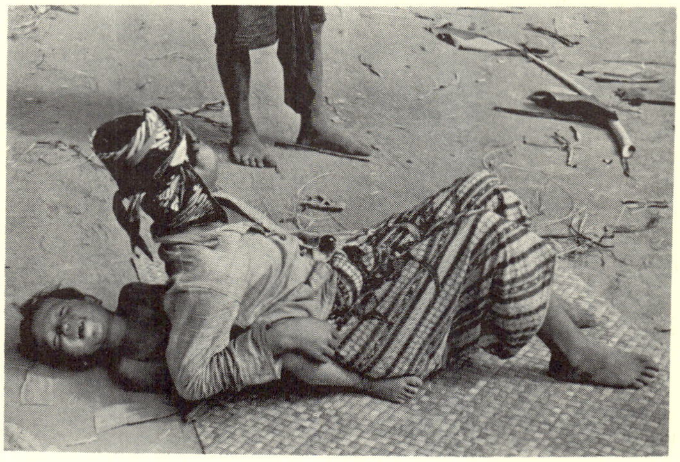
8

1

2

3

4

5

6

7

8

Plate 66
THE DRAGON (*BARONG*)

This plate illustrates how the major themes of the father-child relationship are reproduced in the relationship between the Dragon and mortals. It shows the theme of feeding the Dragon, and the rough play in which the Dragon overruns the mortals who tease him. (A third parallel was illustrated on Pl. 62.)

1. A priest feeds the Dragon. He is here seen holding up food to the mouth of the Dragon's mask, which is supported on posts. In some dance clubs, this feeding of the Dragon is done every day while the club is on tour. Sometimes it is done while the mask is being worn, the man inside the front of the Dragon opening the mouth of the mask and stretching his hand forward to receive the food.
Itinerant troupe from Pengeliangan.
Bajoeng Gede. May 18, 1937.   9 C 24.

2. The Dragon dances. His dancing is very gay in tone and is done by both the men inside the mask dancing in unison. It consists of quickly changing poses of the feet, movements of the head and clapping of the jaws. While the men dance, ripples pass down the length of the Dragon's body.
Pagoetan. Dec. 16, 1937.   20 D 32.

3. The Dragon poses on entering the stage. This was the most handsome Dragon that we saw, and he was especially famous for his black body. Usually the body of the Dragon is made of fiber (as in fig. 1) but this Dragon's body was covered with black crows' feathers, which were said to have been miraculously provided. (The Pagoetan Dragon in figs. 2 and 4 was covered with white feathers, probably fowls' feathers which are less difficult to obtain.)
Tegaltamoe. May 1, 1936.   1 C 15.

4. The Dragon stands poised for a moment in his dance. The men inside the mask are on tiptoe.
Pagoetan. Dec. 16, 1937.   20 D 18.

5. Teasing the Dragon. One of the simplest of the theatrical forms which involve the Dragon is that in which he is teased by clowns (*djaoek*), and then rushes at them. This performance is commonly given as a sort of "curtain raiser" at the beginning of a Witch play (*Tjalonarang*).
Pagoetan. Dec. 16, 1937.   20 E 11.

6, 7, and 8. The Dragon attacks a clown. In fig. 6, the Dragon runs up to the clown who sits with his back turned. In fig. 7, the Dragon pauses, comically threatening and ready to pounce. In fig. 8, the Dragon rushes over the clown.
Itinerant troupe from Taro.
Bajoeng Gede. May 30, 1937.   9 Y 24, 25, 27.

Plate 67

THE DRAGON AND FEAR OF SPACE

A number of themes of Balinese culture which are illustrated elsewhere are relevant to this and the following plate, and are recapitulated here. We have noted that:

A. Fear is in part a pleasant emotion which brings mother and child together, but also, every time this occurs, the child is impressed with the notion that the world beyond the known cultural area is fraught with a great but undefined danger (cf. Pl. 47).

B. In topological terms, Balinese culture is the inverse of our own — it is a system of assured safety and freedom rather than a system of limitations (cf. Pl. 17, figs. 1 and 2).

C. The Dragon can mark out areas which are safe from witchcraft (cf. Pl. 56, fig. 1) and also he can mark out stretches of time, e.g., by opening and terminating the Witch play.

D. The child's regressive attitudes toward the father are expressed by postures in which the back is turned toward the father and the body bent forward (Pls. 63 to 66). The corresponding attitudes toward the mother are the opposite of this (cf. Pls. 49, 58, etc.). Impotent against the Witch, the young man falls backward away from her with bent spine into a catalepsy from which he is revived by the Dragon (cf. Pl. 57).

E. The child is an autocosmic genital symbol (cf. Pl. 39, especially fig. 1, which shows the child with his back to his father).

This and the following plate are concerned with Balinese behavior in vague fear of the unknown, and they show five methods of dealing with this fear: (a) by covering the eyes, or turning the face to the wall; (b) by using the Dragon to delimit space and mark it as safely encircled; (c) by tying some of the Dragon's hair around the wrist; (d) by getting inside a mask and becoming a Dragon; and (e) by going to sleep.

1. A child nurse holding a frightened child. The child was afraid of us and covered his eyes with his hand.
 I Samboet holding I Badera, a neighbor's child.
 Bajoeng Gede. Oct. 25, 1936.   3 A 21.

2. A mother holding her child while a sore on his chest is being medicated. She covers his eyes with her hand, showing that the behavior of the child in fig. 1 is in part taught by the mother.
 Men Goenoeng holding her son, I Raoeh, aged 250 days.
 Bajoeng Gede. Oct. 24, 1936.   3 A 3.

3, 4, and 5. A baby girl walks out into space. She is in the big court of the village temple and has walked out away from her mother or child nurse. This behavior persists for a very short time after a baby has newly learned to walk. It is rapidly extinguished, partly by continual pulling back and partly by the mother's exclamations of fear.
 In fig. 4, the baby is accompanied by her elder sister; and in fig. 5, the elder sister picks her up after she has tumbled.
 I Doemoen with her elder sister, I Kesir; I Belot watching.
 Bajoeng Gede. Mar. 20, 1937.   6 A 28; 6 B 5, 9.

6. A Dragon circles the village. When itinerant troupes of dancers come to the village, they are usually accompanied by a Dragon (perhaps to protect them in their wanderings in strange places). In addition to joining in the theatrical performance in the village temple, the Dragon performs a tour of all the streets of the village. While making his round, the Dragon sells his hair.
 Dragon from Pengeliangan.
 Bajoeng Gede. May 18, 1937.   8 Z 29.

7. A small boy playing at being a Dragon. He stands completely covered by a mat of plaited pandanus leaves. His mother is sitting just behind the camera, selling food on the side of the street.
 I Karsa.
 Bajoeng Gede. May 25, 1937.   9 J 31.

8. Children frightened. They were frightened of us, and stood with their faces turned toward the wall of the street.
 Bajoeng Gede. Aug. 26, 1936.   2 I 33.

9. Wearing a bracelet of Dragon's hair. As the Dragon tours the village, he sells his hair at the houses he passes. It is bought for a few cash and is tied on the wrists of the smaller children — to prevent them from having nightmares about the Witch.
 I Njawa looking at her wrist.
 Bajoeng Gede. May 9, 1937.   8 I 8.

1

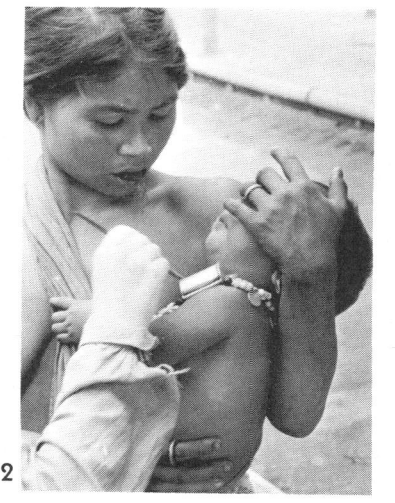

2

3

4

5

6

7

8

9

1

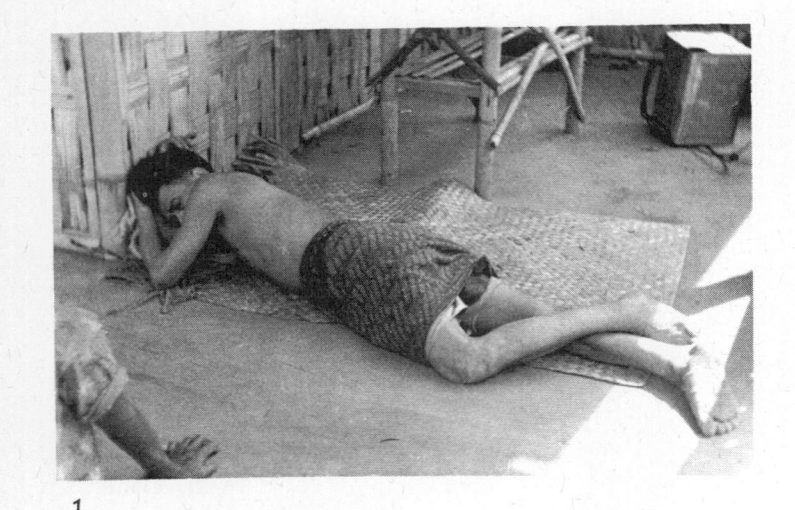

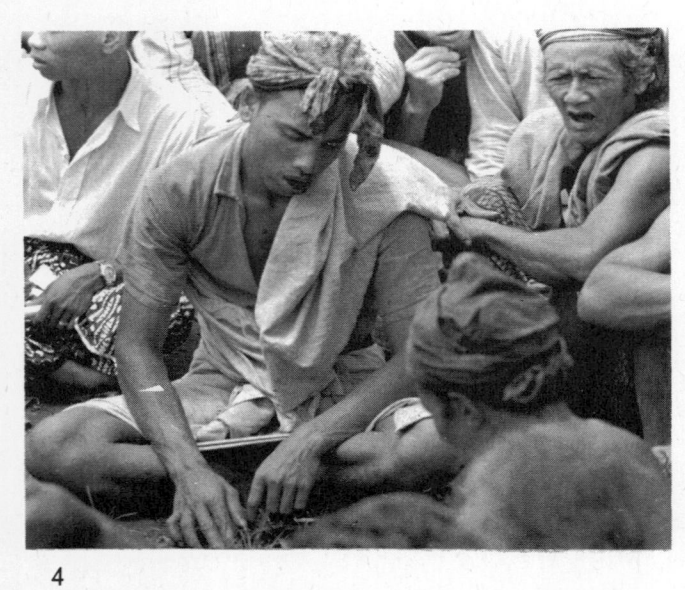

2

3

5

4

6

Plate 68

FEAR AND SLEEP

The Balinese readily go to sleep during the day, and in particular, they go to sleep when they are frightened. This behavior is summarized in the common Balinese phrase, *"takoet poeles"* (literally, "afraid-sleep"). On one occasion we sent our cook boys by omnibus to our Bangli camp, carrying knives and forks and other kitchen equipment. When we arrived we found them all asleep in the Bangli kitchen and no attempt made to open the camp. They had left the knives and forks in the bus and were afraid. Similarly, small children never witness childbirth, not because they are driven away but because they sleep through it, lying sound asleep often on the same bed as the woman in labor.

This handling of fear by means of sleep may be regarded as a regressive technique and is probably comparable to the relaxed regression of the child toward the father.

1. A man asleep. In this case, the sleep was due to fatigue. The man had been out all the previous night carrying a message for us.

I Goesti Kompiang (native of Oeboed, resident in Bajoeng Gede).

Bajoeng Gede. May 4, 1937. 8 A 27.

2. A boy asleep in his mother's arms. The baby, carried in a sling, must learn to be very flexible and relaxed if he is to escape jolts, and swing easily and naturally with his mother's body. This is especially true of babies carried by child nurses, and it is not uncommon to see a baby asleep in the sling, while its nurse is engaging in some boisterous game with other children or even having a temper tantrum.

Men Singin, carrying her son, I Karsa.

Bajoeng Gede. Oct. 13, 1936. 2 Z 5.

3 to 6. Two thieves falling asleep during their trial. Figs. 3 and 4 show one thief; figs. 5 and 6 show the other.

These two men had stolen a considerable sum (about 70 guilders) from the village treasury and had gambled with the proceeds. Later the loss was discovered and a conditional oath (*dewasaksian*) was administered to all the men of the village. Each man had to drink special holy water which would cause painful and disgraceful death in many successive reincarnations if he were guilty. One of the thieves avoided drinking by postponing his participation in the ceremony until next day; the other drank and suffered from pains in the night. Next day, they both confessed.

The citizens then gathered to decide what should be done with the thieves — whether they should be handed over to the Government or punished in the village. The thieves sat with the other men in this discussion, but took no part in it beyond answering one or two questions.

The photographs show both men slowly slumping forward toward sleep. I Ampiag (figs. 3 and 4) actually went to sleep and had to be wakened at one stage in the discussion; Nang Rebo (figs. 5 and 6) only leaned forward on the verge of sleep, without actually achieving this escape. It is interesting that Nang Rebo wore his blanket in the hot sun.

I Ampiag (center in figs. 3 and 4); Nang Rebo (lower left in figs. 5 and 6); I Made Kaler (in white shirt behind I Ampiag); Nang Karma (looking at camera in fig. 5); Nang Djeben, I Ampiag's elder brother (to the right of Nang Karma).

Bajoeng Gede. Jan. 20, 1938. 20 X 29, 35, 5, 10.

Plate 69
SIBLING RIVALRY I

The triangular relationship between the mother, the youngest baby and the dispossessed or "knee" baby is standardized in many different ways in different cultures. The behavior of the knee baby may be hostile or affectionate and either pattern may be directed either toward the mother or toward the new baby.

In Bali, the behavior of the knee baby is preponderantly directed toward the mother and consists of bids for her attention alternating with or mixed with fits of sulky withdrawal. The knee baby rarely resorts to direct aggressive behavior either against the mother or against the younger sibling, though such aggressive behavior is common in those cases where the mother has borrowed another baby as a means of stimulating her own child (cf. Pl. 50). The mother's behavior consists of attention paid to the youngest baby, increasing unresponsiveness to the knee baby, and frequent attempts to make the knee baby pay loving attention to the youngest baby. This, in fact, is the only context in Balinese life in which anything like an emotional expression is articulately demanded.

1, 2, and 3. A knee baby gets attention from her mother on the new baby's 420-day birthday. The mother is holding the new baby, dressed up for the ceremony, on her knee, and in fig. 1 she is attending to the new baby while the knee baby glares at it.

In fig. 2, the mother reaches out to get some cake from a tray on the table and the knee baby's gaze follows her hand. (The knee baby had been trying to steal cakes during the ceremony.)

In fig. 3, the mother's hand has returned to her knee, but her head remains turned as it was in fig. 2, except that now the knee baby has caught the mother's attention and laughs up into her face.

Men Asa with her son, I Asin, 420 days old, and her elder daughter, I Asa.

Bajoeng Gede. Sept. 13, 1936. 2 M 26, 27, 28.

4. A knee baby withdraws from the mother clutching food in its hands. Before the birth of the new baby, the knee baby in this picture was sent away to the house of relatives of his father, because his mother was in a mildly psychopathic state during her pregnancy and insisted on staying indoors and doing nothing. When the picture was taken, the knee baby had only recently returned. He is seen sitting alone on the doorstep of the house while his mother plays with the new baby. In each hand he holds a handful of food (cf. Pl. 70, figs. 4 and 6; Pl. 35, fig. 6 for the baby's habit of holding the mother's breast).

Men Sama with her new baby, I Sami, aged 216 days, and I Sama, her older son.

Bajoeng Gede. April 30, 1937. 7 Q 35.

5. A knee baby pulling at the mother's baby sling. This photograph was taken at the 105-day birthday of the new baby. On these occasions, when the new baby is specially dressed up, the knee baby almost invariably tries to get hold of some of the cloth, either dragging at the mother's clothes as in this picture or holding on to some of the baby's new clothes. In part this is an attempt to attract attention, but it is also a grasping after a substitute satisfaction. In this photograph, the knee baby not only pulls at the mother's cloth, but also holds it against her own cheek.

Men Njawi with the new baby, I Koewat, aged 105 days, and I Njawa, her older daughter.

Bajoeng Gede. July 13, 1937. 12 N 14.

6, 7, and 8. A knee baby seeks substitute satisfaction in the new baby's necklace and in the mother's knee. Throughout the sequence of pictures, the mother pays no attention to the knee baby; in fig. 6, she sits with a vacant expression, and in the other two pictures she attends to the new baby.

In fig. 6, the knee baby plays with the new baby's necklace, pulling it with both hands so that it presses hard against her upper lip. This is the necklace on which the baby cuts its teeth.

In fig. 7, the knee baby leans her head on her mother's lap and closes her eyes. The necklace is now hanging down from the knee baby's hands.

In fig. 8, the knee baby has put on the new baby's necklace, and its string is visible against her hair, and she presses her face deep into her mother's lap.

Men Kesir, with her baby, I Doemoen, aged about 18 months, and her older daughter, I Kesir, aged 3–4 years.

Bajoeng Gede. July 16, 1937. 12 R 8, 21, 26.

1
2
3
4
5
6
7
8

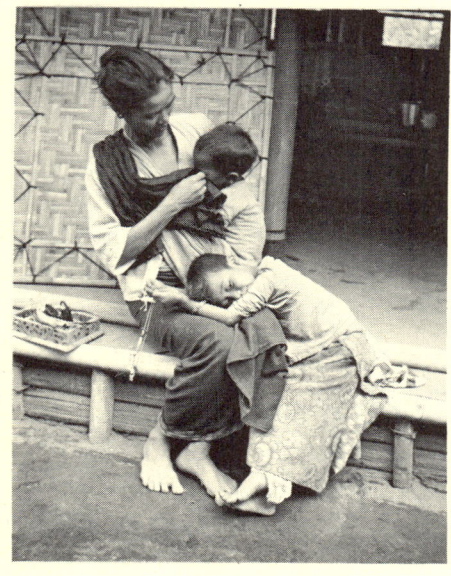

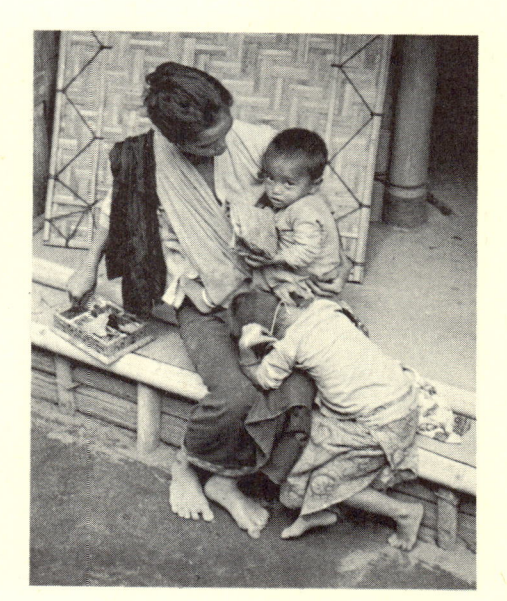

1

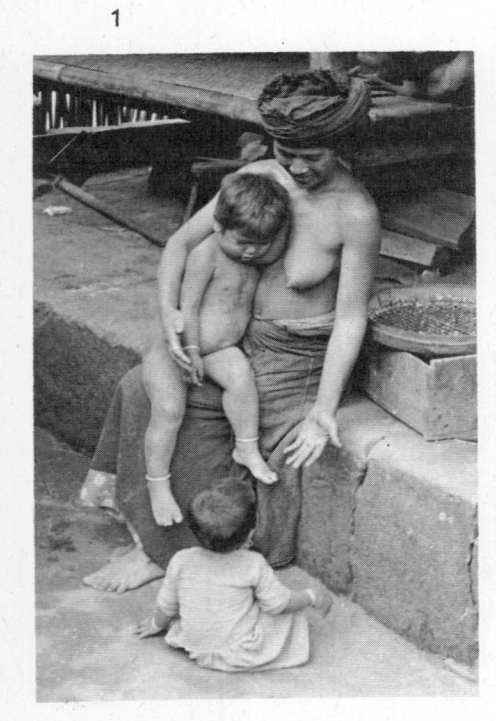

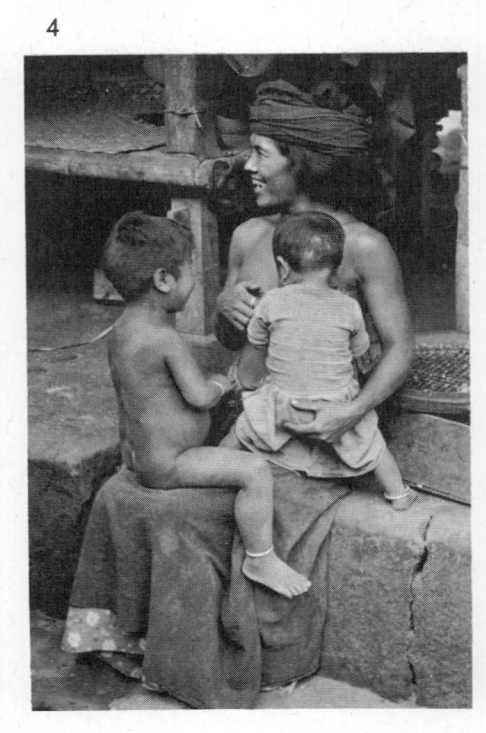

2

3

4

5

6

7

8

Plate 70

SIBLING RIVALRY II

This plate further illustrates the knee baby's reaction to the mother and the new baby, and especially the lines along which this reaction is generalized so that it becomes a theme in Balinese character. We have already noted (Pl. 69) that this triangular relationship is the only context in which conventional emotion is demanded; and we have noted (Pl. 12, fig. 6 and Pl. 13) that in Balinese mythology and in the theater the sibling relationship is a focal point for comical inversions of the conventional patterns of behavior — the elder brother being stylized as awkward and even gross. We shall see (Pl. 75) that the Balinese child very often passes through a gross and sulky unresponsive phase in early childhood, and that this phase is followed by a more impersonal adjustment in later childhood. It is legitimate to suppose that contexts of sibling rivalry play their part in establishing this sulky habit and that this earlier habit underlies the later impersonal adjustment.

1. A native drawing showing sibling rivalry and adult Balinese men engaged in the impersonal activity of carving geometrical designs on a door. This drawing was done for the Pita Maha Club of Balinese artists to be used as a poster advertising a sale of Balinese works of art.
   Painting by I Goesti Njoman Lempad of Oeboed.
   Reduced x ¼ linear.

2. A native drawing of sibling rivalry. This shows the younger child close to the mother, standing on a higher level and drinking; while the elder brother is farther from the mother, on a lower level, kneeling and holding a dish of food in his left hand (cf. Pls. 26 and 37 for the psychological contrast between eating and drinking). The mother's face is turned toward the younger child and she holds a bowl in her hands.
   The bodies of both children are coarse and thick, but that of the elder is much coarser. In addition, the elder holds out his right hand with the index and middle fingers extended and the palm turned upward. (This last feature differentiates the child's gesture from the conventional Balinese scolding gesture described in Pl. 62, fig. 3.)
   Painting by I Goesti Njoman Lempad of Oeboed.
   Purchased Jan. 6, 1938. Cat. No. 029. Reduced x ¼ linear.

3 to 7. A sequence of behavior involving mother, knee baby, and youngest baby in which knee baby is displaced in favor of the younger.
   In fig. 3, the knee baby is on his mother's lap and has his head resting against her breast. Both he and the mother are looking down at the youngest child, a baby girl, who is sitting below them on the ground. The mother's hand is extended downward inviting the baby to come up.
   In fig. 4, the baby girl has risen to her feet and the mother holds her by the upper part of her arm preparatory to lifting her up. The knee baby's response to this is to press his cheek closer to the mother's right breast and to grasp her left breast with his hand.
   In fig. 5, the mother has both children on her lap and has one arm around each of them. Her face is contracted with the effort of settling the two children, but she is already beginning to smile at the situation which she has created. The elder child has now shifted his grasp to her right breast and looks up into his mother's face (cf. Pl. 69, fig. 3). The younger child is settling herself to suck.
   In fig. 6, the knee baby looks round at the photographer but still holds the breast in his hand. His mother watches him, laughing.
   In fig. 7, the knee baby's hand has been displaced, while his mother rubs her breast to make the milk come. She looks away still laughing.
   Men Karma with her son, I Gata (knee baby) and her daughter, I Kenjoen, aged 520 days.
   Bajoeng Gede. Aug. 19, 1937.   14 I 8, 9, 11, 15, 18.

8. The same mother with her two youngest children. In this picture, the mother is standing and the younger child is sucking at one breast and reaching out with her left hand to hold the other. The knee baby is on the ground straining up toward his mother with his arm outstretched to hold her sarong. Note the parallel between this picture and the drawing in fig. 1.
   Men Karma with I Gata and I Kenjoen, aged 460 days.
   Bajoeng Gede. June 20, 1937.   11 U 21.

Plate 71

SIBLING RIVALRY III

The mother's behavior in this and the following plate is a conventional game which is often played — especially when there is an audience of visitors in the house. It consists of putting the new baby in the knee baby's lap and urging the latter to treat the rival as "younger sibling."

M. M.'s verbal record of the sequence of behavior shown in this plate reads as follows:

"Njawa (the knee baby, a girl) runs over and hangs on mother.

"Njawa tries to suck.

"Njawa given the baby to hold by her mother (fig. 1).

"Refuses, elbows sticking out (fig. 2).

"Men Njawi (the mother) says 'Gisiang! gisiang!' ('Hold it! hold it!') (fig. 3).

"Njawa puts her face down by the baby's (fig. 5).

"Njawa's arms tentatively around baby; she plays with her own mouth.

"Men Njawi says 'Gisiang!' ('Hold it!'). Njawa giggles self-consciously" (fig. 6).

(The remainder of the verbal record and discussion of the whole sequence are included in the description of the next plate.)

Men Njawi with her daughter, I Njawa, and new baby, I Koewat, aged 30 days.

Bajoeng Gede. April 30, 1937.   7 V 26, 27, 28, 29, 31, 32.

1

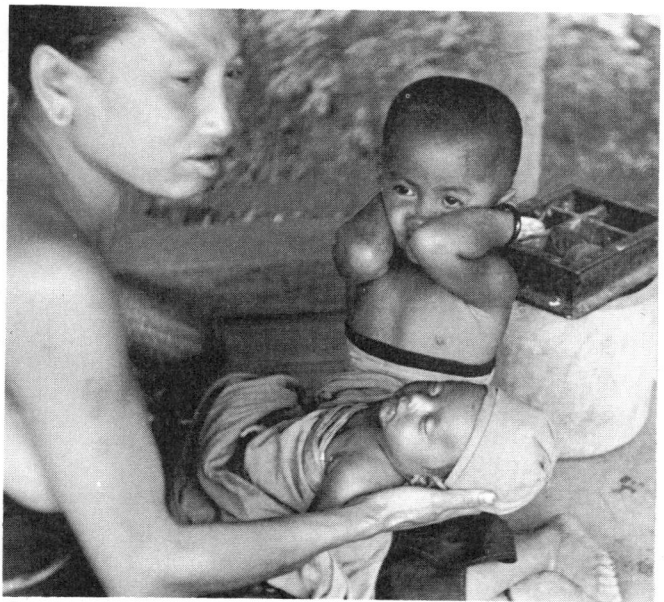

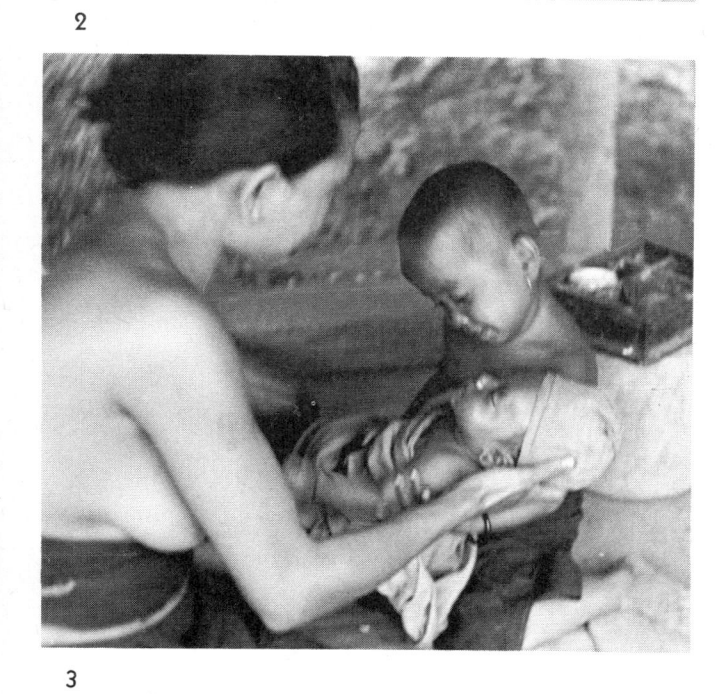

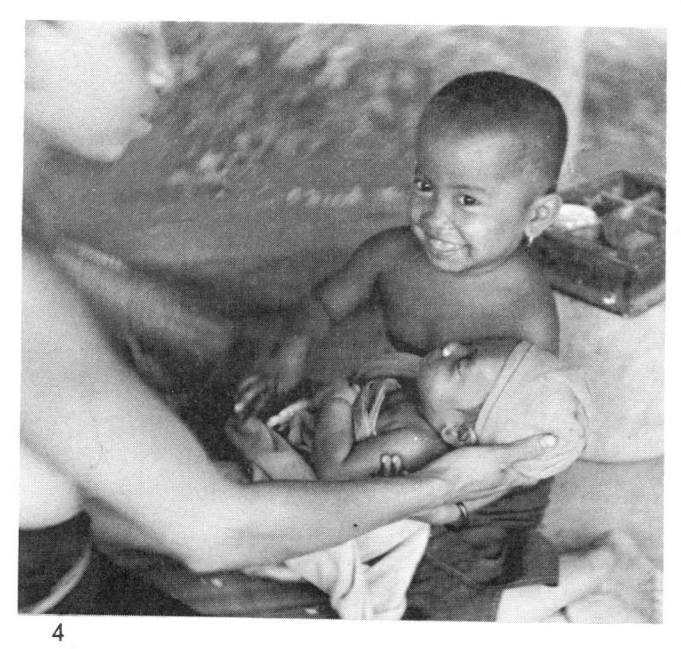

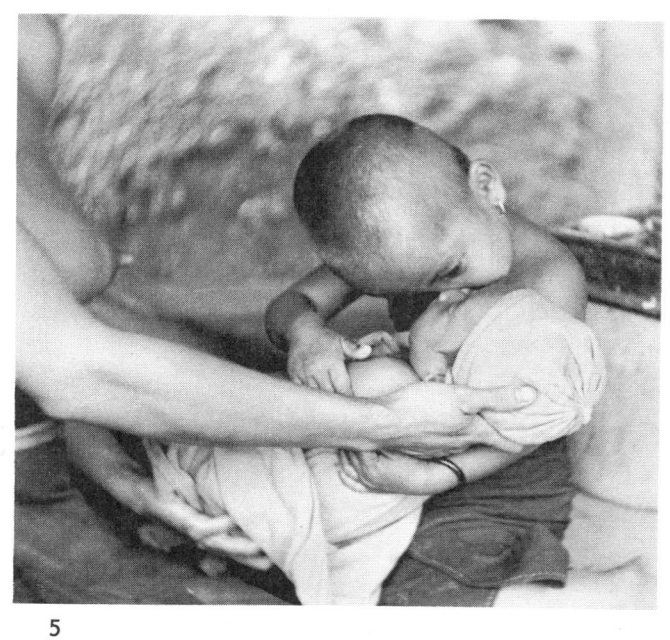

2

3

4

5

6

1

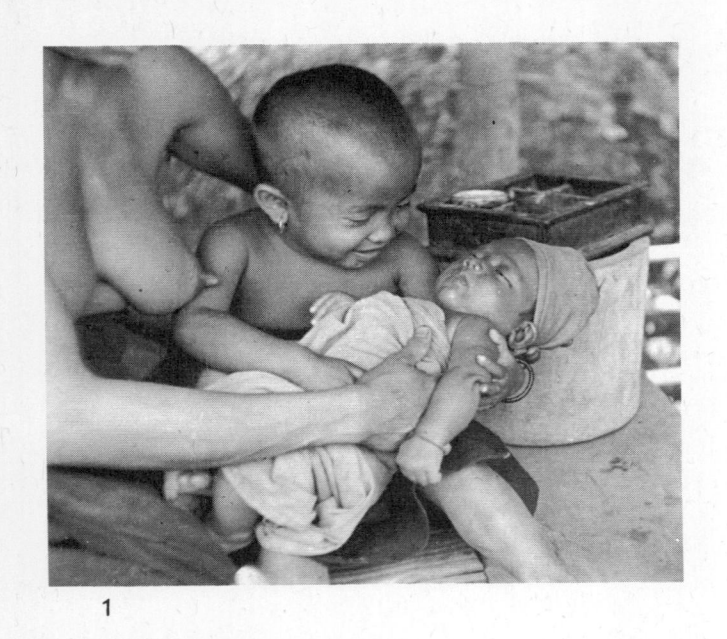

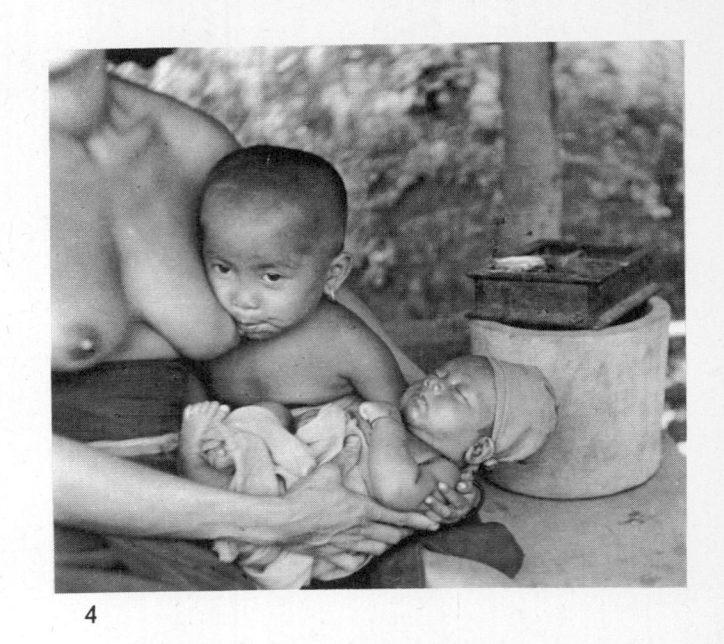

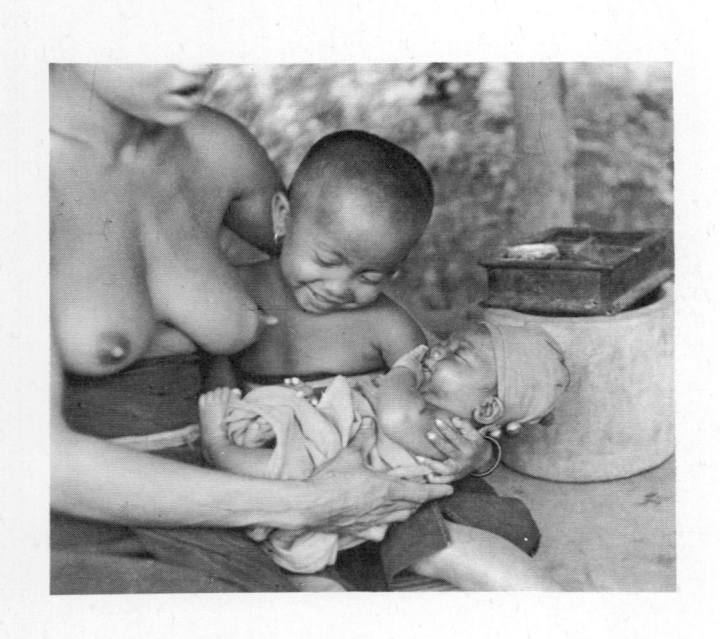

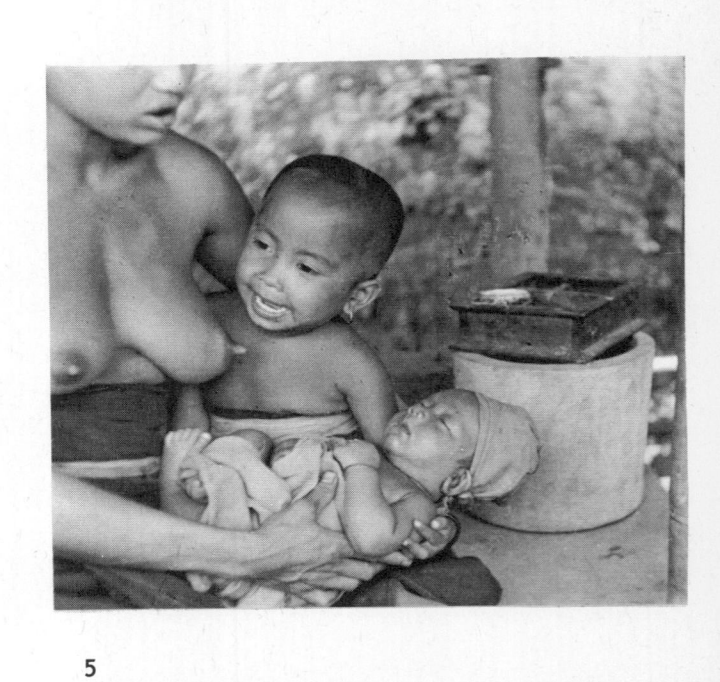

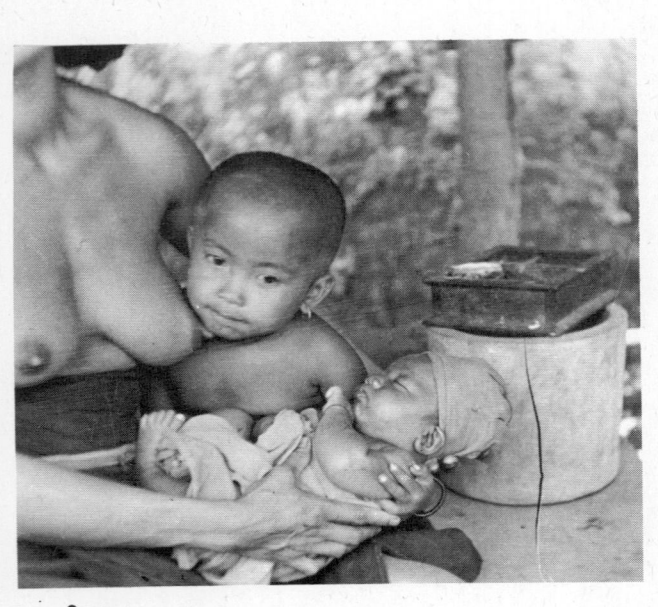

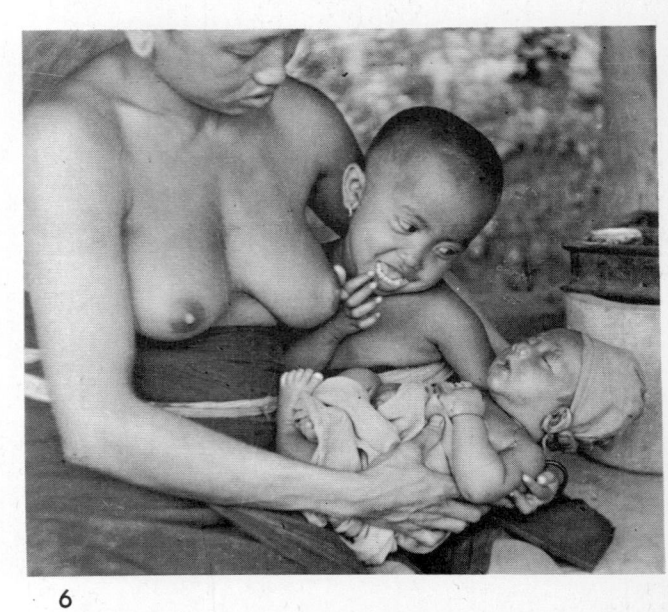

2

3

4

5

6

Plate 72
SIBLING RIVALRY IV

This plate continues the sequence begun on the previous plate.

M. M.'s verbal record of the second half of the behavior reads as follows:

"Njawa puts her face down to baby (no photograph).

"Njawa pokes baby's chest with her finger, and then puts her finger behind her and rubs it off vigorously on the back of her sarong.

"Men Njawi says 'Sit better; put your legs out,' and she straightens Njawa's legs and lays baby on them. Says *'Gisiang!'* Mother stern." (This change of position took place between Pl. 71, fig. 6 and Pl. 72, fig. 1.)

"Njawa says *'Ngelawang'* ('It's resisting').

"Men Njawi repeats this, laughing, 'She says it's resisting.' The baby is really absolutely passive and good.

"Njawa ignoring baby leans against breast (figs. 3 and 4).

"*'Poeles'* ('It's asleep' — probably said by the mother).

"Njawa looks at baby, finger in mouth" (fig. 6).

Putting the verbal record and the photographs together, the events fall into eight groups:

A. Njawa attempts to suck (recorded verbally), and the mother replies by placing the baby in Njawa's lap (Pl. 71, fig. 1).

B. Njawa withdraws (recorded verbally and in Pl. 71, fig. 2).

C. Njawa puts her face down in contact with that of the baby (recorded verbally and in Pl. 71, figs. 3 to 5), and then smiles at the photographer (fig. 6).

D. Njawa withdraws from the baby to play with her own mouth (recorded verbally) and the mother renews her insistence on attention to the baby.

E. Njawa again "kisses" the baby (recorded verbally).

F. Njawa repudiates the baby — poking it and then wiping her finger (recorded verbally). To this the mother responds with a vigorous effort to make her attend to the baby. The mother straightens Njawa's legs, etc.

G. The mother's attention shifts away from the children (Pl. 72, fig. 3) and Njawa sucks at the breast (Pl. 72, fig. 4), which is what she wanted to do at the beginning of the sequence.

H. Njawa looks at the baby with a triumphant expression, showing her teeth (recorded verbally without comment on the facial expression, and in Pl. 72, fig. 6).

The two sets of data complement each other on a number of points, and neither gives the whole story without the other. The camera did not record Njawa's initial attempt to suck nor any of the mother's behavior when she was most energetically trying to make Njawa attend to the baby. While this was happening the photographer had to move and refocus the camera, but the camera did record Njawa's exhibitionistic attention to the photographer, her final successful effort to suck and her facial expression when she looked at the baby at the end of the incident.

The sequence illustrates the knee baby's ambivalence, and her attempt to make loving the baby more palatable by exhibitionism. It also illustrates the characteristic inconsistency of the mother's behavior — in first making a considerable effort to prevent the knee baby from sucking by making her pay attention to the new baby, and later permitting her to suck. It is true that the mother's attention reverts to the knee baby after the sucking, but no rebuke followed, and the photographs show no sharp movement of the mother's body or left hand.

Men Njawi with I Njawa and I Koewat.

Bajoeng Gede. April 30, 1937. 7 V 34, 35, 36, 37, 38, 39.

Plate 73

EACH PARENT WITH THREE CHILDREN

This plate shows a father and mother (Nang and Men Karma) with each of their three youngest children. They have three other children older than those shown here, but they are now past the period of maximum dependence on the parents. The three youngest children, however, illustrate the various stages of diminishing dependence, and especially the fact that independence is achieved by the adoption of different behavioral roles according to the temporary position of the child in the series of siblings.

The behavioral role played by any child and the treatment which it receives depend partly upon the age of the child but still more upon its ordinal position, counting from the youngest. The first (i.e., the youngest) child is in the most favored position so far as the mother is concerned, but is not yet given very much attention by the father. The second child (or knee baby) is passing through a period during which he is sharply prohibited from access to the mother's breast, though he still steals to the breast. He is, however, in maximum favor with the father. The third child is still anxious to get attention from the parents, but gets very little and will soon adopt a new role as nurse, carrying the youngest child around in a sling (cf. Pl. 79).

1. The mother with the youngest child at the breast.
    Men Karma with I Kenjoen, aged 183 days.
    Bajoeng Gede. Sept. 20, 1936.   2 Q 2.

2 and 3. The mother with the second child (knee baby). These photographs were taken on the same day as fig. 1, and they show the second child stealing to the breast, first with his hand and then with his mouth.
    M. M.'s verbal record of this incident is as follows:
    "Gata (the knee baby) went over to the north side of the yard and defecated. Everyone disapproved, mildly crying out a little. Men Karma (the mother) quietly went and got some dry leaves and cleaned it up, then took Gata up gently and without rebuke, and carried him off to clean him with some more leaves. She returned with him in the sling very contented. He has a red fruit in his hand, breaks it open and starts squeezing the juice on the ground; rebuked by both parents and others, who took it away from him (cf. Pl. 32, figs. 1 to 5). He blows bubbles, plays with the edge of the cloth which lies over his mother's breast, but does not touch the breast. Touches nipple, looking away as he does so. Then twists a bit of his own coat into a knot and plays with it. Pats his mother's shoulder rhythmically. . . .
    "Gata finally yielded and started to suck his mother's breast. His mother and everyone else stared with disapproval, and his mother took the flat of her hand and pushed his head away, good-humoredly and absolutely without affect. He repeated this twice and was pushed away. He did not cry but hung onto her shoulder with a blissful expression. Then took her nipple in one hand and again covered it with the other."
    Men Karma holding I Gata.
    Bajoeng Gede. Sept. 20, 1936.   2 Q 3, 9.

4. The mother with the third child and the youngest. The baby is at the breast between the mother and the third child, but the latter is having her head loused by the mother — almost the only form of parental attention that is extended to this child.
    Men Karma; I Gati and I Kenjoen.
    Bajoeng Gede. Aug. 19, 1937.   14 I 39.

5. The third from youngest child hides behind the mother while the mother's attention goes to the second from youngest. This position is one very commonly assumed by the third child (cf. fig. 8), and enables her to keep physical contact with the parent though making no demands on the parent's attention.
    I Gati behind Men Karma, with I Gata in front.
    Bajoeng Gede. Nov. 23, 1937.   19 B 37.

6. The father with the youngest child. At the period shown in fig. 1, this baby was almost entirely in his mother's care, though we have two records of the father suckling the baby at his nipple during that period. Now, six months later, the baby is beginning to displace the knee baby in the father's attention when at home. But it is still the knee baby that the father takes with him when he goes out.
    Nang Karma with I Kenjoen, aged 383 days.
    Bajoeng Gede. April 4, 1937.   6 P 6.

7. The father with the second from youngest child. The father is acting as priest at a trance performance (*sangiang*) while the child is curled up, happy in his lap.
    Nang Karma with I Gata.
    Bajoeng Gede. July 8, 1936.   1 Y 13.

8. The father with the third child. The girl has still not fully accepted the child-nurse position and flirts to attract her father's attention, often taking up a position behind him.
    Nang Karma with I Gati beside him and I Gata in right foreground.
    Bajoeng Gede. Sept. 27, 1936.   2 S 4.

1
2
3
4
5
6
7
8

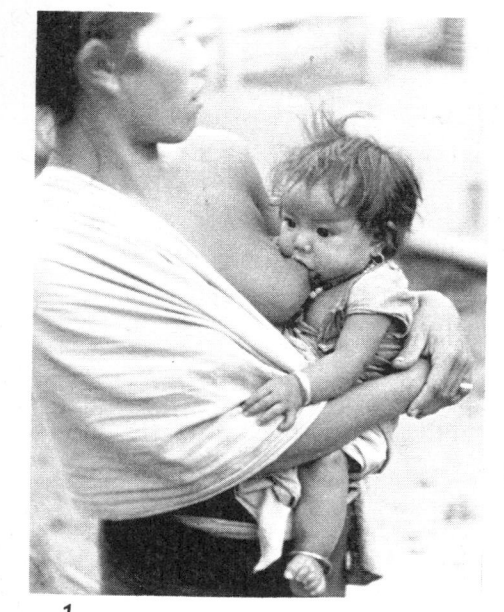

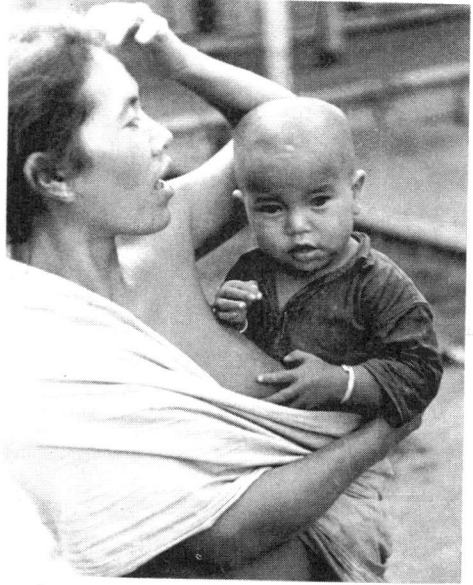

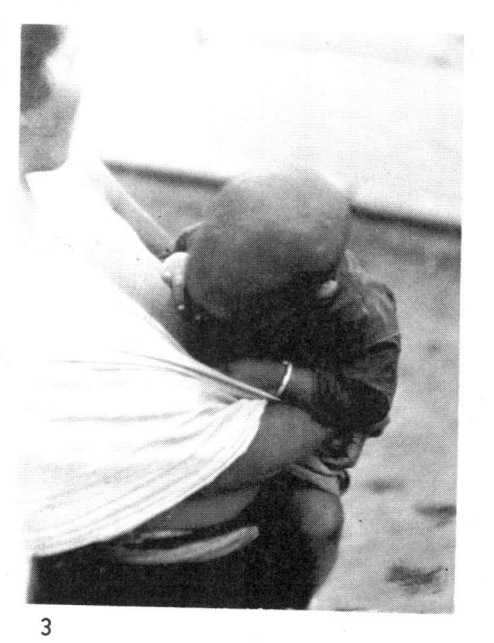

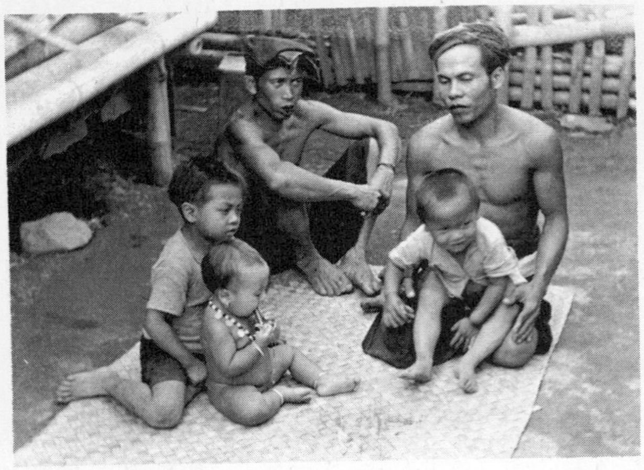
1

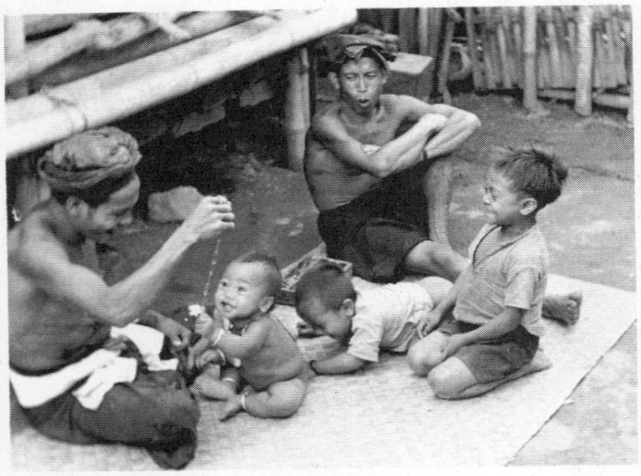
2

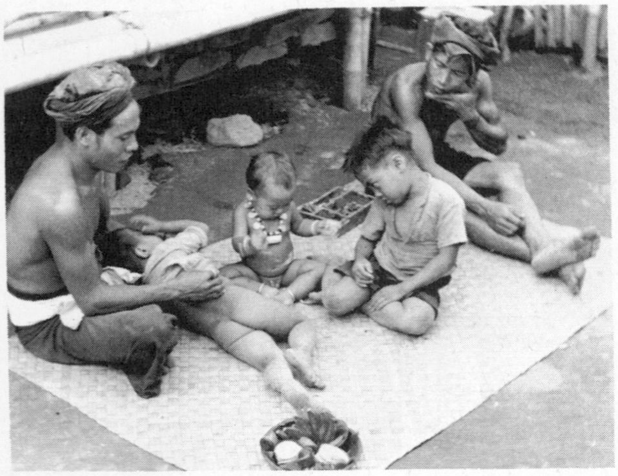
3

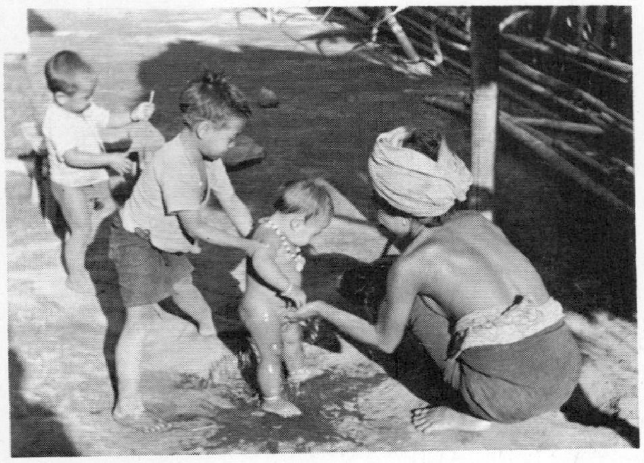
4

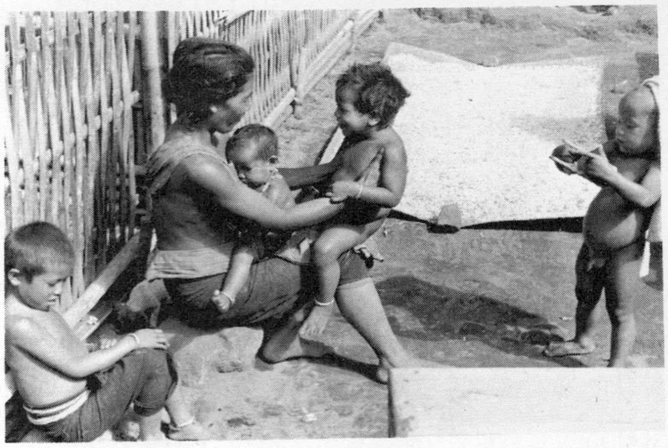
5

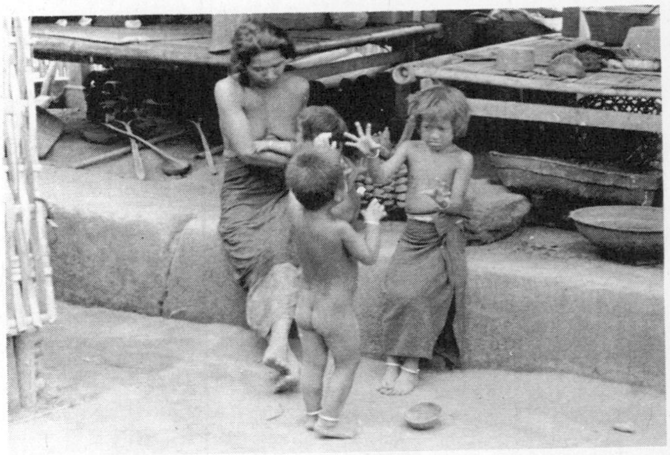
6

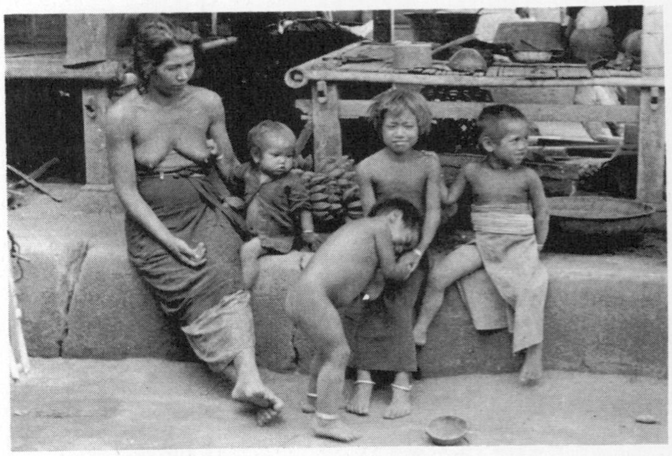
7

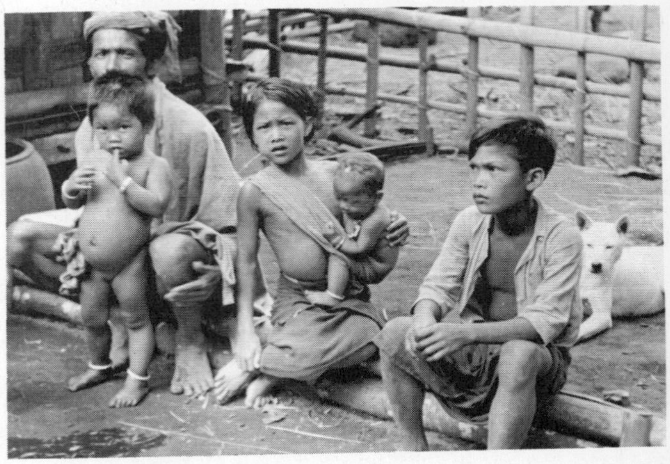
8

Plate 74

ROLES OF SIBLINGS

The position of each sibling in the sequence governs not only his access to parental attention, but also his behavior toward the other siblings. This is most conspicuous in the case of the relationship between first and third sibling (counting from the youngest), where the elder child becomes a parent-substitute. The role of the second child is less clearly defined. He gets all that he can of parental attention, and may, as we have seen, get a great deal of attention from the father. The second child's success with the father is apparently much harder for the third child to bear than is the existence of the youngest child.

1 to 3. Sibling relationships in a family with three boys.

In fig. 1, the oldest child has the baby in his lap, while the second child sits in the father's lap.

In fig. 2, the father plays with the baby while the oldest child watches happily. The second child is crawling over toward the father.

In fig. 3, the second child is sprawling in the father's lap while the oldest child looks on jealously and the baby plays alone.

Nang Degeng, the father, with I Degeng, eldest son (wearing black shorts); I Leket, second son (with shirt but no shorts); I Sepek, the youngest, aged 140 days. In the background, Nang Leket, brother of Nang Degeng, who has partially adopted I Leket. I Leket is therefore in an abnormal status; he is Nang Degeng's second child and Nang Leket's only child.

Bajoeng Gede. April 30, 1937. 7 S 7, 24, 33.

4. The same children with the adoptive mother of the second child. Here the oldest is again behaving like a parent, assisting Men Leket to bathe the baby. He holds him under his arms while she splashes water on him. In the background, I Leket, the second child, is playing by himself.

Men Leket bathing I Sepek, aged 140 days; I Degeng helping. I Leket in the background.

Bajoeng Gede. April 30, 1937. 7 U 29.

5. A mother with her three youngest children. This photograph shows the second child playing a role parallel to that of the youngest. The baby sits astride on the mother's lap and pulls at the breast, and the second child sits, also astride, holding her arms, while she holds him under the armpits. The older third child meanwhile sits, sulky and withdrawn, in the left foreground.

Men Karma with I Kenjoen at the breast, I Gata on her knee; I Gati sitting on the ground. I Karsa, a cousin of these children, stands on the extreme right.

Bajoeng Gede. June 20, 1937. 11 V 37.

6 and 7. Play between the second and third children. In fig. 6, the older sister plays at being the Witch (a parental role) with her fingers splayed out. The fingers of the left hand are bent as if to claw at her brother, and her face is contracted into a scowl. (Children, when they play at being the Witch, usually accentuate the threatening aspects of the part; adults, when they play the Witch's role on the stage, do not flex the fingers into claws, cf. Pl. 60, figs. 1 to 4.) The second child stands facing her, in what appears to be a startled posture. The mother is looking at her youngest child who sucks at one breast and holds on to the other.

In fig. 7, the mother and youngest child have turned to watch the second child who is now burying his head in his elder sister's lap, treating her as a parent.

Men Karma; I Kenjoen; I Gati; I Adjer, a neighbor's child, on the right; I Gata with his head on I Gati's lap.

Bajoeng Gede. Nov. 23, 1937. 19 B 15, 18.

8. A father and his four children. In this photograph, the children have arranged themselves almost schematically according to their roles in the family constellation. The fourth child (counting from the youngest) sits a little apart from the others — he already spends most of his time outside the family with other boys of his own age. The third child, a girl, sits near her father and carries the first (youngest) child in a sling. The second child stands with her back toward her father and in contact with his knee.

Nang Lintar; I Meres (second child); I Ngembon (third child) with the new baby; and I Ngetis.

Bajoeng Gede. Feb. 12, 1939. 36 M 16.

Plate 75

INFANCY AND UNRESPONSIVENESS

Plates 75 to 83 deal with successive stages in the development of the child from infancy to young adulthood, the first two of these stages being shown on this plate.

A baby, according to the Balinese cliché, is most happy at its 210-day birthday. Actually the period of happiness and responsiveness extends considerably beyond this occasion, and most babies do not become unresponsive till they are about two years old. In infancy the baby is played with and stimulated and responds happily to this constant stimulation. Gradually, however, this stimulation becomes a source of frustration, and the child of two or three, traversing a group of adults, will walk carefully, taking long detours to avoid coming within reach of any adult's arm which might reach out to play with the child or pull at his genital.

In addition to this caution, the child's habitual postures and facial expression change toward coarseness. The corners of the mouth become drawn in so that the lips protrude, as though the child were constantly on the verge of tears.

These changes occur regardless of whether another younger child is born to the family, but it is likely that being displaced from the mother's attention would hasten the change (cf. Pl. 70, where it is suggested that the coarseness of the elder-brother stereotype is related to this stage of childhood).

1, 2, and 3. A baby girl at two stages of development.

In fig. 1, she is 289 days old, and her mother is playing with her. The mother holds her high and laughs up at her, enjoying her (cf. Pl. 62, fig. 1).

Fig. 2 was taken on the same day as fig. 1, but shows a momentary fall in the baby's spirits, which we may regard as an indication of how her facial expression will develop.

In fig. 3, she is two years older, sullen and unresponsive, being carried by her elder sister. Child nurses enjoy carrying small babies, and a small baby, especially if it be lively, is eagerly sought after and constantly passed from one little girl to another; but this girl is now too heavy, and is probably carried only by her own elder sister.

Men Karma; I Kenjoen (aged 289 days in figs. 1 and 2; 1062 days in fig. 3); I Karmi.

Bajoeng Gede. Jan. 30, 1937 and Feb. 12, 1939.   4 K 4, 9; 36 D 19.

4, 5, and 6. A baby girl at two stages of development.

In fig. 4, she is playing on her mother's lap; and in fig. 5, taken the same day, she is being carried by her next elder sister.

In fig. 6, taken two years later, she stands between her father's knees with a slightly sulky expression and her arms folded inside her blanket. The elder sister who was carrying her in fig. 5 is now carrying the recently born baby. (Pl. 74, fig. 8 includes another photograph of this child on the same day.)

Men Lintar, the mother; I Ngembon, the elder sister; Nang Lintar, the father; I Meres, the baby girl.

Bajoeng Gede. March 30, 1937 and Feb. 12, 1939.   6 L 26, 10; 36 M 27.

7 and 8. A small boy at two stages of development.

In fig. 7, he is kneeling beside his father and has his hands on his father's shoulder. The next younger child is sitting between the father's knees. The occasion is the birthday of the younger child, actually celebrated on the 315th day (cf. Pl. 74, figs. 1 to 4 for a still earlier series of photographs of this family).

In fig. 8, taken two years later, the same small boy is standing alone with his face puckered and sullen.

Nang Degeng, the father; I Leket, the knee baby; I Sepek, the youngest child, aged 315 days in fig. 7.

Bajoeng Gede. April 30, 1937 and Feb. 12, 1939.   7 S 5; 36 K 9.

9. A mother with two children. The group is sitting at the edge of the houseyard, withdrawn from the confusion of other relatives and neighbors who have come for a marriage feast. Note the mother's disassociated expression, the older daughter's tight mouth, and the younger child's frightened and hostile stare. The old woman on the right has her hand between her face and the crowd.

Men Kesir holding her daughter, I Doemoen; I Kesir, bottom left; and an unrelated stranger on the right.

Bajoeng Gede. Aug. 8, 1937.   13 S 14.

1

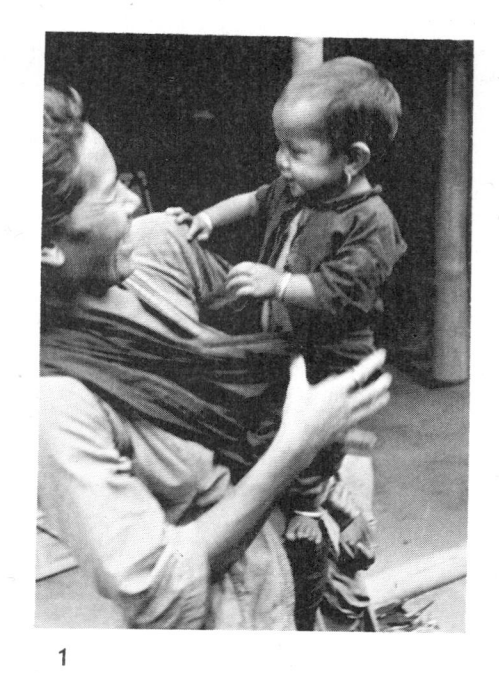

2

3

4

5

6

7

8

9

1
2
3
4
5
6
7
8

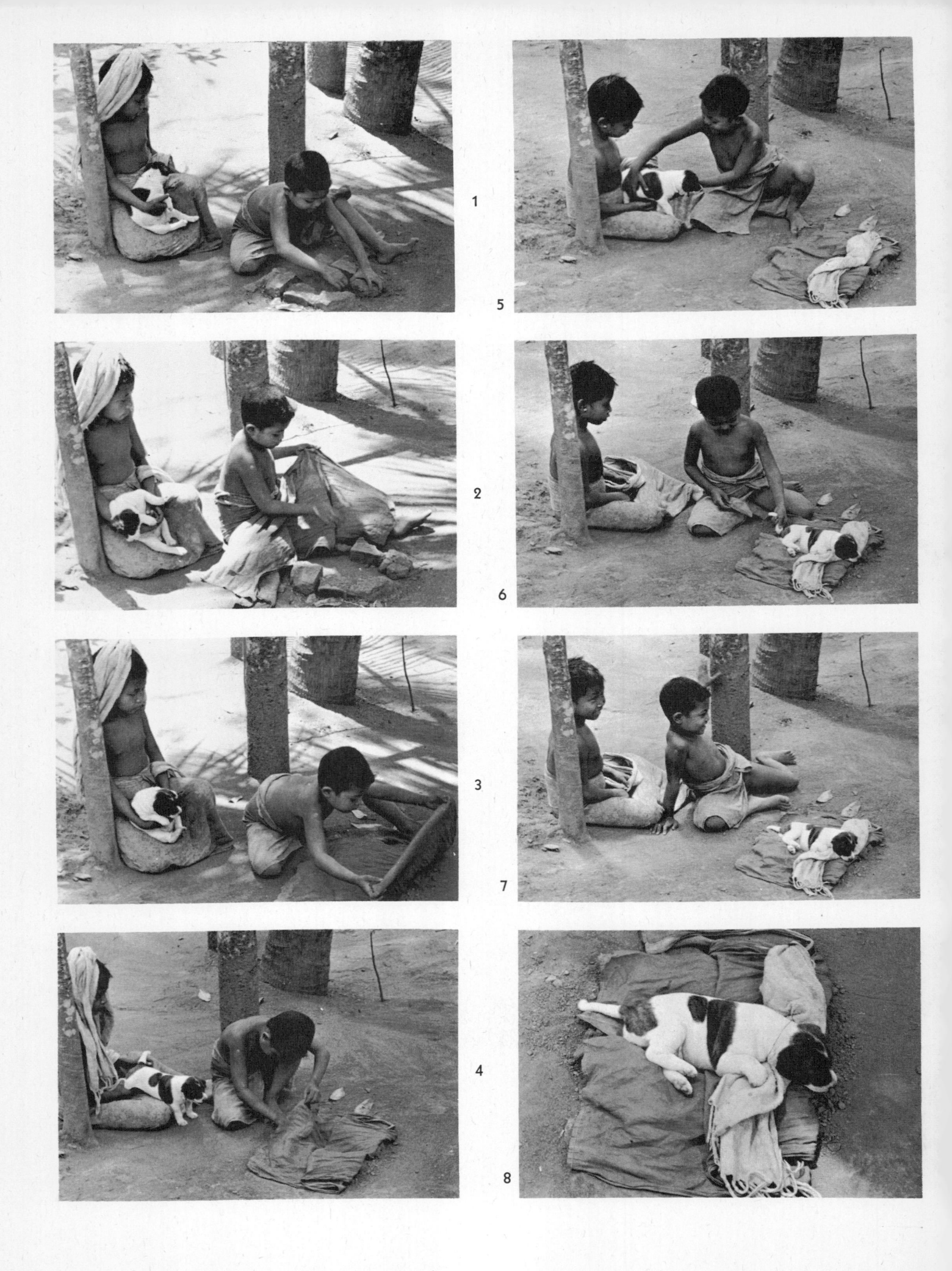

Plate 76

SMALL GIRLS' PLAY I

This and the following two plates show play behavior of small girls soon after they have become a group of age mates, cutting across caste and family lines.

Their play is very largely imitative of the themes of adult culture, but it also contains conventional games of the "crack-the-whip" type, semispontaneous elements (e.g., jumping over the puppy, as in Pl. 77) and a number of elements derived from the handling of babies. These little girls are already acting sometimes as child nurses but this does not eliminate the tendency to play with substitute babies of various sorts (cf. Pl. 38, fig. 3). The puppy in these photographs is mostly cast for the role of corpse, but several times it is treated as a baby.

The play here recorded took place on two successive days. We were doing a detailed study of an adult Brahman artist at work, and the children were playing in his courtyard.

1 to 8. Two small Brahman girls lay out a puppy as though it were a corpse.

In fig. 1, one girl holds the puppy while the other arranges stones on the ground to make a bed or grave.

In figs. 2, 3, and 4, she takes her sling cloth and lays it smoothly over the stones, going back in fig. 4 to adjust the stones under the cloth. The girl who is holding the puppy meanwhile sits quiet, paying very little attention to the preparation of the grave and no attention to the puppy till, in fig. 4, he tries to escape and she holds him tightly by the hind leg.

In fig. 5, the headcloth of the second girl has been laid out as a sash over the sling cloth, and the first girl is about to place the puppy on its prepared grave.

In fig. 6, the puppy is lying quietly on the grave, but the children have for the moment forgotten that they are playing at "funerals." The first girl is pulling the puppy's tail as a means of raising its hindquarters so that she can place a leaf under its anus, treating it as a baby. (The leaf is visible in place in fig. 8.)

In fig. 7, both girls have for a moment lost interest in the puppy and are grinning at M. M.

Fig. 8 shows the lay-out of the puppy. It is interesting to note that they have inverted the standard method of laying out a corpse. They have placed the body on top of its clothes instead of under them (cf. Pl. 92).

I Daijoe Ribek, a neighbor, leaning against tree; I Daijoe Soekra, the daughter of the house, laying out puppy.

Batoean. Oct. 6, 1937.   16 P 3, 4, 5, 7, 9, 11, 12, 13.

Plate 77

SMALL GIRLS' PLAY II

This plate continues the sequence shown on the previous plate.

1 to 8. The little girls leave the puppy covered up and start to draw in the sand. Some small boys come and watch them, and the girls start a game of jumping over the puppy, first jumping forward and then jumping backward.

In fig. 1, the first girl covers the puppy. She has removed the headcloth from underneath and now places it on top of the animal, thus partially correcting the first lay-out in which the puppy was on top of the clothes.

In fig. 2, the girls have left the puppy covered up and have started to draw in the sand. In the bottom right is a group of small boys who have also been drawing in the sand. These are the boys who join the girls in fig. 4.

In fig. 3, the puppy is still lying under its cover and the girls are drawing "hornets' nests" (*taboehan*). This is a conventional design which is begun at the center by drawing a crosslet (i.e., a cross whose arms are themselves crossed). The design is then increased indefinitely by drawing a continuous line around and around the central crosslet.

In fig. 4, the boys have come across the yard to watch the girls, who have started to play with the puppy again.

In fig. 5, the girls stand self-consciously, the second behind the first and with her arms around her. They are laughing and watching M. M.

In figs. 6 and 7, a new game has started. The girls are now jumping over the puppy.

In fig. 8, a variant is added to this game — jumping backward instead of forward.

Daijoe Soekra; Daijoe Ribek; I. B. Terang, the boy with white cloth; I. B. Saboeh, the other boy.

Batoean. Oct. 6, 1937.   16 P 23, 24, 27; 16 Q 5, 8, 9, 10, 11.

1
2
3
4
5
6
7
8

1
2
3
4
5
6
7
8

Plate 78

SMALL GIRLS' PLAY III

This plate shows the same girls playing with the puppy on the day after the behavior recorded on the two previous plates.

1 to 8. The little girls have two hibiscus flowers which they have spiked on the ends of small sticks to make them into umbrellas. The role of the puppy varies. It is a Dragon in fig. 1, a corpse in fig. 2, a baby in figs. 3 and 4.

In fig. 1, one girl holds the puppy in her lap, and she holds one of the flowers in her right hand. Another girl cooperates, holding the other flower, so that the two flowers make an arch over the puppy's head. The puppy is here being honored with umbrellas (cf. Pl. 10, fig. 4), while the girls sing Dragon music.

In fig. 2, the girl who was holding the puppy has now lost interest in it and is using her flower to hit one of the other girls. The girl who held the second flower is now starting to cover the puppy with a cloth, treating it as a corpse.

In fig. 3, the second girl has now taken complete possession of the puppy and holds it on her lap, while the first girl starts to tease it by hitting at it with her flower.

In fig. 4, the second girl is now putting the puppy to bed on her lap and covering it with a cloth. The first girl still teases the puppy with her flower.

In fig. 5, the flowers have been discarded, and the girls are starting to bury the puppy with cloth.

In figs. 6 and 7, they have started to lie on the puppy, apparently using it as a pillow.

In fig. 8, a new game has started. The girl on the right is busy collecting dust in her lap and the little boy (with back to camera) is helping her. Later she went across and put this sand into the hole which had been used as "grave" for the puppy in yesterday's play. After this all the children began to draw in the sand.

Daijoe Soekra; Daijoe Ribek; I Rentjen, on the left in fig. 3; I. B. Toempek, on the left in fig. 7; Daijoe Meser, on the right in fig. 6.

Batoean. Oct. 7, 1937.   16 S 31, 34, 37, 40; 16 T 8, 19, 20, 25.

Plate 79

CHILD NURSE

The major role which small girls play in social life is as nurses. Chiefly they carry around their own younger siblings, but if there is no other baby in the house where a girl lives, she will borrow other babies to carry. There is a great deal of interchange of babies so that, though a baby may leave home in the hands of one girl, it will pass through the hands of many others before one of them brings it back to the mother.

The relationship between child nurse and baby is not of such a kind as would result in introjection of a personalized super-ego. The baby learns limpness — that when the nurse is playing "crack-the-whip" (called *"goak-goakan"* or "flock of crows"), it is best not to stiffen any muscles — and it learns to sleep if the child nurse has a temper tantrum.

The baby is treated mostly not as a person capable of learning by reward and punishment, but simply as a more or less awkward bundle.

Even when the child nurse plays with the baby, her attitude toward it is the characteristically Balinese delight in stimulating some responsive object. She treats the child as an autocosmic symbol (cf. Pls. 38 to 44). This may be described as treating the child as "different from the self" (except insofar as one's own body or its parts are autocosmic symbols), but the relationship between Balinese child nurse and baby is still very far from being comparable to the relationships in which, in Western cultures, the image of some adult is introjected to form a personalized super-ego. For the Western type of character structure, it is surely necessary that there be great contrast between the two persons. This occurs where the baby is looked after by adults, but where the baby is looked after by children only a little older than itself, the contrast is necessarily less.

1 to 8. A child nurse with her younger sister. Both children came to our house to get treatment for some minor infection of the eyes (such infections are very common in the mountains during the extreme dry season), and both were a little fretful on this particular day. In addition, the child nurse was still learning her task, and was not yet fully skilled in the art of fixing the two ends of the sling under the baby.

In figs. 1 to 3, the baby is yelling, and the nurse, trying to quiet her, disturbs the set of the sling.

In figs. 4, 5, and 6, the nurse is adjusting the sling. She has the two ends hanging down from her shoulder, and she raises the baby high. Then she wraps the ends across the baby's nates, and pulls them up between the baby's legs, so that when the baby is again lowered, its weight will hold the ends in place.

In figs. 7 and 8, the baby is limp and asleep.

In fig. 8, the baby has awakened and is crying, but the child nurse now pays no attention — by fixedly looking in the opposite direction.

The whole series covers about two minutes of behavior.

I Gati with her younger sister, I Kenjoen, aged 520 days.

Bajoeng Gede. Aug. 19, 1937. 14 B 1, 2, 3, 4, 5, 6, 7, 8, 9.

1 2 3

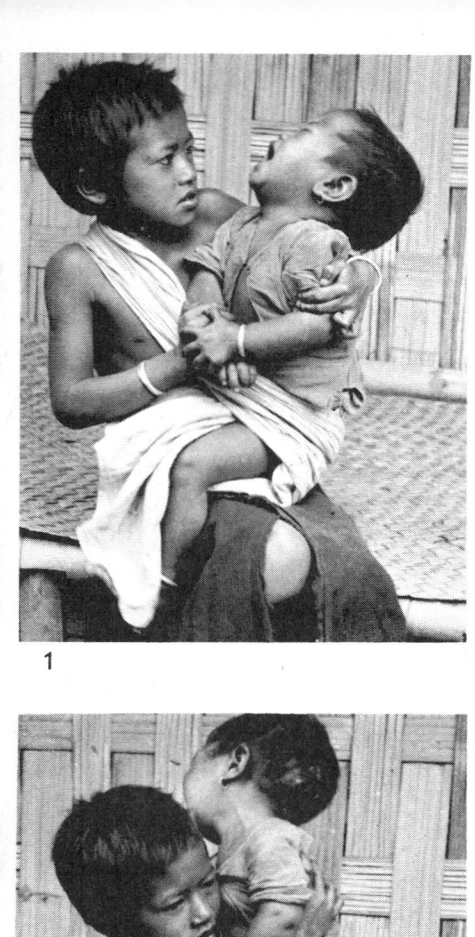

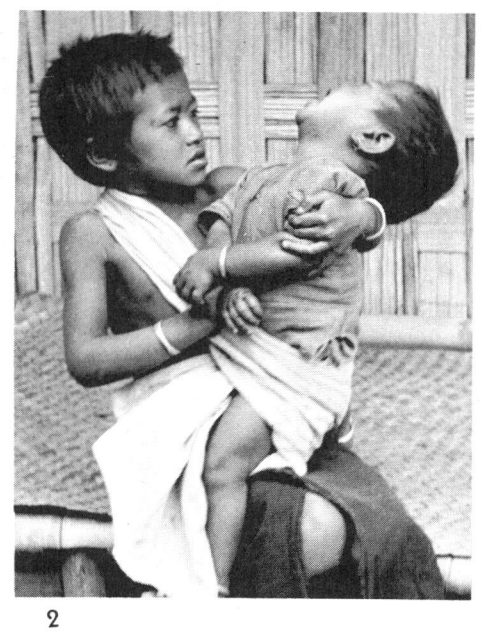

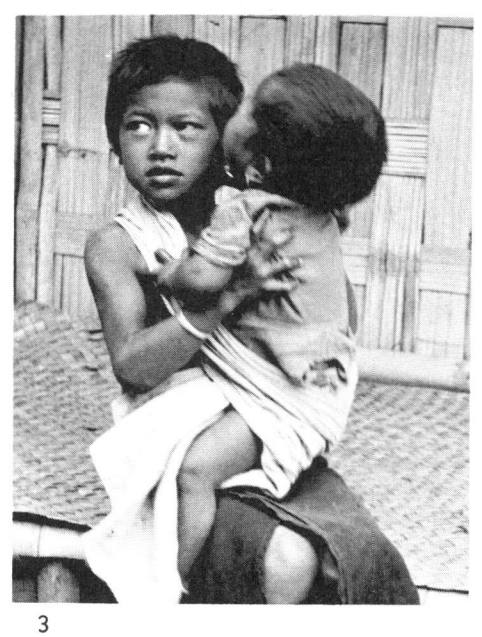

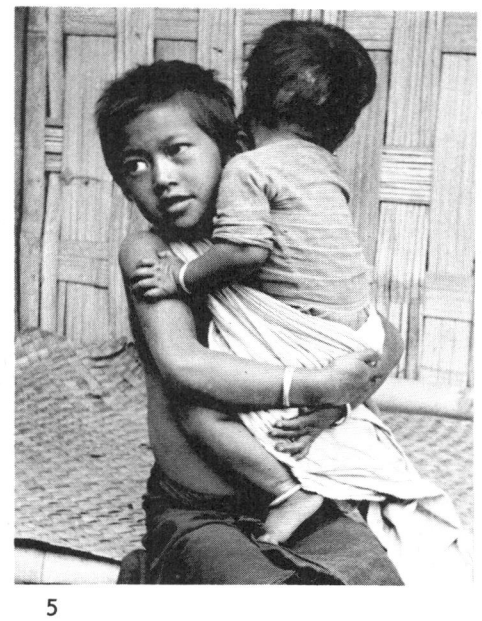

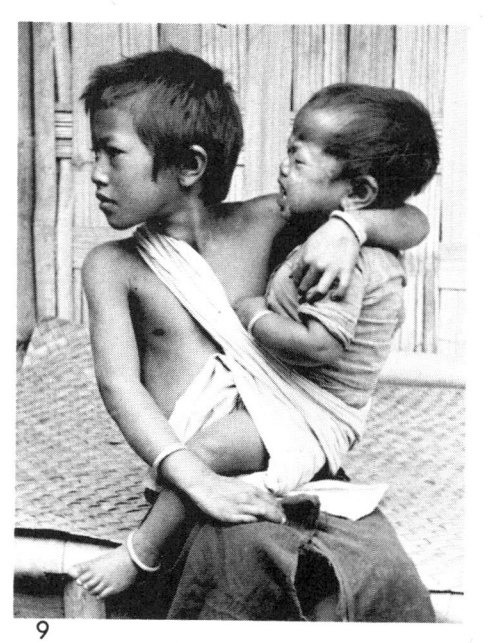

4 5 6

7 8 9

1

2

3

4

5

6

Plate 80

FEMALE CHILDHOOD

During the period between early childhood and adolescence, girls have a very definite part in the social life of the village. In addition to the care of babies, already illustrated, the girls do a considerable part of the work of preparing offerings for temple feasts and ceremonies in the household; they carry the offerings to the temple and remain there as an important part of the congregation. In fact, the business of ritual is carried on chiefly by older people and girls, while the young married people and the boys play a very small part except when they are specially involved in some particular ceremony.

Characteristically, a group at work on the preparation of offerings consists of a few older women and more girls than are necessary for the work, and in such a group any given girl is sometimes working, sometimes watching, sometimes playing either with a baby or with other girls and smaller boys.

The girls also have a number of conventionalized forms of play of the oranges-and-lemons and crack-the-whip types. Here again the typical play group consists of older girls and younger boys, while the boys who would be contemporary with the girls are out with their oxen or playing in separate groups.

1. Girls and small boys at a mudhole. These holes are made by the men in order to get mud for the walls which surround the houseyards. The hard work of puddling this mud is done by the men, but the children also play in it. On this occasion, they left the babies on the bank where they screamed until they were picked up. The play consisted of chasing, mock slapping, wrestling, and teetering on the edge until they lost balance and jumped into the pit. All this was done clothed, but with the sarong tucked up high (cf. the same rowdy behavior associated with water and mud in the carrying of the corpse, shown in Pl. 95).

I Renoe carrying I Malen; I Gedjar on left; I Karsa in foreground.

Bajoeng Gede. May 11, 1937. 8 M 25.

2. Girls at a wedding ceremony. In the intervals of preparing the feast, they have made "long hair" for themselves out of some of the palm-leaf strips which were used in preparing the offerings.

I Renoe on the left; I Karni wearing "long hair"; I Kemit on the right (cf. Pl. 54 for I Karni's tantrum behavior).

Bajoeng Gede. April 14, 1937. 6 V 22.

3. Girls standing on the fringe of the congregation at a ceremony. They have just brought offerings to the ceremony and are still wearing their head cloths as carrying pads.

I Karni sitting; I Njantel with her hands to her head; I Renoe on the left; I Misi on the right.

Bajoeng Gede. Aug. 18, 1937. 13 S 39.

4. Girls in a group working on offerings. They have used some of the white clay prepared for the offerings to paint the faces of the small boys.

I Desak Made Rai painting.

Batoean. Sept. 27, 1937. 16 C 43.

5. Another part of the group shown in fig. 4. The man on the left is laying the base for a high offering, while one girl helps him by steadying the stand. The other two girls play with the baby.

Batoean. Sept. 27, 1937. 16 C 12.

6. High-caste girls playing "crack-the-whip" (*goak-goakan,* literally "flock of crows"). This photograph shows part of a long line of girls running, and each girl holding the girl in front of her. The leader tries to catch the girl on the end of the chain.

Daijoe Poetoe Manis; Daijoe Poetoe Sasih; Daijoe Soekra.

Batoean. Feb. 21, 1939. 36 Q 16.

Plate 81

FEMALE ADOLESCENCE I

In this period, the status of the girl gets formal recognition (in the mountain communities) when she becomes a member of the *daa* group in which she remains until marriage or until the village officials can no longer overlook her sexual indiscretions. Theoretically each household should be represented by one girl in this organization.

The girls' occupations remain approximately what they were at an earlier age — the care of babies, preparation of offerings, weeding the fields, etc. — but as a *daa* she has certain ceremonial duties. She is still ceremonially pure and can enter the special temples from which young married people are excluded. She should become a member of the village maidens' dance group (*redjang*) which performs at temple feasts, but if she is too shy to dance she may choose rather to work on the offerings.

1. The leaders of the *redjang* dance in Bajoeng Gede. The dance is a slow procession with smooth movements of the arms and hands.
I Soka leading; I Teboes behind her.
Bajoeng Gede. Dec. 22, 1937.   20 Q 35.

2 and 3. The whole *redjang* group dancing in two lines. The prettier girls and the better dancers are put at the front end of the column, and it is possible to see in the photograph that the formal precision of the front end is not preserved at the back. A great deal of the audience's attention goes to the new and inexperienced dancers at the back who are self-conscious and shy, and who, if they feel themselves mocked at (*djailina*) will give up the *redjang* and work on offerings instead.
In fig. 3, the dance has just finished, and all are running off the temple court giggling.
I Wandri leading on the left; I Salib leading on the right.
Bajoeng Gede. Nov. 25, 1937.   19 L 4, 5.

4. The *daa* group offering toward the cemetery. Certain details of ceremonial can only be performed by the village maidens, and the girls are shown here, in an incident of wedding ceremonial, offering baskets of food toward the cemetery. The ceremonial acts which fall to the *daa* group are usually performed with giggling.
I Dabdab; I Ngembat; I Roemi; I Karmi; I Moegloek; I Remin.
Bajoeng Gede. Oct. 2, 1936.   2 V 8.

5. Girls dressed up for *redjang* procession. This photograph shows how much more elaborate the ceremonial may become in other communities, as compared with the extreme simplicity of Bajoeng Gede.
Redjang from Boeaijangan in the Karangasem District.
Karangasem. Aug. 8, 1937.   13 G 33.

6. The *daa* group of Bajoeng Gede cleaning the Temple of Origin (Poera Poeseh). This temple is too sacred to be entered by married people unless they have performed certain *rites de passage* (*mesaioet*). The work of weeding and cleaning this temple is a duty of the *daa* group. Once a month the village crier warns them that on the morrow they must perform this task. They are not supervised and do not work very hard at it.
I Karmi holding I Karba; I Tamboen holding rake.
Bajoeng Gede. May 26, 1937.   9 M 17.

1

2

4

3

5

6

1

2

3

5

6

Plate 82

FEMALE ADOLESCENCE II

This plate illustrates the ceremonial routines of the adolescent daughter in a Brahman household. In addition to these acts she also does her share of the work in the household — cooking, sweeping, going to market, etc.

All the photographs are of the same girl, Daijoe Ketoet Siti.

1. She is here seen offering to the god of the Goenoeng Agoeng (the central mountain of the island) at a shrine erected just outside the entrance to the houseyard. The occasion is the feast of Galoengan, which recurs every 210 days. At this season the entrance to almost every houseyard is decorated with an enormous bamboo pendant (*pendjor*), against which the shrine is set.

Batoean. Dec. 1, 1937.   19 M 23.

2 and 3. The same girl offering to the lower demons. This is another part of the Galoengan ceremonial and was taken on the same day as fig. 1. These offerings (*mesegeh*) to the lower demons (cf. Pl. 33, figs. 2, 3, and 4) are a part of almost every ceremonial act. After the cooking of every principal meal, the girls take out a few little leaf trays of cooked rice and lay them on the ground for the demons.

In fig. 2, she has placed the burning coconut shells on the ground, and is about to lay out the decorated trays of betel ingredients (*tjanang genten*). On her arm she has a tray with two glasses of holy water.

In fig. 3, the lay-out is complete with fire in the center, two decorated trays and five little leaf boxes of cooked rice. The girl is shown terminating the ceremonial act with an offering gesture of her right hand with her palm toward the offerings and a flower between her fingers.

Batoean. Dec. 1, 1937.   19 M 18, 20.

4 and 5. These photographs were taken on the calendric feast of Koeningan, which falls ten days after Galoengan. Koeningan is a periodic, 210-day festival which includes special rituals for the domestic animals. In fig. 4, she is sprinkling holy water on the pig; and in fig. 5, she is giving special feast food to a caged fighting cock.

6. The same girl dressed up for her *ngeradjahan* feast which is celebrated at menarche. It took about two hours for an expert high-caste dresser to achieve this result, and the greater part of this time was devoted to the coiffure. The hair at the top of the forehead was shaved off, then the rest of the hair was fixed in exact position with wax, the frangipani flowers were carefully attached, and finally the shaven margin was blacked with paint.

The binding of the breasts with a long spiral sash (*sapoet*) is the correct formal style for both sexes when appearing before superiors or taking part in religious ceremonial. (The girl on the extreme right is wearing a simplified version of this binding; her *sapoet* is just a cloth tied around the top of the sarong and not covering the breasts.)

The plugs in the ear lobes are only worn by unmarried girls. In this photograph they are of gold, but on everyday occasions the girl would sometimes wear plugs of rolled-up palm leaf.

Batoean. Dec. 7, 1937.   19 U 17.

Plate 83

MALE CHILDHOOD

The independence which boys achieve at the end of babyhood is much more complete than that of girls. The boy joins a gang of other boys of his own age, whose occupations no longer center in their homes. They look after oxen, each boy taking out one animal, washing it in the stream, tethering it in the fields, and bringing it in at night. And while the ox is grazing, the boys roam the fields, scare the monkeys out of the maize, and steal bananas from the nearest garden. The boys have virtually no part in the ceremonial life of the village, beyond spectatorship at the theatrical shows. But in Bajoeng Gede, while the girls and older people are offering to the gods, there is usually a gang of little boys chasing each other around the edges of the temple courts, and before the ceremony begins, these boys are out in the middle of the temple court playing mild kicking games. There is actually very little roughness in their rough play. The only hurts that are received result from accidents, and there is almost no aggressive attempt to hurt each other. The kicking games are typical of this nonaggressive play, and the kicking movements which are directed toward the opponent, always fall short of touching him.

1. A small boy on a feast day. This boy has not yet reached independent childhood. He is dressed up in full adult costume and will accompany his mother or child nurse to the temple. Fathers also sometimes take their dressed-up sons to temple feasts. This dressing up for ceremonies will last till he is three or four years old and after that he will be left dirty and unkempt.
 I Karba, aged 654 days.
 Bajoeng Gede. Nov. 25, 1937. 19 G 2.

2. Small boys playing in the street. This is a pushing and pulling game in which, as in the kicking, the boys' bodies scarcely come into mutual contact.
 I Nandoer facing the camera on the left; I Gedjer.
 Bajoeng Gede. April 5, 1937. 8 C 17.

3. Boys playing against a tree trunk. The two bigger boys are playing a hugging game, in which the little boy has joined. This type of play is accompanied by a great deal of roaring and shouting.
 I Repen with his back to the tree; I Reta, the small boy.
 Bajoeng Gede. May 13, 1937. 8 U 39.

4. One boy with his arms around another boy's neck. Physical contact of this sort, in which one boy has his back to the other, is exceedingly common (cf. Pl. 38, fig. 1). Here the larger boy has his hands superposed on the smaller boy's chest, while the smaller boy's left hand holds the index finger of his own hand.
 I Nandoer holding I Karta.
 Bajoeng Gede. May 18, 1937. 8 Z 11.

5. A small boy just beginning to become a member of the gang. The boy on the left in this photograph is I Karba, who is shown in fig. 1. Now, fifteen months later, he is beginning to join other boys a little older than himself. He is still in the unresponsive stage which we noted on Pl. 75, and not until this is past will he become a properly participating member of the gang.
 I Karba, aged 1103 days; I Riboet with arms round I Gata; I Karsa.
 Bajoeng Gede. Feb. 12, 1939. 36 E 8.

6. A group of small boys romping. This scene occurred during a 210-day birthday ceremonial, when the boys were around in the houseyard, but taking no part in the ceremony. The photograph was taken just before the whole mass of boys fell to the ground in a writhing heap (cf. *rame*, Pl. 5).
 Bajoeng Gede. June 4, 1937. 11 E 20.

7. A crowd of small boys at a funeral. Here again, the boys are a part of a crowd which has gathered in the houseyard before taking the corpse to the cemetery, but they have no part in the ceremonial. They spontaneously lined up in this way to watch the preparations. There was a little pushing in the line and other photographs show that the order of the boys continually changed as some were pushed out and started again at the end.
 I Dira; I Toegtoeg; I Sandra; I Madera; I Doeroes.
 Bajoeng Gede. Jan. 17, 1937. 4 C 26.

8. An analogous group of small boys in Batoean. This photograph shows that even among high-castes in the rich villages of the plains, the little boys have the same dirtiness and neglect. They are not quite so shabby as the boys in fig. 7, and they spend rather more of their time in such activities as drawing, painting, learning to read, etc., but the small high-caste boys of Batoean contrast as sharply with their parents as do the boys of Bajoeng Gede.
 The tallest boy is casteless; the others are Brahman and Kesatrya.
 Batoean. Feb. 21, 1939. 36 O 11.

1

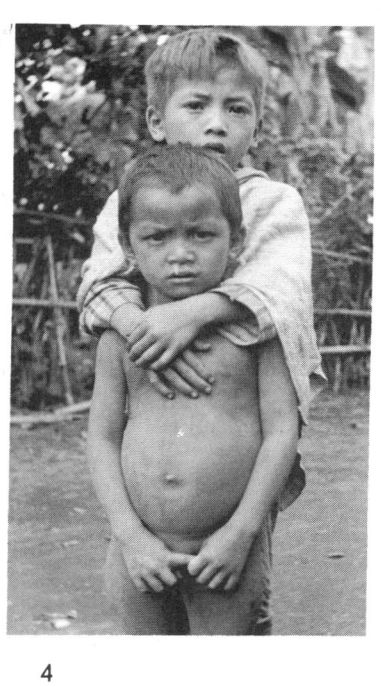

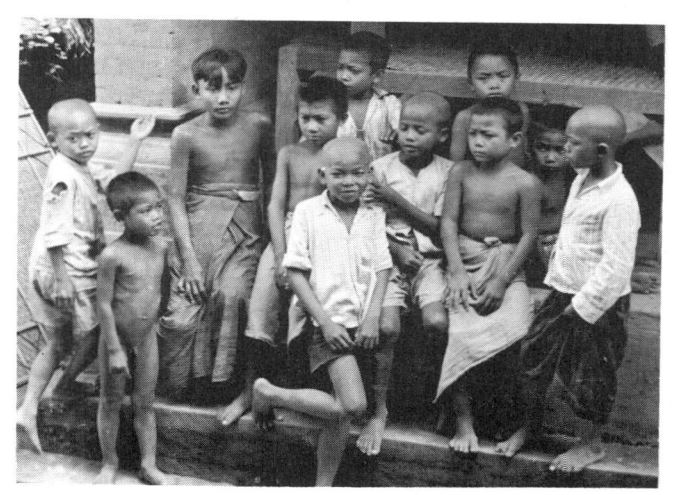

2

3

4

5

6

7

8

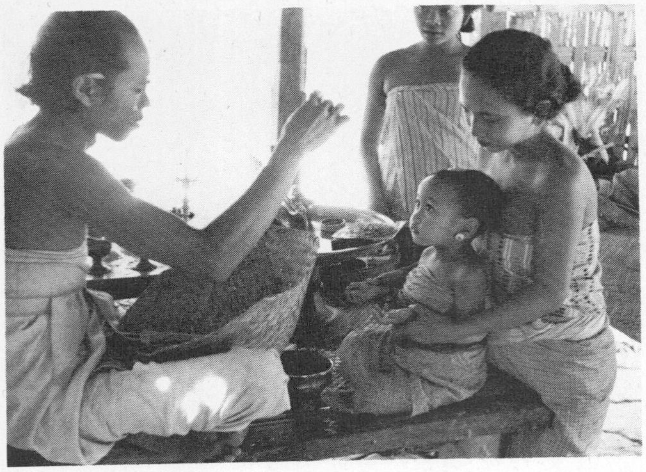

1

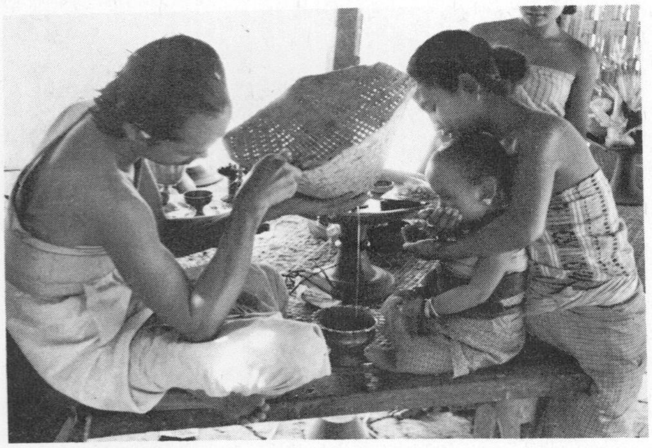

2

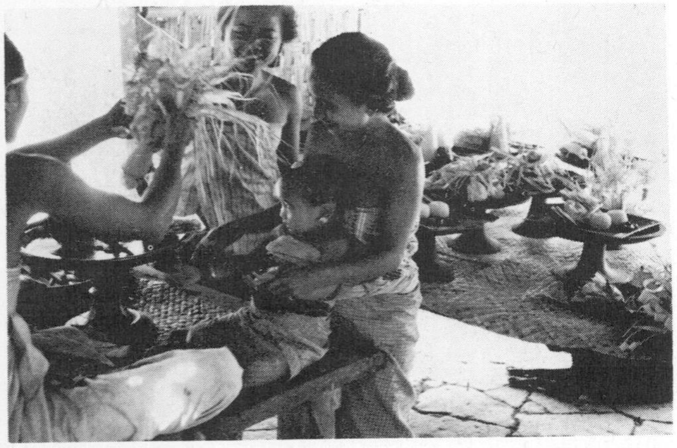

3

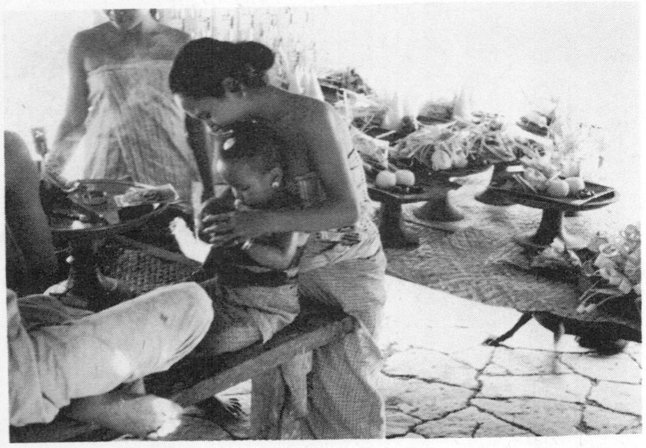

4

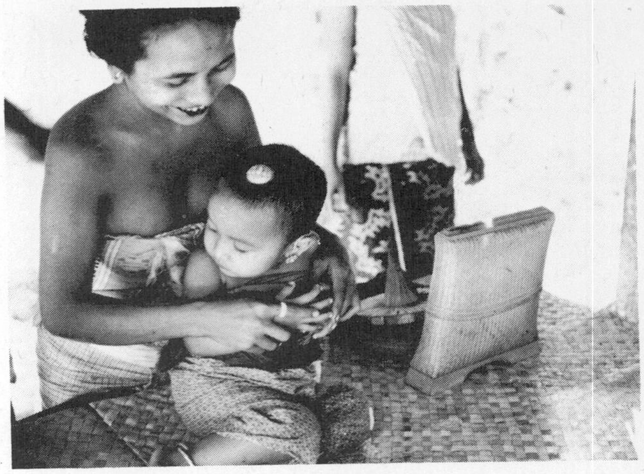

5

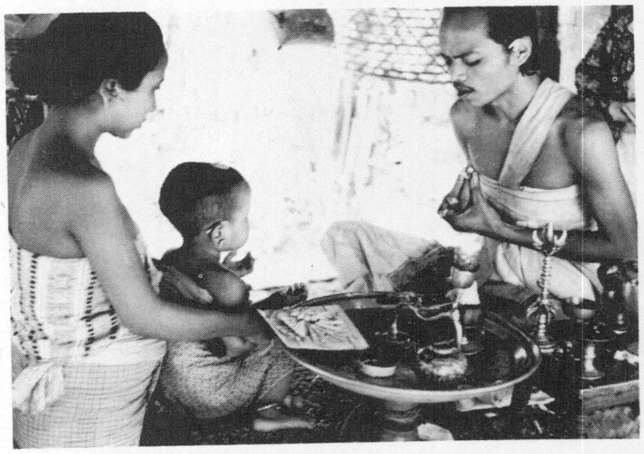

6

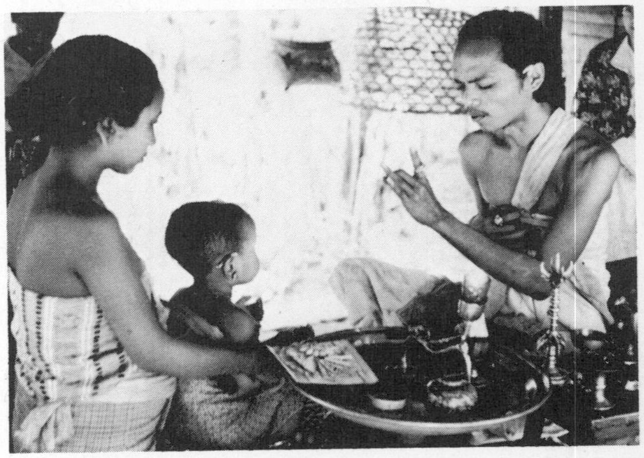

7

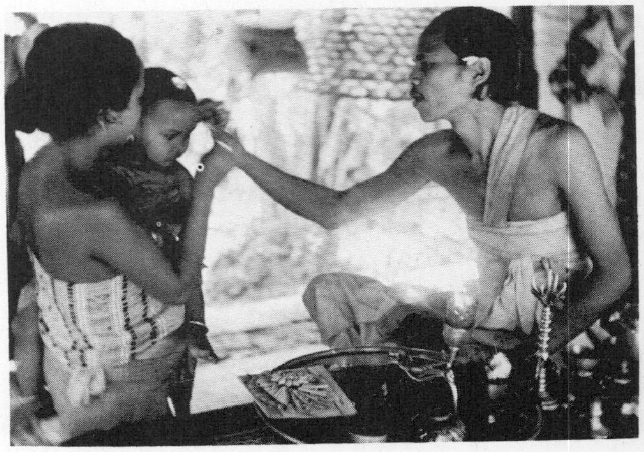

8

Plate 84

210-DAY BIRTHDAY I

Plates 84 to 100 deal with Balinese *rites de passage*, the ceremonials which are carried out at birthdays, tooth-filings, marriages, and after death. As in other parts of this book, we shall examine the rites as occasions for emotional expression, and touch on the formal minutiae only insofar as they throw light on Balinese character. Further, we shall confine our attention to those ceremonies which seem to reveal most of Balinese character and of which we have good photographic records, omitting those connected with birth, with the making of new priests, and with progress in the village hierarchy.

The 210-day birthday is the largest of three more or less similar ceremonies which follow birth and mark stages in the baby's entry into social life. The first of these ceremonies is held on the 12th day after birth (or the 42nd day in case of a first-born child); it marks the end of the period of seclusion and impurity of the parents. The second is *neloeboelanin*, held on the 105th day, at which the baby is given a name (before this date, the baby is given a nickname, such as "Mouse" or "Caterpillar"). The third is on the 210th day, the *otonin*, which is illustrated on this plate. At this ceremony the baby's hair is cut for the first time.

The baby's feet are ritually put to the ground in either *otonin* or *neloeboelanin*, according to the locality and caste.

1 to 8. The 210-day birthday for a baby Brahman girl in Batoean, here being repeated on the fourth such birthday (i.e., the 840th day). This, while not nearly as elaborate as the corresponding ceremony for a baby Kesatrya prince, is much more elaborate than the corresponding ceremony in the mountains. The Brahman ceremony is celebrated by a Brahman priest (*pedanda*) instead of an old woman of the village. The priest sits on a cushion on a raised platform or bed (*bale*), while the mother stands on the earth floor holding the baby on the edge of the bed with no cushion and therefore lower than the priest.

In fig. 1, the priest sprinkles holy water with a frangipani flower, while the mother holds the baby's hands in a receptive posture with the palms upward.

In fig. 2, the baby receives holy water through a filter (*koeskoesan*), a cooking utensil used as a colander in steaming rice. The baby must drink this holy water, and the mother catches some of it in her hands and holds it to the baby's lips.

In fig. 3, the priest holds up a sprinkler (*lis*) made of strips of palm leaf. This is a complex ritual object used in almost all Balinese ceremonies. It contains a large variety of symbolic elements, representations of viscera, etc., and it is bound around with a sash of plaited palm leaf. In the photograph the baby is being made to waft (*natab*) the essence (*sari*) of the *lis* toward herself. Later the *lis* will be dipped in holy water and used as a sprinkler.

In figs. 4 and 5, the baby is being made to place her hands in a position of prayer.

In figs. 6 and 7, the baby waits while the priest intones (*memantra*) a prayer, holding his hands in ritual postures (*moedra*).

In fig. 8, the baby receives *sesarik*, a mixture of chopped spices, which is placed on the forehead.

Ida Pedanda Made; I Daijoe Resi, the mother; I Daijoe Gambar, the baby, aged 840 days.

Batoean. Aug. 4, 1937.   13 B 17, 20, 24, 25; 13 C 1, 3, 5, 9.

Plate 85

210-DAY BIRTHDAY II

The first five figures in this plate are a continuation of the sequence shown on Pl. 84. The others show haircutting at 210-day ceremonies in Batoean and Bajoeng Gede.

1 to 5. Play scenes after the priest has concluded his ritual. The ceremony terminates by giving food to the baby from one of the offerings (*toeloeng oerip*). This feeding of the baby becomes play, in which the father and an old female relative join.

In fig. 1, the mother holds the *toeloeng oerip* by its base, and she holds some of the food from it in her right hand while the baby eats out of her palm.

In figs. 2 and 3, the father takes the *toeloeng oerip*, and, laughing, puts it in the baby's hands.

In fig. 4, the baby sits with the *toeloeng oerip* in her lap, and slowly eats bits of the food.

In fig. 5, the baby sits astride her mother's lap, outside the house in which the ceremony was conducted. She still has the *toeloeng oerip* and is still eating.

I Daijoe Resi, the mother; I Daijoe Gambar, the baby, aged 840 days; I. B. Made Togog, the father.

Batoean. Aug. 4, 1937.   13 C 14, 17, 18, 21, 31.

6. A 210-day birthday in Bajoeng Gede. The man in white in the foreground is a religious practitioner (*balian*) from a neighboring village, who was brought in to perform the ceremony because this particular family had lost four previous babies. Usually in Bajoeng Gede, the ceremony is performed by an old woman (cf. Pl. 100, fig. 1) high up in the village hierarchy, but not a wife of one of the first four citizens, who are too pure to come in contact with a small baby.

In the background, the father of the baby cuts its hair (using our medicine scissors) while the religious practitioner holds the censer in the right hand and rings the bell with the left.

Balian from Lindjong; Nang Oera, the father; I Karba, the baby, aged 210 days.

Bajoeng Gede. Sept. 2, 1936.   2 K 1.

7. A 210-day birthday in Batoean. The baby is sucking at the mother's breast while a Brahman woman cuts its hair with a razor. The female Brahman priestess (*pedanda isteri*) who will perform the ceremony is visible in the background.

Casteless wife of I. B. Tantra holding her son, aged 210 days, while I Daijoe Resi cuts the baby's hair.

Batoean. Aug. 22, 1937.   14 S 2.

1

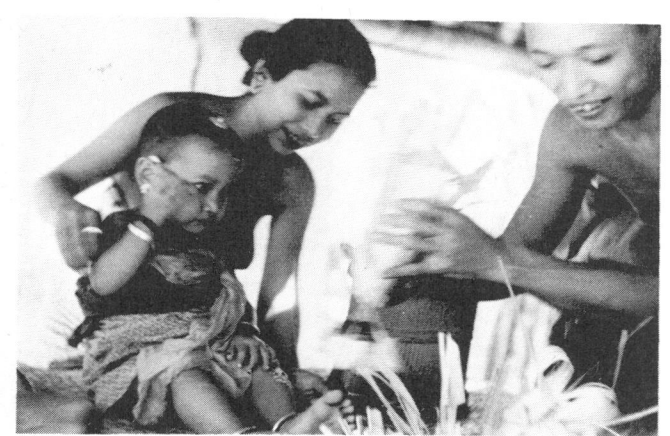

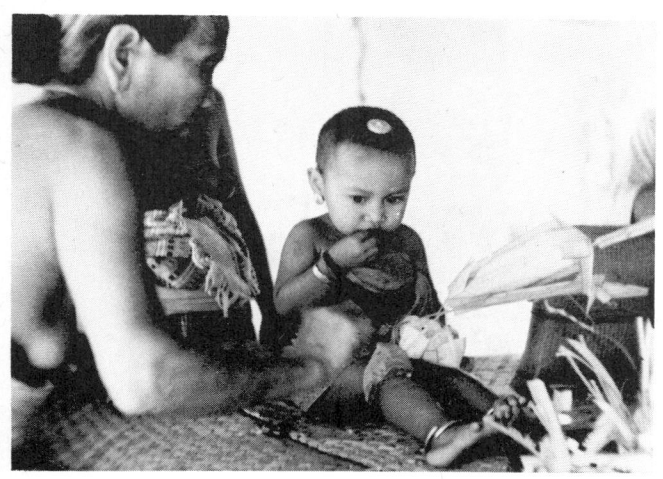

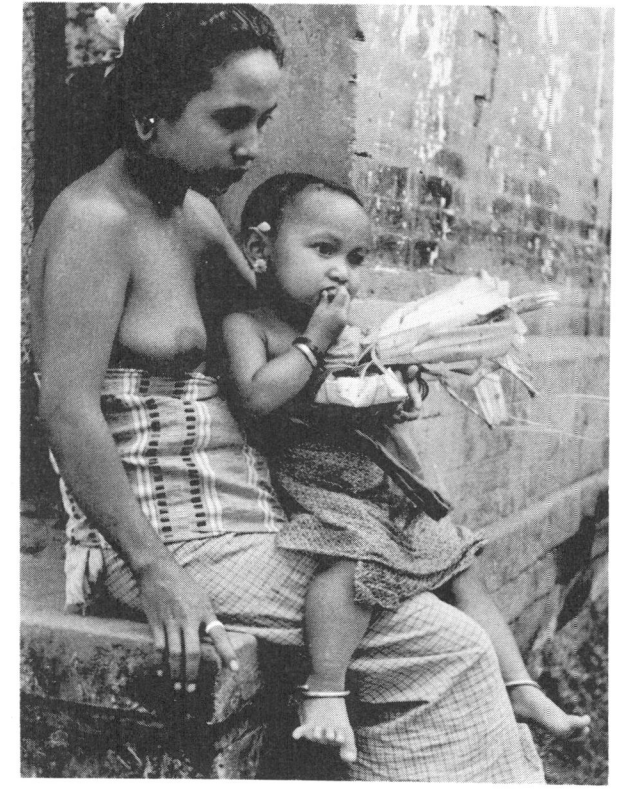

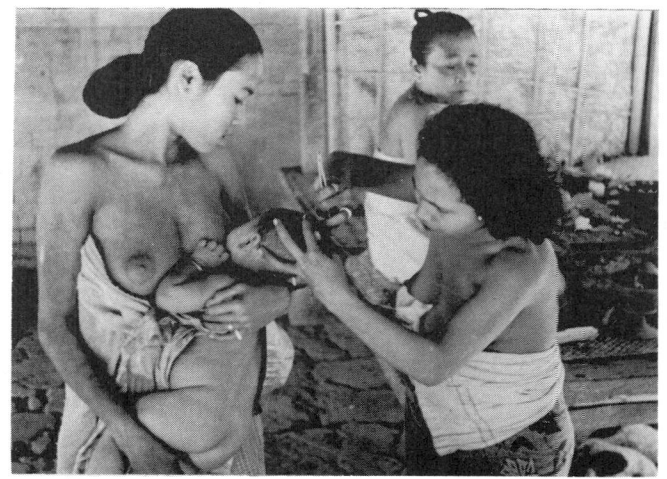

2

3

4

5

6

7

1

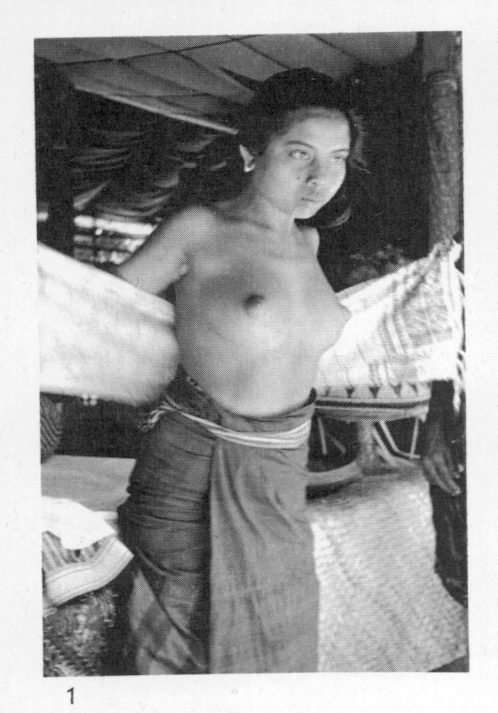

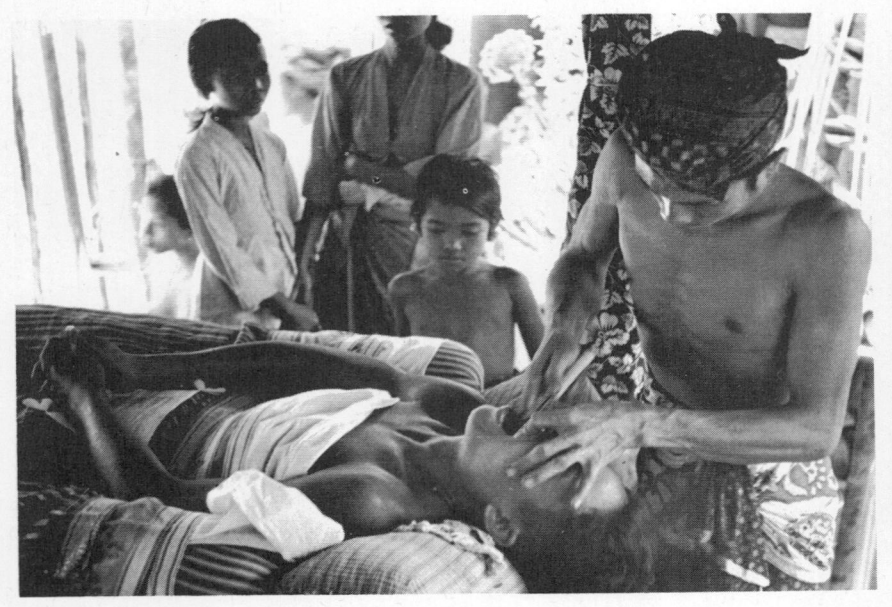

2

3

4

5

6

7

Plate 86

TOOTH-FILING

This is the only common Balinese *rite de passage* in which physical violence is inflicted upon the protagonist (apart, that is, from cases of psychological violence such as occurs in haircutting, cf. Pl. 24, fig. 7, and the mauling of corpses, cf. Pl. 95). And, in tooth-filing the pain is inflicted on the mouth, the region which, as we have seen (cf. Pl. 27) the Balinese feel to be especially vulnerable and which they habitually protect. It is hardly surprising, therefore, that this plate shows more intense and more overt expression of emotion than any other.

Apparently the context of tooth-filing is one which effectively assails the Balinese protection against identification with pain. They can and do avoid being present at real birth scenes (while enjoying theatrical representations of birth) and they avoid witnessing pain in others unless forced by kinship duties to be present. A father holding his child while its scabies is being treated will say, "If this were not my child, I would not dare to be here." But tooth-filing is a ceremonial occasion which relatives attend in their best clothes, and it is especially the bystanders who involuntarily show their sensitivity to the pain located in the protagonist's mouth. The boy whose teeth were being filed was stoical, but his younger sister whose teeth were also to be filed that day showed fear during the period of waiting when she was a spectator.

1. The younger sister of the boy whose teeth have just been filed. She is adjusting her sash (*sapoet*, cf. Pl. 82, fig. 6) before lying down on the bed to have her teeth filed.
   Younger sister of I Keteg.
   Batoean. Sept. 30, 1937.   16 H last.

2. A young Brahman, who is training to become a priest, filing the young man's teeth. The more drastic filing to reduce the edges of all the visible teeth in the upper jaw to a uniform straight line took about 45 minutes, and this was followed by fifteen minutes of polishing.
   Note the set of the operator's mouth, and the widely opened eye.
   I. B. Made Katji operating on I Keteg.
   Batoean. Sept. 30, 1937.   16 H 17.

3. I Keteg's sister whose teeth will be filed next. She is watching her brother undergoing the operation, and feeling her own teeth with some small object.
   Younger sister of I Keteg.
   Batoean. Sept. 30, 1937.   16 H 24.

4. A woman watching the operation. She is a relative or neighbor but her identification with the suffering is evident in her facial expression, wide eyes, flaring nostril, and pursed mouth; and also in her posture with hand to chin.
   Batoean. Sept. 30, 1937.   16 H 8.

5. Gifts brought to the tooth-filing. The conventional presents for this occasion included uncooked rice and a pillow.
   Three women are visible behind the gifts, and their identification with the suffering is evident in the tightness of their mouths. These women are relatives or neighbors of the boy and girl whose teeth are being filed, and the photograph was taken when work was just beginning on the girl's teeth, after the boy's teeth had been done.
   Batoean. Sept. 30, 1937.   16 I 1.

6. The filing of the boy's teeth. The boy is laid out like a corpse (cf. Pl. 92 and Pl. 76, fig. 8) and keeps his hands in a correct posture with the right on top of the left.
   Note the splayed-out position of the operator's fingers.
   I. B. Made Katji operating on I Keteg (cf. I. B. Made Katji in Pl. 90).
   Batoean. Sept. 30, 1937.   16 H 6.

7. I Keteg examining his teeth in a mirror, and feeling them with his fingers during a pause in the filing.
   I Keteg.
   Batoean. Sept. 30, 1937.   16 H 22.

Plate 87

MARRIAGE

The marriage illustrated on this plate occurred between two Brahman families in the village of Batoean, and is typical in marking the end of a period of elopement. It is very wrong in Bali for the parents of the girl to appear to have any part in the arrangement of the marriage unless it be to marry their daughter to a close cousin. Usually the bride's parents are presented with a *fait accompli* and the bride and bridegroom stay "hidden" in the house of some relative until the parents are willing to receive them back. The ceremony here illustrated marks the return of the bride and groom from impure elopement to normal social participation.

In folklore, the distribution of initiative between the sexes swings between tales of forcible abduction of the girl and the folk belief in Bajoeng Gede where it is said that if a girl snatches a man's headcloth, she may demand that he marry her. But though these extremes rarely occur as forms of proposal or courtship, we find both of them symbolically represented in the marriage rituals. In the marriage of Kesatrya princes, the bride is carried completely passive, wrapped from head to foot in white cloth which the bridegroom must remove before he sees her face. In Bajoeng Gede, certain irregular marriages must be formalized by the bride's publicly snatching the bridegroom's cloth under the village gong.

The participation of the bride and groom in the ceremony seems to depend upon the relative importance of citizenship and kinship. We noted that in Bajoeng Gede citizenship is paramount, and there the bride and groom play virtually no part in the ceremonial; there is no dressing up and only one small ritual incident (cf. Pl. 4, fig. 7) which involves them. For the rest, the ceremony is oriented to purifying the village and re-establishing normal relations between the two families and the village. Each side must pay an ox to the village herd together with offerings containing cash, since without these payments the village will be unable to perform any of its calendric ceremonials. The two families must have a formal conversation about the marriage arrangements witnessed by two senior citizens (not, however, the most senior citizens who must preserve their purity), and finally the two families feast together.

1 to 8. A Brahman marriage.

In fig. 1, the bride and groom arrive outside the entrance to the houseyard of the bridegroom's family. Offerings are spread on the ground for the demons, and green bamboos are burned over a fire until they explode. (Similar bamboo explosions are used in mortuary ceremonial.) Both bride and groom stand in very self-conscious postures waiting for the completion of the ritual, after which the bride will walk over the offerings, followed by the groom, and they will enter the houseyard.

In fig. 2, the bride enters the houseyard of the bridegroom's family.

In fig. 3, the bride and bridegroom stand in the same self-conscious attitudes inside the houseyard, waiting for the next step in the ceremony. In the foreground on the right there is a string stretched between two sticks of a special sort of tree (*dadap*). The bride, followed by the groom, will walk through this string, breaking it as she goes; thus symbolizing the finality of the ceremony (cf. Pl. 99, fig. 5, where the same ritual episode is used to "cut off" relations with the dead).

In fig. 4, the bride and groom are about to receive holy water.

In fig. 5, the bridegroom is carrying an offering (*tegenan*) on a pole over his shoulder. A coconut is suspended at one end of the pole and other foods at the other end. This method of carrying is characteristic of men and is a part of the ritual. Similarly, the bride is made to carry "things for market" in the basket on her head. In daily life, Brahmans avoid these methods of carrying in order to preserve their caste position.

In figs. 6 and 7, the bride and bridegroom prepare for a second series of ceremonies which will be conducted by a Brahman priest. They go to a stream to wash. The bridegroom (fig. 6) washes upstream of the bride (fig. 7), and when he takes off his sarong, he lets it float downstream to the bride who picks it up. The sarong is visible in the foreground of fig. 6 and behind the bride in fig. 7.

A crowd of women and children follows the bride; nobody pays any attention to the bridegroom.

In fig. 8, the bride and bridegroom and bridegroom's father sit on a mat in their most decorative clothes. They pray, holding flowers in their hands, while a priest intones the final ceremony.

I. B. Nj. Tjeta, the bridegroom; I Daijoe Langkir, the bride; I. B. Kompiang Koeroeh, the bridegroom's father.

Batoean. Jan. 9, 1938.   20 V 1, 20, 25, 28, 38; 20 W 1, 5, 15.

1

2

3

4

5

6

7

8

1

2

3

4

5

6

Plate 88

DEATH ON THE STAGE

The remaining plates illustrate the Balinese attitudes toward death and the large series of mortuary *rites de passage*.

This plate illustrates the theatrical expression of these attitudes, and it may be argued that these stage representations are in a sense more "real," or more direct, than the conventionalized behavior in the face of actual death. Certainly the theatrical conventions are more comprehensible to the European observer.

The theatrical behavior can be described as based directly upon ways of expressing horror, fear, and grief — ways which are familiar to the European, so that the only unfamiliar elements in the picture are the exaggeration of the expressions and the handling of funeral scenes as broad comedy.

The Balinese are one of the very few peoples in the world among whom mourning is not institutionalized. Neither black nor white garments, no special disfigurements, and no special ornaments mark the person who has suffered a bereavement. Smearing with clay, one of the commonest signs of mourning in this region of the world, occurs on the stage, where it is used to make the clowns more ridiculous. We once saw a person weep at a real funeral, but he was a deaf-mute, and the other people supposed that this was the reason for his unusual behavior.

On the stage death occurs together with birth in the scenes of pestilence which constitute the middle section of the Witch play (*Tjalonarang*), and both death and birth are infested with grotesque minor witches who terrify the performers with practical jokes and pinchings.

Death also occurs occasionally in the plots of other types of drama (e.g., *Ramajana* and *Sampik*) when a beautifully polished hero or heroine is bereaved of a lover. In these cases, the expression of grief is devoid of comedy (unless the clowns intrude) and may even be very moving to the European spectator. The Balinese audience is in general intent upon judging the actor's techniques and do not feel the emotions which the polished actors portray.

1 to 4. Funeral scenes from the Witch play.

In fig. 1, the pregnant woman (whose part is acted by a man) sits wailing loudly beside the rough bier on which the "corpse" is carried, while a man squats leaning over the corpse to inspect it. On the right, a man stands with a torch of palm leaves in his hand to ward off the witches who come to eat the corpse.

In figs. 2 and 3, the men are frightened and start to pray in grotesque attitudes — with fingers clasped and protruding. In fig. 3, a fly switch is visible, lying on the corpse.

In fig. 4, the men carry their worldly possessions. They are plague-stricken refugees fleeing from their village and act as though their baskets of possessions were very heavy.

Dendjalan. May 26, 1936. 1 I 29, 30, 31, 38.

5. Rama, the hero of the classical *Ramajana* epic, weeps for his wife, Sita, who has been stolen.

Itinerant troupe of *Wajang wong* players from Kedoewi.

Bajoeng Gede. May 13, 1937. 8 W 36.

6. A real funeral in the mountains. From this photograph, one might suppose that grief was expressed in real life by bowing the head. Actually these people have their heads down searching for cash which is thrown after the procession as a farewell present to the dead. On the left, there are several people with their blankets spread above their heads to catch the thrown coins.

Funeral of Dong Merada.

Bajoeng Gede. Oct. 9, 1937. 16 Z 20.

Plate 89

FUNERALS

Balinese mortuary rites are repetitive and never complete. The ritual which is performed at the funeral is later repeated with greater elaboration at the cremation, and may be repeated yet again in still more elaborate postmortuary ceremonies (*meligija*, etc.). Only the richest princes attempt to perform these more elaborate rites, but the books of ritual provide for rites even more elaborate and costly than the princes can afford.

The rites consist in purifications of the body followed by its destruction or disposal. The act of destruction is followed by a final farewell to the body. This makes it necessary to dispose of the body-substitute of which the last farewell was taken, and this again must be done by purification and destruction.

The system is circular, like the Balinese calendar, or like the Balinese conception of the life cycle with its alternations of death and reincarnation, and the graded sacredness of the human being which is high in infancy, falls in the middle of life, and rises again in old age as the individual again approaches the supernatural. It is the transitions between the secular and the supernatural, the phenomena of birth and death, which are fraught with horror and impurity, and the transition through death must be endlessly repeated in incomplete efforts to insure finality.

On the purely secular level, however, the death of an individual is followed very rapidly by forgetfulness. The names of the dead are soon forgotten and it is scarcely possible to obtain any description of the character of a dead person. The dead, like the gods, have no personal characteristics.

(For other photographs of funerals, cf. Pl. 34, figs. 6 and 7; Pl. 37, fig. 8; Pl. 76; Pl. 94, fig. 2.)

1 to 3. Scenes at the funeral of the mother of a Brahman priest. High-caste people avoid burying the dead if possible, and keep the body in the house for months or years until preparations are complete and the calendar is propitious for the cremation. It is the rule that a high priest must not be buried. In the present instance, however, the dead was not a priest and the family did not wish to incur the extra expense involved in keeping the body for a long period during which hospitality must continually be shown to visitors. They therefore buried the body in the cemetery.

Fig. 1 shows a group of Brahman women gathered in the houseyard, watching the preparation of the body for burial.

In fig. 2, the priest (the son of the dead woman) is praying over the body which has been laid out on a makeshift bed over which a white sheet is suspended. The body itself is covered except for the face, and a sash is laid across the chest.

In fig. 3, a group of Brahman men are wrapping the body for burial. This work is done hurriedly, almost with violence, and those who cannot reach the body peer at it over the shoulders of the others.

Funeral of the mother of Pedanda Rai.
Batoean. Dec. 5, 1937. 19 R 19, 38; 19 S 14.

4. Brahmans washing a body before cremation. In this case the "body" consists of exhumed bones which have been laid out in a coffin and covered, like a corpse, with clothes and sash. The pouring of quantities of holy water over this body is the final rite before burial, and it is repeated before cremation.

Batoean. Aug. 24, 1937. 14 Z 8.

5. Preparing a body for burial in Bajoeng Gede. In many mountain villages there is no cremation. The body is buried in the cemetery in the woods (or in the bed of a stream if it be the body of a leper or a thief caught in the act). This particular body was of a recent immigrant to Bajoeng and therefore had to be buried in Peloedoe, a suburb outside the village.

In the photograph, the neighbors and relatives are holding their hands over the genitals of the corpse during the washing. M. M.'s verbal record describes the whole process of preparing the corpse as "done with no emotion except a kind of giggling haste — none of the feeling of a surging mass such as there was at two previous funerals." The haste was, in part, due to the need to get the body buried before sunset.

Funeral of Nang Moespa's father.
Bajoeng Gede. Sept. 5, 1936. 2 D 20.

6. Washing the body on the way to the cemetery. This shows the Bajoeng Gede version of fig. 4. The corpse is hurriedly carried to the last field before entering the woods. Here the procession stops for a few minutes while water from a special spring is poured over the dead.

Funeral of Dong Merada.
Bajoeng Gede. Oct. 9, 1937. 16 Z 9.

1

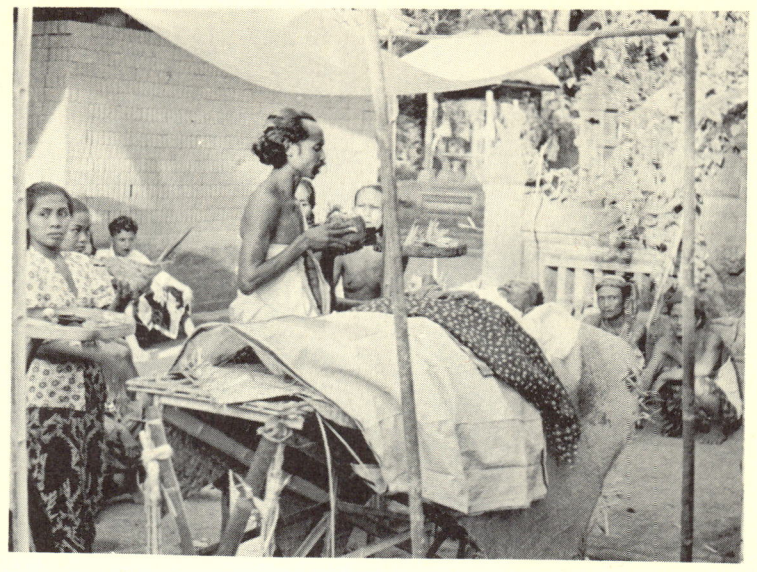

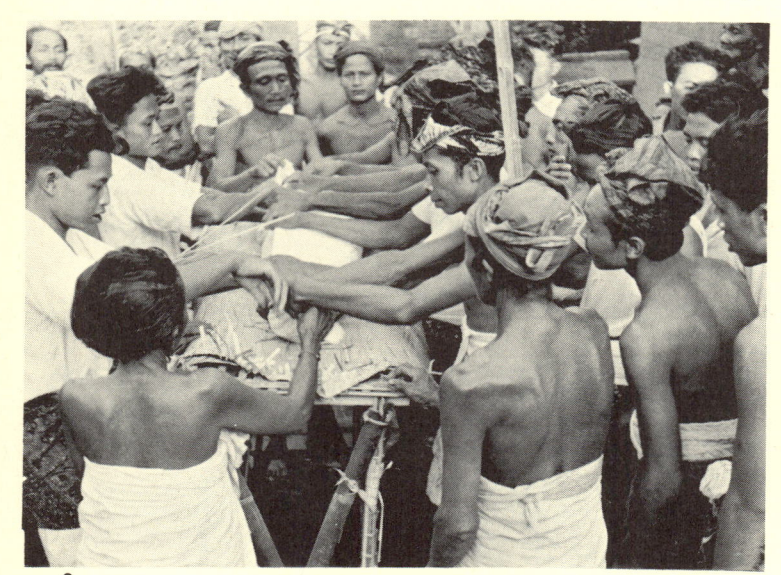

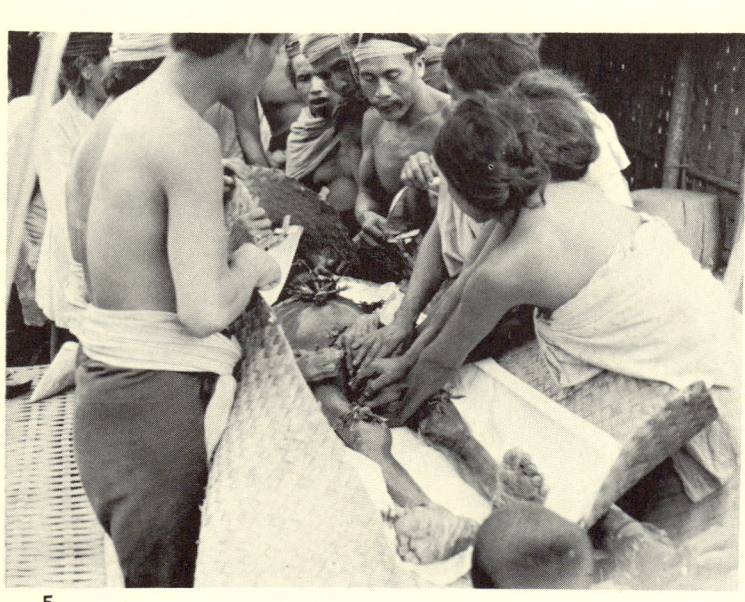

2

3

4

5

6

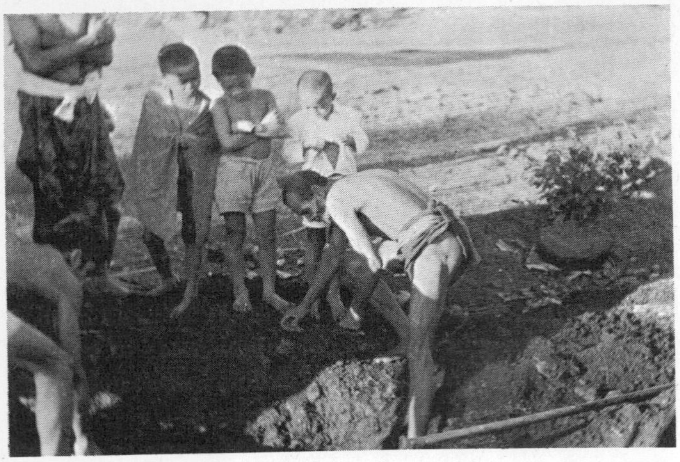
1

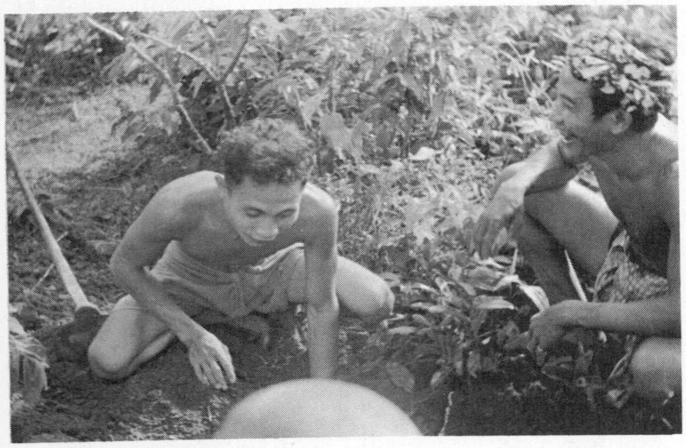
2

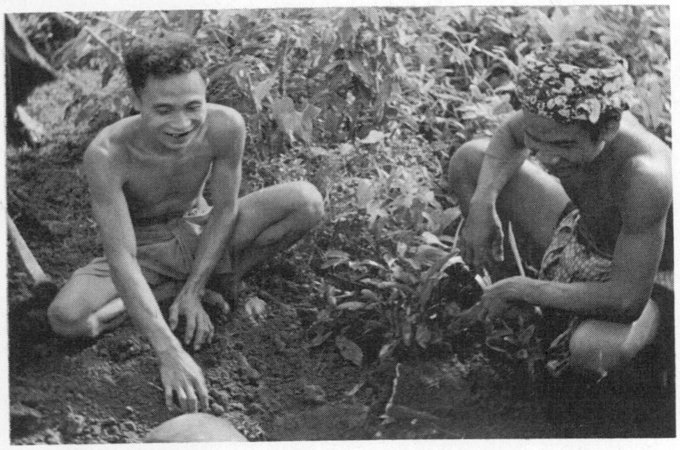
3

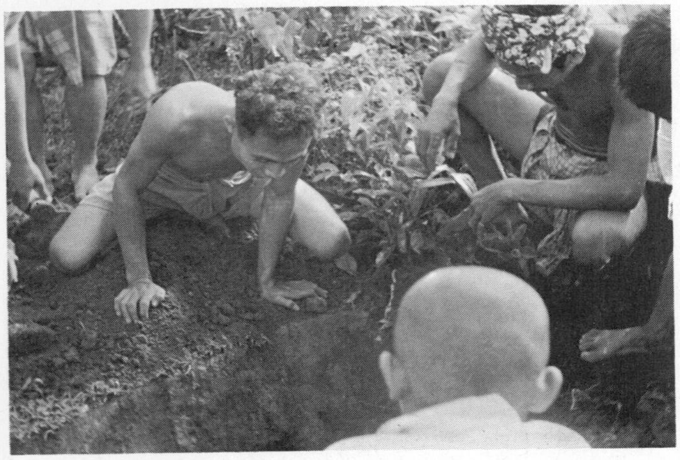
4

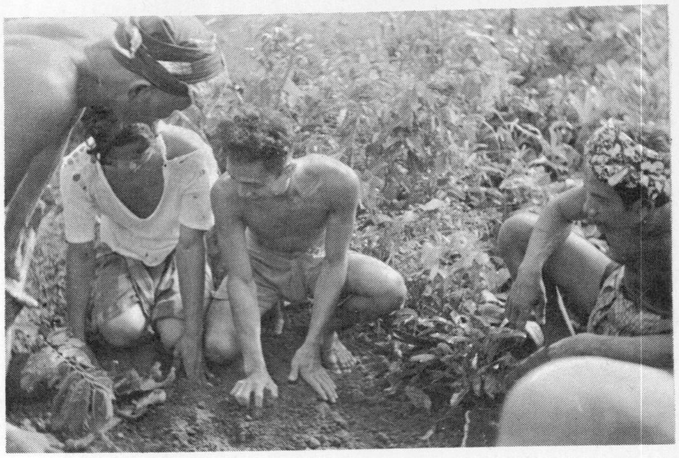
5

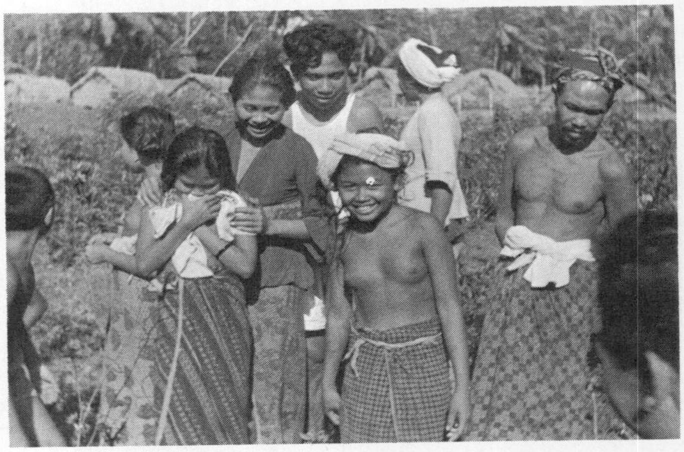
6

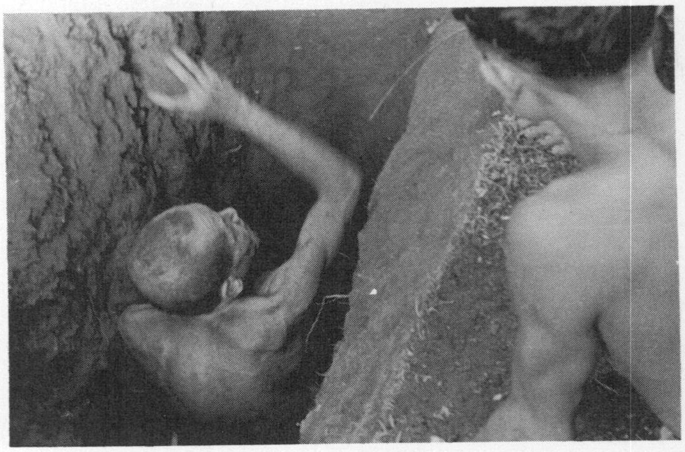
7

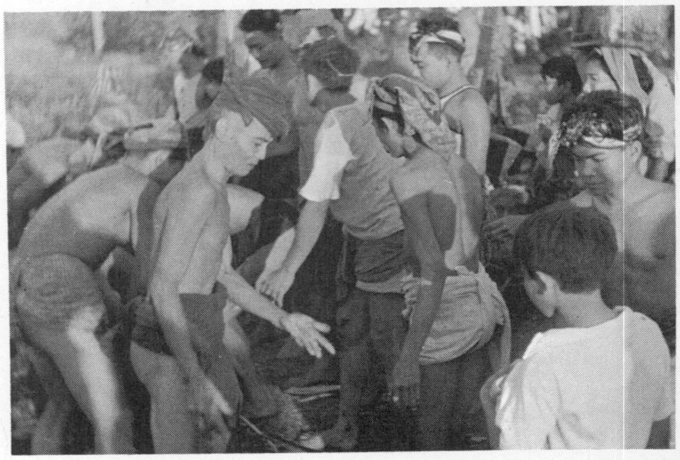
8

Plate 90
EXHUMATION I

Depending on the type of holy water used in the burial, a body may be left from three to twenty-five years in the grave before cremation is necessary. The more expensive holy water has a more enduring effect, but finally, in the plains villages, the body or the bones must be exhumed and cremated.

Exhumation is usually done in the early morning, and the context brings out the attitudes toward death both of those who take part and those who only watch. A Balinese man will boast that he is *sapta* — that he can withstand unclean smells and contact with the unclean without nausea — and whenever there is a corpse to be carried to the cemetery or to be exhumed, he will show off this characteristic by grotesque and violent behavior. (A man who is *sapta* will even dare to carry an adult woman.)

In this way, the horror of the body which is falling to pieces (*beroek,* cf. Pls. 18 to 20) becomes inverted and the body provides a stimulus for exhibitionistic daring — but some men avoid these contexts.

In Bajoeng Gede, the village priestess and the senior citizens have to maintain their purity by avoiding all contact with death; but in the plains the Brahman priests are so holy that they can afford such contact. The Buddhistic Brahmans even underline their freedom to contact the unclean. They will eat beef, and a Buddhistic Brahman priest may have his house in the cemetery.

The people shown in these photographs are Sivaistic Brahmans, except the old man in figs. 1 and 7.

1. An old servant starts to dig up a grave while three little boys look on.
Batoean. Aug. 22, 1937. 14 P 17.

2 to 5. Brahman men squatting on the edge of the newly opened grave joking about the corpse and the money. The old man shown in fig. 7 is working down in the grave passing up the bones and scraps of cloth to the Brahmans. The man on the left with the curly hair was a very conspicuous joker on this occasion and chiefly joked about the money that had been buried with the dead. He would say of some scrap of cloth, "This perhaps contains money. Search it. Perhaps you'll find 25 cents," exaggerating the possibilities since only cash is buried with the dead. (Cf. Pl. 86, fig. 2 for the facial expression of the same Brahman in another unclean context, tooth-filing. The tooth-filer must not touch food with his hands, but in the tooth-filing there is no convention for rowdy and macabre behavior.)
I. B. Made Katji.
Batoean. Aug. 22, 1937. 14 Q 35, 36, 37, 38.

6. A group of Brahman girls and men standing beside the opened grave and joking about the smell. One girl has her cloth to her nose. Actually this was a long-buried body, and there was no smell except that of mold.
Batoean. Aug. 22, 1937. 14 R 4.

7. An old family retainer (casteless) working in the grave and passing up bones to the Brahmans on the edge. This man also played a comedy role in joking about the bones.
Batoean. Aug. 22, 1937. 14 R 12.

8. Washing the bones after exhumation. This work renders the hands impure in a ritual sense, and on this particular occasion the body had not been buried long, so that the ritual impurity was emphasized. The other bodies had all been exhumed in the early morning, but this one was postponed until afternoon because there was some unwillingness to work on it.
The man in the foreground holds his hands away from his body.
Batoean. Aug. 22, 1937. 14 T 25.

Plate 91
EXHUMATION II

When all the bones have been dug up, they are put in water and washed. The long bones are counted and laid out to reconstruct the body in diagrammatic form, and then the smaller bones are heaped on them.

During the exhumation, a second ceremony has been taking place. Small representations (*sanggah oerip*, cf. Pl. 98) of the souls of the dead were brought to the cemetery at the beginning of the exhumation. These are dolls made of palm leaf, and they are carried like babies by the women. The dolls go to visit the home of the dead man and are there ritually fed and given betel, after which they are carried back to the cemetery and placed with the collected bones.

The bones are finally wrapped in matting and laid out under clothes and sashes, repeating the laying out of the body at the burying.

1 and 2. A Brahman washing the bones. Note that he laughs, but works with his arms outstretched to keep his body away from the splashing.
I. B. P. Sentoelan.
Batoean. Aug. 22, 1937.   14 Q 10.

3. A Brahman boy playfully starting to lay out the bones as they are passed to him after washing.
Batoean. Aug. 22, 1937.   14 Q 11.

4. The skull and other bones lying in a heap of plaited coconut mat after washing.
Batoean. Aug. 22, 1937.   14 Q 23.

5. Laying out the long bones and the skull to reconstitute the body. They are laid out on a loose-woven cream-colored fabric with a plaited mat underneath it.
Batoean. Aug. 22, 1937.   14 Q 16.

6. The smaller bones are now heaped on top of the long bones.
Batoean. Aug. 22, 1937.   14 Q 21.

7. The reconstituted body and the doll (*sanggah oerip*), representing the soul, are now placed side by side. The *sanggah oerip* with the cloth (*anteng*) in which it was carried are lying on a mat in the foreground, and the black mass in the top left is the heap of bones.
Batoean. Aug. 22, 1937.   14 Q 32.

8. The final wrapping of the body in mats. This is a repetition of the process of wrapping the body at the funeral (cf. Pl. 89, fig. 3).
Batoean. Aug. 22, 1937.   14 T 40.

1

2

3

4

5

6

7

8

1

2

3

4

5

6

7

8

Plate 92

THE LAY-OUT OF THE BODY

The repetitive nature of Balinese mortuary rites is shown very clearly, if we bring together pictures of the various occasions on which either the body, or the bones, or some substitute for the body, is laid out with its full set of clothes.

1. The lay-out of the body for purification by a priest before burial (cf. Pl. 89, fig. 2).
Funeral of Pedanda Rai's mother.
Batoean. Dec. 5, 1937.   19 R 27.

2. The graves in the cemetery dressed as bodies before the beginning of exhumation. The two graves in the background are completely dressed. In the foreground is another heap of clothes for a grave which had not yet been located, and in the foreground on the left are offerings. This dressing of the grave is called "dressing up the dead" (*ngesehin sang seda*). The clothes for a male body consist of sarong, sash, belt, *sapoet* (an outer sash) and a little ceremonial handkerchief; for a female body, skirt, petticoat, cloth sling, sash, and handkerchief.
Batoean. Aug. 22, 1937.   14 P 3.

3. The dolls (*sanggah oerip*) representing the souls of the dead are set up in a sitting position in the temporary house built in the graveyard. The souls are left here until the exhumation is complete.
Batoean. Aug. 22, 1937.   14 Q 26.

4. A later view of the interior of the temporary house in the graveyard. The exhumation is now complete. The bones have been washed and assembled and wrapped in matting. They have been put with the dolls which represent the souls, and the clothes from the grave have been placed over each bundle which now contains both body and soul.
   A more elaborate version of the funeral ceremony (*noesang*) is performed in this temporary village before these bundles can be taken away for the cremation, and when they are removed, they are lifted over the surrounding fence, not carried through the entrance. (In an ordinary funeral the body is carried through the door of the house and through the entrance of the houseyard.)
Batoean. Aug. 22, 1937.   14 R 24.

5. A body-substitute laid out on a shroud. In this case, the representation of the body is a figure (*oekoer*) made of coins tied together (cf. Pl. 97, fig. 2), and on this figure are laid small conical twists (*koewangen*) of betel-chewing ingredients. These twists are carefully placed on all the nodal points in the body (cf. Pl. 20, fig. 4) — the feet, the knees, the navel, the shoulders, the elbows, and the hands with special subdivided twists to represent the fingers.
   Under the figure is an openwork bamboo lattice (*klatkat soeda mala*) and under this the shroud which is decorated with symbolic designs of the Sivaistic Brahmans. (The analogous shroud in a Buddhist Brahman ceremony would have on it a symbolic picture of the dead.)
Batoean. Aug. 23, 1937.   14 U 38.

6. The body-substitute made of coins, shown in fig. 4, has now been covered with clothes like a real body, and on top of the clothes the sash and handkerchief are visible. The lay-out is, however, still incomplete. On the pillow at the head there is a mass of plaited palm-leaf material which when opened will be three more strips similar to that which is already lying across the sarong. These plaited strips are called *kadjang sinom* and the four of them are said to cover the head, chest, thighs, and legs of the dead (cf. Pl. 93, fig. 1).
Batoean. Aug. 23, 1937.   14 U 39.

7. The ashes after the burning. The remains of the bones are carefully collected from the dying embers, and the heap is wrapped in matting to reconstitute a body.
Batoean. Aug. 25, 1937.   14 Z 35.

8. The body reconstituted from the ashes. In this case, the ashes are that of a casteless person and are placed on a stretcher (cf. Pl. 88, fig. 1) on the ground, whereas the ashes in fig. 7 are those of a Brahman and are put on a high platform.
   In this photograph, the reconstruction is complete. A "house" of cloth is set up around the reconstituted body, and a cloth canopy is suspended over it as was done at the funeral (cf. fig. 1).
Batoean. Aug. 25, 1937.   14 Z 39.

Plate 93

THE HOUSE AND THE CORPSE

There is a very close relationship between the house and the corpse. The picture which is repeated over and over again in the mortuary ceremonies is that of the body lying on a bed in the dwelling house; it is repeated in the houseyard when the body is placed on a bed under a canopy (Pl. 92, figs. 1 and 8), and again on the way to the cemetery when the body is carried in a small portable house (*djoli*). In cremation, the "house" in which the body is carried becomes still more elaborate, and for the dead of rich families an enormous tower (*wadah*) is constructed (Pl. 11, fig. 6), and the body is carried in one of the upper stories of this portable pagoda. On arrival at the cemetery it is placed in an animal figure in another "house."

The Balinese dwelling house is beautifully carpentered out of separate pieces, held together by mortise joints. These pieces are prefabricated and when all are ready, the house is put together in a single afternoon. The house can later be taken apart and carried to another part of the village, and there rebuilt. Such a structure clearly fits with the Balinese fantasy, that the body is made up of separable parts which may fall apart (cf. *beroek*, Pls. 18 to 20).

In carrying the house the same technique is used as in carrying the cremation tower. A lattice of large bamboos is constructed under the frame and the carriers enter this lattice — one man in each square — and lift the bamboos on their shoulders.

1. The house of a Kesatrya family in which a body has been kept until cremation. This photograph was taken just before the carriers came to carry the body to the cemetery for burning. The house is surrounded by a special ceremonial fence (probably the prototype of the *kadjang sinom* shown in Pl. 92, fig. 6) and is decorated with palm-leaf streamers.
House of I Dewa Paijoek.
Batoean. Aug. 24, 1937.   14 X 6.

2. The temporary village in the cemetery. When an important person is being cremated, a large number of other families also cremate their dead. Thus a big cremation may be the occasion for burning fifty or more bodies. Some bodies have been kept in the houses of the rich, but the majority are exhumed. For these a temporary village is built in the cemetery. Each house contains the bodies belonging to one family, and is decorated and fenced like the house in fig. 1.
Batoean. Aug. 20, 1937.   14 N 16.

3. The corpse from the house shown in fig. 1 was first carried in a coffin with the riotous behavior shown in Pls. 94 and 95, but before reaching the cemetery, the corpse was placed in the portable house (*djoli*) shown here. The carriers are running up the slope after crossing a stream.
Batoean. Aug. 24, 1937.   14 Y 19.

4. The house for a Brahman girl's first menstruation ceremonial. It is decorated with palm-leaf streamers and specially fenced like the house in fig. 1. The house is complete in itself, with special washing arrangements (cf. Pl. 37, fig. 5) for the girl, on the wall dividing the house from the place where people go for defecation. In this house she was dressed for the ceremony (cf. Pl. 82), and the house has its special shrine to the Sun, visible in the foreground of this picture.
Batoean. Dec. 5, 1937.   19 U 10.

5. A small cremation tower (*wadah*). This shows the house-like form and the lattice of bamboos which is used to carry the tower with the corpse inside it to the cemetery. (Pl. 11, fig. 6 shows a very much larger tower.)
Kesiman. May 20, 1936.   1 G 21.

6. A house constructed over the body of a woman who died in childbed before the birth of the child. Such a body is left exposed in a house in the cemetery "until the body of the child is expelled." When a body is kept by the family in their dwelling house, a similar but smaller structure is built in the cemetery to contain a pot into which the juices from the decomposing body are poured every day.
Sanoer. Oct. 19, 1936.   2 Z 22.

7. An unfinished dwelling house. This photograph includes one corner of the rectangular frame which supports the roof and the sloping bamboos on which the thatch will be fixed. The elements of the frame are all mortised together and the frame itself is temporarily supported on bamboos. In the foreground is one of the posts which will later support the frame. It is cut to a tenon, and the mortise into which this tenon will fit is visible on the underside of the frame.
Bajoeng Gede. April 14, 1937.   6 S 17.

1

2

3

4

5

6

7

1

2

3

4

5

6

Plate 94

CARRYING THE CORPSE I

This activity, called *"ngarap bangke"* or *"ngarap wadah"* (literally, "working the body" or "working the tower"), is noisy, riotous, and mischievous. When the carriers excel themselves in excitement, laughing and shouting, splashing up the mud in every stream and almost upsetting the cremation tower or tearing the corpse in pieces, it is usually said that they are "very angry with the family of the deceased." Our observations indicate, however, that the degree of intensity of this riotous behavior increases with the social status of the deceased, the size of the tower, the newness of the body, and the number of carriers.

This is the occasion on which a young man especially shows that he is *"sapta,"* that he "dares" to handle the unclean (cf. Pl. 90).

The last two photographs on this plate are the beginning of a sequence which is continued on the next plate.

1. Carrying a cremation tower to the cemetery. This cremation was held in a village near Bajoeng Gede and was organized by a rich low-caste man who was regarded as an upstart. He even constructed a figure of a cow *(lemboe)* in which to burn the body — a high-caste prerogative. On instructions from the local prince just before the cremation, the animal was converted into an elephant.

At this cremation, the reason given for the violence of the behavior and the swaying of the tower was that the people of Sekahan stopped carrying for awhile and left the work to people from a visiting village.

Sekahan. Sept. 19, 1936. 2 N 36.

2. Turning a body in Bajoeng Gede. Here there is no cremation, but a trace of the excited behavior, characteristic of cremations in the plains villages, occurs in the funeral procession to the cemetery. The corpse is carried on a stretcher, and before entering the forest the stretcher is rotated three or four times. The same ritual is followed in the plains with cremation towers at every crossroads and on arrival at the cemetery.

Bajoeng Gede. Jan. 17, 1937. 4 C 32.

3. A man drinking palm beer before working as a carrier under the tower shown in fig. 1.

Sekahan. Sept. 19, 1937. 2 N 13.

4. A closer view of the men under the bamboo lattice carrying the tower shown in fig. 1. The man in the left foreground shows an inebriated facial expression characteristic of men in this activity. The gesturing with the raised hand and the shouting are also characteristic. Actually, though palm beer and even distilled spirits *(arak)* may be provided at cremations, the men are not intoxicated, but rather *acting,* and their excited behavior is very intermittent. A man will be shouting and dancing in the thick of the crowd at one moment, and a few seconds later he will be perfectly quiet and normal in his behavior on the fringes.

Sekahan. Sept. 19, 1937. 2 N 33.

5 and 6. Carrying a body in a coffin containing a Kesatrya body from the house to the cemetery. The coffin has just been brought out of the house shown in Pl. 93, fig. 1. The men crowd around it snatching and pulling first in one direction and then in another. (This sequence is continued on the next plate.)

Batoean. Aug. 24, 1937. 14 X 20, 21.

243

Plate 95

CARRYING THE CORPSE II

A European observer at one of these scenes of violent struggling over a corpse or a coffin is surprised that the men do not get hurt in any way — but a part of the answer to this problem is provided by the photographs. We have noted (Pls. 21 to 23) that Balinese hand postures differ markedly from those usual in Western cultures, and we have noted the large part which fear and startle play in Balinese character (Pl. 46).

In the photographs of men struggling over bodies, we find a very high proportion of these disharmonic hand postures, and this probably denotes preparedness for startle, a high degree of readiness to jump away from sudden danger.

The photographs also show that many of the members of this struggling crowd have their hands on the shoulders of those in front of them, partly using the hand as a sense organ to give warning of sudden swirls in the crowd and partly using the arm as a buffer to save themselves from sudden pressure.

(All the photographs on this plate were taken on the same occasion as the last two on Pl. 96, but they are not arranged in chronological order.)

1. On the banks of a stream. In this photograph, the crowd is going up from the stream where they have been splashing and pulling the coffin this way and that. But while the crowd is going up, there are also men jumping down into the crowd from the banks.
Batoean. Aug. 24, 1937.   14 Y 9.

2. Spectators on the banks watching the scene in the bed of the stream. Several of these men had been taking active part in the struggle a few seconds before, especially the man sitting on the bank and the man who is shouting and pointing down into the crowd. This pointing with the index finger is one of the gestures characteristic of this occasion.
Batoean. Aug. 24, 1937.   14 Y 1.

3 and 4. Fighting over the coffin in a narrow part of the stream. Several of the hand postures in these two photographs are interesting: especially, in fig. 3, those of the men outside the crowd in the top left of the picture and of the man with the white singlet whose fingers are splayed out on the coffin; and, in fig. 4, those of the man in the center of the picture.
Batoean. Aug. 24, 1937.   14 X 30, 31.

5 and 6. Closer views of the struggling crowd immediately after the coffin was brought out of the house. Fig. 5 shows the great range of diversity in the facial expressions, from the laughing expression of the man wearing a comic charcoal moustache to the frightened expressions of the two young men on the extreme right. Fig. 6 shows how the men place their hands on the shoulders of the men in front of them.
Batoean. Aug. 24, 1937.   14 X 23, 24.

1

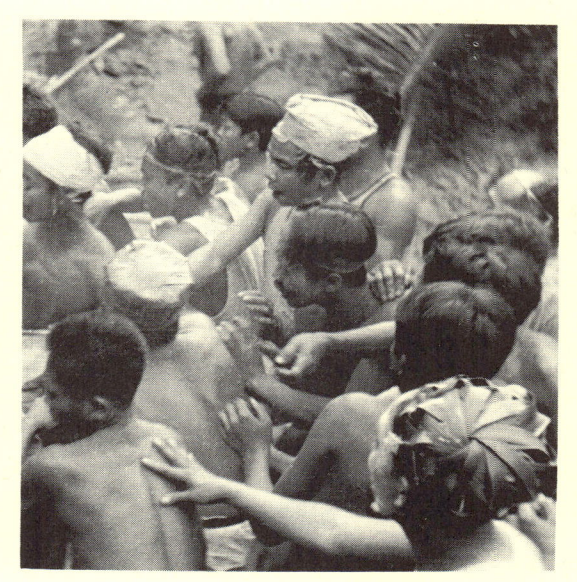

2

3

4

5

6

1

2

3

4

5

Plate 96

BURNING THE CORPSE

The body when it finally reaches the cemetery is placed in a hollow animal figure (*petoelangan*, literally, "a thing for bones") which stands on a high roofed platform (*bale pebasmean*). The body receives a final washing and purification, and firewood is arranged under the belly of the animal figure. A priest lights a torch and from this the many fires are lit.

The burning takes several hours, and the people do all in their power to hasten it by poking the flames and turning over the less combustible fragments.

1. The arrival of the body at the cemetery. This photograph is the last of the sequence shown in Pl. 95. The man with a striped pajama coat, standing on the platform, is the head of the Kesatrya family from whose house the body was brought. He stands passive, surveying the still excited carriers, while one of them, more excited than the rest, stands above him shouting to the carriers.

Batoean. Aug. 24, 1937. 14 Y 22.

2. An animal figure (*petoelangan*) for the burning of a body. The animal in this case is a calf — for the body of a high-caste child.

These figures are carefully carpentered, and the back of the animal lifts off, like a lid, for the insertion of the body.

Kesiman. May 22, 1936. 1 G 25.

3. A general view of the burning in the graveyard. This photograph shows several of the roofed platforms (*bale pebasmean*) each with one or more animal figures burning. The thatched roof on the right is of one of the temporary houses built in the graveyard for the exhumed bodies.

Batoean. Aug. 24, 1937. 14 Z 31.

4. The consecration (*melaspas*) of an animal figure. This photograph shows the head of one of these cows, with an offering (*banten adjoeman*) balanced on its forehead and food placed in its mouth. Its horns are decorated with silver paper.

Batoean. Aug. 22, 1937. 14 T 1.

5. The animal figure after the burning. This photograph shows the figure of a lion standing on the platform, and the remains of the fire underneath the animal's belly. A very little burning is sufficient to loosen the planks of which the belly is made, and the bones then fall down into the fire, where their destruction can be hastened by poking the fire and adding fuel.

Before the embers are dead, the people come to collect the remains of the bones — to make them up into a reconstituted body ready for the next cycle of ceremonial.

Kesiman. May 22, 1936. 1 H 5.

Plate 97

REPRESENTATIONS OF THE BODY

In addition to the body itself, the bones and the collected ashes, the mortuary ritual also involves a long series of ritual objects which represent parts of the body or the body as a whole.

While the body and the doll which represents the soul are lying in a single bundle in the temporary house in the cemetery, a large ceremony (*ngaskara*) is held in the houseyard of a Brahman priest. This ceremony is perhaps a more elaborate analogue of the simpler ritual in which the doll representing the soul was taken home from the exhumation to be fed and to visit the household gods. To it are brought in procession representations of the bodies and the souls of all the dead who are being cremated. After *ngaskara*, the various representations of the dead are taken to the cemetery and placed beside the body.

1 and 2. The materials necessary for laying out the *oekoer* (the figure of the dead made of coins, cf. Pl. 92, figs. 5 and 6). These are carried to the *ngaskara* ceremony, where the figure is laid out as a corpse.

In fig. 1, the *oekoer* is covered by a tray containing a little mattress and pillows, a smaller tray of chopped and scented leaves, eleven folded rice haulms (*keketjer*), etc.

In fig. 2, the tray has been removed to show the *oekoer* figure. On the left is a mass of plaited palm leaf which can be opened to form the strips (*kadjang sinom*, cf. Pl. 92, fig. 6) which are laid across the complete lay-out.

Batoean. Aug. 21, 1937.   14 O 13, 16.

3. An anthropomorphic offering (*poepoehan*) used in a postmortuary ceremony (*meanin*) in Bajoeng Gede. Here, where there is no exhuming and no cremation, there is nevertheless a ceremony which the people equate with the cremation ceremony of the plains. This is called *meanin* and it is held annually.

The "head" of this offering is at the right-hand end of the photograph, and the body is composed of a long mountain of chopped food (*oeraban*) surrounded by leaf platters of cooked rice. This arrangement suggests that the body is divided into many parts (cf. *kawes*, Pl. 9).

This offering is taken to the graveyard and is there divided between the men who attend the ceremony.

Bajoeng Gede. June 13, 1937.   11 Q 4.

4. Offerings for the *ngaskara* ceremony in cremation. These are called *oeriaga* or *basang-basang* (bellies). It is said that the ghosts (*sang pirata*) come at night and reach in through the entrance to steal the food. One Brahman woman described this offering as "*isin awak*" (the contents of the body).

This offering contains: a coconut (*njoeh tjemaning*) surrounded by red, white, and black thread (*seridatoe*); two banana stems tied with similar thread, representing the bones; two eggs, representing the testes (only one egg in case of a woman); one pineapple representing the neck; five cakes representing arms; a piece of plaited palm leaf, called *tetampak*, representing the anus; five measures of rice, representing the contents of the body; 125 cash, representing the "roots"; 1000 cash representing the "cover"; two containers each containing ten onions, representing the fingers and toes; eleven garlic roots (*kesoena*) (only ten of these for a woman, but our informant said these had no meaning); a split gourd, representing the lips; a walking stick; and a number of other ingredients of unknown significance.

Informant: I. B. P. Poeting, a Sivaistic Brahman.
Batoean. Aug. 24, 1937.   14 X 5.

5. *Angenan*, another representational offering in the *ngaskara* ceremony. This is said to be the "*oeloen ati*" ("the head of the liver"). The base is made of a coconut covered with colored paper. To the mast-like structure are suspended four square spools of thread of four colors (yellow, black, white, and red) for the four directions.

The other half of the *angenan* is a support for a little lamp made of an eggshell. This lamp is lit later when this object is set up on the chest of the laid-out body. The Balinese are very little interested in "purpose" and "meaning." For them preparation completely overshadows consumption, and it would be psychologically false to say that the "purpose" of the *ngaskara* ceremony was to prepare or validate the *angenan* and other ritual objects, so that they could meaningfully be placed beside the corpse. A Balinese will say that the *angenan*, etc., are prepared for *ngaskara* and later disposed of by placing beside the corpse (cf. discussion of climax, Pls. 46 to 59).

Batoean. Aug. 21, 1937.   14 N 36.

6 and 7. Figures (*djelema-djelemaan*) of the dead made of clothes. The figure in fig. 6 was taken to a Brahman *ngaskara* ceremony and later placed beside the body. Fig. 7 shows the analogous object used in the great postmortuary *meligija* ceremony performed by the Regent of Karangasem.

Batoean. Aug. 23, 1937.   14 U 29 (fig. 6).
Karangasem. Aug. 9, 1937.   13 I 39.

1

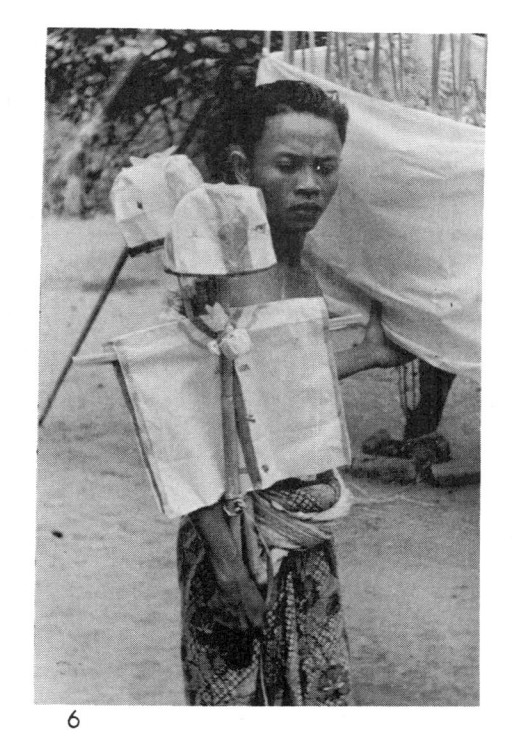

2

3

4

5

6

7

1

2

3

4

5

6

7

Plate 98

REPRESENTATIONS OF THE SOUL

This plate presents the converse of the proposition illustrated on Pl. 45. It was there shown that children are in some sense "gods"; and here it is shown that gods and souls (*atma*) of the dead are in some sense "children." When a man in trance, possessed by a god or soul, addresses an ordinary mortal, he says *"bapa"* ("father") or *"meme"* ("mother"), and when a doll is prepared to represent the soul, it is carried in a sling like a baby, a custom which persists even in Batoean where babies are not usually carried in slings.

1 and 2. Taking the souls home from the exhumation. The souls are represented by dolls (*sanggah oerip*) made of palm leaf and carried in slings by the women.

In fig. 1, the souls are in their home courtyard, in front of the family shrines and are being given flowers with which to pray to the family gods and ancestors. The women go through the motions of prayer, holding up the flowers between their fingers and letting them drop (cf. Pl. 87, fig. 8). Usually after doing this a woman will put one of the flowers in her hair, but in this case a petal is stuffed inside the doll.

In fig. 2, the souls are kneeling beside the grave at the beginning of exhumation.

Batoean. Aug. 22, 1937.   14 T 14; 14 P 10.

3. Representations (*tjili ampilan*) of the soul at the final "sending off" ceremony (*ngirim*). This ceremony follows the burning, and for it all the representations of the dead from the *ngaskara* ceremony are brought out, among which are these *tjili ampilan*. They have faces and fan-shaped headdresses of palm leaf, and the female figures have earrings. Each little figure is set up on a box which is covered with cloth representing the sash, handkerchief, etc., of the dead, and each figure wears 100 cash attached to the string which binds the figure to the box (cf. Pl. 100, fig. 4).

Near Bangli. Aug. 4, 1937.   13 D 16.

4. Figures (*sekah*) which represent the dead in the "sending off" ceremony (*ngirim*). Each figure is built on a green coconut which is opened at the top, and in which a central stick (*toengked aa*) is set up. White cloth is wrapped around the stick and coconut to give the conical form and a fan-shaped headdress of palm leaf is fixed to the front. The figure is further provided with a handkerchief, 225 cash, etc.

These figures are brought out after the burning for the ceremony called *ngereka*, at which the body is reconstituted from the ashes. In this ceremony, a piece of skull, two pieces of humerus, two pieces of radius or ulna, two pieces of femur, and two pieces of tibia or fibula — to make nine pieces in all — are collected together with tongs and put in a little mortar (*sende*). A piece of sugar cane or a piece of *dadap* wood is used as a pestle and the bits of bone ash are ground up with water (*jeh koemkoeman*) in which a precious stone (*mirah codi*) has been dipped. The resulting mixture is poured into the coconut in the base of the *sekah* shown in this photograph.

The *sekah* are later taken to the sea, or to some stream and there thrown away (cf. Pl. 99).

Batoean. Aug. 23, 1937.   14 U 31.

5. Figures (*pererai*) of gods. These little dolls with their handkerchiefs were set up in the house temple (*sanggah*) for a ceremony (*melaspas*) consecrating the temple.

Batoean. Oct. 6, 1937.   16 Q 27.

6. Carrying offerings (*pisang djati*) which represent the soul (*atma*) of the dead at the *ngaskara* ceremony. This consists of a basket (*wakoel*, cf. Pl. 4, fig. 6) fenced around at the top with a palm-leaf barrier in which there is an opening for the ghosts (cf. Pl. 97, fig. 4). The contents are "the same as those of *oeriaga* but smaller."

The *pisang djati* has a high comb-like headdress and hair (made of vegetable fiber). A little of this hair is visible in the photograph, hanging down on the far side of the nearest *pisang djati*.

Pisang djati are carried in slings like babies in the mountain villages.

Batoean. Aug. 23, 1937.   14 U 26.

7. Scene in the priest's house temple, when all the representations of the many dead are gathered for the *ngaskara* ceremony.

The photograph shows a group of *tjili ampilan* (cf. fig. 3) laid out on the right, and a group of *adegan* (another type of representation of the soul with fan-shaped headdress) on the left. In the background is another anthropomorphic offering (*tjanang rebong*, cf. Pl. 4, fig. 1) made of flowers.

Batoean. Aug. 23, 1937.   14 V 11.

Plate 99

FAREWELL TO THE DEAD

This plate illustrates the methods of ending any series of mortuary rites — by caressing representation of the dead, giving money as a farewell gift (*bekel*) to the dead, scrambling over the figure of the dead, taking the ashes out to sea, carrying the doll representing the soul through a stretched string, and leaving this doll tied up to the trunk of a tree.

These methods are, however, not final. There are further series of mortuary rites to be performed if the family can afford it, and these would be carried out with other representations of the body and soul of the dead.

1. Postmortuary ceremony (*meanin*) in Bajoeng Gede. For this ceremony a figure (*adegan*) of the dead is made out of a basket (*wakoel*) covered with a sarong, sash, belt, and headcloth. Its contents include: a measure of rice; ten white cakes (*bantal poetih*); ten other cakes (*bantal badeng*); 25 cash; a kris (or a knife in case the figure represents a woman); and four patterned palm leaves projecting from the basket.

This figure is made in the house. Mourning visitors come and put money into it and rub oil on the four palm leaves which represent the hair of the dead.

For the ceremony, the figure is taken to the village temple and laid out with a spread of offerings as shown in this photograph. Relatives come in turn and lift it up for a moment, as if trying its weight.

After this, the figure is taken to a sacred place (*tegal soetji*) outside the temple, and there it is scrambled over by the young men (cf. Pls. 34 and 95 for other occasions on which scrambling is used as a means of eliminating the unclean).

Nang Salib (son of the dead woman) holding the *adegan*; Nang Dakta (deaf mute) behind him; and I Gina to the right.

Bajoeng Gede. June 13, 1937.   11 Q 12.

2. Farewell offerings to an ox before it is ceremonially killed. This was an incident in one of the purificatory ceremonies connected with reaching high rank in the village hierarchy. The candidate must sacrifice an ox, and his son is here oiling the horns of the ox before it is killed.

The ox is tied with its head between two posts, and the chief priest of the village stands on the left with a handful of money which he will hold up in front of the ox's nose, weighing it in his hand, as a farewell present (*bekel*) to the ox.

Bajoeng Gede. May 5, 1936.   2 L 14.

3. Taking the ashes out to sea. This was a final incident in the Karangasem *meligija* ceremony (cf. Pl. 5, fig. 1). This was a postcremation ceremony, but structurally it was only a more elaborate cremation in which, in place of a body, a figure representing the dead was burned. The ashes were collected and put in another figure representing the dead, and this was taken out to sea.

The man in the front of the canoe has on his knees a tray containing the ashes. He will throw these ashes into the sea a few hundred yards from the shore.

Karangasem. Aug. 9, 1937.   13 K 9.

4. An offering (*pemerasan*) from the *ngaskara* ceremony. This offering illustrates a confusion of sequence common in Balinese ritual. The whole cremation cycle will end with *ngirim*, the ceremony of "sending off," in which the ashes will be thrown in the sea, but, here in one of the intermediate ceremonies we find the double outrigger canoe represented by a toy in one of the offerings at an earlier ceremony.

Batoean. Aug. 21, 1937.   14 O 25.

5. Breaking the string. This ritual (*mepegat*, literally "cutting off") occurs in marriage (cf. Pl. 87, fig. 3), after funerals, and after cremation. Essentially it seems to be a statement of finality and perhaps a symbolic breaking off of contact with a former state. Thus the married couple break off from the impurity which followed their elopement and the dead breaks off his contact with the world.

In this photograph, the ceremony is being held after the funeral of the sister of the woman who is carrying the doll representing the dead (cf. Pl. 34, figs. 1 to 4, for the scrambling behavior on this occasion).

In the cremation ceremony, the original dolls which went to visit their homes after the exhumation are burned up with the bones, but more dolls of the same sort are made for this *mepegat* ceremony.

Batoean. Sept. 29, 1937.   16 F 15.

6. The dolls (*sanggah oerip*), which represent the souls of the dead, after they have ritually broken off their connection with the living, are tied up to a tree trunk by the side of the road and are left there to decay.

Batoean. Sept. 29, 1937.   16 F 19.

1

2

3

4

5

6

1

2

3

4

Plate 100
THE CONTINUITY OF LIFE

The Balinese know the day of the week on which they were born, but they do not know how old they are. Climax is absent from their sequences of love and hate. They are insensitive to interruption, and however strong the emphasis upon finality may be, no mortuary ceremony is ever really final.

All these peculiarities of the culture appear *negative* to us. We have our own ways of punctuating the stream of life, and when we watch the Balinese and try to understand them, we miss the commas and periods, the bar-lines and parentheses, in terms of which we habitually organize the on-going stream. We become dazed when we try to dissect out the scheme which (we think) must underlie the details of the thousands of offerings which go to a single cremation ceremony. We look for a system of ends and purposes, and lose ourselves in a maze which is not constructed on the principles with which we are familiar.

But the Balinese are not lost in this maze. They live in a rigidly organized universe, and what appears to us to be negative — a lack of punctuation — appears to them as *continuity*. The souls of the dead are babies who must be taught to pray; and the babies are souls of the dead, and they too must be taught to pray. The great-grandfather is reincarnated in the great-grandchild, and every individual is somewhere in this three-generation cycle in which his position is determined by tecnonymy. If he is a child he is called "I So-and-So"; if he is a parent he is called "Father of So-and-So"; and if he is a grandparent he is called "Grandfather of So-and-So." Only if a man survives to be a great-grandparent does an overlap occur; and there are conventions to meet this anomaly. In Bajoeng Gede, the birth of a great-grandchild terminates a man's citizenship, and if he meets his great-grandchild, he ought to give him a present before speaking to him.

Every individual is somewhere also on the other great cycle of Balinese life, the cycle which alternates between life and death, between the secular and the supernatural. If he is alive, his position depends upon completed *rites de passage* and upon his age. In infancy and old age he is close to the supernatural, and only attains a measure of secularity in early married life. If he is dead, his position likewise depends upon *rites de passage;* only after *meanin* (Pl. 99, fig. 1) may the ghost enter the temple.

These two continuous cycles are symbolized in Bali by circular skeins of thread held down by money. In various *rites de passage* (including cremation) there is a ritual (*meperas*) in which all the descendants hold a rope in the order of their descent. The soul is tied to its box by a skein to which money is suspended (Pl. 98, fig. 3) and in this plate we see the village priestess in trance, possessed by the souls of the dead, going along the village street held by a similar skein.

1 and 2. A baby praying at its 210-day birthday.

In fig. 1, the baby boy is held by the old woman who is performing the ceremony, and she puts his hands in the position of prayer while he looks at the camera. After this ceremony held in the house temple, the baby may enter the village temple.

In fig. 2, a few seconds later, he repeats the lesson which he has just learned. (We observed this repetition in several babies at the 210-day ceremony.)

I Raoeh held by Dadong Poepoe in fig. 1; and held by his mother, Men Goenoeng, in fig. 2.

Bajoeng Gede. Aug. 15, 1936. 2 G 3, 4.

3. The souls of the dead being made to pray in the *mepegat* ceremony which terminates the cremation ritual. After this ritual, the souls break the suspended string and bamboo firecrackers are burned. In sending the souls away, the Brahman head of the household said, "Finish making trouble! Go home! So that Daijoe Siti may soon be mature." (Daijoe Siti was his daughter and her menarche was late in coming.)

Daijoe Siti at the far end of the kneeling line. I. B. Koeroeh, her father, on her right.

Batoean. Sept. 29, 1937. 16 E 10.

4. The village priestess in trance for the *metoeoen* ceremony (cf. Pl. 6, figs. 5 and 6). This is a postmortuary ceremony which follows *meanin* (cf. Pl. 99, fig. 1). The first part of the ceremony is held in a sacred field (*tegal soetji*) and there the priestess begins her trance. She is possessed by the souls of the dead and speaks first as one and then as another. She is taken in this trance state to the house, and the string apparently marks the continuity of the two halves.

Djero Balian Soekeh leading; Men Margi following.

Bajoeng Gede. July 10, 1937. 13 G 23.

ETHNOGRAPHIC NOTE ON BALI

Bali is a small island with an area of 2905 square miles and a population of approximately one million. It lies just off the east coast of Java. The Balinese are found only on this small island, on the neighboring island of Lombok (the much more numerous Sassak population of which was conquered and held by Balinese from 1692 to about 1740), and in small exile settlements in East Java and on the island of Noesa Penida (both said to have been founded by exiles who had violated the rule against marriage with a woman of higher caste or who had been involved in some other deep social trouble). In appearance the Balinese are enough like the Javanese, so that the style of headcloth and way of movement are superficially the easiest method of telling them apart.

They have an Indonesian culture which has received progressive waves of cultural influence from Buddhist and Hindoo sources, with a less important Chinese impact, a very slight Mohammedan influence, and finally a progressive overlay of older systems of authority by the immigration during the centuries of Javanese high-castes who fled Java before the Mohammedanization. Three castes, Brahman, Kesatrya, and Vesia, are recognized, and hypogamy is permitted to the males of all three castes, the women so married being progressively raised in status by successive generations of higher caste descendants. The bulk of the population is spoken of as "outsiders" (*djaba*), lacking membership in these castes. The language, which is related to Malay, is graded to express differences in caste, status, and intimacy, these gradations depending upon substitution of widely different vocabularies. These substitutions apply to all parts of speech, though personal pronouns are most highly differentiated. A small proportion of the population (priests, seers, diviners, scribes, and clerks) are literate in the syllabic script, which is derived from Sanskrit letters and traced with a stylus on the leaves of the lontar palm, cut into an even series and strung together.

The political organization, before Dutch occupation, consisted of a number of kingdoms, each ruled by a Rajah (*Anak Agoeng*) of the Kesatrya caste, assisted by a large number of his relatives who acted as his provincial representatives and tax collectors. This system overlays a system of autonomous villages, each with its own local laws (*adat*) administered by a village council consisting of full resident males, who also administered the village temples, the system of land tenure, and the elaborate calendrical system of feasts. The Rajahs levied taxes in kind or in corvée, maintained courts which tried a few major offenses, patronized the arts, conscripted the labor of artists, occasionally seized more lands or otherwise expropriated relatively helpless citizens, and exercised an occasional veto on the tenure of office of the Brahman priests. These priests, divided into two principal sects, Buddhistic and Sivaistic, owed a secular allegiance to their Rajahs and respect to the priests who had taught them. Each priest, in loose collaboration with others, served as a religious center, first for his own family and extended family, second for other families from the two other castes, and third for constellations of the casteless people, who superimposed upon their village and family rituals, Brahman rituals when they could afford to pay for them. Brahman priests were tied to the organization of kingdoms, but not to any local organization except through the routine membership of their households in village communes and by their duties to the home temples of their own ancestors.

The three castes maintain extensive kinship relationships with intermarriages between members of different kingdoms, observances of death taboos by the entire relationship group, and periodic offerings in family temples. Among the casteless people, allegiance to the village of residence is the strongest tie, with a secondary tie to the larger patrilineal family group, which often became generalized into membership in a temple. Many people also have membership in one or more temples (other than the village temples) and these subsidiary temples were probably originally the family temples of senior lines, though now this origin is forgotten. Kinship terms are bilateral, with the addition of phrases to indicate collateral distance, so that *reraman* is father, *reraman di misan*, father's or mother's first cousin, and *reraman di mindon*, father's or mother's second cousin. Distinctions are made between elder and younger siblings; and order-of-birth terms in sets of four are the customary modes of address. Tecnonymy occurs systematically among most casteless people and in a modified form, among high-castes, where the appropriate caste term for "father" or "mother" is substituted for the personal name without however including the name of the child, as is done among casteless people.

Kinship ties within the patrilineal family are stressed and given continuity by a variety of customs. If a man has no son, he may adopt a prospective son-in-law who then becomes a son and worships the ancestors of his wife. If a man has several sons, the eldest and the youngest have a somewhat greater share of power than the others; the eldest "because he is senior" and the youngest because, after the others have left home and built up their own establishments with the father's help, he usually inherits the paternal house and most of such land as the family owns privately. The parents endeavor (usually without success, except in the high-caste families) to make their children marry cousins. In the plains villages, the preferred marriage is with the father's brother's child, but in Bajoeng Gede this marriage is regarded as incestuous and the preferred marriage is with a patrilineal second cousin of own generation. There is a strong prohibition against a man's marrying a female relative of ascendant generation. Such a marriage would "cut the [line of] respect," because a man should worship the dead of ascendant generations but a woman should worship her dead husband. The hypergamous sexual union between a casteless male and a high-caste woman would, of course, be a still more drastic breaking of this taboo, and such offenses are punished by death or exile. There are also ceremonial objections (sanctioned by supernaturally caused sickness or disaster) against a stranger's building his house between the houses of close relatives, especially between a man's household and a household containing a senior house temple belonging to the same family.

The economic system of exchange is based on periodic markets which are held in large centers to which both professional vendors and individual peasants with a handful of vegetables take their wares. The cash nexus between individuals is set up from the time a two-year-old child purchases peanuts from a female relative or neighbor who is maintaining a street stall, and continues through life in the payment of fines, levies, and all exchanges of goods between persons. Chinese cash (value in 1938, 1/7 of a Dutch cent) was the only money before Dutch contact, and larger units are formed by stringing the cash on bamboo thongs. Certain villages specialize in certain manufactures, such as pots (made on the potter's wheel), baskets, and metal objects. The iron workers and the indigo workers constitute virtual subcastes of high and low status respectively. Rice, however, is the major product and the irrigated rice crops are staggered so that some districts are harvesting while others are planting, and purchases to cover these discrepancies are made in the markets. Many families sell rice at one period of the year and purchase rice at other periods.

In addition to specialization by localities, there are also specialists in each community in a number of skills, such as tuning orchestral instruments, making masks, weaving fine fabrics, teaching dancing, carving tufa, translating ancient texts, divining, providing magic amulets, etc., and the services of these specialists can be obtained for a fee. A Rajah or wealthy nobleman maintained an entourage of such specialists, and of a number of low-caste hangers-on who thus fell virtually outside of the scheme of village organization.

Land tenure is of many kinds, especially in the mountains. A man may personally own land which was cleared by an ancestor or which he has bought or acquired as security on a lapsed loan from somebody whose ancestor cleared it. But the majority of land around Bajoeng Gede is owned by the community and the rights of usufruct are assigned in various ways. Each full citizen (a man with household and body complete, whose youngest child has not married and who is not yet a great-grandparent) has a strip share of the enormous fields (*laba*) which are redivided every year. He also has a piece of land (*ajahan*) allotted to him in recognition of his work for the village, and may have other extra pieces (*bakti*) if he holds ranking office in the village hierarchy. Other land is shared among men who have retired from citizenship. There are also many forms of share-farming, renting, and mortgaging; and many individuals, who own no land, live as more or less vagrant casual laborers receiving a share in the crop and/or their board and lodging.

The pursuit of wealth, either through trading, lending money on land, or lending money on other securities at high interest, is regarded as one possible vocation, just as are the activities of the artist, the diviner, the priest, the gambler; and all are overlaid upon an agricultural base. The great majority of the population, however, are primarily farmers, and practice other occupations merely as supplementary or temporary avocations. Wet rice fields, cultivated by water buffalo and irrigated by elaborate systems (handled by social organization units called *soebak* in which men cooperatively keep the ditches in repair and supervise the flow and distribution of water), are the rule for most of the island, except in the very mountainous parts, where dry rice fields and cultivation by oxen are substituted. Horses, of which there are a few on the island, are used only for transportation. Herding, except for the half-wild sacred herds which belong to the communes, is an individual matter, with a herding boy for each ox or water buffalo. Other domestic animals include the pig, ducks, chickens, an occasional goose, and the ubiquitous dog which acts as a scavenger. Fighting cocks form an important leisure time item, and princes and peasants alike keep both fighting cocks and caged songbirds.

The diet has a heavy carbohydrate base of rice, sweet potatoes, or maize, garnished with a variety of vegetables and small quantities of dried fish and meat. These garnishings are highly seasoned and "hot" with red peppers and turmeric. In 1936 the Balinese were estimated to consume about two pounds of rice per person per day, as against 0.7 pound for a Javanese. Although there is occasional famine in parts of Bali, due to rats, grasshoppers, floods, etc., they have a form of social organization and a method of using the land which is adequate for feeding the people.

Balinese daily life is organized on a principle of voluntary association with others as a member of a village, a rice club, a temple club, an orchestra, etc., and membership carries with it obligations and privileges; failure to discharge or claim these is punished by fines and finally by expulsion. Within each of these organizations, the participants are arranged in a fixed order of responsibility for the discharge of ceremonial and economic obligations, accompanied in many cases by sacerdotal responsibility.

The religious system is complex, containing a large pantheon of impersonal, polynomial gods, some of whom are equated with the various Hindoo gods. This pantheon merges indistinguishably into cults of personal ancestors and the ancestors associated with larger kinship temples, and into the cults of the gods of the village, the Temple of Origin, and the Temple of Death. Individual trancers and seers may from time to time, in their utterances, particularize the behavior and inter-personal ties of such gods and order that these relationships be expressed as social ties between clubs, temples, or villages. The gods, especially those generalized deities who personify the social organization (Betara Desa, "God of the Village," etc.), are articulated with village calendrical feasts and work rituals. Particular village functionaries may keep (*ngamong*) special gods in their own home temples. The whole pantheon at its various levels of personalization may be variously invoked in ceremonial by the village religious functionaries, the keepers of shrines or family temples, the seers and diviners, and the Brahman priests. None of the sets of ceremonial formulae, with their accompanying offerings and ritual behaviors are regarded as exclusive of the others, and most Balinese ceremonies are a repetitive conglomerate of rituals from different villages, different cults, and different degrees of Hindooistic, Buddhistic, or Indonesian influence.

All conspicuous consumption of food and the performance of theatricals are phrased as "offered" to the gods. And such conspicuous consumption may be resorted to whether the occasion be a village ceremonial, a feast for the household gods, or a ceremonial for the marriage or birthday of some individual. The majority of such occasions are defined by the calendar, but conspicuous consumption may also celebrate some special event. A woman whose pig is sick may even promise the gods that, if it recovers within three days, she will take a pleasure trip on a motor bus at the calendric feast of *Galoengan*. Religious acts are pleasurable, and the making of offerings occupies a considerable proportion of a Balinese woman's time. Every occasion of religious importance in her own household, in that of a relative, or in the village calendar, must be marked by the construction of dozens or hundreds of offerings (*banten*, carefully specified combinations of food, cash, flowers, betel ingredients, etc., cf. Pl. 97, fig. 4 for an example). And in these constructions, an endless number of details are specified as "usual" (*biasa*) or "necessary" (*perloe*): the material used — red rice or white rice, raw or cooked; the method of cooking; the shape into which it should be pressed — circular, square, conical, human or animal; how it should be wrapped; the way in which the wrapping should be tied; the colors of the string; the pattern to be painted or pressed upon the surface; the container in which the specified combination of elements is to be placed — one of scores of different types of baskets, leaf-trays, pots, and coconuts in different colors and degrees of ripeness; the clothes in which the container should be dressed; and the type of pedestal upon which the container should be set — a wooden pedestal, a tray, a mat, or perhaps some special little structure of sticks. Some of the necessary constituent elements are standard and formal, like the little square tray (*tjanang genten*) of flowers and betel ingredients which is called the "pollen" of the offering and is left on the shrine for the gods after the offering is "asked back." Other elements are special to some particular *rite de passage* in a given family in a given village.

Each element is reduplicated a specified number of times in each combination, and each combination is reduplicated a specified number of times for a given ceremony. And the number of combinations "necessary" varies widely, from five or six in a small birthday ceremony for the sixth child of a poor man in the mountains, to many thousands for the cremation of a prince.

In addition to containing the "necessary" ingredients, most offerings are embellished by quantities of stock materials — cakes, fruit, flowers, and intricate cut-outs of young palm leaves — and it is perhaps this embellishment which, more than anything else, gives the characteristic appearance to every large aggregation of offerings. Wherever offerings are spread out — in front of a shrine, inside a house, on the ground of the house temple, or on high tables set up beside the sea — they present very much the same appearance from a distance — a mass of bright colors, towers and plaques and patterns of flowers, colored cakes, patterns made of meat and meal, decorative pieces of cloth, carved and painted wooden supports and pendants, umbrellas, banners, and anthropomorphic figures. It takes a practiced eye to pick out the constant elements — the practitioner's basket with its skein of thread and bell and holy water, the offerings which will be used to lustrate the other offerings and various parts of the premises, the offerings which constitute the toilet articles for the gods or ancestors for whom the feast is being given.

The same apparent confusion and meaningless repetitiveness is also characteristic of the rituals for which the offerings are prepared. It takes experience to recognize the sequences of lustration and purification; the invitation to the gods to come down; the waftings of the essence of the offerings toward the gods and the waftings toward the self (in *rites de passage*) of those offerings which are offered to the candidate or to the soul incarnated in him; the formal trances in which the gods, through the mouth of the religious practitioner, acknowledge receipt of the offerings; the request to the gods to give back the offerings; the invitation to the gods to return to heaven; and the final sharing back of the offerings among those who have made them or contributed to them. Except in cases where the foods are offered to the dead or to demons, or where the style of the ceremony demands that the offerings be so extensive that many of them must be made weeks before, so that they cease to be edible, offerings become food to be eaten informally by the family and distributed to relatives and neighbors, with the careful specification, "This is food which has been asked back from the gods," i.e., it cannot be used for offerings again.

In addition to the elaborate series of pleasant but very mildly emotional acts which constitute the normal religion, there is in Bali a belief (itself not very highly toned) that the black arts of witchcraft are highly emotional. In addition to many of the familiar European beliefs about witches — the belief in witchcraft hereditary in the maternal line, in were-animals, in sympathetic magic, and in reversed or left-handed rituals — there is a curious body of belief about the ways in which witches, wanting to practice their art, go about seeking situations which will make them sufficiently angry. The witch may know *how* to kill by magic, but before she can work her charms she must pick a quarrel (*ngalih lih*) with her selected victim. The problem, for the Balinese, is how to *want* to kill.

Some women are believed to be witches and are to some extent shunned in social life, and some women probably believe themselves to be witches; but the actual disruption of social life due to suspicion of witchcraft and black magic is very slight. For the Balinese, death is a part of life, and in their religious system witchcraft is an elaboration of a minor theme in a religion which recognizes two extremes of the sacred: the highest and purest attributes of the high gods at one end of the scale being no less supernaturally valid than the extremes of horror and impurity down in the cemetery at the other end of the scale. The Witch, *par excellence,* whose disciples are the minor witches and the mortals who transform themselves into monkeys, is *Rangda,* whose mask is that of *Durga* (the Hindoo goddess, Death) and who is the necessary counterpart of the protective Dragon.

The changes resulting from European culture contact in Bali have been determined by Balinese limited compliance and Dutch self-restraint. For hundreds of years the Balinese have been adopting and resisting cultural details from other peoples, especially from Chinese and from higher centers of Hindooism; and two characteristics of Balinese culture are the ready acceptance of those small details of custom and technology which can be absorbed without changing the basic premises of life, and the utter inability and unwillingness to contemplate any more drastic changes. The Dutch, on their side, have shown a preference for using the existing native social structure as fully as possible. They have indulged in no arbitrary interference with native life, and have not allowed themselves to be pressed into supporting missionary efforts among those of their subject peoples who, like the Balinese, espouse the higher oriental religions.

The northern kingdom of Bali with its capital in Boeleleng came under Dutch rule in the period 1849–54. The Dutch seat of government was established in Singaradja, adjacent to Boeleleng, and the whole southern part of the island was taken over in 1906. At that time the Balinese showed the extreme of their noncompliance. Two of the Rajahs of South Bali walked out to suicide dressed in state and accompanied by wives and retainers — a procession into the fire of the Dutch guns. But this initial refusal to accept foreign rule was not followed by years of discontent. The Dutch replaced the dead Rajahs with successors from the same family lines who became Regents, so that the social structure, in which the Rajahs had died rather than live after it was disrupted, was re-established. Attached to each Regent was a Dutch district official or Controleur, and almost the whole of the official contact between Dutch and native governmental systems was concentrated at this point — the Regent retained the old system of local native officials, while the Controleur communicated with this native system only through the Regent. Thus, when we arrived in Bali, we were referred by the Dutch Government to the Regent of Bangli in whose kingdom we proposed to reside. The Regent gave us letters of introduction to his local official or *Poenggawa* in Kintamani, the market town nearest to Bajoeng Gede, under whose supervision we would be. The actual form of the relationship between Controleur and Regent has undergone slow changes since 1906 when, following the military conquest, the Controleur may be supposed to have had "control." Since then his functions have become more and more "advisory" until in June 1938 this change in function was formally recognized by the *Herstel van Zelfbestuur* — a legal change by which full authority was vested in the Regent and the functions of the Controleur became consultative rather than advisory.

Economic aspects of society have undergone more profound changes than the administrative system. The introduction of Dutch money and access to cheap calico, pajamas, lamps, bicycles, and even automobiles, have changed the superficial appearance of the Balinese people. The Regents have begun to express their prestige more and more in terms of automobiles and less by the patronage of the arts. On the other hand, tourists have bought pictures and carvings, and thanks to the wise guidance of European artists resident in Bali — especially Walter Spies who encouraged the Balinese to follow what was best in the new Balinese art — there has been a renaissance rather than a decadence in painting and carving. The tourist traffic has been carefully organized by the Koninklijke Paketvaart Maatscappij, the shipping company, which could not afford to have clients wandering off and complaining when they missed their shipping connections. As a result, the tourists are helped to see the best sights and the best dancing in the island, and but only a few hundred of the one million population come in contact with tourists. Bajoeng Gede, four miles from the main road and a hotel, had never been visited by a tourist and had only twice been visited unofficially by a Dutch Controleur interested in village organization.

In the field of public health, the Dutch have concentrated upon preventing epidemics, and have avoided the constant interference with the population which would be involved in any attempt to deal with the manifold individual ills. The corpses of princes and priests are still kept in houses, and the dogs are still the only (and very effective) sanitary inspectors, but universal vaccination and stringent quarantine rules have eliminated the epidemics. The population was rapidly increasing when we were on the island, and for several years the Government had been encouraging the excess population in the southern and eastern parts of the island to migrate to West Bali where there are large areas of virgin forest and still an occasional tiger.

All in all, from 1936 to 1939, we saw a Bali which had undergone many superficial changes as a result of culture contact. Cheap foreign towels were replacing native woven fabrics, and aniline was replacing native vegetable dyes, but the Balinese were content and gay; they enjoyed the new colors, and the Balinese character remained unchanged, not ground down by exploitation and not outraged by violence. How the Balinese behaved when the island was invaded by the Japanese we do not yet know — probably having had a pleasant experience of dominion by one power, the Balinese were not overfrightened by the substitution of another. But the Dutch have a record of self-restraint and respect for native customs; the Japanese are notorious exploiters of the helpless, and that firm but passive streak of noncompliance in Balinese character may well invoke extra savagery from Japanese invaders. The history of culture contact in Japan through the ages has not been happy, and the Japanese, lacking respect for their own culture, perceive their inevitable inferiority and feel insulted when they meet this self-respect in others.

M. M., G. B.

BIBLIOGRAPHIC NOTE

There is an enormous literature on Balinese culture, most of it in Dutch, and almost all of it is concerned with matters of archeological, linguistic, and scholarly interest very far removed from the subject matter of this monograph. Two bibliographies of the literature on Bali have been published; the first by Lekkerkerker, which covers publications before 1919, and the second recently compiled by Goris and covering the later literature up to 1935–36.

We list here only manuscripts and publications by those collaborators with whom we actually worked in Bali and upon whose insights or concrete materials we have drawn either for matters of actual fact or for those intangible understandings which are more difficult to document. We also list publications of our own containing data or theory based on the Balinese field work.

ABEL, THEODORA M.
"Free Designs of Limited Scope as a Personality Index," *Character and Personality*, VII (1938), 50–62.

BATESON, GREGORY
"An Old Temple and a New Myth," *Djawa*, XVII (September, 1937).
—. "Equilibrium and Climax in Interpersonal Relations" (Paper read at the Conference of Topological Psychologists, held at Smith College, Northampton, Mass., December 31, 1940 – January 2, 1941).
—. "Experiments in Thinking about Observed Ethnological Material," *Philosophy of Science*, VIII, No. 1 (1941), 53–68.
—. "The Frustration-Aggression Hypothesis," *Psychological Review*, XLVIII (1941), 350–355.
—. "Comment on 'The Comparative Study of Culture and the Purposive Cultivation of Democratic Values,' by Margaret Mead," *Science, Philosophy, and Religion*, Second Symposium (published by the Conference on Science, Philosophy, and Religion), New York, 1942.
—. "Morale and National Character," *Civilian Morale*, Second Yearbook of the Society for the Study of Social Issues, Goodwin Watson, Editor. Boston and New York: Houghton-Mifflin, 1942.
—. "Cultural Determinants of Personality," *Handbook of Personality and the Behavior Disorders*, J. McV. Hunt, Editor (in press).

BELO, JANE
"A Study of Customs Pertaining to Twins in Bali," *Tijdschrift voor Ind. Taal-, Land-, en Volkenkunde*, LXXV, No. 4 (1935), 483–549.
—. "The Balinese Temper," *Character and Personality*, IV (December, 1935), 120–146.
—. "A Study of a Balinese Family," *American Anthropologist*, XXXVIII, No. 1 (1936), 12–31.
—. "Balinese Children's Drawings," *Djawa*, XVII, Nos. 5 and 6 (1937).

BELO, JANE AND MERSHON, KATHARANE
"Trance in Bali," New York: Columbia University Press (in press).

Goris, G.
    "Overzicht over de Belangrijste Litteratuur Betreffende de Cultur van Bali over het Tijdvak 1920–1935," *Mededeelingen Kirtya Liefrinck van der Tuuk*, Aflevering 5, 1936(?).

Holt, Claire
    "Les Danses de Bali," *Archives Internationales de la Danse*, Part I (April 15, 1935), 51–53; Part II (July 15, 1935), 84–86.
——. "Théâtre et Danses aux Indes Néerlandaises," *Catalogue et Commentaires*, XIIIe Exposition des Archives Internationales de la Danse (1939). Paris: Maisonneuve, 1939. Pp. 86.
——. Analytical Catalogue of Collection of Balinese Carvings in the American Museum of Natural History, New York (unpublished).

Lekkerkerker, C.
    Bali en Lombok; overzicht der litteratuur omtrent deze eilanden tot einde 1919 (Uitgave van het Bali-Instituut). Rijswijk: Blankwaardt & Schoonhoven, 1920.

McPhee, Colin
    "The 'Absolute' Music of Bali," *Modern Music*, XII (1935), 165.
——. "The Balinese Wanjang Koelit and its Music," *Djawa*, XVI (1936), 1.
——. "Angkloeng Music in Bali," *Djawa*, XVII (1937).
——. "Children and Music in Bali," *Djawa*, XVIII (1938).
——. "Figuration in Balinese Music," Peabody Bulletin (May, 1940).
——. "The Gamelan Music of Bali" (in preparation).
——. "Music in the Air; a Balinese Journal" (in preparation).

Mead, Margaret
    "Public Opinion Mechanisms among Primitive Peoples," *Public Opinion Quarterly*, I, No. 3 (1937), 5–16.
——. "Strolling Players in the Mountains of Bali," *Natural History*, XLIII, No. 1 (1939), 17–26.
——. "Men and Gods in a Bali Village," *New York Times Magazine* (July 16, 1939), 12–13, 23.
——. "Researches in Bali, 1936–39; on the Concept of Plot in Culture," *Transactions of the New York Academy of Sciences*, Series II, Vol. 2 (1939), 1–4.
——. "Character Formation in Two South Seas Societies," *American Neurological Association, Transactions*, 66th Annual Meeting, June, 1940, 99–103.
——. "Social Change and Cultural Surrogates," *Journal of Educational Sociology*, XIV (1940), 92–109.
——. "Conflict of Cultures in America," *Proceedings, 54th Annual Convention, Middle States Association of Colleges and Secondary Schools*, November 23–24, 1940.
——. "The Arts in Bali," *Yale Review*, XXX (1940), 335–347.
——. "Administrative Contributions to Democratic Character Formation at the Adolescent Level," *Journal of the National Association of Deans of Women*, IV (1941), 51–57.
——. "Family Organization and the Super-ego" (read at the Conference of Topological Psychologists, Smith College, Northampton, Mass., December 31, 1940 – January 2, 1941).
——. "Back of Adolescence Lies Early Childhood," *Childhood Education*, XVIII (1941), 58–61.
——. "Community Drama, Bali and America," *American Scholar*, II (1941–42), 79–88.
——. "Educative Effects of Social Environment as Disclosed by Studies of Primitive Societies," in Symposium on Environment and Education (E. W. Burgess, W. L. Warner, Franz Alexander, Margaret Mead), University of Chicago, *Supplementary Educational Monographs*, LIV (1942), 48–61.

——. "Research on Primitive Children," *Handbook of Child Psychology*, Leonard Carmichael, Editor. Boston: Houghton Mifflin (in press).

——. "The Family in Primitive Society: its Role in the Definition of Personality," *The Role of the Family in Contemporary Society*, Science of Culture Series, III. New York: Harcourt-Brace (in press).

ZOETE, BERYL DE, AND SPIES, WALTER

"Dance and Drama in Bali" (preface by Arthur Waley). New York and London: Harper, 1939.

GLOSSARY AND INDEX OF NATIVE WORDS AND PERSONAL NAMES

The personal name is always the last component in the series of words used to refer to an individual. I Karsa is therefore listed under Karsa, I, and Ida Bagoes Made Togog is listed under Togog, I. B. Made, etc.

The following abbreviations have been used for the commonest titles:

B. (Bagoes), a title for Brahman males.

I. (Ida), an honorific personal pronoun, used as a personifying prefix before the titles and names of Brahmans and those Kesatryas who have the title, *"Anak Agoeng."*

I (not an abbreviation), a personifying prefix used before the names of all persons except those entitled to "Ida."

W. (Wajan), P. (Poetoe), and K. (Kompiang), order-of-birth terms applied to the first-born in each series of four children.

M. (Made), the term for the second-born child.

Nj. (Njoman), the term for the third-born child.

Kt. (Ketoet), the term for the fourth-born child. (The fifth child may be called "Wajan" or "Poetoe" or, if no further children are expected to make up the second set of four, the fifth child may be called "Ketoet.")

Among casteless people, parents are usually referred to as "Father of So-and-So" and "Mother of So-and-So," using the name of the eldest child. Thus I Gangsar married I Adjin and their eldest child was I Karma. The parents are therefore now called Nang Karma (the father) and Men Karma (the mother). This system of tecnonymy has been used in the cross references. The members of the most photographed households are listed under the names of the tecnonymous children. Under Karma, I, will be found a list of I Karma's brothers and sisters in order; and under Gata, I, will be found a cross reference to the tecnonymous elder brother, Karma, I.

The spelling of native words and names is that of our native secretary, I Made Kaler.

adegan, an anthropomorphic representation of the soul in cremation ceremonies. Pl. 98.

Adjer, I. Pl. 74.

adjoeman, showing off, decorative. Pl. 96.

agoeli lindjong (*a-,* enumerative singular prefix; *goeli,* terminal joint of finger; *lindjong,* the middle finger), a unit of length. Pl. 21.

agoeng, great, big (*aloes*).

aijoe, beautiful, a term for physical beauty, only applied to females (cf. Daijoe).

ajab, to waft away from oneself, a ritual gesture. Pl. 84.

ajahan (literally, "something for which service is given"), land owned by the village but to which the citizens obtain right of usufruct by *corvée.* Pl. 2.

alas-alasan (literally, "something pertaining to the forest"), a bunch of special leaves, which is an ingredient in many offerings. Pl. 4.

aloes, polished. This word is used metaphorically

to describe the language and vocabulary of respect used between strangers or by an inferior in addressing a superior. In some cases vocabulary is selected according to the status of the owner of the object referred to, or according to the status of the subject of the verb used. Thus it is more polite to use *ngamah* (equivalent to the German *fressen*) when mentioning one's own eating to a superior person. The opposite of *aloes* is *kasar*, rough or coarse, referring to the language and vocabulary used in speaking to inferiors and intimates.

Ampiag, I (see Oera, Nang). Pls. 27, 68.

anak, a person; *Anak Agoeng*, a ruling prince, a Regent. *Anak Agoeng* is also a common title applied to either sex in the Kesatrya caste. Pl. 3.

angenan, a ritual object representing the "head of the liver" of the dead. Pl. 97.

anteng, a long piece of cloth worn as a shawl and used by women in Bajoeng Gede as a sling in which the baby is supported on the woman's hip. It is used in the plains for carrying dolls which represent gods or souls. The same term is used for the Witch's cloth. Pls. 46, 48, 56, 60, 62, 69, 79, 91, 98.

arak, a drink made by distillation of any fermented liquor. Pl. 94.

ardja, a secular theatrical form. Pls. 13, 22.

Asa, I. Pls. 24, 69.

Asa, Men. Pl. 69.

Asin, I, younger brother of I Asa. Pls. 29, 69.

atma, Hindooistic term for the soul of the dead. Pl. 98.

awak, body. Pl. 4.

Badera, I, tecnonymous son of Nang Badera. Pls. 44, 67.

Badera, Nang, formerly I Mebet, tecnonymous son of Nang and Men Mebet. Their children are: Nang Badera; I Gedor (boy); I Gedar (boy); I Gedir (girl); I Geder (girl); I Gedoer (girl); I Gedjer (boy); I Gedjar (boy).

bagoes, handsome, a term for physical beauty only applied to males. This term is used as a title for male members of the Brahman caste.

Bala, I. B. Made. Pl. 33.

bale, house, platform, bed, table. Pls. 12, 84, 93.

Bale Agoeng (literally "great house"), the long house, usually in the village temple in mountain villages, in which the citizens meet for certain ceremonial feasts. Pl. 1.

bale pebasmean, the roofed platform on which the corpse is burned at cremation. Pl. 96.

balian, a professional religious or magical practitioner not attached to any hierarchical group. *Balian*s are of many kinds according to their repertoire of skills, which may include divination, trance, medicine, magic, sorcery, etc. In Bajoeng Gede, the *Djero Balian* is an important religious functionary, a woman who goes into trance at almost all village ceremonies and so represents the gods. Her functions and appointment are independent of her status in the village hierarchy. Pls. 8, 61, 85.

banjoen tjokor (probably a corruption of *baijoe*, life, and *tjokor*, foot), a special sort of holy water. Pl. 11.

bantal, a cake which is cooked in a leaf-wrapper. Many different sorts are named. Pls. 48, 96, 99.

Baoe, title applied to the 3rd and 4th citizens in the village hierarchy in Bajoeng Gede. Pl. 9.

bapa, father. Pls. 62, 68, 98.

baris, a type of dance, usually danced by men in formation carrying weapons (spears, bows, or shields). Most mountain villages have several types of *baris*, which are performed as an embellishment to religious ceremonies. Pl. 40.

Baroe, I. B. Kt. Pl. 40.

Barong, the Dragon mask. Pls. 14, 23, 48, 55, 58, 62, 66, 67.

basang-basang (reduplicated from *basang*, a belly), a type of offering used in cremation. Pl. 97.

batis-batis (reduplicated from *batis*, a leg), a type of spirit which haunts graveyards and which consists of a leg which has a head. Pl. 20.

Bawa, I. Pl. 12.

bekel, a gift to a person who is departing. Pls. 34, 99.

belakas, a heavy chopper made of soft iron. Pl. 40.

Belot, I. Pl. 67.

Berata Joeda, a Hindoo epic. Pl. 20.

beroek, decaying, falling to pieces (of corpses, buildings, etc.). Pls. 17, 18, 19, 20, 90, 93.

Betara, a title for gods.

betel, the leaf of *Piper betle*. This is chewed with the fruit of *Areca catechu*, lime, and sometimes other ingredients.

Bima, I, mythological hero. Pl. 20.

boedjoeh (probably connected with *boedjoe*, an idiot or lunatic), a facial expression. Pl. 58.

Boen, I. B. Poetoe. Pl. 38.

boeta, a species of minor demon. Pls. 9, 33, 58.
Bontok, I (see Rimpen, I). Pl. 28.

daa (also spelled *daha*), an unmarried woman, especially a girl who is a member of the club of village virgins. Pl. 81.
Dabdab, I. Pl. 81.
dadap, a species of tree, much used in Balinese ritual, perhaps because the cuttings take root wherever they are planted. Pls. 87, 98.
dadia, a voluntary membership group, usually associated with a particular temple. Pl. 9.
dadong, father's mother or mother's mother, a term prefixed to the name of a grandchild to give a tecnonymous term for the grandmother.
Dadong Badjang. Pl. 4.
dag, the central figure who acts as master of ceremonies in the modern *djanger* dance. Pl. 21.
Daijoe, a title for Brahman females. The word is usually preceded by the non-honorific personifying prefix, thus: I Daijoe. This combination is probably a corruption from Ida Aijoe (cf. *aijoe* and *bagoes*).
Dakta, Nang, deaf-mute father of Nang Salib. Pl. 99.
dalang, the narrator and manipulator of the puppets in the shadow-play.
Dampoek, I, tecnonymous son of Nang and Men Dampoek. Their children are: I Dampoek; I Wadi (girl); I Rinjin (girl, partly adopted by Djero Baoe Tekek); I Gingsir (boy); I Kemit (girl, lives with Men Poekel); I Sidep (girl); I Karta (boy); I Malen (boy). Pl. 45.
Dana, I (see Loka, I). Pl. 63.
Dangdang Bang, I, comical horse-headed figure in shadow-play. Pl. 22.
Dani, I (see Loka, I). Pl. 17.
Dapet, Djero Balian. Pl. 34.
Darma, I. Pl. 20.
Daweg, I. Pls. 39, 59.
Degeng, I, tecnonymous son of Nang and Men Degeng. Their children are: I Degeng; I Leket (boy, partly adopted by Nang Leket, brother of Nang Degeng); I Sepek (baby boy at breast). Pls. 29, 33, 34, 74.
Degeng, Men. Pl. 12.
Degeng, Nang. Pl. 74, 75.
Delem, I, a comic servant in the shadow-play, elder brother of I Sanggoet. Pl. 20.
desa, the village; sometimes personified as "I Desa."
dewaning dewa (literally "god of gods"), a title claimed by many deities. Pl. 20.

dewasaksian (literally, "a business of which god is witness"), an ordeal ceremony, in which all suspects drink of special holy water, thereby invoking a conditional curse if they are guilty. Pl. 68.
Diding, I. B. Kt. Pls. 10, 24.
Dira, I (see Moespa, I). Pls. 25, 83.
djailina, mocked for some failure or weakness. Pl. 81.
Djaja, I Dewa P. Pl. 16.
Djana, I (see Djani, I). Pl. 15.
djanger, a dance form which has recently become very popular. Boys sit facing inward on two opposite sides of a hollow square; girls on the other two sides. The dance has been influenced by the Malay Opera, and that of the boys consists largely of acrobatics. Pls. 12, 21.
Djani, I, tecnonymous daughter of Nang and Men Djani. Their children are: I Djani; I Djana (boy); I Kanggoen (girl at breast). Pl. 15.
Djani, Nang. Pl. 29.
Djantoek, I (see Karsa, I). Pls. 38, 48.
djaoek, clowns who perform with the Dragon. This word is also used for more polished dancers who wear white masks in various forms of drama. Pl. 66.
Djata, I. Pl. 38.
Djatisoera, I. B. Made, father of I Daijoe Soekra. Pls. 23, 24.
Djeben, I, tecnonymous daughter of Nang and Men Djeben. Their children are: I Djeben; I Nampah (girl). Pls. 15, 44, 45.
Djeben, Nang. Pls. 24, 68.
djelema-djelemaan (reduplicated form of *djelema,* a *kasar* term for a human being). Pl. 97.
djero or *djerone,* term of respect applied to strangers and to superiors without caste, e.g., heads of the village hierarchy, casteless wives of Brahmans, etc. Pl. 45.
djimat, a magical object. Pl. 20.
djoget, a trained itinerant female courtship dancer, usually preadolescent. Pls. 22, 39, 59, 60.
djoli, a small decorated house-like structure used for carrying corpses. Pl. 93.
doelang, a circular stand on which offerings or foods are placed. Pl. 4.
doeloe (derived from *oeloe,* head), a general term for the senior citizens in Bajoeng Gede. Pls. 9, 12.
Doemoen, I (see Kesir, I). Pls. 67, 69, 75.

Doeroes, I, tecnonymous son of Nang and Men Doeroes. Their children are: I Doeroes; I Karti (girl); I Karta (boy at breast). Pls. 44, 83.
Doeroes, Men. Pl. 54.

Endeh, Men. Pl. 54.

Gae, I (see Soewaka, I). Pls. 7, 35.
galoeh, princess in drama. Pl. 13.
Galoengan, a calendric feast which recurs every 210 days when the dead are said to visit the world. Pls. 37, 82.
Gambar, I Daijoe, daughter of I. B. Made Togog. Pls. 45, 84, 85.
Gana, Betara, Balinese name for Ganesha, the elephant-headed god of Hindooism. Pl. 45.
Gangsar, I, unrelated to Men Gangsar. Pl. 44.
Gangsar, I Wajan, carver of Bedoeloe. Pl. 23.
Gangsar, Men, mother of Nang Karma. Pl. 7.
garoeda, a mythological bird which eats mythological serpents (*naga*). Pl. 30.
Gata, I (see Karma, I). Pls. 5, 26, 32, 33, 39, 41, 50, 65, 70, 73, 74, 83.
Gati, I (see Karma, I). Pls. 18, 33, 36, 54, 73, 74, 79.
gede, big, great (*kasar*).
Gede, I. B. Wajan. Pl. 36.
Gedjer, I (see Badera, Nang). Pl. 83.
Gedjer, Ni, unrelated to Nang Badera. Pl. 46.
gegantoesan, a decorated conical container for betel-chewing materials, a common component of offerings. Pl. 4.
Gelis, I (see Kasoeb, I). Pls. 44, 50.
Geloeh, I. Pl. 27.
genten, a virgin.
Gentos, Nang. Pl. 24.
Gerantang, I, younger brother of I Tjoepak. Pls. 12, 20.
Gina, I. Pl. 99.
Giri Poetri, a name for Doerga, Death Goddess, in her beautiful form. Pl. 45.
gisiang (imperative from *gisi,* to hold). "Hold [it] for [me]!" Pls. 71, 72.
goak-goakan (a plural form with substantival suffix, from *goak,* a crow; literally, "a crows-thing"), a game resembling the American "crack-the-whip." Pl. 79.
Goenoeng, I, tecnonymous son of Nang and Men Goenoeng. Their children are: I Goenoeng, a defective boy; I Raoeh, baby boy.
Goenoeng, Men. Pls. 12, 27, 35, 67, 100.
Goenoeng, Nang. Pls. 1, 44.

Goenoeng Agoeng, the central mountain, home of the gods. Pl. 10.
Goewet, I, younger brother of I Roemi. Pl. 44.

isi, contents; *isin awak,* contents of the body. Pl. 97.

kadja, one of the cardinal points, the direction of the Goenoeng Agoeng or center of the island, north in South Bali and south in North Bali. The opposite of *kadja* is *kelod.* The other cardinal points are *kangin,* the direction of the rising sun, and *kaoeh* the direction of the setting sun. Pl. 10.
kadja-kangin, the most sacred direction; northeast in South Bali, southeast in North Bali. Pls. 1, 10.
kadjang sinom, a small fence-like structure laid over the body in mortuary ceremonies. Pls. 92, 93, 97.
kala, a sort of minor demon. Pls. 9, 33, 58.
Kaler, I Made, our secretary, a boy about 21 years old, native of Boeleleng. Pls. 19, 38, 44, 51, 60, 68.
kamben, any woven fabric, especially a sarong. Pl. 60.
kandampat, the "four brothers"; the cord, the blood, the placenta and the amniotic fluid. Pl. 45.
Kanggo, I. Pl. 24.
Kanggoen, I (see Djani, I). Pl. 17.
kangin (see *kadja*).
kaoeh (see *kadja*). Pl. 10.
kapar, gesture of sudden fright or startle, the Witch's posture with arms raised. Pls. 22, 60, 62.
Karba, I, only surviving son of Nang and Men Oera. Pls. 14, 15, 17, 21, 31, 41, 44, 45, 49, 50, 62, 81, 83, 85.
Kari, I (see Karma, Men). Pl. 43.
Karia, I (see Kasoeb, I). Pl. 28.
Karma, I, eldest son of Nang and Men Karma. Their children are: I Karma (adolescent boy); I Karmi (adolescent girl); I Ridjek (preadolescent girl); I Gati (girl); I Gata (boy, knee baby); I Kenjoen (girl at breast). Pl. 26.
Karma, Men, formerly I Adjin, tecnonymous daughter of Nang and Men Adjin. Their children are: Men Karma; Men Lintar; I Kari; Men Kesir; Men Oera; I Kaler (unmarried boy); Men Riboet; Men Singin; I Nanta (adolescent boy). Pls. 5, 32, 35, 54, 70, 73, 74, 75.

Karma, Nang. Pls. 7, 9, 18, 24, 39, 43, 65, 68, 73.
Karmi, I (see Karma, I). Pls. 32, 49, 75, 81.
Karni, I (see Loka, I). Pl. 5.
Karsa, I, only surviving son of Nang and Men Singin, to whom a daughter, I Djantoek, was born in summer of 1938. Pls. 7, 14, 31, 36, 40, 41, 48, 49, 51, 52, 53, 65, 68, 74, 80, 83.
Karta, I (see Doeroes, I). Pl. 54.
Karta, I (unrelated to I Karta, son of Nang Doeroes). Pls. 44, 83.
Karti, I (see Doeroes, I). Pl. 54.
kasar (see *aloes*).
Kasoeb, I, tecnonymous daughter of Nang and Men Kasoeb. Their children are: I Kasoeb; I Gelis (boy); I Karia (boy). (See Modoh, I.)
Katji, I. B. Made, Brahman studying to be a priest. Pls. 27, 86, 90.
kawes, ceremonial distribution of food. Pls. 9, 97.
Kawi, a general term for archaic religious language containing Old Javanese and Sanskrit derivatives. Pl. 62.
kebiar, a solo dance performed sitting. Pl. 16.
keketjer. Pl. 97.
kelod (see *kadja*). Pl. 10.
Keloepoes, I Made. Pls. 7, 23.
Keloepoes, I Wajan, uncle of I Made Keloepoes. Pls. 10, 21.
Kemit, I (see Dampoek, I). Pl. 80.
Keneh, Djero. Pl. 6.
Kenjoen, I (see Karma, I). Pls. 5, 17, 18, 33, 35, 49, 54, 70, 73, 74, 75, 79.
Kentel, Djero Baoe. Pl. 37.
kerama desa, a full citizen of the village. Pl. 9.
keraoehan (a passive substantival form from *raoeh*, to come), a term for supernatural possession; one into whom a god has come. Pl. 18.
kertala, the "younger brother" in a pair of comic servants in Balinese drama. Pls. 10, 13.
Kesatrya (see *Triwangsa*). Pls. 4, 84, 93, 94.
kesela, a sort of sweet potato. Pl. 30.
Kesir, I, tecnonymous child of Nang and Men Kesir. Their children are: I Kesir (girl); I Doemoen (girl at breast, died 1938). Pls. 32, 67, 69.
Kesir, Men. Pls. 38, 69, 75.
kesoena, a sort of garlic. Pl. 97.
ketantrian, a loose theatrical form with a plot. Pl. 46.
Keteg, I. Pls. 27, 86.
kimbul, the mood in which a child finally refuses the thing for which he was crying. Pl. 51.

klatkat soeda mala, a small bamboo frame placed under the *oekoer*. Pl. 92.
Kobot, I Goesti. Pls. 12, 45.
Koebajan, title of the first two citizens in the Bajoeng Gede hierarchy. Pl. 9.
Koeboe, I, tecnonymous son of Nang and Men Koeboe. Their children are: I Koeboe; I Wandri (adolescent girl); I Wandera (boy); I Rendoet (small girl); I Nandoer (small boy partially adopted by Djero Baoe Tekek).
Koeboe, Men. Pl. 7.
Koeningan, a calendric feast, 10 days after *Galoengan*. Pl. 82.
Koeroeh, I. B. Kompiang (see Teroewi, I. B. W.). Pls. 87, 100.
koeskoesan, a wide conical structure of basketwork used as a container for steaming rice over boiling water, and used as a strainer for holy water in many rituals. Pl. 84.
koewangen, a small conical twist of betel leaf containing chewing ingredients, a common offering or component of offerings. The most elaborate *koewangen* have traces of anthropomorphism. Pl. 92.
Koewat, I (see Njawi, I). Pls. 12, 35, 38, 45, 49, 69, 71, 72.
kompek, a basket in which a man habitually carries his small possessions, betel-chewing materials, etc. Pl. 63.
Kompiang, I Goesti. Pl. 68.
kris, Malay word for a double-edged dagger of sinuous form. Pls. 13, 40, 56, 57, 58, 62, 99.

laba, a share of temple land. Pl. 2.
lamak, a ceremonial bib. Pl. 11.
Lana, Dalang. Pl. 20.
Langkir, Daijoe. Pl. 87.
Lanoes, I. Pl. 43.
Lasia, I, son of Men Lasia. Pls. 10, 18, 19, 45.
Lasia, Men. Pl. 11.
latah, Malay word for a psychopathic condition involving imitative behavior. Pl. 19.
lawean, a type of graveyard spirit. Pl. 20.
legong, a type of dance performed by preadolescent girls. Pls. 19, 20, 55.
lejak, a general term for the supernatural forms assumed by those who practice witchcraft, and for the minor spirits associated with graveyards and births. Pls. 14, 17, 20, 55, 61.
Leket, I (see Degeng, I), adoptive tecnonymous son of Nang and Men Leket. Pls. 26, 28, 33, 49, 74, 75.

Leket, Men, sister of Men Njawi. Pls. 49, 74.
Leket, Nang, brother of Nang Degeng. Pls. 28, 74.
lemboe, sacerdotal term for a cow. Pl. 94.
Lemek, Men. Pl. 6.
Lempad, I Goesti Njoman. Pls. 20, 57, 70.
Lintar, I, tecnonymous son of Nang and Men Lintar. Their children are: I Lintar (adolescent boy); I Ngetis (boy); I Ngembon (girl); I Meres (girl); and a baby born in 1938. Pl. 28.
Lintar, Men. Pls. 5, 75.
Lintar, Nang. Pl. 74.
lis, an elaborate broom-like bundle of young palm leaves used as a sprinkler for holy water. It contains a variety of special items representing parts of the human body, and it is bound with a girdle. The "hair" of the *lis* is cut in certain *rites de passage*. Pls. 4, 34, 84.
loeh, a woman, female.
loengsoeran, things asked from a superior, offerings which have been asked back from the gods. Pls. 9, 11.
Loepiah, I Dewa. Pl. 15.
Loka, I, tecnonymous daughter of Nang and Men Loka. Their children are: I Loka; I Dana (boy); I Dani (girl). I Karni, an older daughter of Nang Loka by a previous marriage, lives with her mother's parents. I Njantel, resident with Nang Loka, is a daughter of Nang Oera by divorced wife who is a sister of Nang Loka. Pls. 9, 63.
Loka, Nang. Pls. 44, 63.

Madera, I (see Maderi, I). Pl. 83.
Maderi, I, tecnonymous daughter of Nang and Men Maderi. Their children are: I Maderi; I Madera (boy); I Marsi (girl). Pls. 15, 29.
Maderi, Nang. Pl. 63.
Malen, I (see Dampoek, I). Pl. 80.
Malih, I. Pls. 18, 21.
Manis, I Daijoe P. Pl. 80.
mantenin padi, the ceremony for the commencement of rice harvest. Pls. 4, 32.
mantri, the prince in *ardja* and other theatrical forms. Pl. 13.
maoerip (see *sanggah oerip*). Pl. 21.
Margi, Men. Pl. 100.
Mari, I. B. Pl. 40.
Mario, I. Pl. 16.
Marsi, I (see Maderi, I). Pl. 63.
Marti, I, tecnonymous daughter of Nang and Men Marti. Their children are: I Marti; I Marta (girl, born Jan.–Feb. 1938). Pls. 48, 51, 63, 64.

Marti, Men. Pl. 63.
Marti, Nang. Pls. 51, 63, 64.
matah, raw, unripe, used metaphorically to refer to the Witch when she appears in human form before her transformation. Pl. 55.
meanin, a postmortuary ceremony in Bajoeng Gede, equated with the cremation ceremony of the plains. Pls. 97, 99, 100.
Mebet, Nang (see Badera, Nang). Pl. 37.
medelokin, to visit a house in which some *rite de passage* is being performed, especially a house in which a death has recently occurred. Pl. 10.
melaspas, a ceremony of consecration or validation for a new house, shrine, etc. Pls. 96, 98.
meligija, a very elaborate postmortuary ceremony. Pls. 5, 11, 89, 97, 99.
melis (intransitive or passive form from *lis*), a purification ceremony. Pl. 36.
memantra (verbal form from *mantra*, a prayer or incantation). Pl. 84.
meme, mother. Pl. 98.
memedi, stupid and mischievous spirits. Pl. 46.
memendak (from *mendak*, to go to meet somebody who is coming), the initial part of a ceremony, going to meet or invite the gods. Pl. 11.
mepegat (from *pegat*, to cut off), ritual episode in *rites de passage* in which the candidate breaks a stretched thread by walking through it. Pls. 34, 99, 100.
meperas, ritual episode in *rites de passage* in which the kin of the candidate stand in genealogical order holding a rope. Pl. 100.
Merada, Dong. Pl. 88.
mereh, to acquire supernatural power of the sort associated with witchcraft, graveyards, etc. Pl. 17.
Meres, I (see Lintar, I). Pls. 5, 38, 52, 53, 74, 75.
mesaioet, purification ceremony in Bajoeng Gede. Pl. 81.
mesakapan, a purification ceremony. This term may refer to a large variety of ceremonies (marriage, consecration of a dancer, purification after incest, etc.). Pl. 30.
Mesem, I (see Rimpen, I). Pl. 50.
Meser, I Daijoe. Pl. 78.
metadjoek, a gathering of neighbors and relatives to help in ploughing. Pl. 2.
meteboes (passive or intransitive form from *teboes*, to tie), a ritual episode in various *rites de passage* in which string is used. It is tied around the wrist or placed behind the ear of the candidate. Pl. 4.

metjaroe, a purification ceremony which consists of offerings to the lower demons, a more elaborate ceremonial analogue of *segeh.* Pls. 6, 30, 33.

metoeoen, a postmortuary ceremony in Bajoeng Gede, in which the dead speak through *Djero Balian* in trance. Pls. 6, 29, 100.

Minab, Men. Pl. 6.

mirah codi, a precious stone. Pl. 98.

Mirib, I, daughter of Man Saoe. Pls. 24, 46.

Misi, I, girl, *sangiang* dancer (see Tamboen, I). Pls. 10, 18, 19, 45, 80.

Misi, I, late adolescent boy, unrelated to I Misi (girl). Pl. 50.

Modoh, I, illegitimate daughter of Nang Kasoeb, partially adopted by Djero Baoe Tekek. Pls. 24, 44, 45.

moeani, a man, male.

Moeda, I. B. P. (see Teroewi, I. B. Wajan). Pl. 46.

moedra, ritual hand gestures performed by Brahman priests. Pl. 84.

Moedri, I (see Oera, Nang). Pls. 4, 7, 50.

Moegloek, I. Pls. 44, 81.

Moeka, Bala, a minor demon. Pl. 20.

Moeklen, I Dewa. Pl. 15.

Moerdah, I, younger brother of I Towalen, servant in the shadow-play. Pl. 13.

Moespa, I, tecnonymous daughter of Nang and Men Moespa, settlers in Bajoeng Gede from Manik Adji. Their children include: I Moespa and I Dira (girl). Pl. 25.

Moespa, Nang. Pl. 89.

Mondel, I. Pl. 29.

naga, a mythological serpent. Pl. 40.

Nahoela, I (see Pendawa). Pl. 20.

Nami, Men. Pl. 38.

Nampah, I (see Djeben, I). Pls. 36, 38, 45.

Nandoer, I (see Koeboe, I). Pls. 44, 51, 83.

nangloek-merana, ceremony expelling grasshoppers and rats. Pl. 5.

Neka, I. Pl. 35.

neleb, ceremony in Bajoeng Gede, connected with the annual sharing of temple land. Pl. 1.

neloeboelanin (from *teloe,* three; and *boelan,* a moon or month of 35 days), 105-day birthday ceremony for a baby. Pls. 4, 84.

Ngadang, Sang Kala, a minor demon. Pl. 33.

ngamong, to keep a special god in the house temple. Pl. 11.

ngarap bangke (literally, "to work a corpse"), the riotous carrying of a corpse to the cemetery. Pls. 33, 94.

ngaskara, one of the ceremonies in cremation. Pls. 4, 97, 98.

ngebat, to prepare food by chopping. Pl. 30.

ngelawang, to oppose or resist, especially to resist the decisions of the community. Pl. 72.

Ngembat, I. Pls. 44, 81.

Ngembon, I (see Lintar, I). Pls. 53, 74, 75.

ngempoe, a nurse, a companion of the candidate in various *rites de passage.* Pl. 4.

Ngendon, I, son of Nang and Men Ngendon. Pls. 21, 26.

Ngendon, I, artist, unrelated to Nang Ngendon. Pl. 46.

Ngendon, Men, formerly I Maring. (She did not get her tecnonymous name until the 105-day birthday of her child, which was later than the photographs shown here, but the tecnonymous name is used here for convenience of reference.) Pls. 6, 26, 38.

Ngendon, Nang, settler in Bajoeng Gede, born in Selat, older brother of I Sambeh and father of I Ngendon. Pls. 21, 69.

ngeradjahan, purificatory and validating ceremony. Pl. 92.

ngeragrag (reduplicated form of *raga,* the body, the self), to invent or compose. Pl. 20.

ngereka, a ceremony in the cremation series in which the body is reconstituted from the bones or ashes. Pls. 91, 98.

ngerorasin (from *roras,* twelve), the ceremony held on the 12th day after birth. Pl. 84.

ngesehin sang seda, to dress up the dead. Pl. 92.

Ngetis, I (see Lintar, I). Pl. 74.

Ngetis, Nang, unrelated to I Ngetis. Pl. 18.

ngirim (literally, "to send"), ceremony in which the ashes are thrown in the sea after cremation. Pls. 98, 99.

Nini (archaic word for "mother"), a figure of the Rice Goddess. Pl. 4.

Njantel, I (see Loka, I). Pls. 6, 17, 80.

njapoepoe, a species of graveyard demon. Pl. 17.

Njawa, I (see Njawi, I). Pls. 12, 49, 67, 71, 72.

Njawi, I, tecnonymous daughter of Nang and Men Njawi. Their children are: I Njawi; I Njawa (girl); I Koewat (boy at breast). Pl. 49.

Njawi, Men. Pls. 12, 35, 38, 45, 49, 69, 71, 72.

njoeh, a coconut. Pl. 97.

noesang, a form of funeral ceremony performed with exhumed bones before cremation. Pl. 92.

oekiran, complicated designs of leaves and scrollwork in carving or painting. Pl. 30.

oekoer, a figure made of coins and representing the dead. Pls. 92, 97.

oeloen ati (literally, the "head of the liver"). Pl. 97.

oemah, the house or home in the village, as opposed to the *pondok*. Pl. 2.

oembel-oembel, a pennant carried in procession. Pls. 30, 40.

Oera, Men (see Karma, Men), mother of I Karba. Pls. 28, 49.

Oera, Nang (see Loka, I), father of I Karba. Nang Oera was formerly I Bina, tecnonymous child of Nang and Men Bina. Their children are: Nang Oera; Nang Marti; Nang Singin. Men Bina, by a later marriage, had other children: Nang Djeben; Men Madri; I Ampiag (male); I Njelod (boy); Men Resi; and one illegitimate son, I Moedri. Pls. 2, 15, 41, 43, 59, 60, 62, 65, 85.

oeriaga, an offering representing the viscera of the dead. Pls. 97, 98.

oeroedjah, a hotly spiced drink. Pl. 63.

Oka, I Made. Pls. 20, 22.

Omong, I. Pl. 44.

otonin, ceremony celebrating the recurrence of a special day in the *oton* (210-day) cycle, especially the 210-day birthday of a baby. Pls. 7, 24, 27, 29, 84.

Pageh, I. Pl. 27.

Paijoek, I Dewa. Pl. 93.

pantjoran, a spout for water. Pl. 37.

patokan, a stick or support (from the same root as *tatakan,* a stand for offerings; and *tapekan,* a trance dancer). Pl. 18.

pedanda, a Brahman priest. Pls. 6, 19, 84, 85, 89, 92.

pemangkoe, a priest or religious practitioner attached to a temple, usually of no caste. Pls. 23, 33.

pemerasaan, a species of offering. Pl. 99.

penasar, a general term for comic servants in Balinese theater. Pl. 13.

Pendawa, the five brothers, heroes of the Hindoo epic, Berata Juda. Their Balinese names are: Darma, Bima, Redjoena, Nahoela, Sahadewa. Pl. 20.

pendjor, a decorative pendant. Pl. 82.

penegtegan (literally a "standing thing"), a bamboo which supports the baby while he is learning to walk. Pl. 17.

pepatih, the servant or ambassador of a king in Balinese theater. Pl. 62.

pererai, the *aloes* word for face, the face of a god. Pl. 98.

perloe, necessary, required, prescribed. (This word is used in Bazaar Malay to translate European notions of "purpose.") Pl. 5.

petoelangan (literally "a thing for bones"), the container in which the bones are burned. Pl. 96.

Pindet, I, mother of I Tongos. Pl. 12.

Pinti, I. Pl. 37.

pirata (from the same root as *pitra,* a ghost purified after cremation), a ghost before cremation. Pl. 97.

pisang djati, an offering representing the soul of the dead. Pl. 98.

Pita, Maha, a club of Balinese artists. Pls. 45, 70.

poeles, sleep. Pl. 72.

poenta, the "older brother" in a pair of comic servants in Balinese drama. Pl. 13.

Poepoe, Dadong, mother of Djero Koebajan Poepoe, whose son is Nang Nedeng. Nang Nedeng was I Poepoe until the birth of his son, I Nedeng. Pl. 100.

Poepoe, Djero Koebajan, 2nd citizen in Bajoeng Gede hierarchy. Pl. 9.

poepoehan, an anthropomorphic offering in *meanin*. Pl. 97.

poera, a temple.

Poera Dalem (from *dalem,* deep), the Death Temple, usually located near the cemetery and *kaoeh* or *kelod* of the village. Pl. 17.

Poera Desa, the main village temple. Pl. 1.

Poera di Panti, a minor temple in Bajoeng Gede run by a voluntary association of Bajoeng people. Pl. 9.

Poera Doekoeh (from *doekoeh,* a hermit), minor temple in the fields outside Bajoeng Gede run by the village. Pls. 5, 11.

Poera Medoewe Karang. Pl. 35.

Poera Pemetelan. Pl. 9.

Poera Poeseh, Temple of Origin. Pls. 1, 81.

poesoeh, the heart, a banana flower. Pl. 41.

poetih, white.

Poeting, I. B. P. Pl. 97.

poleng, a checkered fabric used for ceremonials. Pl. 5.

Polih, Nang. Pl. 12.

pondok, a house or farm outside the village. Pl. 2.

pring, a sort of *lis*. Pl. 34.

Radin, I. Pl. 36.
rai, a measure of length, a span. Pl. 21.
Rai, I Desak Made. Pl. 80.
Raksi, I. Pl. 5.
Ramajana, old Hindoo epic. Pl. 88.
rame, crowded, full of things happening, such as fire-crackers, orchestras, dances, etc. Pls. 2, 5, 83.
Rangda (literally, "Widow"), a common term for the Witch. Pls. 22, 23, 45, 55, 56, 60, 61, 62.
Raoeh, I (see Goenoeng, I). Pls. 12, 27, 35, 57, 67, 100.
Raroeng, I, the daughter of the Witch in some *Tjalonarang* stories. Pl. 22.
Rebo, Nang. Pl. 68.
redjang, a processional dance for women and girls. Pl. 81.
Redjoena, third of the *Pendawa.* Pl. 20.
Remin, I. Pl. 81.
Rendoet, I (see Koeboe, I). Pls. 6, 7, 36.
Renoe, I, *sangiang* dancer, daughter of Nang Ringin. Pls. 6, 18, 19, 36, 80.
Rentet, Nang. Pl. 24.
Rentjen, I. Pl. 78.
Repen, I, a native of Malet, relative of Nang Oera. Pls. 65, 83.
reregek, a figure probably representing the candidate or his *ngempoe* in a *rite de passage.* Pl. 4.
Resi, I Daijoe, daughter of I. B. M. Togog. Pls. 84, 85.
Resi, I. Pls. 25, 45.
Resi, Men. Pls. 25, 45.
Reta, I, tecnonymous son of Nang and Men Reta. Their children are: I Reta; and a baby which died unnamed. Pls. 29, 34, 83.
Reta, Men. Pl. 35.
Ribek, I Daijoe. Pls. 76, 78.
Riboet, I, baby daughter of Nang and Men Riboet (see Karma, Men). Pl. 83.
Ridjek, I (see Karma, I). Pl. 32.
Rimpen, I, tecnonymous daughter of Nang and Men Rimpen. Their children are: I Rimpen; I Bontok (boy); I Mesem (girl). Pl. 50.
Rimpen, Nang. Pl. 28.
Ringin, Nang, father of I Renoe. Pl. 6.
Rinjin, I (see Dampoek, I). Pls. 5, 18.
roban, a servant or relative who works for board. Pl. 24.
Roemi, I, elder sister of I Goewet. Pl. 81.
roentoetan, fruit, flowers, etc., added to an offering to make it more showy. Pl. 5.
Roni, Nang. Pls. 2, 29, 37.

saba, a type of annual feast in Bajoeng Gede; Saba Dalem. Pl. 30; Saban Jeh. Pl. 37.
Saboeh, I. B. Pls. 15, 40, 77.
Saboeh, Nang. Pls. 29, 37.
Sadia, I. Pls. 7, 29.
Sahadewa, I (see Pendawa). Pl. 20.
saja, in Bajoeng Gede, the man whose duty it is to provide and lay out food for a village feast. These duties devolve upon a different man each month in rotation. Pl. 9.
sajanganga (passive form from a root meaning "to serve," see *ajahan, saja*), used as an adjective to describe princes, or children who are very much served, or "spoiled" by their servants or parents. Pls. 13, 45.
Salib, I. Pl. 81.
Salib, Nang, son of Nang Dakta. Pls. 43, 99.
Sama, I, tecnonymous son of Nang and Men Sama. Their children are: I Sama; I Sami (boy at breast). Men Sama had numerous children by earlier marriages, none of whom appear in this book. Pl. 69.
Sama, Men. Pls. 21, 26, 69.
Sambeh, I, younger brother of Nang Ngendon. Pls. 21, 38.
Samboet, I. Pl. 67.
Sami, I (see Sama, I). Pls. 21, 26, 50, 69.
Sampik, I, eponymous hero of a Balinese opera. Pl. 88.
Sandra, I. Pl. 83.
sang, archaic personal pronoun used as a personifying prefix in various religious contexts, chiefly for supernaturals, e.g., *sang seda,* the deceased.
sanggah, the house temple, a group of shrines for ancestors and family gods in a small enclosure on the *kadja* or *kangin* side of every houseyard. Pls. 1, 11, 98.
sanggah oerip (*oerip* means "life" or "alive"), a small doll made of palm leaves and representing the soul of the dead. Pls. 34, 91, 92, 97, 98, 99.
sangiang, a pantomimic trance dancer. Many types of *sangiang* occur and are commonly named after the object pantomimed, e.g., *sangiang deling* who imitate dolls; *sangiang tjeleng* who imitate pigs; etc.
Saoe, Men, mother of I Mirib. Pl. 46.
sapoet, wide sash worn by both men and women, obligatory when entering temples or meeting superiors. Pls. 4, 86, 92.

sapta, daring in the face of impurity, uncleanness, etc., able to eat in presence of an unpleasant smell. Pls. 34, 90, 94.

sari, pollen, used metaphorically for that essence of the offerings which is taken by the gods, or for the *tjanang genten* which is left on the shrine when the offerings are removed. Pl. 84.

Sasak, I. B. Nj. Pl. 34.

sasaran, an unfortunate being. Pl. 20.

Sasih, I Daijoe P. Pl. 80.

sate, food smeared or spiked on a wooden skewer and cooked over an open flame. Pls. 6, 30.

Sebeng, Dalang. Pl. 20.

segeh, segehan, mesegeh, etc. (see *metjaroe*), offerings laid on the ground for the demons. Pls. 17, 33, 58, 82.

segseg, to dance with sideways steps. Pl. 19.

sekah, a container representing the soul, into which the ashes are sometimes put after cremation. Pl. 98.

sende, a small mortar, a lamp. Pl. 98.

Sentoelan, I. B. P. Pls. 32, 45, 91.

Sepek, I (see Degeng, I). Pls. 12, 33, 38, 74, 75.

Sepoeng, I (see Soka, I). Pl. 5.

seridatoe, ceremonial thread of three colors, red, white, and black. Pl. 97.

Serijoet, Bala. Pl. 20.

sesarik, a mixture of spices applied to the candidate in *rites de passage.* Pl. 84.

Singin, Men (see Karma, Men), mother of I Karsa. Pls. 7, 31, 32, 36, 38, 48, 49, 51, 53, 54, 63, 68.

Singin, Nang (see Oera, Nang), father of I Karsa. Pl. 6.

sisia, a novice, especially a disciple of the Witch. Pls. 55, 61.

Siti, I Daijoe Kt. (see Teroewi, I. B. W.). Pls. 82, 100.

soegihan (substantive form from *soegih,* rich), land which is privately owned. Pl. 2.

Soekoeh, Djero Balian. Pls. 5, 6, 8, 23, 29, 100.

Soekra, I Daijoe, daughter of I. B. Made Djatisoera. Pls. 76, 77, 78, 80.

soembah, a posture of self-deprecation and respect. Pl. 10.

Soeria, Betara, the Sun God. Pl. 11.

Soewaka, I, tecnonymous son of Nang and Men Soewaka. Their children are: I Soewaka (boy); I Memes (girl); I Gae (girl). Pls. 7, 39.

Soka, I, tecnonymous daughter of Nang and Men Soka. Their children are: I Soka; I Poekel (boy adopted by Nang Poekel); I Soekeh (girl); I Gampiang (boy); I Djoemah (boy); I Paek (girl); I Tjoebling (girl); I Sepoeng (girl). Pls. 19, 45, 81.

Soni, Nang (see Tamboen, I). Pls. 6, 19, 21.

Sri, Betara, the Rice Goddess. Pl. 4.

taboehan, a hornets' nest, the name of a game in which the children dance as "hornets" on a drawing in the sand. Pl. 77.

Tamboen, I, eldest surviving child of Nang and Men Soni (see Poepoe, I). Their children are: I Tamboen; I Misi (girl); I Sari (boy); I Ngenoe (boy). Pls. 45, 81.

tangan-tangan (reduplicated form from *tangan,* a hand), a species of graveyard spirit. Pls. 17, 20.

Tantra, I. B. P. Pl. 85.

Tantra, I Made, unrelated to I. B. P. Tantra. Pl. 35.

Tatah, I. Pl. 38.

Taweng, I. Pl. 38.

Teboes, I. Pls. 17, 81.

tegal soetji, a sacred cleared space. In Bajoeng Gede, it is on the road between the Village Temple and the Temple of Origin. Monthly (lunar) feasts and other ceremonials are held there. Pls. 99, 100.

tegen-tegenan (from *tegen,* to carry on a pole), an offering composed of food and other objects suspended from the two ends of a pole. Pl. 87.

Tekek, Djero Baoe, calendric expert in Bajoeng Gede (see Dampoek, I, Modoh, I, and Koeboe, I). Pls. 1, 51.

Tendo, I. B. P. Pl. 38.

Terang, I. B. Pl. 77.

Teroewi, I. B. Wajan, eldest son of I. B. Kompiang Koeroeh, whose children are: I. B. W. Teroewi; I. B. Nj. Tjeta; I Daijoe Kt. Siti; I. B. P. Moeda.

tetampak. Pl. 97.

tiban, the agricultural year of twelve unequal lunar months. Pl. 97.

Tilem, the feast of New Moon. Pl. 9.

Timtim, Nang. Pl. 27.

Tiroe, I. Pls. 22, 59, 60.

tis. Pl. 37.

Tjalonarang, a name for the Witch, eponymously applied to the Witch play. Pls. 13, 14, 22, 23, 55 to 58, 60, 61, 62, 66, 88.

tjanang genten, a small leaf-tray of flowers, betel-chewing ingredients and cash (see *sari*). Pls. 33, 81.

tjanang rebong, a high pyramidal offering made of flowers. Pls. 4, 98.

tjatjah, a food resembling rice made by chopping and drying tubers of *kesela.* Pl. 30.

Tjerita, I. Pl. 17.

Tjeta, I. B. Nj. (see Teroewi, I. B. W.). Pls. 17, 60, 87.

Tjibloek, I. Pl. 4.

tjili, a human figure with a fan-shaped headdress. Pl. 4.

tjili ampilan, an offering consisting of a human figure tied to a box. Pl. 98.

Tjintjia, Sangiang, a deity, sometimes equated with Betara Soeria, the Sun. Pl. 20.

tjiri, a token, especially a token act, e.g., if it is raining and a dance must be offered, the dancer will posture for a moment as a *tjiri* of the whole dance. Pl. 40.

Tjoengkoeh, I, a schizoid vagrant. Pls. 7, 27.

Tjoepak, I, coarse elder brother of I Garantang in a story commonly shown in theater and shadow-play. Pls. 12, 20.

tjondong, the nurse and servant of the princess in Balinese theater. Pls. 13, 22.

toeak, a drink made by fermenting the juice of a palm. Pl. 30.

toegoe, a simpler form of *lis.* Pl. 4.

toeloeng oerip, a species of offering. Pl. 85.

toembak, a spear. Pl. 40.

Toempek, I. B. Pl. 78.

toempeng, a cone made of rice paste, a common anthropomorphic constituent of offerings. Pl. 27.

Toenggal, Betara, the "Unit" God. Pl. 20.

toengked, a walking stick. Pl. 98.

Toetoeg, I. Pl. 83.

toetoeg kamboehan, ceremony held 42 days after birth of a first baby and terminating the seclusion of the parents. Pl. 84.

Togog, I. B. Made, father of I Dajoe Gambar. Pls. 10, 40, 85.

toja (the *aloes* word for water), holy water. Pls. 6, 37, 56, 82, 84, 89, 98.

Tompelos, I. Pl. 6.

Tongos, I, son of I Pindet. Pl. 12.

topeng, a mask, a theatrical form typically given by a single performer who appears on the stage in a succession of different masks. Pl. 19.

Towalen, I, comic servant in shadow-play, elder brother of I Moerdah. Pls. 13, 20.

Triwangsa, a collective term for the three castes; the first caste is the Brahman from which priests are recruited; the second is the Kesatrya and includes the ruling princes; the third is the Vesia, mostly rich landed aristocracy. Less than 10 per cent of the population are *Triwangsa,* the remainder being *djaba* or "outsiders."

wadah, a container, especially the tower in which the corpse is carried to the cemetery for cremation. Pls. 11, 93, 94.

Wadi, I (see Dampoek, I). Pl. 18.

Wajang, I. Pl. 29.

wajang, the shadow-play, a puppet used in shadow-play. Pl. 20.

wajang wong (*wong* is a Javanese word for human being), a theatrical form in which human actors are substituted for the puppets of the shadow-play. Pls. 13, 60, 61, 88.

wakoel (from the same root as *awak,* a body; *wakil,* an agent or representative, etc.), a cylindrical basket used in the construction of anthropomorphic offerings. Pls. 4, 11, 98, 99.

Wandera, I (see Koeboe, I). Pl. 40.

Wanderi, I (see Koeboe, I). Pls. 25, 81.

Wara, I. Pl. 20.

Of this book 2,000 copies have been printed by E. L. Hildreth & Company, Brattleboro, Vermont. The paper is No. 371 Vellum light natural wove furnished by Miller & Wright of New York. The pictures are reproduced by Fredrick Photogelatine Press, Inc., of New York, and the binding has been done by the J. F. Tapley Company, Long Island City.